# IN PRINT:
# CRITICAL READING
# AND WRITING

# IN PRINT:

Longman Series in College Composition and Communication
*Advisory Editor:* Harvey Wiener, La Guardia Community College
of the City University of New York

# CRITICAL READING AND WRITING

Martin Stevens / Jeffery Kluewer

Longman
New York & London

**In Print: Critical Reading and Writing**

Longman Inc., 1560 Broadway, New York, N.Y. 10036
Associated companies, branches, and representatives
throughout the world.

Developmental Editor: Gordon T. R. Anderson
Editorial and Design Supervisor: Ferne Y. Kawahara
Interior Designer: Antler & Baldwin, Inc.
Manufacturing Supervisor: Marion Hess
Composition: Kingsport Press
Printing and Binding: Fairfield Graphics

**Library of Congress Cataloging in Publication Data**

Stevens, Martin.
  In print: critical reading and writing.

  (Longman series in college composition and
communication)
  Includes index.
  1. English language—Rhetoric.  2. College
readers.  I. Kluewer, Jeffery Dane.  II. Title.
III. Series.
PE1408.S754  1983      808′.0427      82–16201
ISBN 0–582–28291–8

Manufactured in the United States of America

We dedicate this book

to the *third* generation
Paul Allen Williams and Jacob Ryan Stevens

and to the *second*
Jessica, Joshua, and Benjamin Kluewer

# CONTENTS

## Unit III NARRATION 133

## Unit IV EXPOSITION AND ANALYSIS 197

# PREFACE

This book is designed to make college-level writing a lively experience. We write this book out of some dissatisfaction with many writing texts currently available. It strikes us that most of them either concentrate on rules, guides, and mechanical descriptions of composing, to the exclusion of many examples of actual prose, or they offer an anthology of prose masterpieces with little or no accompanying discussion and instruction. Some courses require both a "rhetoric" and a reader, overwhelming student and instructor with 800 to 1000 combined pages, advice often contradicted by practice. With few exceptions these texts are written in deathly prose, as if issued from a committee, the product of some consensus, without distinctive voice or a point of view.

We offer here a single book for the introductory writing classroom, written—we hope—in a distinct voice. The text combines elements of a rhetoric along with elements of an anthology. Many of our selections come from the most popular print media and are ones you might normally read every day entirely out of personal interest: movie reviews, consumer reports, humor columns, exposés, news stories, obituaries. Good writing, we believe, occurs everywhere—in sports columns, editorials, even advertisements. There is no more reason to believe that all popular writing is trashy or "merely journalistic" than that all academic writing is clear and elegant. The popular media of our culture contain much admirable writing produced by professionals who earn their living through their use of language.

While our book is different from most college readers in its contents, it is traditional in its rhetorical headings and instruction. We have matched media writing with the traditional rhetorical categories: narration is demonstrated with sports reports; description is illustrated in travel columns; exposition and analysis are shown as they occur in consumer reports and feature articles; argument and persuasion are seen in editorials, op-ed pieces, and advertisements; the writer's voice is illustrated in news reports and television criticism.

In each chapter and in the book as a whole we move from the familiar to the unfamiliar, and from the simple to the more complex. The book thus attempts to bridge the kind of reading experiences you already enjoy daily, even if casually, with the kind of reading and writing that you will be expected to do in college and as an educated person in your chosen career.

It is a premise of this book that careful critical reading is integrally related to good writing. Thus, along with standard writing instruction you will find introductory material which prepares you to read the selections critically. Early in the book especially, there is also commentary to give you examples of close reading. Commentaries will discuss writing topics associated with the chapter, analyze the structure of the selection, or discuss the implications of the language. In addition to commentary there are also questions at the end of selections to direct your attention both to the content or meaning of the selection and to its writing style.

Exercises in the chapters generally ask you to analyze writing or to find new examples of the rhetorical forms under discussion. You may, for example, be asked to find your own illustrations of logical fallacies among the daily editorial and opinion columns. Writing assignments generally ask you to imitate the various types of writing presented: for example, "Write a vivid sports report." Other assignments ask you to research subjects from standard sources. In these ways your hometown, college town, or campus newspapers and newsstands, as well as the campus library, will become part of our text.

We hope to interest most of you much of the time and to invite you to take seriously what you may perceive now as common and ordinary in your experience. By enticing you to take your experiences seriously, we hope to encourage you to find authentic motives for your own writing and research.

We acknowledge here our debts to Philip Zimbardo of Stanford University and Edward Quinn of the City College of New York for their help with the earliest incarnations of this book, to Harvey Wiener and especially Donald McQuade for the expert editorial guidance which produced this latest incarnation and for contributing the title *In Print*. Over at Longman we received incomparable help and support from Tren Anderson, our editor, who gave this project his unflagging support and who brought us together with our readers over memorable meals for memorable airings of disagreements and wholesome discussion. We are grateful as well to our production editor, Ferne Kawahara, who prepared the book with eagle eye for the compositor. Bette Ryan has worked selflessly and tirelessly with great skill, judgment, and intelligence over the many details that convert a muddled manuscript into a finished typescript. Connie Terrero has been with us longer than anyone. She has been our principal typist and the trustee of the four or five versions through which she has nurtured this book. To our wives,

Rose Zimbardo and Susan Kluewer, we expressly do not make the traditional acknowledgments. While we sharpened our pencils, they did *not*—in the parlance of prefaces—darn our socks or cook our meals, anymore than we did theirs. Instead they pursued their own careers and engaged in their own creative projects. We are grateful not for their support but for their independence. The latter enlivened us all, including this book.

Martin Stevens
Jeffery Kluewer

# ACKNOWLEDGMENTS

## UNIT I

Journal entry by Clare Schweighardt, Suffolk Community College, N.Y. Used by permission of the author.

Sample notes for "Tito Gaona" supplied by Roy P. Clark, used by permission of the author, Peter B. Gallagher.

"Tito Reached for the Sky and Won," © 1978 *St. Petersburg Times.* Reprinted by permission.

"Berkowitz Outbursts Disrupt Court; Sentencing Put Off, Tests Ordered" © 1978 by The New York Times Company. Reprinted by permission.

"Do I Look Like an Animal" was originally published as "Open Admissions and the Inward I" by Peter J. Rondinone. Reprinted with permission from *Change Magazine,* Vol. 9, No. 5 (May 1977). Copyrighted by the Council on Learning, 271 North Ave., New Rochelle, N.Y. 10801.

"The Ride Down" from *Of a Fire on the Moon* © 1969, 1970 by Norman Mailer. Reprinted by permission of Little, Brown and Company.

"The Moon and the Mudball" was originally published as "Installment 35: 1 August 69." Excerpt from *The Glass Teat* by Harlan Ellison. Copyright © 1969, 1970, 1975 by Harlan Ellison. Reprinted with permission of, and by arrangement with, the author and the author's agent, Richard Curtis Associates, Inc., New York. All rights reserved.

Portion of the Index from *The New York Times* © 1981 by The New York Times Company. Reprinted by permission.

## UNIT II

"The Sybarites" by Herbert Siegel, copyright © 1978 by the *Saturday Review.* All rights reserved.

Two ads for Passport Scotch (one using Toledo as background, the other, Estoril). Reprinted by permission of Joseph E. Seagram & Sons.

"Albarracín: In a Little Spanish Town" by Bailey Alexander reprinted from *Travel & Leisure,* copyright © 1978 American Express Publication Corporation.

"New Orleans and Her River" by Joseph Judge, copyright © 1971 by *National Geographic Magazine.* Used by permission.

"Fish Store" by Kate Jennings first appeared in *Poetry,* © 1975 by Modern Poetry Association. Reprinted by permission of the editor of *Poetry.*

## UNIT III

"Ali vs. Frazier, 'The Thrilla in Manila' " Associated Press, October 1, 1975. Reprinted by permission.

"Joe Was Still Coming In" by Red Smith © 1975 by The New York Times Company. Reprinted by permission.

"Griffith vs. Paret" by Norman Mailer from *The Presidential Papers.* Reprinted by permission of the author and the author's agent, Scott Meredith Literary Agency, Inc., 845 Third Avenue, New York, NY 10022.

"Russell, The Bee Expert" by Nat Hentoff. From "Our Vanishing Libraries," *Village Voice,* February 4, 1981, p. 8. Reprinted by permission.

"The Search for Marvin Gardens" from *Pieces of the Frame* by John McPhee. Copyright © 1972, 1975 by John McPhee. This material first appeared in *The New Yorker.* Reprinted by permission.

"Starting Over" from *Too Old To Cry* by Paul Hemphill. Copyright © 1976 by Paul Hemphill. Reprinted by permission of Viking Penguin, Inc.

"A Conversation With My Father" from *Enormous Changes at the Last Minute* by Grace Paley. Copyright © 1972, 1974 by Grace Paley. Reprinted by permission of Farrar, Straus and Giroux, Inc.

## UNIT IV

"How to Make Sure Your Water Is Fit to Drink" by Jane E. Brody, © 1979 by The New York Times Company. Reprinted by permission.

"Briton's Classic I.Q. Data Now Viewed as Fraudulent" by Boyce Rensberger, © 1976 by The New York Times Company. Reprinted by permission.

"How to Decode a Food Label" by Marlene Cimons and Michael Jacobson. Reprinted from *Mother Jones,* Feb/Mar 1978, which is available from Center for Science in Public Interest, 1755 S Street. N.W., Washington, D.C. 20009. Membership is available to the public for $20.00 per year.

"Who Needs a Hamburger Maker?" copyright 1978 by Consumers Union of United States, Inc., Mount Vernon, N.Y. 10550. Reprinted/excerpted by permission from Consumer Reports, July 1978.

From "The Atlantic Generating Station" by John McPhee. Reprinted by permission; © 1975 The New Yorker Magazine, Inc.

"A Cold New Look at the Criminal Mind" by Michael S. Serrill. Reprinted from *Psychology Today Magazine.* Copyright © 1978 Ziff-Davis Publishing Company.

"White Progress" article by Joel Dreyfuss, *Village Voice,* October 1, 1979, pp. 16–17, copyright © 1979.

"bowd·ler·ize" © 1981 Houghton Mifflin Company. Reprinted by permission from *The American Heritage Dictionary of the English Language.*

"Bowdlerize" The Oxford English Dictionary, p. 1031. Reprinted by permission of Oxford University Press.

From "Trouble With Antibiotics" by Jack S. Remington from *Human Nature I* (June 1978). The copyright owner for *Human Nature* cannot be found. Any information will be appreciated.

## UNIT V

"Which Side Do You Believe?" America's Electric Energy Companies ad in *Time* October 13, 1980, pp. 98–99. Reprinted by permission.

"The Nuclear Faithful: Time to Face Reality" by Vince Taylor from Union of Concerned Scientists newsletter *Nucleus.* Reprinted by permission.

"Radiation Ethics: Some Issues" by John W. Gofman. Reprinted by permission of the Committee for Nuclear Responsibility.

"Doublespeak and Ideology in Ads" by Richard Ohmann from *Teaching About Doublespeak,* ed. Daniel Dieterich (Urbana, Ill.: NCTE, 1976), pp. 44–47.

"Mother Nature is lucky her products don't need labels," ad in *The New Yorker,* April 21, 1980, p. 79. Reprinted by permission of Monsanto Company.

"The Cost of Clean Air" © 1981 Mobil Corporation. Reprinted by permission.

"I Was Asleep for 29 Years" ad in *The New York Times,* Monday, October 20, 1975, p. 68. Used by permission of *Psychology Today.*

"mmm mmm good" Bloomingdale's ad from *The New York Times Magazine,* May 2, 1976, p. 33. Reprinted by permission of Stan Shaffer (concept, design, and photography).

Lord Calvert ad, *Time,* October 16, 1978, p. 87. Reprinted courtesy Calvert Distillers Company.

Volvo ad. Reprinted by permission of the Volvo of America Corp.

Chadbourn, Inc. ad from *Cosmopolitan,* March 1970. Reprinted by permission of Stanwood Corporation.

Tsingtao ad. Reprinted by permission of Monarch Import Co.

"Dittos. For Boy Scouting" from *The New York Times Magazine,* August 17, 1980. Reprinted by permission of Hamilton Advertising.

**UNIT VI**

"People Magazine" from *Scribble Scribble: Notes on the Media* by Nora Ephron. Copyright © 1975, 1976, 1977, 1978 by Nora Ephron. Reprinted by permission of Alfred A. Knopf. Inc.

"Synopsis of *Psycho*" from *Filmfacts,* July 29, 1960, p. 153. We have been unable to locate the copyright holder. Any information would be appreciated.

"Synopsis of *Death of a Salesman*" taken from *The Reader's Encyclopedia of World Drama.* Reprinted by permission of Harper & Row Publishers, Inc.

Jacket copy from the Grove paperback edition of the Pulitzer Prize-winning novel *A Confederacy of Dunces* by John Kennedy Toole copyright © 1980 by Thelma Toole. Reprinted by permission of Grove Press, Inc.

Capsule book review of "The Comet is Coming" by Nigel Calder is reprinted from *Library Journal,* March 1, 1981. Published by R. R. Bowker Co. (a Xerox Company). Copyright © 1981 by Xerox Corporation.

Capsule book review of "When Elvis Died" by Neal Gregory and Janice Gregory is reprinted from *Library Journal,* February 15, 1981. Published by R. R. Bowker Co. (A Xerox company). Copyright © 1981 by Xerox Corporation.

Capsule film review of *Hester Street* by Rex Reed courtesy *Vogue.* Copyright © 1975 by The Condé Nast Publications, Inc.

Film synopsis of *City of Women,* in *Saturday Review,* April 1981. All rights reserved. Reprinted by permission.

"Movie Classics: *The Bride of Frankenstein*" by Edward Sorel from *Esquire* (May 1981). Copyright © 1981 by Esquire Publishing, Inc. Used by permission.

"Review of Three Films" by Gene Shalit, from *Ladies Home Journal,* Vol 92, (February 1972), p. 6. © 1972 by Gene Shalit. Reprinted by permission.

"Macbeth Returns" by Frank Rich © 1981 by The New York Times Company. Reprinted by permission.

"Bigotry As A Dirty Joke" excerpt from *This Pen for Hire* by John Leonard. Copyright © 1973 by John Leonard. Reprinted by permission of Doubleday & Company, Inc.

"Fathers and Sons" from *Reeling* by Pauline Kael, by permission of Little, Brown and Co. in association with the Atlantic Monthly Press.

"An Economist with Style" a review of John Kenneth Galbraith's memoirs entitled *A Life in Our Times* by James Fallows © 1981 by The New York Times Company. Reprinted by permission.

"Memoirs of an Unreconciled Liberal Thinker" by Lowell Ponte from *The Book Review, Los Angeles Times,* May 24, 1981, pp. 1 f. Lowell Ponte. Used by permission.

"Architecture for a Fast-Food Culture" by Ada Louise Huxtable © 1978 by The New York Times Company. Reprinted by permission.

Two diner photographs: Bob's Diner and Fireside Diner, from *The New York Times Magazine,* February 12, 1978, "Architecture for a Fast-Food Culture." Used by permission of John Baeder.

Photograph of Colonial Williamsburg used in *The New York Times Magazine* article "Architecture for a Fast-Food Culture," February 12, 1978. Used by permission of Colonial Williamsburg.

Service station photograph. No owner can be found. Any information pertaining to same will be appreciated.

MacDonalds photograph. Reprinted with permission of the MacDonalds Corporation.

Photograph of Shell Gas Station used in *The New York Times Magazine* article "Architecture for a Fast-Food Culture," February 12, 1978, pp. 23 ff. Used by permission of Shell Oil Company.

Two photographs of Jack-in-the-Box Family Restaurants used in *The New York Times Magazine* article "Architecture for a Fast-Food Culture," February 12, 1978, pp. 23 ff. Used by permission of Foodmaker, Inc.

"Solzhenitsyn, Aleksandr" *Book Review Digest* copyright © 1974, 1975 by The H. W. Wilson Company. Material reproduced by permission of the publisher.

# GETTING STARTED

# 1

# THE WRITING PROCESS

**F**ew people look forward to writing with much eagerness, and most probably recall frustrations, both from the difficulties of putting words on paper and from discouraging reactions once those words were finally down. No book can help you with all the problems you will encounter with writing, but we can try to point the way. One step in the right direction is to distinguish between frustrations that are inevitable and frustrations that you can avoid.

In the first place, writing is difficult. It is time-consuming labor, no less for a seasoned journalist used to producing thousands of words of serviceable prose a day than for a writer at work on her thirtieth novel, or for you as you try to describe the scene out the window. This is not to say that there are no rewards for this hard labor, whether it is collecting a paycheck, bringing pleasure to readers, or gaining control over your own language. But it *is* to say that writing will inevitably be frustrating at times. The only consolation is that the more of it you do, the easier it becomes.

One kind of frustration that you can do without, however, comes from believing that only special people, probably genetically gifted, can write. "I can't learn it," you might say, "and no one can teach it." Untrue. If you write conscientiously—daily is best, weekly the minimum—and have the benefit of constructive commentary, you cannot help improving. Belief in your own inadequacy is merely an excuse for not trying.

The opposite kind of frustration comes from believing in your own superiority. The block of perfectionism consists of not writing because you cannot think in advance of the perfect topic, argument, organization, sentence, phrase, or word. "If it can't be perfect," you might say, "I won't write at all."

**3**

The type-A overachiever does, of course, hand a paper in, but its imperfections only make the next assignment more difficult.

Much wasted time and energy could be reclaimed by a better understanding of the writing process. Many writing "blocks" and frustrations derive from the conventional image of writing as a two-step process of first discovering your meaning, your purpose or point, and then expressing it—literally pressing it out—in language. This constipated model is more a symptom of an ailment than a prescription for a cure. Instead of thinking of writing as a *product,* something you are finally able to make after you have thought sufficiently, planned sufficiently, researched sufficiently, and outlined sufficiently, think of it as a *process,* something that is organic, that is messy, that does not develop in straight lines, but that changes and evolves in the act of composing.

We endorse this description of writing from Peter Elbow's *Writing Without Teachers,* an excellent book on the writing process if you are motivated enough to write without the discipline imposed by the classroom:

> Meaning is not what you start out with, but what you end up with. Control, coherence, and knowing your mind are not what you start out with, but what you end up with. . . . Writing is a way to end up thinking something you couldn't have started out thinking. . . . What looks inefficient—a rambling process with lots of writing and lots of throwing away—is really efficient since it's the best way you can work up to what you really want to say and how to say it. The real inefficiency is to beat your head against the brick wall of trying to say what you mean, or trying to say it well, before you are ready. (New York, Oxford University Press, 1973, pp. 15–16)

Instead of trying to write that perfect paper on the first draft, slow down and take the time that writing requires. We ask you to think of writing as proceeding through three more or less chronological phases: *prewriting, writing* or *composing,* and *rewriting* or *revising.*

## PREWRITING

To overcome your belief in the perfect first draft, get used to the idea that there is necessary phase of play, experimentation, and research called prewriting. All successful writing needs this period of preparation. Consider the following kinds of prewriting activity and decide for yourself which ones are useful to you. If you already go through some process like this and do not have trouble getting started, by all means stay with what you do now.

### Unfocused Free Writing

As a way of getting started, unfocused free writing is an excellent exercise. Its purpose is to limber you up, to prepare you for the exertion to follow. You should think of this exercise as wholly private, something akin to keeping a diary, writing that will never be handed in for comment or evaluation. Try this exercise at least three times a week and begin with a ten-minute session, gradually working your way up to longer ones. What you do is put pen to paper and write without stopping for the duration of the session. Write about anything; write what is on your mind or the tip of your tongue. Record the day's events and your impressions of them. Describe the scene in front of you or tell a joke, but keep your pen moving. If nothing comes to mind, write "Nothing comes to mind" or repeat the preceding sentence until something does come to mind. Don't look back, don't cross out, don't search for the precise word, don't worry over the correct spelling. Just write. At the end of ten minutes you should have filled up a page or two.

Since you are not writing to be read by another person, you can be totally spontaneous. As you become used to writing this way, you will see that you can drift into relaxed free association, often bringing to the surface feelings and impressions from the unconscious. Sometimes you may wish to vent your emotional responses, your innermost feelings. Just becoming aware of these feelings is extremely valuable. Your feelings and impressions, your "sense of things," provide an important starting point for thinking and writing. Free writing in this way is useful for tapping into and exercising both your critical and your nonrational intelligences.

Remember not to worry that what comes out is not very coherent or articulate. Free writing is only practice. You are getting practice putting words on paper and gaining confidence in your ability to write without blocking. You will be writing without activating all those fears of making mistakes and getting things wrong that you may have built up over the years. That voice in your head that constantly tells you, "This isn't right," "Don't write that," "They'll laugh if you say this," is your internal editor. Though he may try to tell you that he is saving your reputation, like most tyrants all he is really doing is keeping you mute, inhibited, and fearful. If you practice free writing, you will subvert your internal editor, who may be your greatest enemy in getting started.

### Focused Free Writing/Brainstorming

Brainstorming is usually thought of as a group activity in which people pursuing a common goal or jointly working on a project get together to trade ideas and approaches. It is especially useful in a group when ideas from one person prompt new ideas from someone else. Working by yourself you may be able to do something of the same thing by adapting the free-writing exercise to specific writing tasks.

Focused free writing can be used to develop a specific topic if you have been assigned a general subject, such as "Write the story of a memorable childhood incident." Focusing on your childhood, you should then write as quickly as you can for as long as you can on that subject. At this stage in the writing process everything counts. Don't edit out anything. See what comes to you. At the end of half an hour or so, go back and read what you have written. You will probably be able to find a recurring idea, or you will be pulled especially toward one incident that will become the specific topic for your paper.

Focused free writing can be used again after you have found a specific topic (the day you had a fight in the schoolyard) or after you have accumulated material from researching a specific assigned topic (Write a film review of the movie *A Clockwork Orange*). Again at this stage, everything counts. Try focusing your free writing on the specific topic, using the following devices to provide the focus:

- *The journalistic "Five Ws (and an H)"*: who, what, when, where, why (and how). Whom did you fight? What happened during the fight? When did it happen? Where? Why were you fighting? Who was watching? Who won? How did it start? What happened when it was over? Such questions do not begin to exhaust the possibilities in the experience.

  The same sort of questioning can be applied to the film assignment: Who is the director? What other films has this director made? When was this one made? Why? What is the point or intention of the film? What kind of a film is it? (Does it belong to a particular genre or category?) Who is the main character? What happens to him (her)? Why does he act the way he does? Where does the action take place? And again, this quick list does not begin to exhaust the possible questions one might have after having seen the film and read some background on it.

- A second technique is to *interrogate your five senses:* sight, sound, taste, touch, and smell. What did you see during the fight? What did you hear? Do you remember any tastes or any smells? (Get your nose rubbed in the dirt?) Were blows landed? What did they feel like? And you can expand this list by considering your emotional reactions as well: How were you feeling? Do you remember anger, fear, hatred? What did you say?

  Even in recalling the movie you can interrogate your senses and your feelings to begin accounting for your reactions. What did you hear in the dialogue? The sound track? The music? What did you see? Although you can't, of course, speak of taste, touch, or smell except in a figurative way, you should be attentive to your emotional reactions: Why did a particular scene upset you? Was it designed that way? Why? Or did you find yourself unmoved by acts that you think should have upset you? Why did they have no effect? Was *that* response calculated?

The point here is that if you keep asking and answering such questions as part of a focused free-writing exercise, you will soon generate pages and pages of material from which you can begin the business of writing and shaping a first draft.

Remember, everything counts. Instead of frustrating yourself with premature questions like "Where do I begin?" and "How can I say that?" you are frustrating your internal editor, who has had no opportunity to go into action keeping you from filling up the page with your thoughts, reactions, and questions. If you spend thirty minutes or more in this way, you will have something concrete to show for your time: notes, ideas, phrases, and sentences, many of which may find their way into your final draft. Even if most of what you put down at this stage is unusable, at least you have not stewed unproductively in your own juices for the last hour.

### Journal Writing

Another excellent prewriting activity is to make regular journal entries. Journal entries can be made from anything: overheard conversations, thoughts that cross your mind while you are reading, dreams, a newspaper article, something that happened during the day, a memory. You can play when you write in your journal, tell jokes, try out sound effects, try on different writing voices; you can even do some free writing. But a journal is more formal than free writing. In free writing anything goes; in a journal almost anything goes. You should try for something in your journal: to make a point, record a thought, capture a moment. You can, of course, do the same in free writing; but a journal, unlike free writing, should imply an audience. Unfocused free writing can be like a diary, for your personal consumption only; a journal entry should be something that another person could profit from reading. A journal may still be personal, but it is not private. A journal is still practice, but it is closer to being a coherent paper than free writing is; it is more like a scrimmage than warmup calisthenics.

Another way of judging a good journal entry is to imagine yourself reading it in five or ten years: The entry should be able to put you back

into your experience. Comments like, "What a terrible week it's been. The
new job's a bore and I'll never take another math class. What a drag,"
don't put us anywhere. In a week this entry will be meaningless even to
the writer. You can put yourself back in the experience, though, with an
entry like this one, written by student Claire Schweighardt:

> Everyone was dressed in their leotards even though it was a little nippy.
> The teacher was putting on the music, while we were all stretching
> out our muscles. Some girls were doing splits. Ouch!! Because there
> was no room in any of the other classes, Debbie and I were put in an
> advanced class. Ballet is much more difficult than it looks or than I
> had imagined. We grope for the bar when we try to do a graceful turn.
> We muffle our groans when we stretch. We try not to, but we can't
> help making fools out of ourselves. Last night for instance, I noticed
> that when everyone ended up bowing, arms reaching the ground, we
> were on our toes with our arms over our heads. (We quickly changed
> position.)

### Background Reading and Viewing

We discuss critical reading at greater length in the next chapter, but
we want to talk about it here as a prewriting activity and as subject matter
for journal entries. Many of the writing assignments in this book are based
on writing that appears in the mass media. In some assignments you will
be asked to imitate that writing: to describe people or places; to narrate a
sports report; to compare and contrast rival products; to prepare arguments;
to review a film, book, or musical performance. In other assignments you
will be asked to analyze and evaluate how well others carry out such assignments. In both cases you will find that wide reading and viewing in the
media will help you prepare for these assignments.

As further prewriting activities we recommend that you:

- Read one newspaper daily, and not always the same one; your library
  should keep a variety of them. And don't neglect your college or
  university newspaper.
- Watch with a critical eye if you watch television; take notes if something interesting or especially ludicrous happens; and you might expand your experience by viewing documentaries, discussion programs,
  or serious drama that may not now be part of your regular viewing.
- See films and attend plays both on and off campus, again emphasizing
  the expansion of your experiences.
- Once a week browse through at least one issue of a magazine that

you have never read. Again your library should offer a variety of unfamiliar periodicals.

In order to focus your responses to these reading and viewing experiences, consider a simple, three-part formula:

- What did it say? Do you understand the words and their point or purpose?
- What did it mean? What are the implications or consequences of the material presented? What is the context?
- What do you think about what was said and meant?

You can also, of course, apply the journalistic five Ws and the sense questions from the focused free-writing exercise to this sort of viewing and reading as well.

You should record your reactions in your journal. If you use a small notebook for your entries, you can easily carry it around with you almost wherever you go to have it handy to write in. Or you might carry with you a small supply of 3 × 5 cards on which to make notes that you can later transfer into your journal notebook.

If you follow some of these suggestions as faithfully as possible, you will find, first, that you have more to write about than you ever imagined, and, second, that your level of general awareness of the world and your critical perspectives on it will be sharpened and broadened. And you can do much of this "work" just by approaching your normal reading and viewing habits more deliberately. The important point to realize is that the world at large is your laboratory. The newspaper you read, the TV you watch, and the films you see are part of your textbook. We hope to make the real world in all its dimensions, idiosyncracies, shapes, and forms your writing topic.

## WRITING

After you have chosen a topic, and after you have done some preliminary focused free writing, you are ready to confront the shaping of the first draft.

There can be no orderly procedure during this phase; what happens happens invisibly. What we can do is point out what tasks must be accomplished, leaving to you how to do them and in what order.

- Identify a purpose or point for your paper. A point or purpose stated directly is often called a "thesis statement" or "thesis sentence."

Though it is sometimes difficult to specify a single point, the step is crucial to organizing any paper. Ask yourself, "Why am I writing this?" (not just because it was assigned), "What am I trying to get across to the reader?" "Why would someone want to read this?" The point may be stated or unstated in the final draft, but it must be clear in your mind and come across clearly to your reader.

In reviewing your notes and your focused free writing, you must force yourself to reach a conclusion, to make a decision about what your purpose or point will be. Give yourself a time limit—fifteen minutes—and don't spend time at this stage stewing over whether what you are about to do is right or wrong. Decide and act by beginning to write again, to put words on paper, as soon as possible. Remember, your meaning is not what you start with, but what you end up with; it is what you are working toward. The only way to get there is to begin. There are no shortcuts.

Deciding on a purpose or point will be influenced by what kind of paper you are writing and your intention: Are you trying to describe a place vividly so as to give your reader a sense of being there? Or are you trying to demonstrate the superiority of one product over another? Or are you recommending a film you like? If you are writing an autobiographical piece, your intention may be more subtle: to tell a story from your own point of view, to say what it is like to be in a fight, or in an accident, or on a stage performing.

- Thinking about your audience will help you refine your purpose or point and also help you find an appropriate voice for that audience. How should this audience be approached? What sort of writing voice will get your point across to this audience? Are you describing a place with which they might be familiar or a totally alien environment? Is your subject a product they might use or one that they might never have heard of? Is it a film whose actors they might know or is it a foreign film whose actors are likely to be unfamiliar?
- Thinking about your audience will also help you select details from your prewriting material. What does your audience need to know? You don't want to insult them by saying too much that is obvious, or to leave them bewildered by saying too little.
- Having a purpose or point provides you with a guide for deciding, for example, whether to include a particular detail or not, a particular word or not, employ a particular technique or not. It will also help you find some logical or appropriate organization for the parts of your paper.
- At some point you will want to consider both how to begin and how to end your paper. It is best not to worry too soon about the beginning

and the end, however. Unless something leaps to mind immediately, save them for later. After most of the decisions have been made, work on an attractive or dramatic opening that invites your readers into your paper or compels their attention. Then see if you can find a satisfying ending.

## REWRITING

Rewriting is an ongoing process; technically, it is never finished. It can be divided into two kinds of activity: revising and editing or proofreading. No matter how carefully we may have researched a subject, no matter how much expertise we may have in it, we cannot write effectively without gaining control over our ideas and our language. Revising is the attempt to gain better control over our ideas and their presentation by searching for the right words, the right order of ideas, the proper emphasis, and the most appropriate style and voice with which to express ourselves. Editing involves eliminating unnecessary material and the proofreading tasks of checking for mechanical, grammatical, and spelling errors before handing in a final draft.

We repeat that while it is easy enough in a textbook to separate the several steps in the writing process, we should be aware that in reality these divisions are arbitrary. Certainly acts of writing and rewriting are often difficult to separate.

We urge you not to try to write a perfect paper in one draft, but to think of your first draft as an exploration. A first draft should be full of corrections, cancellations, insertions, and rephrasings. Even "second" drafts are rarely "final" drafts. Second drafts often have to do, but even professional writers will agree that whatever draft has found its way into print, it could have benefited from further redrafting. The poet Robert Lowell is said to have remarked that his poems were never finished, so much as abandoned. All this is to repeat that writing is a process with no preestablished ending; writing is not a product. We make concessions to our imperfections any time we turn in a piece of writing. We may wish to persuade ourselves that a draft is "finished," but we should know that there is always more we could do. Your instructor will obviously have to declare an end to rewriting (a decision that will probably not make you unhappy). The instructor may suggest that some assignments are best left at an early draft stage, while more promising ones should have more attention paid to them. In learning to write well or at least better, you must be willing to rewrite.

The best help you can have at this stage is a sympathetic audience. If your classroom is set up as a workshop, you will have the benefit of group discussion of your draft. Otherwise you will have your instructor's reactions, and you may or may not have the opportunity to revise after the instructor's criticism. If handing in an early draft is not part of the structure of your course, you (or patient friends or roommates) will have to provide the constructive criticism.

In revising you should review the same concerns you had in writing your first draft, plus you should pay special attention to clarity and economy: Have you said things well and with as few words as possible? Whether you work alone or in a group, here are some points to consider in looking over your first draft:

- Review your purpose. Picture your audience (you may assume an audience of your classmates and teacher) and establish just what it is you wanted to get across to them.
- Ask yourself if everything you have written contributes to the effects you are trying to create, the purpose you have in mind. Here is where group work is especially useful; you can ask your audience what point they got out of your writing. If you do not have a group, you will have to ask yourself if the reader will be able to understand your purpose from what you have written. This is often difficult to determine on your own without giving your piece time to "cool" because your own writing will tend to look pretty good to you. Unconsciously you will fill in details that are not really there; you will supply concrete instances behind vague or abstract words.
- If you are still unsure of your purpose, try reading your paper aloud to see if any leading ideas or feelings emerge and consider cutting out everything that does not relate to that lead thought or idea.
- At some point, if you have not done this already, try simply to outline the structure of your paper. Where does it start and end? How do the pieces relate to the purpose of the whole and to each other? Do the parts follow some logical order of time, place, importance, comparison and contrast, problem and solution, and do you maintain that order?
- At some point consider the beginning and the ending. Do they speak to each other or fit together in some way? Look especially to see if you haven't actually started your paper in paragraph 3 or 4. It is a common tendency (if you don't follow the advice we offered in the last section) to get off to a stumbling start before you finally find your voice, stride, and purpose.

The preceding points are "organic" considerations: how the piece functions as a whole. You should consider also more "mechanical" editing questions, sometimes called tightening and sharpening:

- Look for the weak repetition of words, especially words in close proximity, and for the repetition of ideas by mere rephrasing.
- Watch for the excessive use of common words like forms of the verb "to be" (is, are, was, were), including "it is" and "there are." Ask yourself if you really need them.
- Look for weak words and phrases that clutter sentences and fail to add meaning: "kind of," "sort of," "in regard to," "the fact that." These are some of the phrases that George Orwell points to as the ones that come flooding into our heads when we are tired of writing our own words and just want to make our prose sound pleasant: "cannot be left out of account," "deserving of serious consideration," "serve the purpose of." Be ruthless; cut them out.

A final revising step is proofreading:

- Have you avoided grammatical, mechanical, and spelling errors? It is useful to compile a "proofreading checklist" of errors of this kind that you are prone to make. Do you have difficulty distinguishing "affect" from "effect," "lie" from "lay," "there" from "their"? Make an entry on your checklist reminding yourself of your confusion and noting how to clear it up. Similarly, if you habitually misspell "judgment" or "receive" or "a lot," make an entry. Until you have made the correct usage a matter of habit or memory, you have no choice but to proofread carefully, looking for your characteristic mistakes.

## CASE STUDY: ELECTRONIC COMPOSITION AND EDITING

We conclude the section on the writing process with a case study of composition and rewriting by a professional writer. The study is valuable in itself for giving us a glimpse of the electronic technology that has been developed to aid writing and rewriting in the modern newsroom of the daily newspaper. It also demonstrates that professional writers *do* in fact revise. We cannot show you all the revisions this piece of writing went through, and so our example shows us only a small part of the revising process, mostly in wording. Still, it will repay careful study.

Newsrooms in many of our major metropolitan newspapers and in such news-service operations as Associated Press (AP) and United Press International (UPI), which supply copy to broadcast and print media alike, have become automated and no longer contain a single typewriter. Instead, these newsrooms function with computers. In place of conventional typewriters,

they contain numerous "video display terminals" (known as VDTs), or viewing screens with keyboards and optical scanners, which are hooked into a
computerized system with electronic memories that allow reporters to type
out their story, to scan any time what they have written on their private
screen, to revise instantly with a cursor (a spot of light that can move at
will over their "copy") any story being readied for the forthcoming edition
of the paper, and to carry on a wide assortment of compositional adjustments
and updatings. As we shall see in a moment, it is possible at any time to
obtain a printout of a story in the making.

All changes were, of course, recorded on the tapes so that the full genesis
of the story could be traced word for word if one wished to take the time
to study all the versions. Because it would be too cumbersome to present
all twenty-six copies of the text, we have decided to reprint here only key
versions of a single passage, the introduction to the article. So that you
can gain an idea of how a professional writer actually works, we include
Peter Gallagher's notes, a handwritten first copy of the introduction, and
then versions 1, 2, 8, 24, 25, and the final version as it appeared in print.

You will see that Gallagher first wrote brief, unrelated notes, sometimes
just words or phrases, sometimes whole sentences: "A man of action," "fearless," "small hands," "the true idea is to make tricks look pretty—not dangerous." This step is comparable to your own free writing where everything
that strikes you counts and should be written down without concern for
order, coherence, or the final draft.

Gallagher next wrote a first draft that would become the basis for the
first two paragraphs of his story. As a professional with some years of experience, and following the journalistic practice of settling on the "lead" to
the story first, Gallagher comes close to the final version in his first draft.
But there are still many important revising lessons to observe here.

We can gain some idea of the growth of the story by noting the number
of lines in each version, a figure shown at the head of all transcripts. Thus
the first "version"—a draft of the introduction only—consisted of 17 lines,
the sixth of 55 lines, the thirteenth of 125 lines, the twentieth of 202 lines,
and the twenty-sixth and last still of 202. These figures dramatically illustrate
that writing by professionals is typically an ongoing process and is usually
not the outcome of inspiration at a single session. It should be noted, too,
that even as the story grew, its contents were steadily changed. Each time
Gallagher sat down in front of the console he would add more paragraphs,
and as he read over what he had previously written, he would revise or
rewrite here and there. With the electronic cursor it was easy for him to
delete or add without having to disturb the rest of his copy because the
computer would automatically readjust and realign the rest of his text. Between versions 20 and 26, the final draft, he added no new lines. At the

Tito opposite of Codona — pure, sunshine, exalted by his own good fortune, constantly shouting greetings to people.

He speaks Span, Eng, Bulgarian, Russian, Italian, French, Swedish, German, Hungarian, Polish

A man of action    fearless    small hands
his soccer team would win the NASL (if we stayed in the same place)

a rock guitarist, classical pianist, collects antique cars, baker, boatsman, + fisherman high diver —
Chris Craft
Offered movie contract, offer by Mexico for gold medal Olympics
They were adjudged best flying act in world
Travels in style    four room miniature palace
Somber wizardry of Alfredo Cadona
Very athletic, perfectly coordinated
Alfredo    The true idea is to make
beautiful    tricks look pretty - not dangerous
hooded eyes    he describes quad as equal to
7 gold medals or first man on moon

*1.1 Original handwritten notes stemming from interview*

latter stages he spent his entire time tightening, sharpening, and improving his word choices and phrasing, not in reorganizing, adding, and deleting.

Look these versions over carefully. Study the transformation of notes to text, and try to justify the changes that Gallagher made as he brought

*1.2 First handwritten draft*

his story along. It is perhaps noteworthy that while he made minor changes in the early versions, he essentially left his introduction alone until he got to version 25. The changes from 24 to 25, therefore, deserve your special attention, for it was here that he did his most serious rewriting of the passage under examination.

Tito Gaona speaks Spanish English Bulgarian Russian Italian

French Swedish German Hungarian Polish and can say hello in 10
                                                        collector of antique cars
others.  He is a rock guitarist, classical pianist and one of the

best soccer players in the world.  He is an amateur boxer who would
                                                    expert
be welterweight champion of the world.  He is an high diver constantly
                                                  sked by
in search of cliffs and bridges to test.  He was a ~~standby~~ Mexico

to perform gymnastics on the Olympic team, asked by Fox to star in a

movie.  He is a legend in Russia and recognized on the streets of
                and has performed for the Queen
Stockholm.  ~~He-has-been-called-the-gre~~  Sports Illustrated magazine

has called him the world's greatest athlete.

*1.3 Transcription of handwritten notes*

### Version 1

1. Tito Gaona speaks Spanish, English, Bulgarian, Rus-
2. sian, Italian, French, Swedish, German, Hungarian, Polish
3. and can say hello in ten other languages. He is a rock guitar-
4. ist of unquestionable skill, a trained classical pianist,
5. knowledgeable collector of antique cars, and one of the very
6. best soccer players in the world. Built with the broad
7. shoulders and bee waist of an Adonis, he is an amatuer
8. boxer of such prowess he could be welterweight champion
9. of the world. He is a high diver constantly in search for
10. cliffs and bridges to daredevilize. He has been asked by
11. Mexico to perform gymnastics on its Olympic team and
12. tempted with contracts by MGM and Fox to become a dra-
13. matic actor. He is a legend in Russia and recognized on the
14. streets of Stockholm and has performed for kings and
15. queens. Sports Illustrated magazine has called him the
16. world's greatest athlete.

### Version 2

1. Tito Gaona speaks Spanish, English, Bulgarian, Rus-
2. sian, Italian, French, Swedish, German, Hungarian, Polish
3. and can say hello in ten other languages. He is a rock guitar-
4. ist of unquestionable skill, a trained classical pianist,

5. knowledgeable collector of antique cars, and one of the very
6. best soccer players in the world. Built with the broad
7. shoulders and bee waist and sculptured visage of an Latin
8. Adonis, he is an amateur boxer of such prowess he could be
9. welterweight champion of the world, an Alcapulco-class
10. high diver constantly searching for cliffs and bridges to
11. daredevilize, a gymnast who has been asked by Mexico to
12. perform on its Olympic team and a ladies man sought vigor-
13. ously by MGM and Fox to become a dramatic actor. He is a
14. legend among the acrobats in Russia, recognized on the
15. streets of Stockholm and a favorite performer of kings and
16. queens. Sports Illustrated magazine has called him the
17. world's greatest athlete.

*Changes from Version 1 to 2:*

| line 7 | *from* | "bee waist of an Adonis" |
|---|---|---|
| | *to* | "bee waist and sculptured visage of an Latin Adonis" |
| | *from* | "amatuer" *to* "amateur" |
| line 9 | *from* | "He is a high diver constantly in search" |
| | *to* | "an Alcapulco-class high diver constantly searching" |
| line 10 | *from* | "He has been asked by Mexico to perform gymnastics" |
| | *to* | "a gymnast who has been asked by Mexico to perform" |
| line 11 | *from* | "and tempted with contracts by MGM and Fox" |
| | *to* | "and a ladies man sought vigorously by MGM and Fox" |
| line 13 | *from* | "He is a legend in Russia" |
| | *to* | "He is a legend among acrobats in Russia" |
| | *delete* | "and" |
| line 14 | *from* | "and has performed for" |
| | *to* | "and a favorite performer of" |

**Version 8**

1.    Tito Gaona speaks Spanish, English, Bulgarian, Rus-
2. sian, Italian, French, Swedish, German, Hungarian, Polish
3. and can say hello in ten other languages. He is a rock guitar-
4. ist of unquestionable skill, a trained classical pianist, dis-
5. cerning collector of antique cars, and one of the very best
6. soccer players in the world. Built with the broad shoulders,
7. bee waist and sculptured visage of a Latin Adonis, he is an
8. amateur boxer of such prowess he could be the welter-
9. weight champion of the world. He is an Alcapulco-class
10. high diver in constant quest for cliffs and bridges to

11. daredevilize, a gymnast who has been asked by Mexico to
12. perform on its Olympic team and a ladies man sought vigor-
13. ously by MGM and Fox to become a dramatic actor. He is a
14. legend among the acrobats in Russia, recognized on the
15. streets of Stockholm and a favorite performer of kings and
16. queens. Sports Illustrated magazine has called him the
17. world's greatest athlete.

*Changes from Version 2 to 8:*

line 5   *from*   "knowledgeable"
         *to*     "discerning"
line 7   *from*   "shoulders and"
         *to*     "shoulders,"
         *from*   "an Latin"
         *to*     "a Latin"
line 9   *from*   ", an Alcapulco-class high diver constantly searching"
         *to*     ". He is an Alcapulco-class high diver in constant quest"

**Version 24**

1.   VENICE   Tito Gaona speaks Spanish, English, Bul-
2. garian, Russian, Italian, French, Swedish, German, Hun-
3. garian, Polish and can say hello in 10 other languages. He is
4. a rock guitarist of unquestionable skill, a trained classical
5. pianist, discerning collector of antique cars and one of the
6. very best soccer players in the world.
7.   Built with the broad shoulders, bee waist and sculp-
8. tured visage of a Latin Adonis, he is an amateur boxer of
9. such prowess he could be the welterweight champion of the
10. world. The man is an Acapulco-class high diver in constant
11. quest for cliffs and bridges to daredevilize, a gymnast invit-
12. ed by Mexico to perform on its Olympic team and a ladies
13. man sought vigorously by MGM and 20th Century Fox as a
14. dramatic actor. He is a legend among the acrobats in Rus-
15. sia, recognized on the streets of Stockholm and a favorite
16. performer of kings and queens. *Sports Illustrated* maga-
17. zine has called him the world's greatest athlete.

*Changes from Version 8 to 24:*

line 3   *from*   "ten" *to* "10"
line 6   *from*   no paragraph *to* paragraph

line 9     *from*    "He" *to* "The man"
line 11    *from*    "who has been asked"
           *to*      "invited"
line 13    *from*    "Fox to become"
           *to*      "20th Century Fox as a"
line 16              "Sports Illustrated" into italics

### Version 25

1.    VENICE   Tito Gaona speaks Spanish, English, Bul-
2. garian, Russian, Italian, French, Swedish, German, Hun-
3. garian, Polish and can say hello in 10 other languages. He is
4. a rock guitarist, a classical pianist, a collector of antique
5. cars, one of the best soccer players in the world, an amateur
6. boxer who could be welterweight champion of the world, an
7. Acapulco-class high diver, a gymnast invited by Mexico to
8. perform on its Olympic team and a ladies man sought by
9. MGM and 20th Century Fox as a dramatic actor. He is a
10. legend among the acrobats in Russia, recognized on the
11. streets of Stockholm and a favorite performer of kings and
12. queens. *Sports Illustrated* magazine has called him the
13. world's greatest athlete.

*Changes from Version 24 to 25:*

All changes are deletions of words appearing in Version 24.
line 4          *delete*    "of unquestionable skill"
                            "trained"
line 5                      "discerning"
                            "and"
lines 7–8                   "Built with the broad shoulders, bee waist and sculp-
                            tured features of a Latin Adonis, he is"
lines 8–9                   "of such prowess he"
line 10                     "The man is"
lines 10–11                 "in constant quest for cliffs and bridges to daredevilize"
line 13                     "vigorously"
two paragraphs are combined

### TITO REACHED FOR THE SKY AND WON

VENICE—Tito Gaona speaks Spanish, English, Bulgarian, Russian, Italian,
French, Swedish, German, Hungarian, Polish and can say hello in 10 other
languages. He is a rock guitarist, a classical pianist, a collector of antique

cars, one of the best soccer players in the world, an amateur boxer who could be welterweight champion of the world, an Acapulco-class high diver, a gymnast invited by Mexico to perform on its Olympic team and a ladies man sought by MGM and 20th Century-Fox as a dramatic actor. He is a legend among the acrobats in Russia, recognized on the streets of Stockholm and a favorite performer of kings and queens. *Sports Illustrated* magazine has called him the world's greatest athlete. (Peter B. Gallagher, *St. Petersburg Times,* January 2, 1978.)

### Questions

*Content/Meaning*
1. A large part of Gallagher's article has to do with Tito Gaona's attempt to do the very difficult quadruple somersault on the high wire. Do you feel that the introduction Gallagher has written prepares in a general way for the treatment of this topic? If not, what exactly does the introduction prepare for? Do you think it is effective?

*Style*
1. Examine closely all the revisions made by Gallagher from version 1 to the final copy. What are the most significant changes made? Apart from mere mechanics (such as spelling errors), do you think that all the changes were for the better? Isolate three changes and comment on them, both for what they were apparently meant to accomplish and whether they succeeded.
2. From version 24 to 25, comment on the paragraphing change that the author contemplated. Why, for example, might he have felt the need to divide the paragraph in version 24 in two? What would have caused him to return to a single paragraph in version 25?

## Exercises

1. You may have a different view of Gallagher's introduction once you know what the author says in the second paragraph. Here it is for you to read:

But forget all that. A hint, perhaps, of immortality in such impressive credits. Fleeting mortal glories all. But the God who is sometimes unfair in the delegation of good fortune has made insurances for Tito's shrine in the memory of time. Victor Daniel "Tito" Gaona dares to perform the quadruple somersault from the flying trapeze. For that alone his name will live on.

The paragraph quoted here asks the reader to forget what he was told in paragraph 1 and bear in mind only the one great gift that God has given to Tito Gaona. It is, therefore, quite directly a thesis sentence for the article. Nevertheless, because we obviously will not forget what we have already been told about Gaona, the first paragraph may be more arresting than it should be. Gallagher may have gone too far in trying to create reader interest. In an effort to provide an alternative opening that approaches the reader more directly, try to revise the two paragraphs in order that the thesis can be incorporated in the first paragraph.

2. As a way of beginning your journal, note your reactions to at least *three* mass media communications that especially interest you. Try in your entries to be critical; that is, stress *what* you heard, saw, and felt, and *why* you liked or disliked it.

3. Assume that you have been asked to write a 300-word paper on a topic of your choice. The only requirement is that this topic involve a personal experience of yours. You are to:

  *a.* List three or four subjects that you might choose. Indicate how long it took you to think up these topics. Did you consult your notebook? Was it far enough along to be helpful at this stage?
  *b.* Settle on one of these topics. Explain why you chose it in preference to the others.
  *c.* Write the paper.
  *d.* Keep a record of the difficulties you encountered in "getting started." Be prepared to discuss them in class and to exchange views on how to overcome them.

# 2

# CRITICAL
# READING

To read intelligently, you must read actively and must bear in mind the basic principles that apply to writing. Just as it is important to know what purpose, point, or main idea you will develop as a writer, so it is important to understand what purpose or point is developed in an essay you are reading. Just as it is important to gain control over your ideas, your writing style, and the voices you use in your writing, so it is important to be able to identify the ideas, voices, and styles in what you read.

Active, critical reading can be summarized in three simple steps:

- Find out what the selection *says*. Do you understand what all the words mean?
- Find out what the selection *means*. What is the point, purpose, or main idea of the selection? What are the implications of what the selection says? How does the author's attitude or voice influence the meaning?
- Decide what you *think* about what the selection says and means. What are your reactions to the ideas and implications of the essay? What specific words, sentences, and ideas prompted your reactions?

Let us examine, in more detail, how to go about taking these steps.

## REREADING

Read any essay or article you are asked to analyze at least twice. The first reading can be fairly quick. Don't stop to underline or take notes; try simply to grasp the main points that the writer is making. You might plan to make mental notes of certain parts in the essay, including the introduction for any clues it may give you to the thesis or purpose of the piece, the topic sentences of paragraphs, crucial or frequently repeated words or phrases, headings if they are included, and summaries such as often appear in conclusions. If you encounter crucial words that you do not know, look them up. You are reading to analyze a piece of writing, and for that purpose it is important to know everything that is being said.

## MARGINAL NOTES

The second reading should be done with pencil in hand. You should be willing to mark up your book or at least to photocopy the passage in question and put your marks on it. Underline crucial sentences and words, and make marginal notes wherever you think these might help. You should clearly know what the main idea of the piece of writing is and where it is stated. Be prepared to stop often—if the piece is complex perhaps after each paragraph—and note the main assertions that are being made. The latter are frequently signaled by such phrases as "most important," or "significantly" or "in the first place." You might also note what attitudes the writer is expressing toward the subject and identify segments of the essay that give an indication of the author's point of view. In the same manner you should note appeals made to the reader attempting to figure out for whom the essay was written.

## READING ANALYSIS

After you have made marginal notes and underlined the most important passages, you should try to answer as many of the following questions about the selection as you can:

- What is the main idea or point of the essay? Did the writer introduce more than one main topic? What supports the main idea?
- How well did the writer organize the topic? Were clear signals given to indicate major subdivisions? Were ideas developed coherently? What seemed to be the writer's favorite devices for providing linkage between ideas or points?
- Do you think the selection is interesting? If so, how does it achieve its effect? Are there arresting examples or incidents? Are any really startling or original statements made? Does the author have an interesting writing voice? Is the language and style of the writing attractive?

- What, finally, did you learn from the piece? Did it change your attitude, add to your knowledge, anger you, or simply entertain you? Was your time well spent reading it? What specifically makes you feel that it was or was not worthwhile?

It is, obviously, not necessary to read everything critically; your pace will vary according to the type of reading you are doing. In this book, especially in the early chapters, we have sometimes inserted commentaries designed as examples of close critical reading. The exercises and illustrations, in turn, will provide you with opportunities to practice such reading collectively and on your own.

George Orwell is the pen name of Eric Blair, an English novelist, critic, and socialist who is perhaps most famous for his novels *Animal Farm,* a satire of Stalinist Russia, and *1984,* a vision of a future totalitarian society. The following passage from his famous essay, "Politics and the English Language," will give you some practice in critical reading.

Most people who bother with the matter at all would admit that the English language is in a bad way, but it is generally assumed that we cannot by conscious action do anything about it. Our civilization is decadent and our language—so the argument runs—must inevitably share in the general collapse. It follows that any struggle against the abuse of language is a sentimental archaism, like preferring candles to electric light or hansom cabs to aeroplanes. Underneath this lies the half-conscious belief that language is a natural growth and not an instrument which we shape for our own purposes. [*A Collection of Essays* (Garden City, N.Y.: Doubleday, 1954), p. 162.]

### Questions

*Content/Meaning*
1. What does the word "decadent" mean? The word "archaism"? All good dictionaries include etymologies of words in square brackets following the definitions. Etymology is the study of a word's history and origin using, in part, that word's basic elements. What are the basic elements of "decadent" and "archaism"? To what other words are they etymologically related?
2. What does the phrase "sentimental archaism" mean? What examples of it does Orwell give? Can you think of other examples?
3. What is the "thesis statement" of this paragraph?
4. What are the different implications of thinking of language as a "natural growth" and of thinking of it as an "instrument"? How does Orwell think of it? How do you know?

*Style*
1. How would you characterize the language in this paragraph?
2. Does the paragraph make you want to read the rest of the essay? Why or why not?
3. If you found this paragraph difficult to read, how would you rewrite it to get its point across more easily?

# 3

# THE WRITTEN VOICE

It seems contradictory to talk about a writer's voice when so clearly voice is what generates speech, not written language. But the world of speech and writing are very closely related. Interestingly, a good many terms by which we describe the writing process have been borrowed from speech—words like *audience, tone, figure of speech,* even *rhetoric* (which comes from a Greek verb meaning "to speak"). Writing is, after all, a secondary form of communication, one that is in many ways modeled on the speech act and that is usually acquired well after a person has learned both to speak and to read.

## ROLE PLAYING

The writer's voice is the device by which we discover the personality that the writer wishes to project on the written page. It is the way in which writers signal the particular roles they wish to play before their unseen audiences. We speak here of more than one role because writers, like speakers, have many voices by which to reveal themselves. Most if not all of us use one vocabulary and tone when we speak with a lover, another with a parent, another with the corner druggist, and yet another with a prospective employer. The vocabulary we use—ranging from profanity to elevated abstractions (and most educated people make use of the whole range)—is usually different from one situation to another, as are the tone of our voices, the complexity of our thoughts, and even our social or regional dialect. Role playing, or assuming voices, is only a way of coordinating our lives with the lives of

**27**

others, of providing the means to integrate ourselves in different social situations.

The same sort of role playing is evident in entire publications, newspapers, and magazines, which are attempting to project a certain relationship with their target audiences. No one voice is by nature "better" than another; it is simply more "appropriate" to some situations than to others, or it is more effective at accomplishing its intended goals. Consider the example of newspapers. They can be classified into two general kinds: the standard format papers, such as the good, gray *New York Times,* staid and serious, and addressed primarily to well-educated, upper-income, middle- and upper-middle-class audiences; and the tabloids, such as the *New York Daily News,* addressed primarily to the less well educated (for years its nickname for itself was "the picture newspaper"), lower-income, lower-middle and working classes. Stories in standard format papers tend toward national and international political news; the tabloids tend toward stories about violent crimes, natural disasters and accidents, life threatening or unusual hospital operations, sex, money, and the bizarre.

## Reading Selection

It is not surprising that the standard format newspaper and the tabloid, which differ so greatly in look, intention, and audience, should also speak in distinct voices. What follows are the headlines and opening paragraphs for the same news story in a standard format newspaper and a tabloid.

### Berkowitz Outbursts Disrupt Court; Sentencing Put Off, Tests Ordered

David R. Berkowitz, who was scheduled to be sentenced yesterday for the six "Son of Sam" murders, battled officers before entering the courtroom, then walked in chanting, "Stacy is a whore."

The courtroom erupted in turmoil, and, only minutes after he entered, Mr. Berkowitz was dragged out by half a dozen guards. His sentencing was postponed for three weeks, and a new psychiatric examination on his competency—the third ordered by the court—was scheduled.

The 24-year-old defendant arrived at State Supreme Court in Brooklyn shortly before 10 A.M. and was taken to the seventh-floor office of Dominick Ruocco, the chief court officer. Inexplicably, he rushed toward a large window.

Court officers battled to stop him, and one, Capt. Thomas O'Toole, suffered a torn leg muscle. Another, Capt. Joseph Murphy, was bitten on the arm.

From *The New York Times,* May 23, 1978.

## BERKOWITZ GOES WILD IN COURT

### Screams: "I'll Kill Them All"

His eyes flashing and his voice a clear singsong, David Berkowitz went berserk
at his sentencing hearing in Brooklyn Supreme Court yesterday, throwing
the proceedings into pandemonium as he chanted, "Stacy is a Whore, Stacy
is a Whore" about the last of his six murder victims.

His sentencing was delayed until June 12.

It was the second violent outburst of an emotion-packed morning by
the confessed .44-caliber killer, who earlier, in a possible suicide attempt,
had broken from guards and tried to plunge from a seventh-floor window
onto Court St. The melee left one court officer hospitalized and another
injured.

From the *New York Daily News,* May 23,
1978.

The world of the *Daily News* is exciting and thrilling because the voice
of the reporter is excited and thrilled. Notice that the *News* version uses
more and simpler words to describe the events and at the same time is shorter
and carries less information, though more emotional impact. What in the
*Times* were described with reserve as "outbursts" are in the *News* described
with the informal and hysteric "goes wild" and "went berserk"; whereas in
the *Times* Berkowitz disrupted court, in the *News* he threw "the proceedings
into pandemonium," perhaps reminding us that the defendant once explained
his actions as being directed by demons. The *News* voice sounds urgent,
perhaps even threatened, a writing strategy designed to affect readers emotionally, to draw them into the "emotion-packed morning." The *Times* reports
coldly, dispassionately, and specifically that "Capt. Thomas O'Toole suffered
a torn leg muscle. Another, Capt. Joseph Murphy, was bitten on the arm."
The *News,* by contrast, is vague and alarming: "The melee left one court
officer hospitalized and another injured." What is lost in specificity is made
up for by the suggestion of greater violence and danger. Another incident
that the *Times* can only describe as an inexplicable rush toward a large
window, the *News* breathlessly describes as "a possible suicide attempt" and
then as a potential "plunge from a seventh-floor window onto Court St.,"
the report suddenly becoming more specific in order to enhance the sense
of danger. The traditional news voice of the standard format newspaper is
calmly factual and addressed to readers seeking information; the tabloid voice
is livelier, not so restrained, and aimed at entertaining an audience as much
interested in vicarious emotional involvement as in being informed.

The tone of voice, then, is determined by the intentions and talent of
the writer and by the audience the writer is addressing. That tone is expressed

in the style of the writing: the details the writer selects, the emotions revealed (or concealed), the word choices the writer makes, even the length and rhythm of the sentences.

## DENOTATION/CONNOTATION

The tone of the writer's voice depends in part on word choice. Choosing the precise word to carry the intended meaning depends in turn on knowing the distinction between denotative and connotative meaning, and on being able to distinguish among words with similar meanings. *Denotation* is usually taken to mean "dictionary definition," agreed-upon primary meaning; it is meaning without emotional color. *Connotation,* on the other hand, refers to suggested meanings, the impressions and feelings that a word or phrase arouses. Connotative meaning is sensitive to context and often carries positive or negative judgments about what it describes. The charge of charged language comes from connotative meaning. The writer can say "He *strode* into the room" and create a positive impression by suggesting that the man is strong and assertive or he can say "He *stumbled* into the room" and create a negative impression by suggesting clumsiness or even drunkenness.

Another way of thinking about denotation and connotation is to understand the connotative meaning as what distinguishes each word in a group of roughly synonymous words from each other. Thus, while "plump," "obese," "paunchy," "fat," and "overweight" all denote a body whose shape deviates from the trim ideal of advertising images, each connotes a slightly different condition and carries slightly different feelings.

The British philosopher Bertrand Russell made up a word game based on the range of connotative meaning found in groups of roughly synonymous words. On a British Broadcasting Company radio show called "The Brain Trust," Russell gave the following "conjugation" of an "irregular verb":

I am firm.

You are obstinate.

He is a pig-headed fool.

All of the descriptive adjectives denote someone who will not give in to another's opinion. The game is in arranging a group of words in connotative progression according to the pattern: I am better than you are are, but you are better than he is.

| | |
|---|---|
| I am discriminating. | I am cautious. |
| You are prejudiced. | You are timid. |
| He is a bigot. | He's a coward. |

With a little practice, you should be able to devise some "irregular verbs" of your own.

## Exercises

1. See if you can match the voices you hear in the following passages with the characters listed. Be as specific as you can about your reasons for assigning a particular voice to a particular character. The list:

| | |
|---|---|
| teenage girl | southern belle |
| teenage boy | southern preacher |
| 7-year-old girl | salesman |
| mind-reader | John F. Kennedy |
| a mother | Richard M. Nixon |
| English teacher | high school principal |
| Ronald Reagan | businessman |
| confessional poet | New York City taxi driver |

The passages:

  *a.* So when I draw the Lord, He'll be a real big man. He has to be to explain about the way things are.
  *b.* Mister Hoyle made a deck of cards with fifty-two cards in the deck, representin' the fifty-two weeks in the year, and the three hundred and sixty-five spots on the cards represented the three hundred and sixty-five days in the year. Mister Hoyle remembered that there was sometimes extra games played in these cards, an' he thought about the leap year, an' Mister Hoyle put a Joker in the deck of cards that you could play every now and then.
  *c.* Some day, you are going to learn that the two greatest joys of being a man are beating the hell out of someone and getting the hell beat out of you.

    *d.* You must stay alert at all times. Never believe the way things look. The garbage collectors believe everything is simple and that's why they're garbage collectors.

    *e.* I should like to have Lionnet back. I'd like to see it fixed up again, the way Mama and Papa had it. Every year it used to get a nice coat of paint—Papa was very particular about the paint—and the lawn was so smooth all the way down to the river, with the trims of zinnias and the red-feather plush.

    *f.* America is full of beautiful towns and fine, upstanding people. And they know me, they know me up and down New England. The finest people.

    *g.* With faith in God and faith in ourselves and faith in our country, let us have the vision and the courage to seize the moment and meet the challenge before it slips away.

    *h.* They come here day and night, so many people . . . fashionable folk, mocking and ravenously credulous, and skeptics bent on proving me a fraud for fear that some small wonder, unexplained, should leave a fissure in the world, and all Saint Michael's host come flapping back.

    *i.* If I could go through it all again, the slender iron rungs of growing up, I would be as young as any, a child lost in unreality and loud music.

2. Try your hand at putting on a voice:

    *a.* Choose a role, then write a short passage of dialogue from which a reader could discern your identity; don't refer directly to your role in the dialogue.

    *b.* Find a news story from a serious, standard format newspaper that attracts your attention. Take several paragraphs and rewrite them for a lurid, sensation-mongering tabloid. Rewrite the headline as well.

    *c.* Transform a tabloid story to a standard news story.

## THE FIRST-PERSON SPEAKER

    Writers who use the first person have a great deal of freedom. They are not restricted by a formula, like the one used to write a news article, and the first person can be adapted to all kinds of writing: description, narration, explanation, argument, or criticism.

    The writer should at some point imagine the audience to be addressed and then decide on the tone of voice to adopt. Will the writer speak with tongue in cheek? Adopt the role of an expert? Defer to the wisdom of the reader and speak as one merely using common sense? Will the writer be angry, ludicrous, self-critical, arrogant, deferential, wise, naive? Is the aim to shock the reader or to bludgeon him with the writer's own viewpoint? Or is the goal, above all, to be seen as judicious and fair-minded? The decisions a writer makes in answering these kinds of questions will determine the writing voice.

## Reading Selection

The essay that follows, a successful first-person narrative, was first published in *Change* magazine, a journal of limited circulation geared to a college-educated readership and focusing on issues related to higher education. The version printed here is cut down from the original, which was a feature-length article. The subject to which the writer relates himself is "open admissions," a social experiment instituted by the City College of New York in the late 1960s and then abruptly stopped in 1976 as a result of a fiscal crisis. It is clear from the article that Peter Rondinone looks upon himself as a beneficiary of the open admissions system. While the whole story of his own experience gradually leads to a persuasive premise, he saves his argument for the end. If it moves us, it does so because we have been "hooked" by the authenticity of the writer's voice. Pay special attention to the quality of Rondinone's voice and to the way he uses his personal drama in developing his point.

### "DO I LOOK LIKE AN ANIMAL?"

#### *Peter J. Rondinone*

The fact is, I didn't learn much in high school. I spent my time on the front steps of the building smoking grass with the dudes from the dean's squad. For kicks we'd grab a freshman, tell him we were undercover cops, handcuff him to a banister, and take his money. Then we'd go to the back of the building, cop some "downs," and nod away the day behind the steps in the lobby. The classrooms were overcrowded anyhow, and the teachers knew it. They also knew where to find me when they wanted to make weird deals: If I agreed to read a book and do an oral report, they'd pass me. So I did it and graduated with a "general" diploma. I was a New York City public school kid.

I hung out on a Bronx streetcorner with a group of guys who called themselves "The Davidson Boys" and sang songs like "Daddy-lo-lo." Everything we did could be summed up with the word "snap." That's a "snap." She's a "snap." We had a "snap." Friday nights we'd paint ourselves green and run through the streets swinging baseball bats. Or we'd get into a little rape in the park. It was all very perilous. Even though I'd seen a friend stabbed for wearing the wrong colors and another blown away with a shotgun for "messin'" with some dude's woman, I was too young to realize that my life too might be headed toward a violent end.

Then one night I swallowed a dozen Tuminols and downed two quarts of beer at a bar in Manhattan. I passed out in the gutter. I puked and rolled under a parked car. Two girlfriends found me and carried me home. My overprotective brother answered the door. When he saw me—eyes rolling toward the back of my skull like rubber—he pushed me down a flight of stairs. My skull hit the edge of a marble step with a thud. The girls screamed. My parents came to the door and there I was: a high school graduate, a failure, curled in a ball in a pool of blood.

The next day I woke up with dried blood on my face. I had no idea what had happened. My sister told me. I couldn't believe it. Crying, my mother confirmed the story. I had almost died! That scared hell out of me. I knew I had to do something. I didn't know what. But pills and violence didn't promise much of a future.

I went back to a high school counselor for advice. He suggested I go to college.

I wasn't aware of it, but it seems that in May 1969 a group of dissident students from the black and Puerto Rican communities took over the south campus of the City College of New York (CCNY). They demanded that the Board of Higher Education and the City of New York adopt an open-admission policy that would make it possible for anybody to go to CCNY without the existing requirements: SATs and a high school average of 85. This demand was justified on the premise that college had always been for the privileged few and excluded minorities. As it turned out, in the fall of 1970 the City University's 18 campuses admitted massive numbers of students—15,000—with high school averages below 85. By 1972, I was one of them.

On the day I received my letter of acceptance, I waited until dinner to tell my folks. I was proud.

"Check out where I'm going," I said. I passed the letter to my father. He looked at it.

"You jerk!" he said. "You wanna sell ties?" My mother grabbed the letter.

"God," she said. "Why don't you go to work already? Like other people."

"Fuck that," I said. "You should be proud."

At the time, of course, I didn't understand where my parents were coming from. They were immigrants. They believed college was for rich kids, not the ones who dropped downs and sang songs on streetcorners.

My mother had emigrated from Russia after World War II. She came to the United States with a bundle of clothes, her mother and father, a few dollars, and a baby from a failed marriage. Her first job was on an assembly line in a pen factory where she met my father, the production manager.

My father, a second-generation Italian, was brought up on the Lower East Side of Manhattan. He never completed high school. And when he wasn't working in a factory, he peddled Christmas lights door to door or sold frankfurters in Times Square.

My family grew up in the south Bronx. There were six children, and we slept in one room on cots. We ate spaghetti three times a week and were on welfare because for a number of years my father was sick, in and out of the hospital.

Anyhow, I wasn't about to listen to my parents and go to work; for a dude like me, this was a big deal. So I left the dinner table and went to tell my friends about my decision.

The Davidson Boys hung out in a rented storefront. They were sitting around the pool table on milk boxes and broken pinball machines, spare tires and dead batteries. I made my announcement. They stood up and circled me like I was the star of a cockfight. Sucio stepped to the table with a can of beer in one hand and a pool stick in the other.

"Wha' you think you gonna get out of college?" he said.

"I don't know, but I bet it beats this," I said. I shoved one of the pool balls across the table. That was a mistake. The others banged their sticks on the wood floor and chanted, "Oooh-ooh—snap, snap." Sucio put his beer on the table.

"Bullshit!" he yelled. "I wash dishes with college dudes. You're like us—nuttin', man. He pointed the stick at my nose.

Silence.

I couldn't respond. If I let the crowd know I thought their gig was uncool, that I wanted out of the club, they would have taken it personally. And they would have taken me outside and kicked my ass. So I lowered my head. "Aw, hell, gimme a hit of beer," I said, as if it were all a joke. But I left the corner and didn't go back.

I spent that summer alone, reading books like *How to Succeed in College* and *30 Days to a More Powerful Vocabulary*. My vocabulary was limited to a few choice phrases like, "Move over, Rover, and let Petey take over." When my friends did call for me I hid behind the curtains. I knew that if I was going to make it, I'd have to push these guys out of my consciousness as if I were doing the breaststroke in a sea of logs. I had work to do, and people were time consuming. As it happened, all my heavy preparations didn't amount to much.

On the day of the placement exams I went paranoid. Somehow I got the idea that my admission to college was some ugly practical joke that I wasn't prepared for. So I copped some downs and took the test nodding. The words floated on the page like flies on a crock of cream.

Before class we had rapped about our reasons for going to college. Some said they wanted to be the first in the history of their families to have a college education—they said their parents never went to college because they couldn't afford it, or because their parents' parents were too poor—and they said open admissions and free tuition ($65 per semester) was a chance to change that history. Others said they wanted to be educated so they could return to their neighborhoods to help "the people"; they were the idealists. Some foreigners said they wanted to return to their own countries and start schools. And I said I wanted to escape the boredom and the pain I had known as a kid on the streets. But none of them said they expected a job. Or if they did they were reminded that there were no jobs. . . .

In math I was in this remedial program for algebra, geometry, and trigonometry. But unlike high school math, which I thought was devised to boggle the mind for the sake of boggling, in this course I found I could make a connection between different mathematical principles and my life. For instance, there were certain basics I had to learn—call them 1, 2, and 3—and unless they added up to 6 I'd probably be a failure. I also got a sense of how math related to the world at large: Unless the sum of the parts of a society equaled the whole there would be chaos. And these insights jammed my head and made me feel like a kid on a ferris wheel looking at the world for the first time. Everything amazed me!

That made my freshman year difficult. The administration had placed me in all three remedial programs: basic writing, college skills, and math. I was shocked. I had always thought of myself as smart. I was the only one in the neighborhood who read books. So I gave up the pills and pushed aside another log.

The night before the first day of school, my brother walked into my room and threw a briefcase on my desk. "Good luck, Joe College," he said. He smacked me in the back of the head. Surprised, I went to bed early.

I arrived on campus ahead of time with a map in my pocket. I wanted enough time, in case I got lost, to get to my first class. But after wandering around the corridors of one building for what seemed like a long time and hearing the sounds of classes in session, the scrape of chalk and muted discussions, I suddenly wondered if I was in the right place. So I stopped a student and pointed to a dot on my map.

"Look." He pointed to the dot. "Now look." He pointed to an inscription on the front of the building. I was in the right place. "Can't you read?" he said. Then he joined some friends. As he walked off I heard someone say, "What do you expect from open admissions?"

I had no idea that there were a lot of students who resented people like me, who felt I was jeopardizing standards, destroying their institution. I had no idea. I just wanted to go to class.

In Basic Writing I the instructor, Regina Sackmary, chalked her name in bold letters on the blackboard. I sat in the front row and reviewed my *How to Succeed* lessons: Sit in front/don't let eyes wander to cracks on ceilings/take notes on a legal pad/make note of all unfamiliar words and books/listen for key phrases like "remember this," they are a professor's signals. The other students held pens over pads in anticipation. Like me, they didn't know what to expect. We were public school kids from lousy neighborhoods and we knew that some of us didn't have a chance; but we were ready to work hard.

Like biology. In high school I associated this science with stabbing pins in the hearts of frogs for fun. Or getting high snorting small doses of the chloroform used for experiments on fruit flies. But in college biology I began to learn and appreciate not only how my own life processes functioned but how there were thousands of other life processes I'd never known existed. And this gave me a sense of power, because I could deal with questions like, Why do plants grow? not as I had before, with a simple spill of words: " 'Cause of the sun, man." I could actually explain that there was a plant cycle and cycles within the plant cycle. You know how the saying goes—a little knowledge is dangerous. Well, the more I learned the more I ran my mouth off, especially with people who didn't know as much as I did.

I remember the day Ms. Sackmary tossed Sartre's *No Exit* in my lap and said, "Find the existential motif." I didn't know what to look for. What was she talking about? I never studied philosophy. I turned to the table of contents, but there was nothing under E. So I went to the library and after much research I discovered the notion of the absurd. I couldn't believe it. I told as many people as I could. I told them they were absurd, their lives were absurd, everything was absurd. I became obsessed with existentialism. I read Kafka, Camus, Dostoevski, and others in my spare time. Then one day I found a line in a book that I believed summed up my unusual admittance to the college and my determination to work hard. I pasted it to the headboard of my bed. It said: "Everything is possible."

To deal with the heavy workload from all my classes, I needed a study schedule, so I referred to my *How to Succeed* book. I gave myself an hour for lunch and reserved the rest of the time between classes and evenings for homework and research. All this left me very little time for friendships. But I stuck to my schedule and by the middle of that first year I was getting straight A's. Nothing else mattered. . . .

I once watched a network television crew interview a campus newspaper staff for a documentary on open admissions. An interviewer from "60 Minutes," notebook on his lap, sat like he had a box of Cracker Jacks, opposite

three campus editors who looked as if they were waiting for the prize. I
stood in a corner. He passed a remark: "I was down at the Writing Center
today. Those kids are animals. They can't write." The editors, who were a
conservative bunch, shook their heads as if they understood this to be their
terrible legacy. I wanted to spit.

"Hey you!" I said. "Do I look like an animal?"

He closed his notebook and looked down his long nose at me. I felt
like an ant at the mercy of an aardvark. The editors got puffy. "Who is
this kid?" they mumbled. "Who do you think you are?" I yelled back. "Those
kids you are talking about are not only willing to learn, but they are learning.
They've written some beautiful essays and stories. You stupid fuck!"

God, those early days were painful. Professors would tear up my papers
the day they were due and tell me to start over again, with a piece of advice—
"Try to say what you really mean." Papers I had spent weeks writing. And
I knew I lacked the basic college skills; I was a man reporting to work
without his tools. So I smiled when I didn't understand. But sometimes it
showed and I paid the price: A professor once told me the only reason I'd
pass his course was that I had a nice smile. Yes, those were painful days.

And there were nights I was alone with piles of notebooks and textbooks.
I wanted to throw the whole mess out the window; I wanted to give up.
Nights the sounds of my friends singing on the corner drifted into my room
like a fog over a graveyard and I was afraid I would be swept away. And
nights I was filled with questions but the answers were like moon shadows
on my curtains: I could see them but I could not grasp them.

Yet I had learned a vital lesson from these countless hours of work in
isolation: My whole experience from the day I received my letter of acceptance
enabled me to understand how in high school my sense of self-importance
came from being one of the boys, a member of the pack, while in college
the opposite was true. In order to survive, I had to curb my herd instinct.

Nobody, nobody could give me what I needed to overcome my sense
of inadequacy. That was a struggle I had to work at on my own. It could
never be a group project. In the end, though people could point out what
I had to learn and where to learn it, I was always the one who did the
work; and what I learned I earned. And that made me feel as good as being
one of the boys. In short, college taught me to appreciate the importance
of being alone. I found it was the only way I could get any serious work
done.

But those days of trial and uncertainty are over, and the open-admission
policy has been eliminated. Anybody who enters the City University's senior
colleges must now have an 80 percent high school average. And I am one
of those fortunate individuals who in a unique period of American education
was given a chance to attend college. But I wonder what will happen to

those people who can learn but whose potential doesn't show in their high school average; who might get into street crime if not given a chance to do something constructive? I wonder, because if it weren't for open admissions, the likelihood is I would still be swinging baseball bats on the streets on Friday nights.

From *Change* 9, no. 5. Reprinted in *The Clarion* (PSC/CUNY) 7, no. 4 (December 1977).

### Commentary

The quality that attracts immediate attention when one finishes reading Rondinone's essay is its literacy. Now, literacy is usually a minimal requirement for essays in a journal like *Change*. But what is so important in this essay is that the acquisition of literacy is exactly what the writer is describing. The voice of the writer is, therefore, first and foremost, "educated" and at times even learned. We watch it develop with every "breaststroke in a sea of logs." In the beginning, as the writer describes his unenlightened precollege life, he mimics his former language, telling us about "grass," "dudes," and "downs," and freely using profanities and street language. The essay is very much concerned with the acquisition of a new vocabulary—in English class to "make note of all unfamiliar words"—and when he now uses words like *perilous, premise, consciousness, existentialism, legacy,* and *absurd,* we have all the evidence we need from his own voice that his remedial training was gloriously successful. Another point needs to be noted: Rondinone tells us that none of the students with whom he associated went to college expecting a job. His own purpose was to shed the "herd instinct" and become self-aware and cultivated. The contrast between his former and his present days is made particularly in these terms. His former life was essentially that of an animal who engaged, with his buddies, in "a little rape in the park" for amusement on Friday nights. He was a member of a herd. The anger that the interviewer's question aroused was naturally focused on blindness to the accomplishments of open admissions and on his prejudice. The interviewer was not referring to—because he could not know about—incidents like the ones in the park, but to verbal deficiencies. If Rondinone and others like him had been "animals" in their precollege days, then they were something far different and better at the Writing Center.

The essay is a beautifully controlled dramatic demonstration through an enlightened first-person voice of what it means to become self-aware. The writer's voice is at times rough, angry, self-denouncing, and resentful. But it is finally altogether positive and full of justified pride in achievement. Here is a writer who has conquered drugs, boredom, and ignorance through the power of language. His own resonance proves that for him, words will never again float "on the pages like flies on a crock of cream." These words are themselves proof of his transformation: Even his language has shed its animal shapes.

## Reading Selections

What follows are three different accounts of the Apollo 11 moonlanding. As you read, pay special attention to differences in voice and style.

### MEN WALK ON MOON

#### *John Noble Wilford*

HOUSTON, Monday, July 21—Men have landed and walked on the moon.

Two Americans, astronauts of Apollo 11, steered their fragile four-legged lunar module safely and smoothly to the historic landing yesterday at 4:17:40 P.M., Eastern daylight time.

Neil A. Armstrong, the 38-year-old civilian commander, radioed to earth and the mission control room here:

"Houston, Tranquility Base here. The Eagle has landed."

The first men to reach the moon—Mr. Armstrong and his co-pilot, Col. Edwin E. Aldrin, Jr. of the Air Force—brought their ship to rest on a level, rock-strewn plain near the southwestern shore of the arid Sea of Tranquility.

About six and a half hours later, Mr. Armstrong opened the landing craft's hatch, stepped slowly down the ladder and declared as he planted the first human footprint on the lunar crust:

"That's one small step for man, one giant leap for mankind."

His first step on the moon came at 10:56:20 P.M., as a television camera outside the craft transmitted his every move to an awed and excited audience of hundreds of millions of people on earth.

From *The New York Times,*
July 21, 1969, p. 1.

### THE RIDE DOWN

#### *Norman Mailer*

Now their landing lights burn down on the sunlit moon ground to beam through the dust, and now comes the dust. At thirty feet above the ground, a great amount blows out in all directions like an underwater flower of the sea and the ground is partially visible beneath as if "landing in a very fast-moving ground fog," and the fuel gauges almost empty, and still he drifts forward. "Thirty seconds," calls out the Capcom for warning. And in a murk of dust and sunlight and landing lights the Eagle settles in. Contact lights light up on the board to register the touch of the probes below her legs. Aldrin's voice speaks softly, "Okay, engine stop. ACA out of detente. Modes control both auto. Descent engine command override off. Engine arm off. 413 is in."

Capcom: "We copy you down, Eagle."

Armstrong: "Houston, Tranquility Base here. The Eagle has landed."

Then was it that the tension broke for fifty million people or was it five hundred million, or some sum of billions of eyes and ears around a world which had just come into contact with another world for what future glory, disaster, blessing or curse nobody living could know. And Armstrong and Aldrin, never demonstrative, shook hands or clapped each other on the back—they did not later remember—and back at Mission Control, Charley Duke said, "Roger, Tranquility, we copy you on the ground. You've got a bunch of guys about to turn blue. We're breathing again. Thanks a lot."

From Norman Mailer, *Of a Fire on the Moon* (NY: MAL, 1971), p. 335.

## THE MOON AND THE MUDBALL

### Harlan Ellison

Ambivalence, the curse of keeping your mind open and receptive to new ideas, assails me this week. The Apollo 11 went up, came down, went up again, and came down again. Like you, I sat Elmer'd (as in the glue) in front of various TV screens, watching us engaged in our first activity on alien soil: dropping litter. It scared the ass off me.

(A reader of this column sent along a copy of *I. F. Stone's Weekly,* with the following circled for my attention, and I pass it on to you:

(PLAQUE FOR THE MOON LANDING

(Here Men First Set Foot Outside The Earth On Their Way To The Far Stars. They Speak Of Peace But Wherever They Go They Bring War. The Rockets On Which They Arrived Were Developed To Carry Instant Death And Can Within A Few Minutes Turn Their Green Planet Into Another Lifeless Moon. Their Destructive Ingenuity Knows No Limits And Their Wanton Pollution No Restraint. Let The Rest Of The Universe Beware.)

In the background, as I write this, Jeff Beck is singing, and all that nice stuff gives me hope that perhaps I'm grown too cynical, and there may be hope.

But . . . ambivalence!

You see, I'm a science fiction writer, among other things. I've been a reader of the form since I first came upon Jack Williamson's story *Twelve*

*Hours To Live* in a 1946 issue of *Startling Stories.* I remember very well, back in 1952, when I was 17 and in high school in Cleveland, a reporter for the *Cleveland Press* coming to interview me and the other members of the fledgling Cleveland SF Society. I remember this clown's unrestrained laughter when I told him (and this was pre-Sputnik) that we would surely have men on the moon within fifteen years. He wrote an article that made us all look like morons, made us seem to be coocoos who probably believed in ghosts, elves, a flat Earth and other improbables like an actor becoming Presidential timber. A few years later, when Sputnik went up, I took my copy of that article and went to find the reporter, at the *Press* offices, to rub his porcine nose in it. But he'd died. It was a bitch of an anti-climax.

So you see, I've been dreaming—along with all the other sf fans—about that moment when the first men would get Lunar dust on their boots. Unfortunately, for me, it was another anti-climax.

I'll admit I was knocked out by Buzz Aldrin bounding about the Moon like a kangaroo, but there were so many negative vibes attendant on the project that it really brought me down.

For instance, nitty-gritty, we did it like jerks. It cost us I can't remember how many billions to put all that scrap metal up there, merely to haul men, when a mechanical probe such as the Russians postulated could have done the same thing, and achieved the very same results. But the plain fact is that we wouldn't have gotten the appropriations for the project if it *hadn't* hauled the three astronauts. People just don't get excited about machines going to the Moon, but they do about other men. The Russians correctly bummed us for risking lives in a flamboyant publicity gig that could have been accomplished as easily by a robot.

But a robot wouldn't have been as inspiring for Nixon and his carnival. "Participation Day," indeed! And that simpering buffoon on board the *Hornet* when they splashed down. The insipid remarks he made were almost as stultifying as the dumb things the astronauts themselves said from space. (I, for one, am sick to the teeth of hearing the Bible quoted to me from Out There. It's bad enough we have to put up with so much outdated philosophy back here on the mudball. It would have pleasured me no end had they landed and come upon the First Church of Throgg the Omniscient, there in the Sea of Tranquility. Wow, can you see the seizure Bishop Sheen would have had!?!) (Or maybe, simply, God appearing in a burning bush and saying, "Okay, you guys, knock off that shit!")

You see, it just sorta killed all the adventure for me. Maybe because I'd taken that first journey so many times being led by Ray Bradbury and Robert Heinlein and Isaac Asimov and Arthur C. Clarke, who dreamed all these dreams twenty years ago. I can see why all the rest of you dug it . . . inherently it is the single most exciting thing that's happened since

Christ splashed down on Calvary, but for the guys who knew without a doubt that it was coming—all the science fiction fans and writers—it was a letdown . . . I guess. At least a little.

But I understand there were some marvelous serendipitous benefits: such as the crime rate in the country dropping to almost nothing. All the crooks and heist-men and cat-burglars were in front of *their* sets, too. Right up to the point where Nixon said the Apollo 11 flight had brought the world closer together than ever before.

After which point the crooks turned off their sets, and went out to mug old ladies for seventy-four cents.

From the *Los Angeles Free Press,*
August 1, 1969

### Questions

*Content/Meaning*
1. Do you know the meaning of or can you identify these words from Ellison's essay: "Sputnik," "porcine," "serendipitous"?
2. Both Wilford and Mailer report the first words spoken on the moon. Do the words have different impact in the two selections? What is different about the contexts in which they occur?

*Style*
1. What features of each selection constitute its style?
2. What effects is each selection trying to create? How does each one create those effects?
3. Can you describe the voice of each selection and the audience to which each is addressed?

## Exercises and Assignments

Find a first-person voice for one of the writing roles below. As you prepare to write these pieces, you should note the following:

- Autobiographical writing need not center on an earthshaking event. Good writing often involves drawing significance out of the seemingly insignificant.
- As a writer you should have a clear idea of what you want to say about the events, ideas, experiences, or objects to which you wish to relate yourself and your audience.
- As a writer you should decide at some point during the writing process what voice you want to adopt and then use it consistently.

1. At many junctures in our lives, we are asked to write an autobiographical statement (or, as it is sometimes called, a *vita*). For example, many applications for jobs or for admission to special education programs need to be accompanied by such summary statements. Usually, the vita is a short, compact, and informative sketch, which may best project something about the writer by not presenting its information in chronological sequence ("I was born. . . . I started school," etc.). Write such a sketch for one of the following purposes:

    *a.* to apply for a part-time job
    *b.* to seek admission to a major field of concentration
    *c.* to join a social organization (fraternity, sorority, club, etc.)
    *d.* to run for some type of office
    *e.* to introduce yourself to a friend of a friend or to a member of your family you have never met

2. Focus on a single event from your childhood that has meaning for you and that might interest others and write the story of that event.

# 4      **RESEARCH**

**Y**ou will rarely be able to write well about any subject beyond the autobiographical without doing at least some research. No one knows everything or can remember all that he once knew. Luckily, there are libraries to fill in for these shortcomings.

## PRELIMINARIES

There is no magic formula to doing research. All research is time-consuming and, from a narrow point of view, "inefficient" because you cannot know before you begin your research what you need to know, what you do not know, and what there is to know about your subject. In its preliminary stages, before you actually sit down to write, research requires that you explore books, people, or places (depending on your subject); that you read a good deal; and that you take useful notes.

If your project requires that you *explore* books and articles, you must become familiar with the holdings and layout of your campus library. Be sure to consult with the reference librarians because they are experts on the particular library you are using and can help you immensely in locating the sources of information on whatever subject you are researching.

Once you locate sources of information, *read.* Read everything you can find and have time for. If you do not have much time or if you have many books, skim them looking for relevant information. Use the table of contents in the front of books and the index in the back to locate special topics, people, or events that pertain to your work.

*Take notes* on each source that you consult, either on 3 × 5 cards or in a notebook, noting author, title, publisher, year and place of publication and general contents. As things strike you as interesting or important, write down the information and note the page number, again using 3 × 5 cards or a notebook.

The most important factor in doing research well is allowing yourself enough time. For many projects that require research you need to compile a good deal of information, much more than you will ever be able to use in your final paper. Having many details at your disposal will enable you to make informed and intelligent decisions about what is important to the topic you are studying and about what is important to include in your final paper. Research is a process by which you gradually become more and more informed about a particular subject. If you wait until a week or a day before your paper is due, you will not have had enough time to become very knowledgeable or to allow your subject to simmer and percolate in your mind. Instead of being able to present your best understanding of your subject, you will include only whatever information you happened to have stumbled upon in the brief time you allowed for your project.

## GENERAL SOURCES

In later chapters of the book we refer you to various specific reference works; here we introduce you to two of the most common general sources, *The New York Times Index* and *The Reader's Guide to Periodical Literature*. These two references alone will give you access to most of the periodicals in the reading room of the library.

Let us take up *The New York Times Index* first. In the words of the *Times* editors, "the *Index* is the only service that presents a condensed, classified history of the world as it is recorded day-by-day in *The New York Times*." Because of the completeness of its news and editorial matter (including the texts of most major speeches and documents), *The New York Times* is the closest we have to a newspaper of record. The *Index* of this record goes back to 1913 in annual bound volumes, and the most recent issues are printed biweekly. Since the *Times* itself has a continuous publication history back to 1851, it provides most libraries with an indispensable record of world and national affairs for well over a hundred years. It is also the source to which to turn in order to locate a given story. If, for example, you are interested in finding a contemporary report about the burning of the dirigible *Hindenburg,* and if, let us say, you know that this disaster occurred sometime in the 1930s, you would at most have to look up the name "Hindenburg" in the ten indexes for that decade (you would find the date to be May 6, 1937). Thereafter, if you wished to read further, possibly in the newsmagazines of the times, you would know the date for which to search in *The Reader's Guide.* Indeed, because the news in the *Index* is abstracted, you sometimes need not read the news report itself; this would be the case when you are looking for simple headline-type facts. If, for example, you simply wanted to know the number aboard a hijacked Lufthansa plane that landed in Somalia on October 17, 1977, you could glean that information from the *Index* as given in the sample entry under the bold heading *Somalia* (the number, as you can see, was 87):

> SOMALIA. SEE ALSO Ethiopia, 0 17, 19, 22, 23, 24. Kenya, 0 23
> *Hijackers of Lufthansa airliner in Dubai with 87 hostages aboard land in Somalia . . .*

The following entries from *The New York Times Index* will provide an explanation of the most common abbreviations and conventions you will need to know:

*Main Heading* ----- ROMAN Catholic Churches

Cathedral of Notre Dame des

Marais de La Ferte Bernard

(Le-Mans, France) 3 alabaster      *Abstract of news story*

statues and 15th-century alabaster

altarpiece are stolen from Rosary

*J1 31 = July 31*    Chapel of Cathedral of Notre Dame

*12:3 = page 12,* ---- (S), J1 31, 12:3 ----------------- *(S) = Short item;*

*column 3*    ROMAN Catholic Churches    *half column or less*

Queen of Angels Roman Catholic

Chapel (Dickinson, Texas): See also

Roman Catholic Church—France,

J1 17 St Patrick's Church

(Anchorage, Alaska): See also

Oil—US, J1 30

ROMAN Catholic Religious Orders

Jesuits: See also Salvador, E1, J1 21

El Salvador's right-wing White

Warriors Union threatens to kill

50 Jesuits unless they leave

country; threat comes at time of

confrontation between ch and mil

Govt; Jesuits, led by Rev Cesar

Jerez, say they will stay to help
peasants fight what they charge is
exploitation (See also Salvador,
E1, J1 18 ff) (M), J1 18, 5:1 ------- *(M) =*
ROMERO, Carlos Humbarto (Pres). *Medium-size item;*
See also Salvador, E1, J1 21, 25 *up to two columns*
ROMERO, Oscar (Msgr). See also
Salvador, E1, J1 25
RONAN, William J (Chmn). See
also Port Auth, J1 29
ROOS, Ronald R. See also
Crime—US, J1 17
ROOSEVELT, Franklin Delano Jr.
See also Fresh Air Fund, J1 31
*Cross-reference*
*entry* ----- ROOSEVELT, Theodore
(1858–1919). See also Numismatics,
J1 24

*(L) = Long story; over*
*two columns (not shown)*

As you can see, many of the entries are cross-references; for example, the
last entry in the sample on "Theodore Roosevelt." If you were to pursue
that citation, you would find the following main entry under "Numismatics":

NUMISMATICS
   Article on 9-coin proof set struck
by Paris Mint in '77, which contains
designs from original hand-cut die
made by Augustin Dupre at time of
French Revolution; illus (M) J1 17,
II, 33:1

> Article on coin sculptor Augustus
> Saint-Gaudens focuses on
> his personal relationship with Pres            *Cross-referenced*
> Theodore Roosevelt, who was a                        *article*
> subject of many of Gaudens coin
> works; illus (M), J1 24, II, 31:1
>     31st ed of Yeoman's Red Book
> entitled A Guide Book of US Coins
> is released (S), J1 31, II, 31:1

Note that in this instance only the second article under "Numismatics" actually mentions Theodore Roosevelt; hence, it is the entry to which we were referred. This particular article is indicated to be of medium length, it was illustrated, and it appeared in the July 24 issue, Section II, p. 30, col. 3. It should be noted that roman numerals in entries refer to the sections in the Sunday edition of the *Times*.

*The Reader's Guide to Periodical Literature* is another vital source of information that you must get to know if you do not know it already. Like *The New York Times Index,* its sole purpose is to provide bibliographical information; in other words, it gives you references to published works, in this case to articles appearing in any of over 160 general periodicals published in America. Chances are good that more periodicals are indexed by *The Reader's Guide* than your library carries. But this situation is to be expected—at least in most smaller public or undergraduate libraries—when one considers some of the more unusual titles included in the *Guide's* list: *American West, Bulletin of the Atomic Scientists, Ceramics Monthly, Conservationist, Horn Book Magazine, Natural Gardening Magazine,* and *Sky and Telescope,* among many others. Naturally, *The Reader's Guide* is the source to which to turn for coverage of subjects in most general and mass circulation magazines. While its list includes some little-known periodicals, it also classifies virtually every magazine carried on drugstore shelves or circulated by subscription to the general public, including such standbys as *Atlantic, Better Homes and Gardens, Ebony, Esquire, Fortune, Good Housekeeping, Ladies Home Journal, Nation, New Yorker, Newsweek, Popular Mechanics, Reader's Digest, Seventeen, Time,* and *U.S. News and World Report.* (*The New York Times*

*Magazine* is included in *The Reader's Guide* even though it is also indexed in *The New York Times Index.*) Obviously, *The Reader's Guide* list is a constantly changing one; you will find now defunct magazines like *Life* or *Liberty* once having been included and new magazines constantly being added. If you are in doubt about the inclusion of a particular magazine, check the list at the beginning of each volume.

Unlike *The New York Times Index, The Reader's Guide* will not provide abstracts or summaries of the articles which it lists. It is essentially an author and subject index. Thus, you might wish to check what popular articles Norman Mailer wrote, say, in the year 1974. You will find any and all entries under the main head *Mailer.* Or you may wish to know what articles have appeared in general periodicals about "Norman Mailer"; in that case, *Mailer* will appear as a subject entry. If there are both author and subject entries under one listing, author entries always come first. Here is a series of entries as illustrations:

> COLD weather
>> Coldest winter? il Newsweek 82:6–9 D 31 '73
>> December 1972 freeze and its effect on the
>>> eucalyptus forest in the Oakland-Berkeley Hills. J. P.
>>> Monteverdi and B. L. Wood. bibliog il Weatherwise 26:160–
>>> 7 Ag '73
>> Freeze: right where you are! B. Stainback.
>>> il Todays Health 51:50–5+ Jl '73
>>> *See also*
>> Winter

This subject entry for "Cold Weather" includes three articles and a cross-reference (to "Winter"). Here is the information given for each of the entries.

*The first article* listed was entitled "Coldest Winter?" It was illustrated and appeared in *Newsweek,* Volume 82, pages 6 to 9, in the issue of December 31, 1973.

*The second article* was entitled "December 1972 Freeze and Its Effect on the Eucalyptus Forest in the Oakland-Berkeley Hills." It was written by J. P. Monteverdi and B. L. Wood; it was illustrated and included a bibliography. It was published in *Weatherwise,* Volume 26, pages 160 to 167 in the August 1973 issue. A reference to the same article could be found as an author entry under Monteverdi, J. P., in the proper alphabetical sequence. Second-authors' names are usually cross-referenced to the first; thus *Wood, B. L.,* will be referred to *Monteverdi.*

*The third article* was entitled "Freeze: Right Where You Are!" Its author was B. Stainback; it was illustrated and appeared in *Today's Health,* Volume 51, pages 50 to 55 (as well as some additional ones, indicated by the plus sign—probably as a result of some advertisements intervening). The article appeared in the July 1973 issue of the journal.

With a general acquaintance of *The New York Times Index* and *The Reader's Guide*, you will be ready to examine a wide variety of coverage in the mass media, and you will undoubtedly have two good sources to consult on any subject that might interest you to read or write about.

## Exercises

1. This exercise is designed, first, to provide you with experience in the use of *The New York Times Index* and relevant back issues of the *New York Times*, and, second, to allow you to browse in one old issue of a newspaper to discover what sort of news was current in the time that the event you are researching took place. Old newspapers can give us a great deal of information about their times: news, ads, reviews, sports news, and other odds and ends that every newspaper issue includes. Your instructor may wish to assign one of the following topics to you:

a. In 1955, a subtropical bittern was discovered in New York City. What is a "bittern"? Give the date and the exact location of this discovery.

b. In June of 1972, President Nixon took issue with the U.S. Supreme Court decision on the death penalty. What two crimes did he feel should not be ruled out? He was able to read the statement of only one dissenting justice. Which one?

c. In 1959, two National League baseball teams finished the season in a tie. Who were to be the starting pitchers for the two teams in the playoffs, and where was the first game to be played?

d. In June 1920, the Democrats nominated Warren G. Harding for President, Calvin Coolidge for Vice-President. Where did the convention take place, and what was the final vote of delegates for Coolidge and his nearest rival?

e. In September 1974, President Gerald Ford pardoned former President Nixon for all federal crimes he may have committed. Give the full name of President Ford's spokesman. Quote the last sentence in the statement made by Nixon responding to the presidential pardon.

f. In August 1965, riots broke out in the Watts section of Los Angeles. Give the number of injured and arrested as reported that day on the front page of the *Times*. Who was responsible for proclaiming a curfew for the next night?

g. Give the name of the man who signed the unconditional surrender for Germany in May 1945. Copy the headline for that day's edition of the *Times*.

h. In 1926, a Mrs. Frances S. Hall was arrested for the murder of two people. Give the names and identify the alleged victims. Who was the arresting officer, and what was the actual time of arrest?

i. John F. Kennedy was nominated on the first ballot in the Democratic National Convention of 1960. Give the vote of the two top candidates on this ballot and the name of the man who moved to make the vote unanimous in favor of Kennedy.

j. In 1972, the U.S. Navy in an unprecedented move bought stock in a private corporation. What was the name of the company? Why was this aid necessary? What was the main headline on the front page of the *Times* on that day?

k. In 1942, Corregidor surrendered to the Japanese. Where is this island located, and who, according to the official release, surrendered it for the Americans?

l. Give the exact date of the death of Pope John XXIII (it occurred during the 1960s). Of what did he die? How long had he been Pope?

m. Give the full names of the two men who were the first to land on the moon in 1969. Upon landing their craft, what message did they send back to their home base? Whose poem was printed on the front page of *The New York Times*?

n. Give the precise date in 1920 when peace was signed between the Allies and Germany to end World War I. How many nations participated on the side of the Allies? Who was the U.S. representative?

o. In one of the more bizarre reports in election history, the *Chicago Daily Tribune* reported in its early edition in 1948 that Dewey had defeated Truman. What was the headline for the same date in *The New York Times* (admittedly the paper preserved in the archives is a later edition)? According to the *Times* report, what major state was still hanging in the balance? If Dewey had retained the majority vote in that state, what, according to the *Times* report, would have happened to the election?

p. In May 1937, Mrs. Eleanor Roosevelt, wife of the President, made a startling recommendation in a radio interview—one that was years ahead of its time. What was it?

q. The Nazis in Germany experienced an uprising of some of their radical leaders in 1934. What personal role did Hitler play in quelling this uprising? Who was the leader of the conspiracy, and what happened to him? What inference did the *Times* report about the real power behind this revolt?

    *r.* An assassination attempt is reported in the *Times* in February 1933. Who was the target? Who was the assassin, and what was his conjectured motive? Was anyone hurt?

    *s.* Give the date in 1953 when the Rosenbergs were executed. Where did the execution take place? What was the President's response? Was there any noticeable reaction in New York City?

    *t.* A U.S. Supreme Court ruling was made in 1976 concerning the personal appearance of police officers. What was the decision? What was the vote of the Court, and who delivered the majority opinion?

    2. After you have completed your research topic, read the issue of *The New York Times* published on the date of your birth. Make notes of some of the more important events as well as editorials, reviews, ads, movies, radio and television programs, obituaries, and sports stories featured or mentioned in that issue of the paper. Then write an "introduction" placing yourself in the world of your birthday.

# DESCRIPTION

**D**escription appears widely in all kinds of writing. One encounters it everywhere: in sports columns, nature writing, advertisements, gossip columns, poetic characterizations, news columns, interviews, passages from novels, travel stories, and countless other forms and areas of our daily communication. The popular journalist has to describe people and places that form the subject or background of news reports, editorials, opinion columns, obituaries, and numerous kinds of features. In turn, description also occurs widely in the reading and writing of other college courses. Scientists are called upon to describe what they see in the microscope; historians must recount the setting of events or characterize people; psychologists frequently describe behavior patterns by examining case histories; architects have a special vocabulary to describe buildings like cathedrals or temples. This unit is devoted to a study of descriptive writing because it forms a basic part of our recreational and professional lives.

# 5      CONCRETE
##           LANGUAGE

**D**ictionary definitions, like the one in *Webster's New World Dictionary*, tend to put the emphasis on the visual element as the basic feature in description; accordingly they define description as "picturing in words." But lively description usually engages more than one of our five senses, and while we live in a sight-oriented culture (we even use *see* for *understand*), we will do a far more effective job of describing when we make a deliberate attempt to appeal to all five senses—sight, touch, smell, taste, and hearing. Descriptive language depends on the writer's ability to perceive, not merely to see, and to translate those perceptions into concrete language. We use the term "concrete" here to denote something that can be perceived by one or more of the five senses. Concreteness can be achieved by the use of adjectives, adverbs, nouns, and especially verbs. The selections in this chapter are notable for their use of concrete language and their attempt to reach readers on various levels of sensual perception.

The passage that follows comes from a description of ancient Sybaris, a city located on the arch of the Italian boot, which 2,500 years ago was the center of luxurious living—so much so, that to this day we have a noun, *sybarite,* which describes "a lover of luxury, a voluptuary," as well as an adjective, *sybaritic,* which means "luxurious, self-indulgent, opulent." The passage shows how the typical Sybarite arose from sleep and was gently prepared for the invariable event that would follow, the feast. Note the concentrated appeal to *all* the senses; note also that the language, in contrast to the scene described, is not extravagant. The effectiveness of the passage depends far less on ornateness and exotic diction than it does on the writer's obvious concern to let the reader experience, not just see, what the life of a Sybarite was like. In reading the passage, make a point of noting where and when it appeals to each of the five senses. Underline specific words of

concrete language (like *silver bed* and *sponge mattress* in the second sentence)
that help create the desired atmosphere.

## THE SYBARITES

*Herbert Siegel*

. . . the typical Sybarite rises in the evening. He has spent his day sleeping
in a silver bed on a sponge mattress strewn with rose petals. His blankets
and pillows are scented and perfumed. His day's sleep has been undisturbed
by the crowing of cocks or by noisy laborers or craftsmen, for all these are
banned by law from the city. When he arises, his portable silver chamber
pot is brought to him. He is then bathed in his tub by servants who wear
leg-irons to ensure their slow and careful movement in order not to scald
their master by spilling the hot water they carry. After his bath, he enters
a steam room—the first sauna in history—where a servant brings him a
golden goblet of wine drawn from a pipe directly connected to the vats of
the master's country estate. After his sauna, he is carefully depilated, and
his skin is polished. His servants then dress him in a lavish yellow-and-red
toga, which is bound by an elegant sash. His wife, equally fastidious, has
mascara, powder, and rouge applied while her servants adjust her hairpiece
(invented in Sybaris and not in Paris). She delights in a pair of fashionable
high-heel cork shoes, which her husband has presented to her.

From "The City That Danced to<br>Destruction," *Saturday Review,* May 27,<br>1978, p. 16.

The passage you have just read depends in part for its effect on the
careful selection of details (e.g., the "leg-irons" of the servants worn for
the comfort of their lord). Obviously, descriptive writing demands attention
to the specific. It also requires discrimination in the choice of language,
and often it is well served by the search for especially expressive words
and by colorful and lively, even surprising, figures of speech.

Here are two short paragraphs describing the same subject, the small
town of Albarracín in the southwest corner of Spain. Read them with close
attention to the choice of language used in each and then answer the questions
that follow:

1. Cars drive down the narrow, twisting streets. Houses are close together, sometimes attached to each other, and they smell of dust
   and smoke. During rush hours, mules with carts line the streets.
   Old people watch the children play.
2. Tiny cars hurtle down contorted streets, bare inches of clearance
   on either side. Bent and huddled houses nearly touch overhead, and

harbor the distinctive regional aroma of stone dust and smoke from fires of olive tree branches. Rush hours are parades of mule-drawn carts with farmers departing for, and returning from, their fields in the valley, twice each way, every day. Old men lean over their canes in the sun, berets tugged down to their ears, watching children clatter and yelp over soccer balls. (From Bailey Alexander, "Albarracín," *Travel and Leisure,* May 1978, p. 88.)

## Questions

*Content/Meaning*
1. Study the two paragraphs. Which gives a more specific impression of the town? What is that impression?

*Style*
1. Single out the verbs, nouns, and descriptive adjectives in the first paragraph.
2. Look at the second paragraph in contrast to the first. Examine each of the sentences. How and why does the second version improve on the first? Why, for example, is "hurtle down" a better choice of verb than "drive down"? What does the substitution of "bare inches of clearance on either side" add to the concept of "narrow"?
3. How many of the five senses are engaged in the language of the two paragraphs?

## Exercise and Assignment

The ads shown in Figures 5.1 and 5.2 use towns like Albarracín (only a good deal larger) as background to sell Passport Scotch.

1. Examine the ads and point out the similarities you find in the setting and the short paragraph describing Albarracín. What, do you suppose, is the purpose of the ad-maker in using this setting to sell Passport Scotch?

2. Find another magazine advertisement that emphasizes setting as a means of selling its product. Write a 300-word paper in which (*a*) you describe the setting in concrete language, and (*b*) you discuss the use of the setting to sell the product. Be sure to turn in a copy of the ad with your analysis.

*5.1*

5.2

## Reading Selection

The description of Albarracín on pages 58–59 was extracted from an essay that appeared in *Travel and Leisure,* a magazine addressed to the reader with an interest in different and distant parts of the world. The usual point of its articles is to provide descriptions of places to visit and some interesting, often historical, background. Here is the complete essay.

## ALBARRACÍN

### In a little Spanish town . . .

#### *Bailey Alexander*

Ardent travelers collect exotic hamlets and villages as rock hounds do agates. They snatch up Chipping Campdens and Portofinos, hoard them, polish their recollections and haul them out for display to like-minded friends. Veteran Spanophiles are no less enthusiastic, but they are more secretive. They want their cherished pueblos to remain unspoiled. With an annual tourist in-migration that often outnumbers the native population, it is not an irrational fear.

It is with justifiable trepidation, then, that I reveal the existence of a heretofore undiscovered mountain town that is one of the most appealing on the entire Peninsula. My motivations for this disclosure are complex— the ego-lift of seeming knowledgeable, the desire to share good fortune with others. But there is security, too.

For whatever the attractions of this secret village are: (*a*) it is very inconveniently situated, far from major tourist centers; (*b*) English is barely spoken or understood by its inhabitants, and (*c*) its name is hard to pronounce and therefore difficult to remember. With all that in its favor, perhaps it will remain unexploited.

So here goes: The town is Albarracín. It is hidden in the southwest corner of Spain's least-visited province, Teruel, tucked away in the folds of its own mountain range. In many ways, it is the quintessential Aragonese town. People there are ignorant of the world beyond their hills, yet intensely curious about strangers. (Say you're an American, and they ask if you know their cousin in Caracas.) Tiny cars hurtle down contorted streets, bare inches of clearance on either side. Bent and huddled houses nearly touch overhead, and harbor the distinctive regional aroma of stone dust and smoke from fires of olive tree branches. Rush hours are parades of mule-drawn carts with farmers departing for, and returning from, their fields in the valley, twice each way, every day. Old men lean over their canes in the sun, berets tugged down to their ears, watching children clatter and yelp over soccer balls.

But Albarracín has more. The government has declared the entire village a National Historic Monument, an appellation reserved for the likes of Toledo and Salamanca. Few new buildings are permitted. When they are, they must conform to the prevailing Medieval style, as must any exterior renovations. Architecturally, Albarracín is frozen in the moment of its highest glory— two centuries before Columbus. The shambling nearby villages of meaner aspect are of the modern epoch, and resemble Albarracín not at all.

The rose-colored houses of Albarracín perch upon—*cling* to—a high, narrow ridge which is nearly encircled by the Guadalaviar River. Lords of the Moorish Almoravid Aben Razín dynasty established the small kingdom, building a wall to protect the town against a rival Moslem faction. These 11th-century ramparts are nearly intact, echoing the curve of the river and snaking over one of the area's nearby mountains.

After a time, the kingdom was absorbed by a larger neighbor. In the middle of the 12th century, the "Wolf King" of Murcia, to the south, sought protection from the incursions of his enemies in Castile, Navarre and Aragon. He reinstated the independent status of Albarracín so it could serve as a buffer state athwart the only pass through the forbidding sierra.

There is a reason for this spoonful of history. The community became an open city, into which poured merchants and refugees of all three warring religions—Moslems, Christians, Jews. To avoid excuses for intervention by any of the larger states, the rulers of the enclave mandated absolute harmony between the religionists. A communal bathhouse was built, and Moor, Catholic and Jew were ordered to use it, together, at least three times a week. Freedom of worship was assured, and churches, synagogues and mosques were erected without conflict. Many of these buildings survive, despite the four centuries of suppression that followed Queen Isabella's expulsion in 1492 of unrepentant non-Christians.

A rich heritage remains. Here, a defiant Star of David adorns a door; there, the flying Star of Islam. Moorish and Christian notions of architectural design melded in the hybrid Mudejar style unique to the region. The lacy iron grilles and the roofline galleries with their carved wooden balustrades are artifacts of Islamic Spain, rarely seen this far north. Coats of arms are inset over doors protected by brass lizards and dragon heads. An annex to the cathedral is filled with Flemish tapestries and gold and crystal treasures from the New World.

There are an uncommon number of amiable bars in which to reflect upon these beguilements. Especially agreeable are the Bar Alcazaba, a block above the main square, and the Bar Los Gavilanes, just beyond the entrance to the ancient tunnel which burrows beneath the town. Both blessedly eschew the pinball machines and jukeboxes endemic to rural Iberian cafés. Tomás Collado, son of the owner of the Alcazaba, strains to understand wisps of his language, and to respond. He is a self-taught painter. With coaxing, he shyly brings out his paintings and drawings of the streets and plazas in which he grew to adulthood.

Bearded, barrel-chested José Luis Narro is the patron of Los Gavilanes. When a stranger arrived one night for after-dinner coffee and brandy, José Luis was leaving his kitchen with an immense skillet, its contents snapping and steaming. He placed it in the middle of a large table ringed by a dozen friends. As he passed out forks and wine, he noticed the stranger at the bar.

"Join us," he said warmly. The invitation was accepted, out of curiosity, if not hunger.

"What is it?" said the stranger, after a judicious taste.

"Gazpacho," was the answer.

"But gazpacho is a cold Andalusian soup."

"Not in Albarracín. Here, when a pig is killed, we take the liver and cook it with potatoes, garlic, onions, olive oil, bread, perhaps a little rabbit or lamb. You will never see it in a restaurant or anywhere away from here. It is special. Something you share with friends."

"But I am not a friend."

"Now, you are."

From Travel and Leisure, May 1978, pp. 88, 91.

## Questions

*Content/Meaning*
1. What is the purpose of the first three paragraphs? What is Alexander saying about "ardent travelers"? How do "Spanophiles" differ from them? In which category would you place Alexander?
2. What points summarize the history of Albarracín as related in paragraphs 5 to 7? Why does the author include this historical information in his article?
3. The article ends with an anecdote, partly in dialogue, about an aspect of the night life in Albarracín. How does this passage fit into the overall description? What is its point? Would you say that the article is rather selective about the impression it wants to create? What sorts of things does Alexander *not* tell us about life in Albarracín? Is Albarracín the sort of place you would want to visit but not live in?

*Style*
1. Analyze the descriptive language of paragraph 6.
2. In Unit I you learned how to identify and characterize the writer's voice. Can you describe Alexander's voice in the foregoing essay? What sort of person does he represent himself to be?

3. On at least two occasions, Alexander uses phrases that some handbooks warn should be avoided in edited English:
   *a.* In paragraph 8, sentence 3, he speaks of "harmony between the
   religionists."
   *b.* Paragraph 10 begins with the phrase "There are an uncommon
   number of amiable bars. . . ."
   What would the handbooks find wrong with these usages? How could
   the sentences be changed to make them more acceptable to users of
   "correct" English? How important are such lapses in usage to your
   overall estimate of Alexander's style?

# Reading Selection

The selection that follows comes from a rather typical "nature" passage in *National Geographic:*

## NEW ORLEANS AND HER RIVER

### *Joseph Judge*

I will not forget one extraordinary moment. We were sitting silently in the
boat shortly after dawn while the sun made a huge rainbow in the deep
mist around us. Out of the rainbow a squadron of jacksnipe suddenly banked
and veered in perfect formation, their white wing patches flashing. As if on
cue, shrill whistles, pipes, booms, flutes, trilling cadenzas broke out as
gallinules, coots, rails, woodcocks, and ibises joined a thunderous chorus.
Then geese snows and blues bugled like massed battalions from within the
white veil before us. Never have I heard such music as I did then, blind in
a blinding rainbow. When the sun finally burned the mist away, the geese
got up, and an endless skein threaded out against the horizon, fluttering
blue-black clouds streaming toward Breton Sound.

From *National Geographic* 139 (February
1971): 185.

### Questions

*Content/Meaning*
1. How many different kinds of birds are described in this short paragraph? Can you group them by their location in relation to the writer?
2. What is the overall impression that the writer chooses to emphasize?

*Style*
1. What are the action words in the passage?
2. To how many of the five senses does the writer appeal?

## Reading Selection

The following selection is a descriptive poem written in free verse (i.e., without rhyme) in irregular lines and stanzas. Its immediate purpose is to provide a graphic and richly imagistic description of a fish store, as its title implies. Kate Jennings has published many poems in such journals as *Poetry, Hudson Review,* and *The American Scholar,* and in two books, *Second Sight* and *Thirtieth Year to Heaven.*

### FISH STORE

*Kate Jennings*

Pisacano's window's a nightmare tangle
of seafood, shellfish, protein, energy:
squid, scungili, fish heads, soft shell
crabs, eels, cod, clams. Flawless bass
bedded on ice chips, their colors vein
vivid—muted purple, pure blue—lie
in perfect layers like nine dead cats.

Inside sawdust squeaks under my feet.
King crab chunks and lumps in tin cans
line the walls where the men are busy
and efficient, making fish bits fly
through the marine-scented air. Blood
splatters their white aprons as they
fillet the thin flounder. A lobster
flinches, then freezes under the knife,
his black and green shell stilled,
lichened tones stalled now in amber,
static, waiting for the boiling bath.

The oysters open with a chalky gritty
creak. In their bin the crabs rattle
and scrabble. I lift a limp pink shrimp
like a curled embryo, a headless curve
or line of raw crunch, scaled. Perch,
haddock, halibut, mackerel, snapper,
sole: fins, flippers, feelers, claws.

This poem appeared in *Poetry,* April–Sept. 1975, p. 208.

## Questions

*Content/Meaning*
1. Although, except for one brief moment, you never see the writer directly inside her poem, she provides a very clear progression of her movement from beginning to end. Can you describe that movement? (You might wish to relate it to the stanza division of the poem.)
2. Besides drawing a vivid word-picture of the fish store, what feelings does the poet seem to express about the atmosphere and activity of the store?

*Style*
1. What are all the words describing color in the poem? What part of speech (adjective, adverb, noun, verb) predominates?
2. What words describe sound and motion?
3. How many sentences do you find in the poem? Does each contain a subject and a predicate? What special effects in pausing and emphasis are created by the breakup of word or phrase groups at the end of lines?
4. To what extent does the sound of various words reinforce the meaning they describe? Can you provide some examples?

# Exercises and Assignments

1. Write a 300- to 500-word critical review of a travel story in a magazine or newspaper. Comment on the writer's use of concrete descriptive language, on the reliance on personal observation (if any), on the apparent audience at whom the article is aimed, and on the central impression that the article leaves in the reader's mind. Magazines like *Saturday Review, Travel and Leisure,* or *National Geographic* and the Sunday travel section of your newspaper are good potential sources in which to look for appropriate articles. Be sure to turn in a copy or xerox reproduction of the article with your paper.

2. Choose four or five main news stories of the day in your newspaper for a given issue. Read each carefully and mark all the descriptive passages. How much of the detail in these reports is strictly descriptive? What kind of news stories seem to emphasize description? How important does setting seem to be in the reporting of the news? Did you find an instance in which there was either too little or too much description for the needs of the story? Bring a clipping or a xerox copy of the best descriptive passage you have found to class and be prepared to write a 300- to 500-word essay in analysis concentrating on one aspect of the writer's use of concrete language.

| SIGHT | | |
|---|---|---|
| Color | Motion or Position | Shape |
|  |  |  |

| Sound | Touch | Smell | Taste |
|---|---|---|---|
|  |  |  |  |

*5.3*

3. Look for a descriptive passage in one of your textbooks. Comment on the atmosphere and the effect created by the passage. Note especially the choice of concrete words and figures of speech.

4. Write a description of a place based on personal observation. Select any place you wish and observe it closely, perhaps in several sessions over the span of some days. The place can be anywhere; it can be the scene of human congestion, or it can be secluded. It should not be your purpose to look for something to happen—we are for the moment not interested in narrative, only in setting and atmosphere. You may, if you wish, seek out a favorite landscape or natural retreat on campus. Or you may wish to concentrate on your room, the cafeteria, a street corner, a bridge—any setting that is sufficiently restricted to allow a short but specific description. Obviously, if the scene is populated, you should find selective details about the people who form a part of it, but make the people subservient to the place, as Alexander did in the paragraph we quoted about Albarracín. The passage you finally write can be simply a paragraph. It need not be packed with details. It will need vividness accomplished through concrete language.

To carry out this assignment, you should take selective notes, perhaps on a chart, shown in Figure 5.3, which will help you organize your perceptions.

5. Write a description of your hometown or neighborhood for the general reader, a person who does not share your intimate familiarity with the setting. You might wish to aim your description at the reader of a travel section in a newspaper or magazine.

# 6

# FIGURATIVE LANGUAGE

In addition to such concrete language as multiple-concept verbs and specific adjectives or nouns, effective descriptions usually depend on a variety of figures of speech, or figurative language. While expert critics are able to identify a long list of such figures, we need, for our purposes, to single out only a few. Let us examine the nature and function of three figures of speech: *simile, metaphor,* and *personification.*

The figure of speech known as *simile* makes a direct comparison frequently using the preposition *like* or the subordinate conjunctions *as* or *such as.* We can find a good example of a simile in the very first sentence of Bailey Alexander's account of Albarracín (see p. 62): "Ardent travelers collect exotic hamlets and villages *as rock hounds do agates*" (italics added). This sentence likens travelers to collectors of rocks. What they have in common is that both search for valuables: Travelers seek "exotic hamlets and villages"; rock collectors seek agate stones. The value of a well used simile is its connection of two kinds of experiences or objects—one that refers literally to the subject at hand ("ardent travelers" and "villages and hamlets") and another that depicts an imagined realm ("rock hounds" and "agates"). The figure of speech thus not only adds variety and interest to the description but it also deepens or broadens the significance of the literal subject. For travelers, Bailey Alexander says, the abstract experience of discovery is very much like the concrete find of treasure seekers. The simile makes us understand the intensity with which "ardent travelers" prize their experience.

For another example of a simile, you might examine Kate Jennings' statement, "I lift a limp pink shrimp/like a curled embryo. . . ." (see p. 66). Ask yourself what level of meaning is added to the description of the pink shrimp by the phrase "like a curled embryo."

*Metaphor* is an implied comparison. Instead of pointing to a likeness of two otherwise unrelated concepts as does the simile, metaphor states that one thing *is* another. Metaphor, because it contains an implied rather than a stated comparison, is the more complex figure of speech. Here, once again, is an illustration from Bailey Alexander's essay (see p. 62): The town of Albarracín is "tucked away in the folds of its own mountain range." The image projected by the metaphor "tucked away in the folds" is a piece of cloth lying loosely over a surface. The mountain range in which Albarracín is located is implicitly likened to such an undulating cloth. The figurative, as opposed to literal, meaning of the metaphor associates the location of Albarracín with safety and comfortable secrecy. It also gives us a vivid "faraway" picture, which travelers see as they approach the town.

*Personification* is a figure of speech that gives a special kind of animation to objects or concepts in descriptions. For example, the travel poster that refers to an ocean liner as "the queen of the seas" is designed to have us associate the ship with the beauty and grace of royalty (perhaps suggesting also that travelers aboard this ship will, by psychological transfer, live a royal life). We often personify abstract concepts: The United States becomes Uncle Sam; justice is represented as a lady with scales; "Everyman" is a stage character who personifies the common man. Personification takes place virtually any time that we use a verb describing a strictly human action and we apply it to a thing, an idea, or even an animal. If, as in Joseph Judge's description of bird life on the Mississippi, we are told that geese "bugled like massed battalions" (see p. 65), we instantly ascribe a human action to animals (while also adding through the simile "like massed battalions" a reinforcement of the personification). The same happens with adjectives referring essentially to human activities. Thus, when Bailey Alexander speaks of "a defiant Star of David," he employs the adjective *defiant* to personify the "Star of David." Personification as a figure of speech, like metaphor, makes an implicit comparison. But the comparison, in this instance, is restricted always to converting a nonhuman or an abstract concept into a human referent. Personification thus serves typically to intensify or humanize an inanimate descriptive passage. It makes us associate with objects, concepts, and abstractions on more intimate terms.

Figurative language appears in a wide variety of forms in all kinds of writing. The incorporation of figures of speech in our writing usually adds depth and interest to the statements we make, and in descriptive passages particularly, figurative language is an important ingredient. One real danger in the use of figures of speech is the risk of confusing the reader with consecutive images. The mixing of metaphors can, on occasion, interfere with clear and direct communication. For example, it is one thing for Bailey Alexander to describe the Star of David as "defiant"; it is another to say that it "adorns" a door. Something defiant rarely can be thought of as an adornment. In this instance the figure of speech needs to be integrated more naturally with its context. One solution might be to say "a defiant Star of David protects a door"; another is to simplify the statement into "a defiant Star of David is placed on a door."

Another danger is to bombard the reader with too many figures or to allow figures of speech to call undue attention to themselves. Here, for example, is a paragraph from the *Los Angeles Times* in which a staff writer wishes to describe how a member of the food catering industry maintains his composure to meet the demands of his profession.

> Pennington's eye-of-the-hurricane nerves have served him well in an industry where the weak in spirit, in social know-how or in operating capital melt away as quickly as ice-carvings at a Death Valley barbecue party. (*Los Angeles Times,* November 10, 1981, p. 1.)

The images in this sentence are distracting. They ask us to visualize too much; hurricanes and Death Valley barbecue parties are simply so remote from each other that the reader is hard put to respond with mental images of both in one sentence. The "eye-of-the-hurricane" metaphor, moreover, does not aptly describe the unflappable manager of a catered affair in which there is a rush of activity to serve a large number of guests all at once. Pennington represents the calm at the center of the storm. In itself, that image is a good one. But should the catering activity be visualized as a hurricane? One hopes not, for that image can only bring havoc and destruction to mind. The metaphor suggests that Pennington presides in calmness while his waiters and busboys create a whirlwind of debris.

The second figure is a simile meant simply to suggest that persons who are not as unflappable as Pennington will meet instant failure. The simile incorporates another figure of speech, known as *hyperbole* or exaggeration (many figures of speech combine in such a way), and it is, of course, meant to be humorous. True, the image of ice carvings at a Death Valley barbecue party has a certain relevance to the catering business. It suggest implicitly what extremes the caterer might have to meet in the way of challenges. If the image were to be applied to the unflappable Pennington directly, it might be quite successful and certainly humorous. But here it is used as a way of intensifying the failure of caterers who lack Pennington's control. The image is so overwhelming that our attention is focused on it rather than the point it makes or supports. The reporter has simply overwritten here. He is more interested in attracting our admiration than in communicating his central thought.

The reading selections that follow make fairly extensive use of figures. Try to decide how successfully the two writers employ figurative language. Ask yourself whether various dominant figures add to or detract from the descriptive passages.

# Reading Selection

The following selection appeared originally in *Rolling Stone*. It was taken from an extended essay describing the city of Washington, D.C., as it appeared in 1974, just after the resignation of Richard Nixon. Jan Morris is a gifted travel writer whose essays have appeared in various journals about such widely differing cities as Dublin, Singapore, New York, and Oxford.

### FAME'S STAMPING GROUND

#### *Jan Morris*

The sentries of the Tomb of the Unknown Soldiers are mounted by an infantry regiment known as the Old Guard, and for myself I found them more haunting than the shades. I suppose new arrivals at Arlington are, so to speak, cosmeticized before burial, but however assiduously they are touched-up for their last roll-call, they could hardly be more theatrical than those soldiers still alive. Apparently shaven-headed beneath their peaked caps, ominously sunglassed when the day is bright, expressionless, ritually stooped, they move with an extraordinary gliding motion that seems to require no muscular activity at all, but is controlled electronically perhaps from some distant command post—a slow, lunar motion, to and fro before the gaping crowds— a halt, a click of the boots, a stylized shift of the rifle from one shoulder to the other, a long pause as though the electrodes are warming up, and then, with an almost perceptible buzz, that slow spectral lope back to the other side of the memorial, while the tourists suppress a shudder.

Behind their dark glasses, I suppose, the soldiers know nothing of the sinister chill that surrounds them, and indeed when I later came across some of the Old Guard off-duty at their barracks, they seemed nice cheerful fellows. In the same way the obsessive nature of Washington is not always apparent to those who form part of it. "When I was just a little kid," a friend of mine told me at lunch one day, "I guess I wasn't more than six or seven years old, I used to dream to myself I could see my name there on the bedroom door—Senator W——!" I could hardly conceive such a fancy in a child's mind, but she saw nothing remarkable about it, and it is probably commonplace in Washington. Politicians are politicians everywhere, but only here is the political addiction so ingrained and so frank. Here one can observe its pursuit in every fanatic detail, from the dream of the visiting debating society president to the attendant hush when the great man speaks, from the swivelling eye over the canapés to the sweep of the big black cars at the Senate side.

To avoid getting hooked myself, for it is catching as well as habit-forming, sometimes I took the day off from politics, and did the tourist rounds: but for all the grandeur and meaning of the city, for all the endearing pride of my fellow visitors, still these experiences only heightened my sense of intrusion upon some immense private performance. Inorganic by origin, Washington is unnatural in behaviour: but far from heightening everything as New York does, it spreads everything out, memorializes it, puts it in a park and reflects it in an ornamental pool. In New York I feel more myself than usual, in Washington much less, for when I look for my own reflection in this city, statues and symbols look back at me.

It is an alienating city. It lacks the corporate gift of hospitality. It is like one vast smokeless zone. Was ever genius less at home than in the National Gallery of Art, where the enigmatic Giorgione, the mad Van Gogh, the lusty Picasso hang for ever antiseptically among the Garden Courts? Did ever Marlowe or Molière find a less likely stage than the Center for the Performing Arts, which suggests to me a cross between a Nazi exhibition and a more than usually ambitious hair-dresser? I thanked my good fortune that this time I had arrived in September; at least those interminable cherries weren't in blossom.

Nowhere in the world is so inexorably *improving*. Elevating texts and aphorisms, quotations from statesmen and philosophers, Thoughts for All Eternity nag one from every other downtown wall, and make one feel, especially perhaps if one has come in a High School excursion bus, awfully insignificant. What giants there were in those days! How grandly they expressed themselves! How thickly they stand about! Innocent III, Napoleon, Blackstone and St. Louis supervise the Senate subway; clumps of heroes wrestle with their standards, horseback generals revise their strategies, on plinth and plaza across the capital. "Where Law Ends," booms the Department of Justice, "Tyranny Begins." "Taxes Are What We Pay For A Civilized Society," retorts the Internal Revenue Service. "Here Are The Ties That Bind The Life Of Our People," the National Archives cry, and across the avenue the Mission responds, with a chime of the carillon: "Come To Me!"

When we came down from the top of the Washington Monument, even the elevator operator dismissed us with a parting injunction. "Let's all work," he said, "to clean up our country for the 200th anniversary just coming up." "Yes sir," we dutifully replied, "you're darned right—you hear that, kids?" He had not, however, finished yet. "And I'm talking," he darkly added, "about the mental aspects as well as the physical."

We had no answer to that.

From Jan Morris, *Travels* (New York: Harcourt Brace Jovanovich, 1976), pp. 133–135.

## Questions

*Content/Meaning*
1. How are the first two paragraphs related to content? What point do the paragraphs make together?
2. Altogether, how many main points about Washington, D.C., does Morris develop in this excerpt from her article? Does she seem to like the city?
3. What does Morris mean in paragraph 4 when she likens Washington to a "vast smokeless zone"? How does this metaphor relate to what follows in the paragraph?
4. What point is made with the anecdote about the elevator operator in the Washington Monument in paragraph 6?

*Style*
1. How many figures of speech can you find in Morris's article? Which of them is a simile, metaphor, or personification?
2. Interpret two of the figures. What is their meaning and their relationship to the point they are meant to support? How effective is each figure as a stylistic device?
3. Are there any figures that you consider obscure or ineffective? (If you find any, bring them up in class discussion for clarification or criticism.)

## Reading Selection

Jimmy Cannon was for many years one of the top syndicated sports columnists in America, and his tough-guy style was widely admired. Here is one of his columns, written at the time of the Kentucky Derby in 1962.

### THE BIG HUSTLE

#### *Jimmy Cannon*

Churchill Downs is an immense hovel of a race track which resembles a lodging for bats and spiders. It has the dour appearance of a place which anticipates being haunted. In glorious testaments to the Kentucky Derby, this tremendous hogan has been described as the Taj Mahal of racing.

It is a slander against the elegant monument to love because this sucker foundry is a monstrosity of a woodshed which is a ramshackle tribute to con. Holding a thrilling horse race in this squalid environment is similar to hanging Rembrandts in a tenement basement. It is a mean joint that persecutes the animals who run across the creek of dust that is its racing strip. The people who watch them would consider this hard time if they were sentenced to serve a day here under the exact conditions by a judge.

The grandstand seems to have been built to keep the occurrences on the race track a secret. A good seat is one a man can stand on and get a view of his neighbor's neck. I arise from my bench in the press box every year with my pants full of splinters.

This is the only racing plant in this country that makes Derby horse owners pay for their boxes. The jockeys' quarters are located in a bungalow which looks upon the back end of the grandstand. One rider bitterly remarked it was erected here so the riders couldn't watch the races for nothing.

The horses run over a thoroughfare which a mountain goat would assess as difficult. On rainy afternoons, it is a gullied street cobbled with rocks of slime. When the sun shines, the dust creates the impression they're racing in the sack of a vacuum cleaner. There are depressions along the way that are deep enough to conceal the tomb of Pharaoh.

It is strictly a one-day grab. The joint is operated as if the owners were going to pack their keisters and take the next train out of town. But this pitch has been on the clip every spring for eighty-eight years.

The race itself is generally exciting because its purpose is to bring together for the first time the best of the three-year-old colts. But this time it isn't a championship race. It can't be one today because such as Jaipur, Vimy Ridge, Cyrano and Nassau Hall are not in it.

There is an obvious trend for trainers to keep their horses in the barns until later stakes, when colts of this age have stamina to run a mile and a quarter. This theory has been substantiated by the design of racing traced by Tom Barry in previous springs. He ignores the Derby and drops fresh colts into the Belmont, which he won with Cavan and Celtic Ash.

The latest victim of this evil track was Sir Gaylord, which would have been the favorite if he hadn't fractured a bone after working Friday morning. This track is less an arena than an ambush for colts. The trainer who gets a sound horse out of it is a lucky man. Only the horses of the picadors in bullfights take more risks.

The defenders of this big hustle offer numerous reasons for Derby winners breaking down after they struggled across this serried mile and a quarter which would be an ideal course for pigeon racing if the birds flew over it.

But the evidence dissolves their protests when you inspect the roster of the maimed. The casualties include Dark Star, Count Turf, Tomy Lee, Venetian Way, Tim Tam, Iron Liege and Hill Gail. They didn't disintegrate on the track, but they broke down in later races and some never moved in competition again.

There is bust-out action Downtown at night. Steers accost the strollers on Fourth Street and offer to escort them to dice games. Agents for prostitutes make whispered pitches from doorways. The waitress who doesn't attempt to shortchange you qualifies as Kentucky's first saint. The vice is mean and despicable. The streetwalkers are the ugliest of their kind. The touts are the scum of every track from Tanforan to Rockingham. The hotels and tag restaurants slug the marks with tripled prices as the politicians croak about the grandeur of Blue Grass hospitality.

I achieved a small victory here last year. A packet of mutuel tickets was lifted out of my pants pocket as I pushed my way through the files of players marshaled in front of the windows. My only consolation was the horse lost.

Management is as furtive as a candy store bookmaker.

The size of the crowd is never disclosed. It is always announced as "over 100,000," although I'm positive I've been here when there were less than 65,000 on the premises.

It is the claim of the old poets of the press box that their eyes get moist when the band plays "My Old Kentucky Home" as the horses mince out on the track. But the only people I've seen weeping have been music lovers who are offended by the atrocities committed against Stephen Foster's song by the high school bands.

This, I imagine, is an historic event. But so was the pain of the soldiers at Valley Forge. But Washington's troops only did it once. A lot of people take this every year. Their numbers diminish. Since the Derby has been televised, the Derby party at home has become as popular as New Year's Eve rumbles.

They hawk sentiment here with disgusting banality. But there isn't a race named in memory of Matt Winn, the man who made the Kentucky Derby a national fete.

From *Nobody Asked Me, But . . .* , *The World of Jimmy Cannon,* ed. Jack Cannon and Tom Cannon (New York: Berkley, 1979), pp. 239–241.

## Questions

*Content/Meaning*

1. In plain language, what are the major complaints that Cannon voices in this column? What was the event that apparently triggered the

column? How does the analogy of "hanging Rembrandts in a tenement basement" (paragraph 2) relate to one of Cannon's major points?

2. To what extent are the points made by Cannon in paragraphs 7 and 8 relevant to his main argument?

*Style*

1. Obviously Jimmy Cannon does not like the Kentucky Derby. One might say that Cannon creates, in his complaint, a repetition by variation—in other words, he uses many descriptive words and figures of speech to make the same points over and over again. What are all the figures of speech he uses for each of the following: the grandstand, the racing strip, the Kentucky Derby?

2. How effective is Cannon's use of figurative language? Would you call it a main feature of his style? Compare Cannon's use of figures with Morris's. Which of the two do you prefer?

3. How would you describe the range of Cannon's vocabulary? From what sources does he draw the various synonyms that you found in answer to question 1? Cannon wrote for a time as the syndicated sports columnist for the *New York Daily News*. Would that fact explain such words or phrases as "joint," "bust-out," "keisters," and "on the clip"? (If you don't know what they mean, look them up in a dictionary. Note especially their origins and the kind of usage they represent.) What, if anything, do these words have in common?

## Exercises and Assignments

1. Select either an article in a newspaper or a magazine or an advertisement and study its use of figurative language. In making your selection, use as your chief criterion the variety and effectiveness of its figures of speech. Write a paper describing the nature and evaluating the effectiveness of the figurative language used in the selection. You should plan the paper as follows:

*a.* Describe the subject, the central point, and summarize the argument of the article or ad.

*b.* Remark generally on the figurative language. What are the chief figures of speech used by the writer? How dominant is the use of figures?

*c.* Select two particularly interesting figures, preferably not of the same type, and, in a paragraph devoted to each, examine the meaning and its relevance to the point being developed.

2. Write a paragraph about a person or a place in which you use at least two effective figures of speech to develop your description.

# 7

# THE
# CENTRAL
# IMPRESSION

In preceding chapters of this unit, we have given attention to the choice of language by which writers can achieve concreteness and liveliness in rendering their descriptions. Now we wish to examine another important feature of descriptive writing: finding and developing the central impression.

Like all other kinds of writing, effective description must have a purpose. It may, of course, be subordinate to a larger design—as we have mentioned, description is vital to many kinds of writing. The historian can hardly expect to explain to a reader General Eisenhower's strategy in the invasion of Normandy without describing the terrain of the beachheads, the positioning of the defending armies, the weather conditions, and numerous other factors that would ultimately influence the outcome of the invasion. In this instance, description would serve as background for the writer's larger purpose of explaining and analyzing a historical event. But the description itself should nevertheless develop a perspective of its own, one that would give point to the details the writer has selected to focus on in the scene. In this instance, the stress might be on the invulnerability the Germans perceived in their defensive position. The description, in consequence, could focus on the slope of the beaches, the placement of the artillery, the rockiness of the shore, the shelter provided by hillocks and vegetation.

The foregoing example demonstrates the need for the writer to select a central impression that will govern choice of detail and attitude toward the subject. Since description is concerned with conveying sensory observations, its organizing purpose must be to allow the reader to perceive what feelings toward the subject the writer wished to record. In a descriptive passage, those feelings collectively are the impression that is being conveyed.

**79**

And that impression is, of necessity, the unifying element that holds the description together.

Until now we have restricted our illustrations of descriptive writing to places. Now we wish to examine some descriptions of people, a topic that readily allows the discovery of central impressions. We often call the description of people by such words as the *sketch, profile,* or *portrait.* While these terms borrowed from painting give the impression that the emphasis should be on external appearance, the best descriptions of people inevitably are more than outward renderings (as indeed the best paintings are, too). They must necessarily be *subjective* by acquainting us, at least in some measure, with the inner person and not merely with appearances.

Our interest, then, in the reading selection that follows is to discover the writer's central impression of her subject. As you proceed in reading the essay, ask yourself what sort of persons the writer is portraying and what central impression she seems to want to leave with her reader.

## Reading Selections

This article was the cover story in one issue of the popular magazine *People,* which is marketed to be read fast and to include a good many pictures in developing its articles. Its coverage, as the name tells us, is devoted to people—it often verges on gossip or, at least, intimate information about the rich, notorious, and famous.

### HOW DID STAN DRAGOTI LAND CHERYL TIEGS?

#### Because She Thinks He's "The World's Most Liberated Man"

*Suzy Kalter*

He created the Alka-Seltzer "Try It You'll Like It" ad campaign and as a board member of the go-go Wells, Rich, Greene agency became a millionaire at an unseemly age. But if the name Stan Dragoti lives—in infamy, envy or at all—it's probably because he was the hulk who, incredibly, resisted Cheryl Tiegs' marriage proposals for three years. Or worse, finally did marry her in 1970, and the damn thing worked, to the fury of a nation of male fantasists. What does the $2,000-a-Day Woman—the world's hottest model, ABC-TV's rookie of the year and Farrah Fawcett-Majors' major opponent in the pinup poster sweepstakes—see in her dark but not so tall (6′1″ to her 5′10″) or handsome geezer 15 years her senior (45 to 30)?

"I never get tired of looking at him," beams Tiegs. So *that's* it, Cheryl's lost in some kind of Trilby trip? No way. A Dragoti could package Tic Tac "Mouthwhack," but only Cheryl and God could make a Tiegs—or this one anyway.

"There are plenty of girls more beautiful than I am," she says as if she believes it, "but people will never know their names, and five years from now they'll be waitresses in a coffee shop." As for herself: "I had to have brains to go as far and as high as I did in modeling. Stan's helped," she concedes, "but instinctively I have a better business sense, and I consider myself the equal of any man." Yet the marvel of Tiegs is that she has got not only more body (34–24–35) than the Golden Girls of decades past but also more soul. "People can look at me and know I'm married, successful and not neurotic—I'm a nice person and it shows."

That self-assurance she *does* credit to Dragoti. "I would go out to dinner and just sit there," she recalls. "It never occurred to me that I was supposed to contribute to the conversation. Stan got me believing in myself." What makes their marriage "happier than most I know," she adds, is that he has no ego hang-ups. "I don't think I could ever find anybody better for me than Stan," she says, noting that Stan's the "most liberated man in the world." He wouldn't be threatened if she became the family's main breadwinner.

It hasn't happened—yet. That $2,000 a day is top price for models, and counting residuals for ads ranging from Cover Girl cosmetics to Virginia Slims to Lincoln-Mercury Cougar, she's bumping the $300,000 bracket. And that was before the $50,000-plus advance for her health-and-beauty book due out next spring and—most important—her estimated five-year, $2.5 million contract with ABC. So far she has offered fashion tips Thursdays on *Good Morning America* and done sports commentary on a Kentucky Derby special with Frank Gifford (by next month she may even be ready to work with Howard Cosell at Forest Hills).

Why TV and not movies? "When I turned 30, Stan and I sat down and figured out how to make the best out of what I've accomplished so far," Tiegs explains. "How would it look to go from being a top model to being a flop in a movie? I'd be right back at the bottom again." With characteristic shrewdness, she's going to take lessons to correct her little girl's voice and is steering clear of variety-show gigs until she can handle them. Similarly, though she negotiated the right to merchandise products under her name, she's being superprotective of her credibility. "There's a Farrah doll," she points out, "but there's no Phyllis George doll."

Cheryl developed that sense of dignity as the daughter of a Quaker undertaker in Alhambra, Calif. "I was a cheerleader in high school," she recalls, "but not the popular kind. I was the shy one." Yet by 16 she was on the covers of *Teen* and *True Romance* enroute to *Seventeen* and *Glamour*. Three years later she dropped out of California State College at Los Angeles and headed for New York to model full-time.

Within a year Tiegs was introduced by a photographer to Dragoti, then art director for Wells, Rich. "I can tell you everything about the moment

I met him—what the room looked like, what I was wearing, everything," rhapsodizes Tiegs. "I called my mother and asked her how to know when you're in love." She insists it had never happened before. The otherwise outgoing Dragoti, whose first marriage had broken up after 18 stormy months, was still altar-shy. But, he admits, "It really did happen just like that—*boing!* After you're through admiring the physical characteristics, you can see she has splendid character. There are little imperfections that make her real, like that silly little laugh. I was determined to get involved immediately."

Dragoti had come a long way from his Depression Era beginnings as the son of Albanian immigrants who settled in New York and ran a garage. He showed artistic talent early—at 7 he went, portfolio in hand, looking for a job as a cartoonist. He dropped out of school at 19 to join the Navy during the Korean war, serving in Manhattan. Then came the School of Visual Arts, and a launch into advertising at Compton's.

Over three years—and three breakups—Dragoti and Tiegs lived together while he resisted marriage. By then he was determined to move up from commercials (he's now won more than 20 Clios, Madison Avenue's Oscars) to feature films. The Dragotis zipped off to California. While he directed a stinkeroo Western called *Dirty Little Billy,* Cheryl quit her career and settled into the role of hausfrau.

The sleek vision in the swimsuit ads ballooned to 155 pounds and developed a skin problem—not, she insists, out of unhappiness. "I was always eating nonstop as a kid and never gained any weight," she explains. "But my metabolism changed in my early 20s and I had to change my eating habits." Off came 35 pounds. "It's no mystery," she shrugs. "I just stopped eating." Plunging back into the modeling game in 1972, she virtually never said no to an assignment. "I traveled way too much," she concedes. "Our marriage wasn't in serious trouble—I've never thought of leaving Stan—but it wasn't healthy to do what I was doing. Now we're together 90 percent of the time—my marriage is my top priority."

Dividing their lives between a $450,000 Spanish villa in Bel Air and a corporate suite at the Sherry-Netherland Hotel on Fifth Avenue, the Dragotis pursue separate but equally flourishing careers. In addition to his consultancy creating tough-case commercials like the current "I Love New York" campaign, Stan has written the screenplay for Irving Wallace's best-seller *The Fan Club* and is negotiating the movie deal with Sophia Loren. Both Cheryl and Stan put their sizable earnings into a corporation called Sunday (after their favorite day of the week), which pays them salaries. It is Cheryl who handles day-to-day finances. "Stan wouldn't even know where the checkbook is," she laughs. (He keeps losing the key to their digs and to his if not her Mercedes.)

They average five nights a week at home alone, she usually deep into a book like Graham Greene's *The Human Factor* that she picks from the *New York Times* Sunday review section. The two other nights they may party till dawn with friends like the Tony Curtises and the David Janssens, but Cheryl never goes out on the eve of a model assignment. Arising as early as 5 A.M., she washes her hair, letting a conditioner settle in while she shaves her legs. She reads the morning paper and breakfasts on hot water with lemon, a bran muffin and orange juice. Then, sans makeup, she goes to her gym, the Anatomy Asylum. She tries to play tennis daily, including all day Saturday and Sunday. While working, Tiegs often forgets lunch, and for dinner has a glass of wine, salad, meat or chicken and a vegetable.

Amazingly, she seems indifferent about clothes, hates shopping and usually buys in bulk. Recently she indulged in a $750 silk nightie, but she generally sleeps in the buff. Her ABC segment on "How to Buy a Wardrobe for $150" notwithstanding, she dropped $2,000 within minutes one day at Beverly Hills' chic Charles Gallay boutique. But that is not necessarily the most serious revelation about Tiegs the network faces. Children are definitely on the Dragotis' drawing board. "I've been carrying around a baby picture of Cheryl for years," says Stan. "It's in my wallet to remind myself that I want one of those before it's too late." Cheryl agrees. "We've been saying next year, next year about a baby. Now it's really going to be next year."

From *People,* June 19, 1978, pp. 104 ff.

### Questions

*Content/Meaning*

1. What central impression does the writer wish to form of Stan Dragoti and Cheryl Tiegs? Is the focus on the two characters designed to make essentially a statement about their marriage?
2. What do we know of the background or personal history of the two personalities? How does the background information support the writer's central impression? Is this information similar in kind for the two subjects?
3. To whom, Tiegs or Dragoti, does the article give more attention? Why?
4. As an afterthought to the piece in *People* magazine, read the following news clipping which appeared a year later in the *New York Post.* To what extent did the article in *People* prepare you for the turn of events described in the news story? Does the report from the *Post*

make you skeptical about the central impression registered in Suzy Kalter's article? Explain.

## CHERYL'S AFFAIR DROVE HUBBY TO DRUGS

### Sam Rosensohn

Stan Dragoti, director of the hit Dracula movie "Love at First Bite" and husband of super-model Cheryl Tiegs, says marriage on the rocks drove him to cocaine.

A Frankfurt court yesterday levied a 21-month suspended jail sentence and a $54,350 fine against Dragoti, who wrote the "I Love New York" TV commercials.

Dragoti, who confessed to smuggling more than three-quarters of an ounce of cocaine into West Germany, said he has taken large doses of the drug since he learned Cheryl was having an affair with photographer-socialite Peter Beard.

"I confronted her with the situation, and it was my understanding that these rumors were largely true," Dragoti said, referring to Cheryl's trip to Africa where she filmed a TV documentary with Beard.

"It was at this time that I started getting involved with cocaine.

"I was very depressed during this period, and needed something to take away the pain," Dragoti said, explaining why he tried to smuggle some coke to the Cannes Film Festival this spring.

"I panicked at the thought of being away from home and not being able to get cocaine."

So Dragoti said he lined a bathing suit with about $2900 worth of the drug for his use during the film festival in the south of France.

"Now I know that was an insane thing to do," said Dragoti, who pleaded guilty in court.

From the *New York Post,* July 5, 1979.

*Style*

1. To what extent does the description of Cheryl Tiegs and Stan Dragoti depend on concrete and figurative language? List some examples of figures in the description of each. How apt are they? What do they add to the overall descriptions?

2. Dialogue is an important part of the article. Note that questions are not asked directly by the writer, though they seem to stem from a personal interview, a good source for sketches or portraits. Study the direct quotations. Do they reveal attributes of Cheryl Tiegs that we do not get in the rest of the article? How are they integrated into the article? Note especially how they are introduced.

## Reading Selection

The biographical sketch that follows originally appeared in *American Heritage,* a glossy, high-quality journal that features popular background articles on American history and culture. Richard F. Snow regularly contributes articles, often on little-known but influential figures, in a feature called "American Characters." As you read the article, note especially the central impression that Snow creates of Dewey.

### MELVIL DEWEY

#### *Richard F. Snow*

He began life as Melville Louis Kossuth Dewey, but soon dropped the two middle names and shortened the first to Melvil. For a while he even tried to spell his surname "Dui." He felt that, like most things in the world, his full name was a disorderly waste of time, and he devoted his life to setting things in order and saving time.

Melvil Dewey was born in upstate New York in 1851. His niece says that as a child "it was his delight to arrange his mother's pantry, systematizing and classifying its contents." His reformer's zeal was fully developed by the time he was fifteen, when he badgered his father into dropping from the stock of his tiny store that notorious thief of time, tobacco. His father acceded, the store failed, but Dewey rejoiced in being "morally ryt."

On his eighteenth birthday he was already fretting over lost time. He had, he wrote, "accomplished during those eighteen years what I hope my children will accomplish better in fifteen or less. . . . As far as education or discipline and development of the mind are concerned I am very sure fourteen years might accomplish it all." He carried this interest in education with him into Amherst college, and in his annual character summary for his twenty-first birthday he announced "—my World Work—Free Schools & Free Libraries for every soul."

As he studied the libraries nearby, he became increasingly distressed. They were citadels of disorder, with books classified by size, title, or name of author, by accession date, sometimes even by color. All that duplication of work from library to library, all that wasted time. "For months I dreamed night and day that there must be somewhere a satisfactory solution." It came to him suddenly one Sunday while he was sitting through a "long sermon" without hearing a word. "I jumpt in my seat and came very near shouting 'Eureka'! It was to get absolute simplicity by using the simplest known symbols, the arabic numerals as decimals with the ordinary significance of nought, to number a classification of all human knowledge in print." After graduating in 1874, he continued to work in the Amherst library, perfecting his system. In 1876, at the age of twenty-four, he published the first of nineteen editions of *A Classification Subject Index for Cataloguing and Arranging the Books and Pamphlets of a Library.*

That same year he became a founder of the American Library Association. As its first secretary, he had the opportunity to promote his system. This he did relentlessly, and he continued to spread the word when, in 1883, he became librarian of Columbia College in New York. He immediately started reclassifying the college collections, established the first library school in America, and defended his stand with fierce eloquence when the administration got mad at him for admitting women.

With the school under way, he left Columbia to serve as director of the state library, where the legislation he proposed served, according to a contemporary, to "remove the reproach that New York had about the worst laws of any State in the Union for establishing and maintaining free public libraries and give it . . . the best."

While Dewey was racking up these successes, he was campaigning to overhaul the greatest time-waster of all. "Skolars agree," he wrote, "that we hav the most unsyentifik, unskolarli, illojical & wasteful spelling ani languaj ever ataind." With orthography as vexing as that of nineteenth-century comic monologues, Dewey went on to call for the simplification of English. He insisted that once spelling was freed from the complexities and absurdities of the past and made uniform, three years could be saved in any child's education. His zeal was such that he would correct his mail as he read through it.

While he campaigned, he and his wife Annie bought land in Lake Placid, New York. In 1895 they founded the Lake Placid Club, which grew to become one of the best-known resorts on earth. Part of its fame came from its exclusivity. With his obsessive categorizing, Dewey classified members according to degree of desirability even after they were admitted. And some people could not be admitted at all. "No one," Dewey wrote bluntly in 1901, "will be received . . . against whom there is physical, moral, social or race objection. . . . This invariable rule is rigidly enforced; it is found impractical to make exception to Jews. . . ." As vigorous in the defense of a bad cause as a good one, Dewey stuck by his prejudice with the same belligerent tenacity he brought to all his affairs. In the end it forced his resignation from the State Library and ended his effective working life in 1906.

He continued as president of the Lake Placid Club, trying to keep his guests from smuggling in liquor and making sure all the menus were in his simplified spelling. One long-time visitor remembered that after a couple of weeks there, "a guest would have trouble spelling 'mayonnaise' for the rest of his or her life."

After Dewey's death in 1931, the menus returned to regular English spelling. His decimal system fared better. He lived to see it in use throughout the world and adopted by 96 per cent of the public libraries and 89 per cent of the college libraries in America. Roger Howson, librarian of Columbia University at the time of Dewey's death, wrote: "Who among us can specify exactly the place that Dewey, who prepared a place for everything, holds himself? He needs no wreath of laurel (583.931), no stained-glass window (729.84), no pyramid (913.32). Go into any library and look around. From 010 to 999 the books are there in serried ranks, drawn up in regiments of knowledge, marshalled according to his plans of organization. He has made the lights so shine that the whole field is equally to be surveyed."

From *American Heritage,* December 1980, p. 73.

### Questions

*Content/Meaning*

1. In detailing the professional life of Melvil Dewey, Richard Snow focuses on three major interests during Dewey's adult years. What were these interests? How does Snow use these interests as illustrations of Dewey's character? Could you derive from them a central impression of Melvil Dewey as a man?

*Style*

1. One important feature of Snow's style is that he refrains from sharply criticizing his subject, even though there may be reason to do so. This avoidance of expressing a strong opinion occurs especially in paragraph 7, which describes Dewey's association with the Lake Placid Club. How would you characterize Snow's use of descriptive language in this part of the article? Does he make much use of figures of speech? of action verbs or concrete adjectives or nouns? Does he express any judgments? What key words help to give a characterization of Dewey in paragraph 7? What do you perceive to be Snow's technique of describing his subject?

2. Coherence is an important characteristic of effective expository writing. An article is coherent when it connects its thoughts—from sentence to sentence and paragraph to paragraph. How does Snow provide coherence to his article by referring repeatedly to Dewey's zeal for spelling reform?

## Reading Selection

The following article was written by an undergraduate student at Baruch College of the City University of New York for publication in a student magazine, *Dollars and $ense,* which specializes in reports on the business world.

### LISA KRYSTINE—PUNK SINGER

#### *Claire Hearns*

A few heads turned as she walked down 8th Avenue by 20th Street wearing outrageous black and white psychedelic glasses, a short black and red coat, and black leotards with calf-length high-heeled boots. Once inside her apartment, she takes off her coat, places it on her antique sofa, and bends over to pick up a purring cat, while the other two felines affectionately rub against her legs.

The small apartment is filled with knick-knacks, Peter Max type drawings, and clothes—everything from a leopard skin jumpsuit to a see-through lace minidress. Poking out of at least three closets are about 20 pairs of shoes—all spike-heeled and pointy-toed, and the top of a dresser and a night table are covered with all types of accessories, such as gloves, gauntlets, wigs and jewelry. This apartment seems to have everything that a budding punk rock singer would need to get her career off the ground.

Lisa Krystine and her band, Future Flashback, are starting to gain some recognition in the punk rock scene. Ms. Krystine, who describes her music as "a cross between high energy, soul and punk," has appeared at Mudd Club, as well as a few other smaller places, and is hoping to appear at more clubs in the near future. As a performer, Ms. Krystine is forceful, dynamic, and quite theatrical. On the stage, she dances as well as sings—utilizing all the skills she learned as a go-go dancer and in her voice lessons. (She is still taking voice lessons because she feels that "no matter how good a singer is, there is always room for improvement.")

Future Flashback has been together a little over two months—and as for the money to be made by such a new punk band, it is practically nil. Ms. Krystine said that most of the punk clubs pay as low as $50 for a gig. This is because the club does not know how big a crowd will be drawn in by a relatively unknown band. As far as the band is concerned, the exposure could prove to be quite profitable. Ms. Krystine feels that Mudd Club and Hurrah's are the best to perform at money-wise. When Future Flashback appeared at Mudd on November 26, 1979 they received $300 for the gig. Comparing this to most other clubs, the pay was high, but when you realize that the $300 had to be split among the six members of the band—well, anyone can see that they do not survive by these gigs alone.

Ms. Krystine, who will be 27 years old in March, works as a waitress in the English Pub part-time to earn money to live on. Besides the usual expenses of food and rent, she must pay for a rehearsal studio for the band out of her own pocket. That costs her $10-$12 an hour, and two three hour sessions a week takes a big chunk out of her part-time check. As for keeping up her wardrobe, Ms. Krystine finds no problem with that. She's a thrift shop fanatic, and buys most of her punky clothes, shoes, and accessories for $2 or $3 a piece.

Although she sometimes finds it hard to get by money-wise, Ms. Krystine would never give up the band. She feels that she's just beginning to get a chance to fulfill her dream of reaching people through her music, and with Future Flashback's hard-hitting, energy-packed sound, Lisa Krystine ought to be turning a few heads in the near future—without the aid of her psychedelic glasses!

From Dollars and $ense: Baruch College<br>Business Review 2 (April 1980): 6, 7.

### Questions

*Content/Meaning*
1. On what aspect of Kyrstine's personality does this article concentrate? Is this concentration appropriate to the specialization of the journal in which the article appeared?

*Style*
1. How does the writer characterize Krystine's wardrobe? What words contribute most sharply toward particularizing her clothes?
2. Linking the ending of an article or essay to the beginning is a useful stylistic device. How is that device used in this article?
3. Paragraph 4 is probably the weakest in the article stylistically. Here is an attempt to revise it.

> Future Flashback has been together for less than two months. As an unknown band, it has little chance to make much money; in fact, the total fee for all six members is likely to be no more than $50 a gig at a typical punk club. Yet, Krystine's band has accepted dates at such clubs to gain exposure. Recently that practice paid off, for Future Flashback was asked to appear on November 26 at the Mudd Club, one of the more famous night spots on the punk scene in New York. That gig paid $300, but even at that rate, the compensation is too low for the members of the band to survive.

Do you think the revised paragraph is an improvement over the original. If so, in what way? If not, can you offer a better revision? What weaknesses do you see in the original version?

## Exercises and Assignments

1. Select a well-known personality and search for three character sketches of him or her. The person may or may not be currently in the news. To locate the sketches, use *The New York Times Index* or *The Reader's Guide* (see pp. 46–51). When you have found three interesting articles, read them closely and be prepared to discuss in class the central impression created in each of the articles. Compare and contrast the three treatments, and conclude your analysis by presenting the point of view and focus you would provide in writing a sketch of the person.

2. Write such a sketch in no more than 250 words.

3. Write a 300- to 500-word "Man (or Woman) in the News" story for your local or college newspaper. You may consider any achievement—academic, physical, social—as worthy of a report, and you may choose a faculty member or a student or even a person living in the community as your subject. Concentrate on creating a dominant impression. It will be essential for you to interview the person and possibly to ask questions of others about him or her. To facilitate your interview, you should prepare a string of questions in advance. This implies that you should know something about the person even before you conduct your interview. If the subject is a professor, you might wish to read something he or she has written. If a fellow student, you might wish to speak with others first. In some instances, there may even be local news reports about the person, particularly if he or she is an outstanding athlete.

# 8

# SELECTION
# OF DETAILS

**W**e have seen that descriptive writing demands the articulation of a central impression. Obviously, our impressions are governed by what we know about a person prior to writing about him or her. The reporter who interviewed Cheryl Tiegs or Lisa Krystine not only gathered a good deal of information on the spot but also may have read about or heard of the person before beginning the interview. The process of reading, interviewing, or both thus provided the writer with much more information than she could finally use. The writing process—and what we say here applies to all kinds of writing, not just descriptions—demands that we prune our information to fit the central impression or idea we wish to develop. It is, therefore, important to *include* the relevant details and *exclude* the irrelevant from among the information we have collected.

Clearly, we have already seen the effects of that pruning process in all of the preceding selections. Take, for example, the article about Melvil Dewey (see pp. 85–87). In that instance, the writer chose to tell us details about Dewey's work in the classification of books, about his penchant for spelling reform, and about his experiences as the founder and president of the Lake Placid Club. He told us nothing about Dewey's love life, his marriage, his children (if he had any), or his death. The central impression the writer wished to convey made those subjects irrelevant, and so he excluded from his sketch details that did not fit his emphasis. We say "excluded" deliberately, for the writer, no matter what the subject, must of necessity collect more details than can be used.

The two articles that follow are about the same person, Phyllis Schlafly, a leading activist in opposing the Equal Rights Amendment (ERA), which for some years now has been before state legislatures for ratification as an amendment to the U.S. Constitution. ERA is designed to provide equal protection by the law and in turn equal legal responsibility for women and men. The amendment states that "Equality of rights under the law shall not be denied or abridged by the United States or by any state on account of sex." The two articles both present portraits, but they differ widely in purpose and approach.

As you read the two portraits, note first the central impression created in each. Then pay particular attention to the details the writers chose in developing their subject. As you read, make marginal notations or keep notes of coverage that is peculiar to one or the other article. Note also those points that are covered in both. Then turn to the questions that follow.

# Reading Selection

This article appeared as part of a news report in *Time,* a publication that calls itself "the Weekly Newsmagazine." Many readers tend to accept reports in *Time* as objective and to regard them purely as information rather than as a mixture of facts and opinion. This response is especially likely when the *Time* report is not given a byline; readers thus must rely on an anonymous, presumably unopinionated, voice for their reactions to the article. In this instance, the article clearly intends to characterize Phyllis Schlafly to the reader. Much of the article is not news but background and opinion.

### ANTI-ERA EVANGELIST WINS AGAIN

#### Feminine but Forceful, Phyllis Schlafly Is a Very Liberated Woman

Looking crisp and composed in a red shirtwaist dress, red-white-and-blue scarf and frosted hair, Phyllis Schlafly arrived last week at the Illinois capitol with 500 followers. To symbolize their opposition to the Equal Rights Amendment, which was about to be voted on in the house, the women had brought loaves of home-baked bread—apricot, date nut, honey-bran and pumpkin. But as she climbed onto a kitchen stool to address the cheering crowd, Schlafly the demure housewife turned into Schlafly the aggressive polemicist. The passage of ERA, she declared, would mean Government-funded abortions, homosexual schoolteachers, women forced into military combat and men refusing to support their wives.

For the past six years, Schlafly, 53, has been delivering similar exhortations to similar gatherings, helping to turn public opinion against ERA, which is still three states short of ratification. After passing 35 state legislatures in five years, ERA was defeated last year in Nevada, North Carolina, Florida and Illinois. Last week the amendment lost once again in Illinois when the house narrowly defeated it. With no other state legislature scheduled to vote on ERA, the amendment will expire on March 22, 1979 unless Congress agrees to extend the deadline.

ERA's decline has been largely the result of Schlafly's small (20,000 members) but highly disciplined organizations, Stop ERA and Eagle Forum. While the feminists have splintered over the issues of abortion and lesbian rights, Schlafly's troops have centered their efforts on ERA. They have evolved into a formidable lobbying force, allied with local and national right-wing groups, including HOW (Happiness of Women) and AWARE (American Women Are Richly Endowed).

Flying from state capital to state capital, the savvy, disarming Schlafly matches the feminists' rhetoric phrase for phrase. She bluntly proclaims that "all sensible people are against ERA," and dismisses the liberationists as "a bunch of bitter women seeking a constitutional cure for their personal problems." In many of her speeches, she continues to insist that "women find their greatest fulfillment at home with their family."

Schlafly, however, is hardly a typical housewife. Author of nine books, a three-time candidate for the U.S. Congress, full-time law student at Washington University in St. Louis, editor of a monthly newsletter, twice-a-week syndicated newspaper columnist and regular speaker at anti-ERA rallies, she acts very much like a liberated woman. By her own reckoning, she is away from her family at least once a week. She employs a full-time housekeeper to care for her six-bedroom Tudor-style mansion overlooking the Mississippi River in Alton, Ill.

How does Schlafly reconcile her career with her stay-at-home dogma? "My husband lets me do what I want to do," she says. "I have canceled speeches whenever my husband thought that I had been away from home too much." Besides, she adds, "when I fill out applications, I put down 'mother' as my occupation." She boasts that she breast-fed every one of her six children and later taught each of them how to read. Says she: "I work all the time. I'm organized. I've learned to budget every minute."

Schlafly developed her organizational talents early. Raised in St. Louis, the daughter of a failed inventor, she put herself through Washington University ('44) by working 48 hours a week testing machine guns at a local arms plant. After earning an M.A. in political science from Radcliffe in 1945, she returned to St. Louis to edit a conservative newsletter.

After marriage in 1949, to Fred Schlafly, a wealthy corporation lawyer, she became increasingly involved in right-wing Republican politics. In addition to writing the bestselling book *A Choice Not an Echo* for Barry Goldwater's 1964 presidential campaign, she started her own national newsletter, the *Phyllis Schlafly Report.* She was a delegate to three G.O.P. conventions and served as president of the Illinois Federation of Republican Women. When she ran for the presidency of the National Federation of Republican

Women in 1967, she lost in a bitter campaign against a more moderate candidate. Schlafly's own next-door neighbor in Alton, a housewife and active Republican, accused her at the time of being "an exponent of an extreme right-wing philosophy—a propagandist who deals in emotion and personalities where it is not necessary to establish facts or prove charges."

Undaunted, Schlafly ran for Congress in 1970 (she lost). When her role as wife and mother became an issue, she retorted: "My husband Fred says a woman's place is in the house—the U.S. House of Representatives." A similar line was used that same year by another woman politician of considerably different views—Bella Abzug.

Schlafly started fighting ERA when she wrote an article denouncing the amendment in her newsletter in 1972. After that, she says, "it just snowballed." She began tireless rounds of debating feminists, making appearances on talk shows and speaking at rallies. Ahead lies a bitter fight against the feminists' drive to win an extension of the amendment's deadline. Vows Schlafly: "We will bury ERA on March 22, 1979." Her opponents claim that she is using the ERA issue to aid her own career, but she denies having further ambitions for political office. Still, given her record, she seems unlikely to retire to hearth and home.

From Time, July 3, 1978, p. 20.

# Reading Selection

The selection that follows is undisguised opinion. It comes from a regular column in the Thursday issue of *The New York Times* entitled "Hers." As its title indicates, this column is written by women and usually about women, women's perspectives, or topics related to the new consciousness encouraged by the women's movement. The "Hers" column is frankly subjective. This article was one of a series on prominent women written by Gail Sheehy, a well-known "new" journalist whose popular successes include the former best seller *Passages.*

## WOMEN & LEADERSHIP: PHYLLIS SCHLAFLY

### *Gail Sheehy*

She rose out of the milling of drones and idlers unmistakably, poised against the coarse background of an airline terminal in alto relievo. Phyllis Schlafly it was, her sculptural figure folded into a champagne suede coatdress, her hair swept up into the chiseled curls of a goddess, her smile a study in alabaster control. She looked for all the world like the Screen Gems lady who used to preside, on a pedestal, over the opening of Columbia Pictures movies.

In the last eight years, Phyllis Schlafly has set herself up on the national level as the moral leader battling to block the proposed Equal Rights Amendment. Moving about the country to debate "the libs" two or three times every week, Mrs. Schlafly had to meet me on the fly between Bethlehem and Tampa. Nevertheless, wrinkling her nose at the vulgarians stirring their coffee with wooden sticks nearby, she was determined to walk the length of the terminal to find "a better coffee shop" before settling down to discuss the grim row hoed by herself and her mother in times past.

"My mother would have been in her mid-30's when the Depression hit and she had to get a job," she said.

"Was your father out of work?" I asked.

"Yes." The screws around her smile tightened suddenly into an arch of contempt. "He had a fair job with Westinghouse, which folded. There were hard years, then he was in his 50's and too old. . . ."

Even though her mother had earned two degrees before she married, she was confined the next 30 years in St. Louis to jobs for which almost no men applied—sales clerk, elementary schoolteacher, librarian. Today, elderly and infirm, her mother lives with Phyllis Schlafly.

"There are no benefits from the years before my father's death," Mrs. Schlafly said, "because he wasn't in Social Security."

Asked why not, her reply was caustic.

"Because he didn't have a job."

Money was scarce. The family was poor, she said. Once a cousin offered to buy her either a winter coat or a bicycle. She knew she had to take the winter coat.

"I never had a bicycle."

"Never, in the whole time you were growing up?" I asked.

"Never had a bicycle. Never had a bicycle."

"Do you have one now?"

"No, can't ride," she laughed bitterly. "You don't learn to ride a bicycle after you're grown."

Never had a friend, never had a date, all through her college years. Knowing that brains were her ticket, she went to work on her 18th birthday at an arms plant and labored through the nights so she could attend Washington University during the day. She put herself through in three years.

"I didn't belong to a sorority, didn't go to any parties," she said. "It was a strictly budgeted, time-managed life."

When I asked if she felt envious of students who had the time and money to enjoy their salad days, she characteristically hammered out the same reply several times, as if hoping to nail it down.

"No. I thought what I was doing was better. Better. Better."

Thus did Phyllis Schlafly convert what might have been a debilitating envy into a stony cast of superiority.

The premise behind her leadership today is based on the next chapter in her own story. "The E.R.A. is the biggest fraud that ever came down the pike," she has said, defending the existing legal structure. "The law is beautiful. He is liable. She is not. Is that fair? Sure. That's the beautiful way men treat women in this country."

And indeed, once a lawyer from a wealthy Catholic Illinois family came along, found her researching an obscure quote in the back of the bank where she had worked without a raise for three years, and made her Mrs. John Schlafly Jr., she was liberated from paying jobs and hasn't held one since.

"Forever," she said, "not for 30 years. It feels wonderful—the greatest life in the world."

Phyllis Schlafly's formula for the better life, then, is based on marrying a rich professional, climbing the pedestal to lady of leisure, and pulling up the rope ladder behind her, thereby breaking any painful identifications with women who are still powerless, women who didn't have the wits to find a high-status male or the initiative to bind him legally into taking "beautiful" care of them. In short, women like her mother.

She refers to her four stints as delegate to Republican National Conventions and her three races for election to Congress as "the great hobby of my life."

But when she lost out on succession to the presidency of the National Federation of Republican Women in a nasty fight with liberals in 1967, she all but abandoned the democratic political process. She mastered a more efficient leadership style.

It would be hard to name another nationally known woman who is against the proposed Equal Rights Amendment. Phyllis Schlafly is La Duce, and there is good reason why.

"You are called chairman of Stop E.R.A.," I said. "Who elected you?"

"Nobody," Mrs. Schlafly said. "I started it myself, appointed myself."

"Is there any mechanism for transfer of leadership?"

"No."

"Isn't it customary in any volunteer organization for there to be elections?"

"It is. But I look upon ourselves as a movement, rather than an organization."

Stop E.R.A. has no members, only chairmen in 45 states, all appointed by Mrs. Schlafly to serve at her pleasure.

Eagle Forum, a tax-exempt organization over which Mrs. Schlafly also presides as chief indefinitely, operates out of her home in Alton, Ill., and allows her to publish the monthly Phyllis Schlafly Report—one woman's political opinions.

Her tactics are effective, if exotic to most Americans. Controlling all communications from under her own roof, she has fomented a countermovement and assumed an unchallengeable position as its moral leader. Fundamentalist religious leaders have had considerable success with such a model, the extreme example being the Ayatollah Khomeini, who from exile committed a revolution by cassette. What, I wondered, did Phyllis Schlafly have to say to her masses?

"But what advice do you have for women who do not enjoy your fortunate circumstances?" Again and again I pressed the question.

Mrs. Schlafly's answers were curt and inconsistent: "It's their own problem, not the government's." She reprimanded such women for lack of "private initiative," contradicting herself by saying that "the biggest problem women have today is inflation, with which the individual can't cope."

It was not an intellectual failure. At work here was a well-known psychological principle, seen in people who elevate themselves through the status of another while denying identifications with powerless figures in their past. The byproduct is often a severe lack of empathy. If the escapee were to permit herself to look back—to imagine how *they* feel—she might be undone.

One finds in Phyllis Schlafly's family history the same lesson that has mobilized so many women to champion the proposed amendment, yet she herself, having had no model of male-female cooperation, comes out demanding it be replaced with a model of male obligation. Not one notch can be loosened on the yoke binding men to take care of women, she is saying. And insofar as it is legally possible, men must be forbidden to fail. As her father did.

Today, unencumbered by empathy on a personal level or by the democratic process on a political level, Phyllis Schlafly is brilliantly successful as a moral boss. There is but one fatal flaw in her style of leadership. If she is run over by a truck, there are no survivors.

From *The New York Times,* January 24, 1980, p. C2.

## Questions

*Content/Meaning*
1. The two essays differ in their approach to their subject mainly because one was written in response to a specific occasion while the other took Schlafly as a subject for its own sake. How do these circumstances influence the focus of the two articles? Do they also influence the nature of the portrait they render of Phyllis Schlafly?
2. What details about Schlafly are shared by the two articles? Does this tell you something about viewpoints shared by the two writers? What qualities in particular do these shared details emphasize about Phyllis Schlafly?

*Style*

1. Examine the direct quotations attributed to Mrs. Schlafly in the two articles. Do they project the same personality? Do you detect in these quotations any biases on the part of the questioner/writer? Be specific in your answer.
2. What concrete or figurative language is used to describe the appearance of Phyllis Schlafly in the two articles?

## Exercises and Assignments

1. On the chart in Figure 8.1, make a listing of details (not attitudes or points of view) that you learn of Phyllis Schlafly from the two articles. Place the details under the appropriate headings. Study the list, and on the basis of what has been included and excluded, try to determine what main topics were of most interest to each of the two writers. Also show whether there are details in one or the other article that might either have received more attention or that could well have been omitted.

2. Here are some additional facts about Phyllis Schlafly. Use these and any other information you have collected from the reading selections or elsewhere and write a 200- to 300-word portrait of her. Make sure that you begin by formulating in your mind a central impression with which you wish to leave your reader.

   a. Her father, John Bruce Stewart, was so conservative he was teased about being a monarchist.
   b. Phyllis Stewart (Schlafly) was educated at a Roman Catholic parochial school in St. Louis.
   c. She was valedictorian of her high school class, and was graduated Phi Beta Kappa from Washington University in St. Louis. She earned a $500 scholarship to Radcliffe College, from which she received an M.A. in Political Science.
   e. She did research for several congressmen in Washington after her graduation and worked as an aide to Republican Claude I. Bakewell.
   f. Her husband, John Fred Schlafly, Jr., came from a wealthy Alton, Illinois, family.
   g. Mrs. Schlafly, during the 1950s, was president of the Radcliffe Club of St. Louis, a director of the Alton YWCA, and director of the local chapter of the National Conference of Christians and Jews.
   h. In 1952, she won the Republican primary and ran unsuccessfully against Melvin Price in a congressional election in Illinois.

## CHART OF DETAILS

| Time article only | Sheehy article only | Both articles |
| --- | --- | --- |
| | | |

*8.1*

i. As a strong anticommunist, she worked as an aide to Senator Joseph McCarthy in the early 1950s.

j. She published two pamphlets called *Reading List for Americans* and *Inside the Communist Conspiracy,* compiling titles of interest to patriotic Americans.

k. Her first book, *A Choice Not an Echo* (the Goldwater campaign biography and guidebook) was published by her own company, Pere Marquette Press.

l. Mrs. Schlafly, often in partnership with U.S. Navy Rear Admiral Chester Ward, published many more books, mostly under the imprint of Pere Marquette. Among these were *Strike from Space* (1967), and *The Betrayers* (1968).

m. In a book under her sole authorship, *Safe—Not Sorry,* she argues that the urban ghetto riots were instigated by communists.

n. In 1977, she published a book entitled *The Power of the Positive Woman* with Arlington House Press. Its subject is her opposition to the cause represented by what she calls the "femlib fanatics."

o. She has argued that ERA "will make a wife equally responsible to provide a home for her family and to provide 50 per cent of the financial support of her family." She has further maintained that ERA would make homosexual marriages legal and would require unisex toilets in public places.

3. The sketch or profile often occurs in textbooks. History, psychology, and sociology texts in particular need to pause from time to time to introduce real or hypothetical people either to illustrate a point or to provide background information. Choose one of your textbooks, and find one illustration of an extended sketch or portrait. Decide what central impression is conveyed and write a short evaluation of the description. Be sure to turn in a xerox copy of the original with your evaluation.

# 9 DOCUMENTATION: PORTRAITS AND THEIR SOURCES

**U**ntil now in our concern with descriptive writing, we have more or less taken for granted that the essays we have read are authoritative and accurate in the information they present to us. We have taken our information on trust. In popular writing, where deadlines must be met from day to day and even from hour to hour, that is as it should be. Surely most reporters and commentators are responsible persons; they have no desire to mislead us. Yet the popular press often does give us inaccurate information. The most notorious illustration of that unhappy fact is the headline published on election eve of 1948 by the *Chicago Daily Tribune,* "Dewey Defeats Truman." No doubt that erroneous report resulted from the rush, in those preelectronic days, to beat the competition with the latest scoop. At the time of the headline, Dewey was indeed leading, but later returns brought a reversal. Veteran critics of the *Chicago Daily Tribune,* a conservative newspaper that favored Dewey editorially, were less charitable in ascribing the reason for the faulty headline; they believed that it expressed a bias resulting from wishful thinking. But whether the result was due to practical circumstances or to willfulness, the headline was wrong. And so are many less dramatic reports in our newspapers and magazines. Too often, we get only partial reports, and as events unfold, more and better information is made available to us.

One major difference between popular and academic writing is that the latter requires us to reveal our sources so that readers can evaluate the accuracy and dependability of a piece of writing for themselves. It is, for example, difficult to know the personality of our leaders or to understand not only why something happened but also how. Why did Richard Nixon choose to tape his conversations in the Oval Office? Why did he not destroy them before their presence was made known to the public? What kind of man was the Richard Nixon who finally was forced to resign the office of President in disgrace? Many writers have professed to give us answers—some because they were there and knew intimate details of the story, others because they wished to defend their leader, still others because they were paid to bring as complete a report of Watergate to the public as was possible. Whom do we finally believe? That is the sort of question that research and scholarship is concerned with.

## PRIMARY AND SECONDARY SOURCES

We certainly try to collect as much firsthand information as we can obtain. Sources of this category are called *primary*. Henry Kissinger or John Mitchell are primary sources for at least some events of the Nixon presidency. So is Judge Sirica, who presided over the Watergate hearings. So also was Rose Mary Woods, Nixon's trusted secretary. And so, in a somewhat less direct sense, were the two famous reporters from the *Washington Post,* Carl Bernstein and Robert Woodward. Clearly, a source that is primary is not necessarily accurate. We must determine what each had to gain or lose from telling the whole truth. But, even though we are obliged to evaluate reports, we must nevertheless make every effort to get information from eyewitnesses and participants.

*Secondary* sources are those that are removed in time and place from the actual event. Secondary sources are, by their nature, more distant from their subjects than primary sources. But that does not mean we should distrust them or even regard them lightly. Historians are usually secondary sources. They will have studied all the primary sources, and on the basis of their full analysis of all events and personalities, they may well provide us with more accurate accounts than the less open-minded primary source might have. At their best, academic reports—whether in history, political science, psychology, economics, or whatever field—try to present as full a body of information without bias as they possibly can. Their aim, especially when they are concerned with re-creating an event from the past or when they look into actions of individual people, is to be *objective*. They must, as much as possible, leave their preferences or ideas outside their search for information and outside their drawing of conclusions. This is not to say that scholars should refrain from expressing opinions. They must do that, too; but if they are true scholars, they will not do so until they have ascertained for themselves what the facts are.

In this chapter we are concerned with the role of research in descriptive writing. We wish to examine various ways by which the researcher can gather facts in writing portraits of well-known people, whether living or dead. Unlike authors of popular articles, who because of the constraints and conventions placed on them rarely reveal their sources, we shall not only examine the means for gathering sources but shall practice acknowledging them in footnotes and bibliography listings. We shall, therefore, turn our attention from single to multiple sources to gain a fuller understanding of the persons about whom we are writing. We shall also learn to differentiate between those sources that are trustworthy and those that might lead us astray. This chapter, then, is designed to make a bridge between the demands of popular writing and academic writing.

## BIOGRAPHICAL REFERENCE SOURCES

There are many handy reference tools that help researchers obtain biographical information. Foremost among these is the *Biography Index,* which is in the same family of bibliographical reference works as *The Reader's Guide* (see pp. 49–51) or *The Book Review Digest* (see pp. 430–432). The *Biography Index* is a cumulative alphabetical reference guide to biographical material published in a wide range of periodicals and books. It is published in monthly pamphlets and bound annually as well as triannually. Coverage is generally restricted to American subjects, though some figures with international reputations are included. Besides articles and books, the *Biography Index* lists obituaries, collections of letters, diaries, memoirs, and bibliographies. It can give you references to any biographical material written in major journals and books over the specific period indexed. Subjects may be living or dead. If, for example, you had looked in Volume 10, covering the period from September 1973 to August 1976, for published material on the late Senator Joseph McCarthy from Wisconsin or on the former Beatle Paul McCartney, you would have found the following listings:

> MCCARTHY, Joseph Raymond, 1908–1957,
> senator
> Fried, Richard M. Men against McCarthy,
> (Contemporary Am. hist. ser) Columbia
> univ. press '76. 428p bibl
> Goldston, Robert. American nightmare;
> Senator Joseph R. McCarthy and the
> politics of hate, Bobbs '73 202p bibliog
> il pors

Jenkins, Roy. Nine men of power. Hamilton
'74 p 109–31 il pors

Oshinsky, David M. Senator Joseph McCarthy and the American labor movement.
Univ. of Mo. press '76 206p bibl

MCCARTNEY, Paul, 1942–  , English singer
and song writer

Gallagher, D. Paul McCartney; growing up,
up and away from the Beatles; interview.
il por Redbook 143:78–9+ S '74

Greenfield, J. All our troubles seemed so
far away, por Biog News 2:373–4 Mr '75

McCartney comes back. il pors Time
107:40–4 My 31 '76

Mellers, Wilfrid. Twilight of the gods; the
Beatles in retrospect. Faber '73 215p

Now they're a lot richer, some are sadder,
all wiser. por Biog News 2:375 Mr '75

Orth, M. Paul soars. il por Newsweek 87:100
My 17 '76

People. pors Time 105:36 F 24 '75; 107:46–
7 My 17 '76

Sparn, E. On the road with Paul McCartney.
il pors Sr Schol 103:32+ S 27 '73

Tremlett, George. Paul McCartney story.
Futura pubs. '75 192p il pors

Von Faber, K. Paul McCartney: acting his
age. il por Biog News 1:670–1 Je '74

Weber, D. . . . And Paul is on the road
again. por Newsweek 82:113 O 29 '73

**Juvenile literature**

Keenan, Deborah. On stage the Beatles; design concept: Larry Soule. Creative educ.
'76 47p il pors

Pirmantgen, Patricia. Beatles; il. [by] Dick
Brude; design concept: Mark Landkamer.
(Rock'n pop stars) Creative educ. '75 31p

The following explanation for reading entries is provided by the *Biography Index:*

Sample entry: ULLMANN, Liv, 1939–  , Norwegian  actress
Ullmann, Liv. Changing. Knopf  '77  177p
—Excerpt. il por McCalls 104:131+ F '77

Explanation: The Norwegian actress Liv Ullmann has written an
autobiographical book, titled Changing. The book
was published by Alfred A. Knopf, Inc. in 1977 and
has 177 pages

An excerpt of this book can be found in McCalls magazine, volume 104, February 1977 issue, beginning
on page 131, continuing on later pages. The excerpt
is illustrated with a photograph of the actress.)

From these entries, we learn the following information covering the years 1973–76:

- Three full-length books (but no journal articles) have been published about Senator McCarthy.
- One book, by Roy Jenkins, includes McCarthy as the subject of a chapter: He is one of *Nine Men of Power.* The chapter appears on pages 109–31 together with a portrait. (Information of this sort— that is, coverage of chapters within a book—can be found only in the *Biography Index*).
- Single articles on Paul McCartney appeared in *Redbook* and *Biography News,* and two articles each were published in *Time, Newsweek,* and *Senior Scholastic.* The piece in *Redbook* was an interview.
- One book by George Tremlett, entitled the *Paul McCartney Story,* was published during this period.
- Two pieces geared for juvenile readers were published about McCartney.

The system of documentation and bibliographical form are the same as in the sister publication, *The Reader's Guide.* In addition to the main body of biographical information given by the *Biography Index,* there is a listing at the end of each bound volume indexing names of biographies covered under various professional headings. Suppose, for example, that you wanted to find whatever was written in the sources covered by Volume 10 about any and all Peruvian generals during the years 1973–76. You would look under the heading "Generals," would find a subhead "Generals, Peruvian," and would note that, indeed, two Peruvian generals were subjects of articles or books: General Manuel Apolinario Odria and General Juan Velasco Alvarado.

In addition to such purely bibliographical sources as the *Biography Index,* you may also find the following dictionaries and encyclopedias useful for your purposes. We shall list and give only short descriptions of a number of the more important volumes in these categories. You should attempt to become familiar with these and other biographical sources in the general reference room of your library:

*The Dictionary of National Biography:* originally in 63 volumes (1885– 1901), reissued in 22 volumes in 1908–9, with supplements issued periodically, bringing coverage up to date to 1960. The *DNB,* as it is usually referred to, covers famous deceased English men and women.

*The Dictionary of American Biography,* or the *DAB,* published in 22 volumes (1928–58). This reference work is the American counterpart to the *DNB;* it covers famous deceased Americans.

*Who's Who,* published from 1849 to date. Consult the latest volume for short résumés of famous living Englishmen. Entries are prepared by subjects and are simply listings of vital information.

*Who's Who in America,* published from 1899 to date. The up-to-date reference for famous living Americans.

In addition to these well-known biographical sources, there are also more limited *Who's Who* volumes covering a variety of specialties and published at varying intervals. Here is a sampling:

*Who's Who in Atoms*
*Who's Who in Communist China*
*Who's Who in Consulting*
*Who's Who in Engineering*
*Who's Who in France*
*Who's Who in German Politics*
*Who's Who in History*
*Who's Who in Music*
*Who's Who in New York*
*Who's Who in World Jewry*

There are also a good many biographical dictionaries, including *Webster's Biographical Dictionary,* which are strictly quick reference sources (see the entry for Genghis Khan on p. 107). Such dictionaries should serve only to give the most essential facts. If you wish a more detailed treatment, say of Genghis Khan, you should consult a source like the McGraw-Hill *Encyclopedia of World Biography,* which consists of 11 volumes, heavily illustrated, written for the nonspecialist, with each entry including a short reference list. Another invaluable source of biographical information is the cumulative *Current Biography,* published monthly (except in December) and bound annually under the title *Current Biography Yearbook.* This publication concentrates on people "who are prominent in the news—in national and international affairs, the sciences, arts, labor, and industry." The biographies are based on information from books and articles in newspapers and magazines. One final work deserves mention: *The New York Times Obituary Index,* which gives the dates of obituary notices or articles in the *Times* for the period 1858 to 1968. It lists over 353,000 names and is, by admission of the editors, inconsistent in its inclusions and exclusions. You will find, for example, a listing for Mrs. Abraham Lincoln but not for Abraham Lincoln. This spotty coverage is the result of incomplete instructions given to the computer (some headings simply were not picked up). Nevertheless, *The New York Times*

**Gen'ghis Khan** (jĕng'gĭs kän'). *Also* **Jen'ghiz** (jĕng'-gĭz) *or* **Jin'ghis** (jĭng'gĭs) *or* **Chin'ghiz** (chĭng'gĭz) *or* **Chin'giz** (chĭng'gĭz) **Khan.** *Original name* **Tem'u·jin** (tĕm'û·jĭn) *or* **Tem'u·chin** (-chĭn). 1162–1227. Mongol conqueror, b. near Lake Baikal. At age of 13 succeeded his father as tribal chief; proclaimed khan of all the Mongols (1206); consolidated his authority among Mongols (1206–12); made his capital at Karakorum. Invaded northern China (1213) and conquered the Kins; subdued Korea (1218); soon embarked on wider conquests in west (1218–22), overcoming shah of Khwarazm (modern Khiva), plundering northern India, and overrunning and subduing what is now Iran, Iraq, and part of Russia; drove Turks before him, who later invaded Europe. A bold leader and military genius, but one who left few permanent institutions. Had four sons: (1) Juji, or Juchi, who died during his father's lifetime, but whose son Batu Khan (*q.v.*) was later khan; (2) Jagatai (*q.v.*), or Chagatai, founder of dynasty that later ruled in Turkestan; (3) Ogadai (*q.v.*), who succeeded his father as khan (1229–41); (4) Tului, or Tulĕ, whose three sons were all great Mongol leaders (see MANGU KHAN, KUBLAI KHAN, HULAGU).

*9.1 Entry from* Webster's Biographical Dictionary

*Obituary Index* is an invaluable reference volume that you should get to know.

## Exercises and Assignments

1. Using the reference sources mentioned in this chapter, make a bibliography of at least ten references covering some famous person, living or dead. Annotate three of your entries. That is, after giving the bibliographical listing, write a sentence to indicate the coverage and the value of the work.

2. Choose any well-known person and look him or her up in at least three of the biographical dictionaries mentioned in this chapter. Make notes of vital information regarding the person's life, achievements, and character. If you prefer and if possible, make xerox copies and underline the important data. Make marginal notations where useful, then write a 250-word thumbnail sketch. Try to make it as interesting as possible. You need not footnote or annotate your sources, but you should be sure to turn in your notes or xerox copies.

## THE OBITUARY AS
## BIOGRAPHICAL ESSAY

As a way of linking the work of the popular press with the special report writing often demanded in the classroom, we have decided to concentrate in this chapter on the obituary. Obituaries are a special form of biography. They appear as regular features in virtually all newspapers, and sometimes, when the person who died is famous, they are front-page news. Normally, when a very well known person has died, someone like Pablo Picasso or Groucho Marx, newspapers and magazines carry full-scale biographical essays that not only cover the person's life but also give a ranging appraisal of his or her accomplishments. To cite one example, the death of Winston Churchill occasioned a sixteen-page special section in *The New York Times* on his life and thought.

The writing of these obituaries is not as spontaneous as it might appear to the casual reader. Alden Whitman, for many years the obituary writer of *The New York Times*, states that when he took over the job, he "drew up a long list of advance obits" that he thought he would eventually have to write. While the writing of an obituary about a person who is still living may seem a bit ghoulish, good newspapers cannot afford to rely on spontaneity when famous persons suddenly die. Below is a select list of persons for whom the Associated Press carried advance obits in 1982. Some of these people have died in the meantime, but a good many are still living.

Abstracted from Associated Press Biographical Service Index of Sketches 1982 Edition

Abernathy, Ralph D., Civil Rights Leader
Agnew, Spiro, 39th Vice President
Albert, Carl Bert, House Speaker
Aleman, Miguel, President of Mexico
Anderson, Marion, Contralto
Annenberg, Walter H., Publisher, Diplomat
Armstrong, Neil A., Moon Explorer
Astaire, Fred, Dancer
Banzer, Hugo, President of Bolivia
Baryshnikov, Mikhail, Ballet Dancer
Bates, Mary Elizabeth, Physician and Surgeon
Baudouin I, King of Belgians
Baum, William Wakefield, Roman Catholic Prelate
Beauvoir, Simone de, French Writer
Beck, Dave, Ex-Labor Leader
Beckett, Samuel, Poet, Novelist
Begin, Menachem, Prime Minister of Israel
Berlin, Irving, Composer
Bernstein, Leonard, Conductor
Black, Shirley Temple, Diplomat
Blackmun, Harry A., Supreme Court Justice
Bok, Derek, Harvard President
Bradley, Thomas, Mayor of Los Angeles
Brando, Marlon, Actor
Bricker, John W., Politician

Brown, Edmund G. Jr., Governor of California
Brzezinski, Zbigniew, National Security Adviser
Burger, Warren Earl, Chief Justice
Burton, Richard, Actor
Bush, George, Vice-President of the United States
Cagney, James, Actor
Carson, Johnny, Television Personality
Carter, Jimmy (James Earl), 39th President of the U.S.
Castro, Fidel, Cuban Prime Minister
Chagall, Marc, Artist
Clark, Mark W., General, U.S.A.
Connally, John B. Jr., Cabinet Officer
Cooke, Terence James, Roman Catholic Prelate
Cooley, Denton A., Physician
Copland, Aaron, Composer
Cousins, Norman, Editor
Cousteau, Jacques-Yves, Marine Explorer
Cronkite, Walter Leland, Journalist
Dali, Salvador, Artist
Daniel, E. Clifton, Journalist
Dempsey, Jack, Ex-Heavyweight Champion
Dietrich, Marlene, Actress

DiMaggio, Joe, Baseball Player
Doolittle, James H., Aviator-Executive
Eberle, Gertrude (Trudy), English Channel Swimmer
Elizabeth II, Queen of England
Feinstein, Dianne, San Francisco Mayor
Fonda, Henry, Actor
Fonda, Jane Seymour, Actress
Fong, Hiram, Former U.S. Senator
Fonteyn, Margot, Ballerina
Ford, Gerald R., 38th President of the United States
Fulbright, J. William, U.S. Senator
Fuller, Richard Buckminster, Geometrician
Funston, George Keith, Stock Exchange President
Galbraith, John K., Economist
Gandhi, Indira, India's Prime Minister
Garbo, Greta, Actress
Gardner, Ava, Actress
Glenn, John H. Jr., U.S. Senator
Godfrey, Arthur, Radio-TV Star
Goldwater, Barry, Politician
Goodman, Benny, Clarinetist
Gosden, Freeman F., Amos of "Amos & Andy"
Graham, Billy, Evangelist
Graham, Martha, Dancer
Gromyko, Andrei A., Soviet Diplomat
Haig, Alexander M. Jr., U.S. Army General
Hall, Gus, Communist Leader
Hallstein, Walter, Common Market Executive
Harris, Fred R., U.S. Senator
Heifetz, Jascha, Violinist
Heiser, Dr. Victor, Physician-Author
Hess, Rudolph, Ex-Nazi Leader
Hirohito, Emperor of Japan
Hiss, Alger, Ex-Official
Hogan, Ben, Golfer
Holtzman, Elizabeth, Congresswoman
Hope, Bob, Actor
Hufstedler, Shirley A., Government Official
Iacocca, Lee A., Industrialist
Inouye, Daniel K., U.S. Senator
Jackson, Henry M., U.S. Senator
Johnson, Mrs. Lyndon B., Former First Lady
Juan Carlos I, King of Spain
Kahn, Alfred, Economist
Kennan, George F., Diplomat
Kennedy, Edward M., U.S. Senator
Kennedy, Mrs. Joseph P. (Rose), President's Mother
Khomeini, Ayatollah Ruhollah, Iran Religious Leader
Kosygin, Alexei N., Soviet Leader
Landon, Alf M., Ex-Politician

Leinsdorf, Erich, Conductor
LeMay, Curtis E., Air Force General
Lindbergh, Anne Morrow, Author-Flyer
Lindsay, John V., Ex-Mayor of New York City
Lodge, Henry Cabot, Public Official
MacLeish, Archibald, Poet
Margaret Rose, Princess
Marshall, Thurgood, Supreme Court Justice
Martin, Billy, Baseball Manager
Martin, William McChesney, Monetary Expert
McGovern, George S., U.S. Senator
Mellon, Paul, Philanthropist
Menninger, Karl A., Psychiatrist
Menotti, Gian-Carlo, Composer
Michener, James, Novelist
Mills, Wilbur E., Politician
Mitchell, John N., Attorney General
Molotov, Vyacheslav, Soviet Diplomat
Mondale, Walter F., 42nd Vice-President of U.S.
Mugabe, Robert, Zimbabwe Leader
Muskie, Edmund S., U.S. Senator
Niarchos, Stavros S., Shipping Magnate
Nickerson, Albert L., Oil Executive
Niemoeller, Rev. Martin, German Clergyman
Nixon, Richard M., 37th President of the U.S.
Nixon, Mrs. Richard (Pat), Former First Lady
North, John Ringling, Circus Executive
Onassis, Mrs. Aristotle (Jacqueline)
Ormandy, Eugene, Orchestra Conductor
Paley, William S., CBS Founder
Palme, Olof, Swedish Politician
Parton, Dolly, Entertainer
Peale, Norman Vincent, Clergyman
Pei, I. M., Architect
Pepper, Claude D., Politician
Philip, Prince, Duke of Edinburgh
Price, Leontyne, Opera Star
Reagan, Ronald, 40th President of the United States
Rehnquist, William H., Supreme Court Justice
Rickover, Hyman G., Naval Officer
Rockefeller, David, Banker
Rogers, Ginger, Actress
Rooney, Mickey, Actor
Rubinstein, Arthur, Pianist
Rusk, Dean, Ex-Secretary of State
Sabin, Dr. Albert B., Virologist-Researcher
St. John, Adela Rogers, Journalist-Author
Sakharov, Andrei D., Physicist
Salk, Jonas E., Scientist
Schmidt, Helmut, West German Chancellor
Segovia, Andres, Guitarist
Sills, Beverly, Opera Singer
Sinatra, Frank, Singer-Actor

Singer, Isaac Bashevis, Author
Smith, Kate, Singer
Stone, Leland, Foreign Correspondent
Symington, W. Stuart, Executive
Taft, Robert Jr., U.S. Senator
Thatcher, Margaret, Prime Minister of Britain
Thieu, Nguyen Van, Ex-President of South Vietnam
Tho, LeDuc, North Vietnamese Leader
Trudeau, Pierre Elliott, Canadian Statesman
Truman, Margaret, President's Daughter
Turner, Stansfield, Director of Central Intelligence Agency
Udall, Stewart Lee, Secretary of Interior
Umberto II, Ex-King of Italy
Vance, Cyrus R., Secretary of State

Veeck, Bill, Baseball Executive
Vorster, John, Prime Minister of South Africa
Wade, Wallace, Football Coach
Walcott, Joe, Ex-Heavyweight Champion
Waldheim, Kurt, Secretary General of the UN
Wallace, George C., Politician
Weaver, Robert C., Cabinet Officer
Westmoreland, William C., General U.S.A.
White, Byron R., Supreme Court Justice
Whitney, Cornelius V., Capitalist-Sportsman
Williams, Tennessee, Dramatist
Wilson, James Harold, British Statesman
Windsor, Duchess of
Wyeth, Andrew N., Painter
Young, Andrew J. Jr., U.S. Ambassador
Young, Coleman, Mayor of Detroit

## Reading Selection

The following obituary comes from *The New York Times* where it appeared on the front page, a not uncommon occurrence when the subject is considered of ranking importance. In this instance the article, on Groucho Marx, continues for almost an entire page (a total of five full columns including two pictures) in the front section of the paper. Note that the first part of the article is in essence the news story of his death with a "Los Angeles, Aug. 19" dateline. It briefly reviews the circumstances of Groucho's death and includes only a very brief paragraph about his major accomplishments. There follows a long, contemplative account of Groucho's life, entitled "Master of the Insult," written by Albin Krebs. It is more than likely that the lengthy essay was written in advance of Groucho's death and kept on file at the *Times*. The information it gives us is clearly collected from many sources, including perhaps the writings of Groucho himself and the biography by his son, Arthur Marx. But, as is true of newspapers in general, sources and background information are not cited or footnoted; they are simply incorporated for easy consumption by the reader. Some of the information no doubt came from biographical sources like the ones mentioned in this chapter, though more than likely the library of the *Times* had collected its own clipping file through much of Marx's noteworthy career. When you read the essay, try to list the kind of information that Krebs has included in his account. It might be useful to make an outline of the main topics.

### GROUCHO MARX, COMEDIAN, DEAD; MOVIE STAR AND TV HOST WAS 86

LOS ANGELES, Aug. 19—Groucho Marx, the comedian, died tonight at the Cedar Sinai Medical Center here after failing to recover from a respiratory ailment that hospitalized him June 22. He was 86 years old.

Marx, whose entertainment career began almost 70 years ago and ranged from vaudeville to television, slumped into semiconsciousness late last night and failed quickly, the doctors said.

His death was attributed to pneumonia.

Marx, with his brothers Chico, Harpo, Gummo and Zeppo, conquered Broadway in such shows as "The Cocoanuts" and "Animal Crackers," and then moved to Hollywood where they started an almost legendary series of movies, highlighted by such pictures as "A Night at the Opera" and "A Day at the Races."

At Groucho's death, Zeppo became the only survivor of the five brothers.

Groucho first entered the hospital in March, suffering from a hip ailment. Following surgery to repair a damaged hip joint, he was released in late March. Subsequently he reinjured his hip and returned for more surgery.

He stayed 11 days, was released, and was readmitted after only one day, suffering from a respiratory condition. He did not leave the hospital again. During his hospitalization, he was not made aware of a bitter court battle over the stewardship of his estate.

With him when he died were his son, Arthur; Arthur's wife, Lois, and Groucho's grandson, Andrew.

A hospital spokesman said no funeral arrangements had been made as of tonight.

## MASTER OF THE INSULT

### Albin Krebs

Effrontery, of the most lunatic, unsquelchable sort, was the chief stock in trade of Groucho Marx. As the key man in the most celebrated brother act in motion pictures, he developed the insult into an art form. And he used the insult, delivered with maniacal glee, to shatter the egos of the pompous—and to plunge his audiences into helpless laughter.

The comedy world of Groucho Marx and his brothers Harpo and Chico was wildly chaotic, grounded in slapstick farce, lowbrow vaudeville corn, free-spirited anarchy and zany assaults on the myths and virtues of middle-class America.

The private world of Groucho Marx was not far removed from his public image. He was the kind of man who could, during his wedding ceremony, fling insults at the minister and, 21 years later, when his wife was leaving him for good, shake hands with her and say, "Well it's been nice knowing you; if you're ever in the neighborhood again, drop in."

Groucho was larger and more antic than life. He was the gruesomely stooped man in the swallowtail coat who took great loping steps across the stage or screen, holding a long, plump cigar behind him. His seemingly depraved eyes rolled and leered from behind steel-rimmed glasses. Below his large nose a smudge of black greasepaint passed for a mustache.

His humor was based on the improbable, the unexpected, the outrageous. In a Marx Brothers play he would interrupt a scene by stepping to the footlights to inquire urgently, "Is there a doctor in the house?" When an unsuspecting physician rose, he would demand to know: "If you're a doctor, why aren't you at the hospital making your patients miserable, instead of wasting your time here with that blonde?" And during one of his television quiz shows, which were immensely popular in the 1950's, when a contestant was asked her age and said she was "approaching 40," he replied, "From which direction?"

But Groucho's expertly delivered, rapid-fire insults were more mad than maddening; they really weren't unkind, for they evolved from his interest in humor that deflated rather than annihilated. This quality was, in fact, the distinguishing mark of the comedy so richly dispensed by Groucho Marx, his brothers and their great contemporaries, such as Charles Chaplin, W. C. Fields and Buster Keaton.

"It was the type of humor that made people laugh at themselves," Groucho said in 1968, "rather than the sort that prevails today—the sick, black, merely smart-aleck stuff designed to evoke malicious laughter at the other fellow."

Throughout his hectic life the comedian remained able to laugh at himself. He even appeared not to take seriously the fact that his early years were passed in extreme poverty. For example, when it was suggested that his rags-to-riches rise bore Lincolnesque overtones, he said, "There weren't any rails to split in the neighborhood around 93d Street and Third Avenue. Just the third rail on the El, and there wasn't much of a future in fooling around with that."

Julius Henry Marx was born Oct. 2, 1890, in a tenement on East 93d Street. His Alsatian-born father, Samuel Marx, was an unsuccessful tailor; his mother, the former Minnie Schoenberg, was the stage-struck sister of Al Shean, of the comedy team of Gallagher and Shean.

Mrs. Marx pushed all five of her sons into show business, partly because she was the embodiment of the "stage mother," but also because every member of the family had to be a breadwinner. At 10, Groucho was singing soprano with the Gus Edwards vaudeville troupe, and at 14 he completed his formal education by quitting P.S. 86. "If I intended to eat, I would have to scratch for it," he wrote years later.

Still in his teens, Groucho got a $4-a-week job with the Le May Trio, an act that broke up in Denver, leaving him penniless. He worked in a grocery store long enough to earn train fare back to New York, where his mother was putting together an act called the Six Musical Mascots.

It consisted of Groucho and two of his brothers, Adolph (later Harpo) and Milton (Gummo), an attractive soprano named Janie O'Riley, Mrs. Marx and her sister Hannah. Mrs. Marx soon realized that she and her sister were so bad that the act was doomed unless they left it. They retired from show business.

What was left was the Four Nightingales, an act that, in the course of its travels through whistle-stop towns, in the South and Midwest, changed its name to the Marx Brothers and Co. Harmony singing, popular on the vaudeville circuit at the time, was the basis of the act before the brothers fairly stumbled onto the format that was to make them famous.

They did so when they played a seedy little theater in Nacogdoches, Tex., in 1914.

"Our act was so lousy," Groucho said, "that when word passed through the audience of numbskull Texans that a mule had run away, they got up en masse to go out and see something livelier. We were accustomed to heckling and insults, but that made us furious, so when those guys wearing ten-gallon hats over pint-size brains came back, we let them have it. It wasn't the best line I ever ad-libbed, but I recall I told them 'Nacogdoches—is full of roaches.' And—ultimate insult—I called those Texans 'damn Yankees.' "

The audience loved the insults and the ad-libs, and from that point on, the Marxes sang less and worked in more jokes, puns and one-liners. They used carefully plotted sketches, but never hesitated to throw in topical ad-libs.

The Marx Brothers perfected their style and characterizations over several years of one-night stands. They got their nutty names from Art Fisher, a monologuist whose hobby was making up nicknames. Harpo's name came from the instrument he played, Gummo's from his gumshoes, Chico's from his reputation as a lady-killer, and Zeppo's from Zippo, star of a chimpanzee act. Because of his saturnine disposition, Groucho's name was a natural.

Groucho first wore his famous frock coat in a sketch called "Fun in Hi Skule," in which he played the professor. He adopted the omnipresent cigar because he liked to smoke cigars in the first place, and they served as useful props. "If you forget a line," he said, "all you have to do is stick the cigar in your mouth and puff on it until you think of what you've forgotten."

The painted-on mustache, which was Groucho's chief trademark for 30 years, until he grew a real one, resulted from a dispute with the manager of the Fifth Avenue Theater. One night he arrived too late to put on his paste-on mustache. Instead he drew one on with greasepaint. After the show the manager demanded "the same mustache you gave 'em at the Palace," so Groucho handed him the fake mustache. The greasepaint smear was thenceforward substituted.

The Marxes' first Broadway hit was "I'll Say She Is," in 1924. It was a success largely on the strength of a rhapsodic review in The New Yorker by Alexander Woollcott, who spent the rest of his life pouring praise upon the brothers, Groucho in particular.

In 1929 Groucho very nearly suffered a nervous breakdown. He and his brothers filmed "The Cocoanuts," which had been their second Broadway hit, on Long Island during the day, and appeared nightly in the stage version of "Animal Crackers" (which was committed to film in 1930). He had invested all his savings, $240,000, in the stock market, and lost it all in the crash. Under the strain of too much work and worry over finances, he developed insomnia, which plagued him the rest of his life.

"Animal Crackers" gave Groucho his most celebrated character, Capt. Jeffrey T. Spaulding, the bumbling African explorer, as well as a monologue that Groucho aficionados have loved over the years. The monologue depended heavily for its humor on Groucho's wildly comic delivery, but even in print, it suggests the outrageousness of the Marx manner.

The monologue is a lampoon of the African adventure saga, delivered by Groucho (Spaulding) before guests at a rich woman's soiree. "Africa is God's country, and He can have it," Groucho begins. "Well, sir, we left New York drunk and early on the morning of Feb. 2. After 15 days on the water and six on the boat, we finally arrived on the shore of Africa. . . . One morning I shot an elephant in my pajamas. How he got in my pajamas, I don't know. . . . But that's entirely irrelephant. . . ." And so on.

Groucho, the master of the ad-lib, refused to follow the scripts of his plays and movies, although some of them were turned out by such masters of comedy writing as George S. Kaufman, Morrie Ryskind and S. J. Perelman. Some of his ad-libs worked so well that they were incorporated into the script. For example, in "Horse Feathers" (1932), an actor said to Groucho, "Jennings has been waiting for an hour and he is waxing wroth," to which Groucho replied, "Tell Roth to wax Jennings for a change." The line went into the script.

In "Animal Crackers," as well as eight other Marx Brothers pictures, Groucho's long-suffering comic foil was Margaret Dumont, whose haughty demeanor suggested the epitome of the grande dame. In their scenes, Groucho was invariably the mangy lover intent on fleecing the rich society matron of her last cent, while at the same time hurling at her the most ungentlemanly insults.

"You're the most beautiful woman I've ever seen, which doesn't say much for you," he ardently told Miss Dumont in "Animal Crackers." In "Duck Soup" (1933), as he, Chico and Harpo fended off Miss Dumont's enemies, he said of her, "Remember, we're fighting for her honor—which is probably more than she ever did."

The most popular of the Marx movies was "A Night at the Opera"

(1935), produced for Metro-Goldwyn-Mayer by Irving Thalberg, who quickly learned he was dealing with zanies. After he kept the Marxes waiting in his office for more than two hours, Groucho instructed his brothers to disrobe. When Mr. Thalberg finally came out to greet them, he found Groucho, Chico and Harpo before the fireplace, roasting marshmallows in the nude.

Groucho was the quack Dr. Hackenbush in "A Day at the Races" (1937). It was his favorite role because, he said, "It tickled up the medical profession, and I think it can stand a bit of lampooning now and then."

By 1939, with the release of "The Marx Brothers at the Circus," he and his brothers were tiring of making movies. "I continued to appear in them" he said, "but the fun had gone out of picture-making. I was like an old pug, still going through the motions, but now doing it solely for the money."

The Marx Brothers wound up their M-G-M contract with "Go West" (1940) and "The Big Store" (1941). They were idle until 1946, when they made "A Night in Casablanca," and broke up the brother act for good in 1949 with "Love Happy."

(Gummo had left the act many years previously, even before the brothers made their Broadway debut, to become a theatrical agent. Zeppo quit the act after "Duck Soup" in 1933, also to become an agent. Chico died in 1961, Harpo three years later.)

With "You Bet Your Life," a radio-television quiz show that began in 1947 and lasted a decade, Groucho forged a new career for himself as a single. The program, at one time the highest-rated TV show in the country and the winner of several broadcasting awards, featured the quizmaster's irrelevant insult humor rather than jackpot cash awards.

On one program, when a contestant developed mike-fright and was unable to utter a word, Groucho said, "Either this man is dead, or my watch is stopped." Interviewing a tree surgeon, he asked, "Have you ever fallen out of any of your patients?"

Groucho's eccentric antics carried over into his private life. He kept an air rifle beside his bed, and when he heard a howling dog, he would bound to the window to shoot at it. He drove his family to distraction, according to his son Arthur, by practicing on the guitar for stretches of six hours, or playing Gilbert and Sullivan recordings into the wee hours.

He tried to master golf, with results so unsatisfactory that on one occasion, while playing on a course overlooking the Pacific, he walked to a cliff, dropped his golf balls one by one into the sea and then tossed his bagful of clubs after them. "He turned away with a benignly happy look on his face," a fellow player reported.

The comedian married his first wife, the former Ruth Johnson, in 1920, not long after he and his brothers opened in an act called "Home Again" at the Palace Theater—and landed at last in the big time. The wedding ceremony was as chaotic as Marx Brothers routine. While Chico and Harpo skittered about the room carrying potted palms, Groucho harangued the minister with remarks such as, "Why are you going so fast? This is a five-buck ceremony. Aren't we entitled to at least five minutes of your time?" The marriage, which produced two children, Miriam and Arthur, lasted until 1942.

In 1945 he married the former Catherine Gorcey and they had a daughter, Melinda, of whom he was inordinately proud. When Melinda was prevented from swimming with friends in the pool at a country club that excluded Jews, her father wrote the club president an indignant, highly publicized letter in which he said, "Since my little daughter is only half-Jewish, would it be all right if she went in the pool only up to her waist?"

His second marriage ended in divorce in 1950. He married a former model, Eden Hartford, in 1953, when he was past 60 and she was 24.

That marriage broke up in 1969, and Groucho did not marry again. Still, for a number of years, he sought to maintain his image as a leering satyr and seldom let himself be seen in public without the company of a young and beautiful woman.

In 1972, when he returned to the New York stage for the first time in 43 years to give a one-man, one-performance show at Carnegie Hall, he was accompanied by Erin Fleming. Miss Fleming had been his "secretary-companion," as she was described then, since his third divorce.

By the time of the Carnegie concert, Groucho, who had shaved four years off his actual age for decades, was no longer lying about the fact that he was past 80. He looked it, too. His voice was feeble and he could hardly hear, even with his hearing aid, but his eyes were still merrily bright.

Last November, he was to have been lionized in Washington, where he intended to present Marxian memorabilia, including the pith helmet he wore as Captain Spaulding in "Animal Crackers," to the Smithsonian Institution. But the trip was canceled at the last minute, ostensibly because Miss Fleming had the flu and he would not go anywhere without her.

Groucho went to the hospital for an operation on his hip last March. As he was recuperating, confined to his Beverly Hills home, an unpleasant court battle went on over the management of his estate, which was estimated at $2.5 million at the time he divorced his third wife.

Three years ago, Miss Fleming was appointed his guardian. She also was temporary conservator for the estate and Groucho's son, Arthur Marx, sought to replace her in that position. According to the testimony, Miss Fleming, now 37, had exerted a baneful influence over Groucho, even threatening his well-being, though others declared that she was the only reason he was clinging to life then.

The court compromised by appointing Groucho's friend of 45 years, Nat Perrin, the screen writer, as temporary conservator pending a final decision. Groucho's grandson, Andrew, 27, was later named permanent conservator.

Early in 1973, Groucho's son, Arthur, published "Son of Groucho," a memoir. In it, he recalled his father as a singularly penurious man who, when going out to dine in an expensive Hollywood restaurant, would park blocks away to save a parking fee.

His stinginess notwithstanding, and despite the pains he took to make himself financially secure, Groucho, his son reported, was not terribly well off in his old age, chiefly because of the expensive alimony and property settlements resulting from his three divorces.

Groucho's irresponsibility in his personal dealings was legendary. It was not unusual for him to call a friend in the middle of the night—this was one of his ways of taking the boredom out of his insomnia—and launch into a barrage of abuse:

"This is Professor Waldemar Strumbelknauff. Aren't you ashamed of yourself, beating your children that way? If you were a man you'd come over here and knock my teeth out. If you were half a man you'd knock half my teeth out. . . . This is Groucho. How are you? As if I really care." And then he'd hang up.

He grew up to hate New York, because he was expected to wear a tie when he went out. He was so addicted to informal wear that he shunned parties, developing, immediately upon being told he was expected to go to one, "a grippey feeling." When he himself entertained, he often took leave of his guests at an early hour, telling them to "go ahead and get drunk on my booze and make fools of yourselves—I don't care because I'm going to bed."

The comedian, who supplemented his meager formal education by reading omnivorously, greatly admired writers. He considered George Bernard Shaw's observation that "Groucho Marx is the world's greatest living actor" as the compliment of his lifetime. For some years he carried on a correspondence with T. S. Eliot, and in 1965 was invited to speak at a memorial service for the poet. Typically, he used the occasion to say something outrageous: "Apparently Mr. Eliot was a great admirer of mine—and I don't blame him."

He was a compulsive letter writer. In 1964 he wrote Gov. William Scranton of Pennsylvania to tell him he had heard him, during a broadcast, mispronounce a Yiddish term. "If you are going to campaign in Jewish neighborhoods," he counseled the Governor, "rhyme mish-mash with slosh."

A collection of his correspondence was published as "The Groucho Letters." The Library of Congress asked him for his letters and papers, which included the manuscripts of two books he wrote, "Groucho and Me" and "Memoirs of a Mangy Lover."

Groucho Marx was actually a moody man, those who knew him best said. They insisted that beneath his brash, fast-talking exterior, he was thoughtful, shy and kindhearted. His longtime friend, the songwriter Harry Ruby, said, "The guy doesn't mean to be insulting; it's an involuntary notion with him, like a compulsion neurosis." And to his son, Arthur, Groucho was "a sentimentalist, but he'd rather be found dead than have you know it."

Groucho himself admitted that "my trouble is that I don't like to let just everybody get in a word edgewise, and can't stand anyone else having the last word." To make sure this wouldn't happen to him ultimately, he took the precaution of writing his epitaph in advance: "I hope they buried me near a straight man."

From *The New York Times*, August 20, 1977, p. 1, 7 *ff*.

## Questions

*Content/Meaning*
1. While the obituary is essentially organized chronologically (from birth to death), it comments widely on Groucho's appearance and character. What details does it stress? What specific paragraphs concentrate on description of his person and mannerisms?
2. Was Groucho simply a slapstick comedian? If you feel that he was more than a slapstick comedian, can you give examples of his wit? What kinds of targets did he aim at? Did he have a sense of humor about himself?
3. Much is made in the article about the similarity of Groucho's real life and his stage parts. Can you find at least three anecdotes that touch on this point?
4. What seems to be the central impression of Groucho left by the obituary? Is it incongruous that it recites by means of anecdotes so much of Groucho's humor? Apart from the length of the article, is there any evidence that *The New York Times* considered his life important and his death a significant loss?
5. Although no direct sources are mentioned for the obituary, where, most likely, did the *Times* staff find its facts about Groucho?

*Style*
1. The article is notably journalistic because it consists of so many short pragraphs. What seems to be the principal basis for paragraph divi-

sion? Can you comment, for example, on the divisions that discuss Groucho's marriages (between paragraphs 36 and 40)?

2. We are told in the first paragraph of the article that Groucho "developed the insult into an art form." What allusions and elaborations of this point can you find in the balance of the article? Note the variation of language with which this point is made.

3. The *Times* is noted for its relatively educated vocabulary. Even in popular writing, as in this article, it occasionally includes fairly learned words, like "saturnine disposition" in paragraph 18. Can you find other examples? What are some words whose exact meanings you would have to look up in a dictionary?

## THE OBITUARY AS RESEARCH PAPER

You have now studied a model of the obituary essay. Like all other biographical forms of writing, the obituary, especially of a famous person with many accomplishments, involves the gathering of information from diverse sources, the choice of relevant details, and the use of expressive language—aspects of writing stressed in this chapter. While biographical writing often verges on narration, its essential requirement is nevertheless to describe a person as fully and as dramatically as possible. We have, consequently, included the obituary—one of the two most popular features in the daily newspaper (the other is the weather report)—in this unit. But apart from its value as an exercise in descriptive writing, the obituary is also an appropriate subject for a research report.

What follows, therefore, is the assignment of a research paper. In essence, you will be asked to write an extended "report of reports"—a paper that will give a summary account of the life of a famous person. Its most important requirement will be its verifiability. That is, the facts gathered must be footnoted to their sources. The reader of a research report has the right, even the obligation, to ask how the writer has acquired information.

The report of reports we are asking you to write is not meant to be advanced research. It will require you to read in a wide range of sources; to separate the credible from the unbelievable; to take notes (preferably on note cards); to footnote all quotations and little-known facts or ideas, even if not quoted, that you gathered from specialized sources; and to present a working bibliography, that is, a list of sources arranged in alphabetical order to show your reader at a glance what books or articles you read as background for your paper. The report of reports is a handy document, not merely an empty academic exercise. It will, incidentally, teach you much about the gathering of information, about the library, and about the difficult task of ordering a wide range of information into a readable paper. Learning this process will help you to write term papers in other classes and eventually to write research reports as part of your graduate education, the requirements of your profession, or both.

# Reading Selection

We have written the following obituary of John Lennon as a research report to serve as a model for this assignment. You will see that our paper, "The Death of John Lennon," differs from the obituary of Groucho Marx in two important ways. First, we cited all our sources of information (for reasons already discussed). Second, we gave much heavier emphasis to the circumstance of Lennon's death than Krebs gave to Groucho's death. Obviously, the subject made this slant necessary: Groucho died of old age; Lennon was murdered in his prime. You will have to determine on the basis of your subject and your interests where you need to put the emphasis.

## THE DEATH OF JOHN LENNON

It was an unusually warm December night in Manhattan. The Dakota apartment house, named by its builder in the late nineteenth century because it seemed so far away from the center of New York City, stood in its stately splendor as if it were a Gothic fortress on Central Park West, sheltering the privileged and the famous in its luxurious quarters. Those who lived there included Lauren Bacall, Leonard Bernstein, Roberta Flack, Gilda Radner, Rex Reed, and, perhaps its most famous tenants, John Lennon and his wife Yoko Ono, who occupied five apartments spread out over twenty-five rooms. The night was December 8, 1980; the time shortly before 11:00 P.M.[1] On ABC's "Monday Night Football," Howard Cosell was the first to inform a stunned nationwide audience that John Lennon, the most talented member of the famous Beatles, the "Fab Four" of the 1960s, had just been shot, from four to six times (depending on the report of various witnesses)[2] as he entered the Dakota on his return from a recording session. Shortly later, special bulletins reported that Lennon was dead.

1. Patrick Doyle et al., "John Lennon Slain Here," *New York Daily News,* December 9, 1980, p. 3.
2. Several witnesses heard four shots, while another, Jeff Smith, a neighbor, heard five; see Les Ledbetter, "John Lennon of Beatles Is Killed," *The New York Times,* December 9, 1980, p. 1. The *New York Post* reported that witnesses heard six shots, while doctors at Roosevelt Hospital later established that "there were seven wounds in his chest, back, and left arm"; see Cynthia R. Fagen and Leo Standora, "John Lennon Shot Dead," *New York Post,* December 9, 1980, p. 2.

The tragic event of that night can best be re-created from the vantage point of Jay Hastings, one of the doormen on duty at the Dakota. Hastings, at 27, had been a long-time Beatles fan. In the two years on his job at the Dakota, he had gotten to know John and Yoko, and John, in turn, knew him by name, often greeting him with a cheerful "Bon soir, Jay," when he returned late at night to his apartment. This evening, Jay looked forward to presenting Yoko with a red Plexiglas rainhat that an eager promoter had left for her. Jay planned to ask her to guess what it was. At 10:50 P.M., Jay was reading a magazine when suddenly he heard what sounded like several shots and shattering glass outside his office. Someone was staggering up the office steps. Lennon stumbled in, with Yoko following, screaming out, "John's been shot." Lennon collapsed, the cassette tapes from his last recording session smashed against the floor and scattered. The anguished doorman called 911, instantly removed his blue uniform jacket and placed it on Lennon, who had blood streaming from his mouth and chest. Using his tie, Jay tried to apply a tourniquet, but there was no place to put it. Lennon vomited blood and flesh. His eyes were unfocused. A low, gurgling sound came from his throat.[3]

Within minutes two police cars pulled up in front of the Dakota's entrance. Hastings had already rushed out to find the gunman. The outside doorman pointed to a gun lying on the sidewalk, while its owner, a heavy-set young man, was standing unperturbed on West 72nd St. reading J. D. Salinger's novel *The Catcher in the Rye*. When four cops slammed out of the squad car, they screamed at Hastings, who was bloodstained and wild-eyed, to freeze and put up his hands. Quickly the other doorman shouted, "Not him . . . that guy over there." And instantly two cops rammed the placid Mark David Chapman against the red-stoned facade of the Dakota. Meanwhile, Hastings led the other two through the entranceway where the shooting took place up to the office where Lennon lay in his death throes.

Against Yoko's wishes, police turned Lennon over to assess his wounds. They said they couldn't wait for an ambulance and gingerly hoisted him off the floor. Hastings, gripping Lennon's left arm and shoulder blade, heard shattered bones crack as they moved him out the door. Lennon's body was limp; his arms and legs akimbo. They put him into a police car for the trip to Roosevelt Hospital. Yoko climbed into a second cruiser. Hastings walked back to the building and waited in the office. Thirty minutes later, word reached the Dakota: John Winston Ono Lennon, forty-year-old husband and father, was gone.[4]

3. Gregory Katz, "Inside the Dakota," *Rolling Stone,* January 22, 1981, p. 17.

4. Ibid.

An unbelieving world was incapable of assimilating the shocking news: John Lennon, the personification of youth to a whole generation of the young in the 1960s, the most widely acclaimed composer-performer of a whole new style of pop music, lay dead in a New York hospital.[5] Vin Scelsa, disc jockey over WNEW-FM, had heard about the Cosell report. He refused to believe it. When finally confirmation of Lennon's death came in, he spoke in a subdued voice, frozen before the mike, "I have the sad task to inform you that John Lennon is dead." Almost unconsciously, he played "Let It Be" and then Bruce Springsteen's "Jungleland." He read the bulletins, canceled all commercials, then played nothing but Beatles songs, and finally put countless callers on the air to share their grief with a stunned audience. "The same thing happened all over the country. . . . There was a sense of sharing that hadn't been felt in radio in ten years."[6]

Why was John Lennon shot down? Who was the deranged gunman, Mark David Chapman? These questions punctured the air almost instantly, and at least partial answers came forward over the media. Chapman at age 25 had been, ironically, a Beatles fan for fifteen years. He was devoted to John Lennon, whom he emulated not only in playing the guitar but also in marrying a Japanese woman. He was known to possess an extensive collection of Beatles albums. Born and raised in the South, he had moved three years ago to Hawaii. In Honolulu he applied for a gun permit and on October 27, 1980, he bought a five-shot Charter Arms .38 special for $169. The manager of the store, in an interview, blithely called him "just a normal dude."[7] Four days before buying the gun, Chapman had quit his job as a security guard in a Honolulu condominium, where he had signed himself out as "John Lennon." Shortly after leaving his job, he borrowed $2,500 from the credit union of Castle Hospital, where he had worked previously in the print shop. Apparently, this money helped him finance a trip to the mainland, first to Atlanta, and finally—fatefully—to New York. He seemed to have arrived at his destination on December 6, 1980, and to have stayed overnight at the West Side YMCA, fewer than ten blocks from the Dakota. The next night, his last before the shooting, he spent at the much more lavish Sheraton Centre on the 27th floor, from which he could easily see the Dakota at the

5. Lennon was pronounced dead on arrival at Roosevelt. A team of seven surgeons worked feverishly to revive him, but to no avail. He had lost nearly 80 percent of his blood volume from the point-blank gunshots. Yoko, wanting to be with John, was told by Dr. Stephen Lynn, "We have very bad news. Unfortunately, in spite of massive efforts, your husband is dead. There was no suffering at the end." Yoko could not grasp the news. "Are you saying he is sleeping?" See "Death of a Beatle," *Newsweek,* December 22, 1980, p. 36.

6. Chet Flippo, "Radio: Tribal Drum," *Rolling Stone,* January 22, 1981, p. 19.

7. "Death of a Beatle," p. 33.

western perimeter of Central Park. Chapman clearly had planned his murderous mission. Although never noted as particularly aberrant in his behavior—he was a fundamentalist Christian and once carried a "Jesus Notebook"—he had twice tried to commit suicide. His identification with Lennon, however, had been a fact throughout the past fifteen years of his life.[8]

The immediate events before the killing can be summarized fairly accurately. Apparently, Chapman "hung out" in front of the Dakota for the few days he was known to have been in New York. He also told tall tales. On Saturday night, he hailed a taxi and boasted to the driver that he had just delivered the tapes of an album that Lennon and McCartney had made that very day. On Monday afternoon, he noticed Lennon and Yoko coming out of the Dakota; they were on their way to what turned out to be their last recording session. Chapman produced Lennon and Yoko's latest album, "Double Fantasy," and asked Lennon for an autograph. As Lennon scrawled his name on the cover, a Beatles fan and amateur photographer, Paul Goresh, from North Arlington, N.J., snapped an extraordinary picture, showing the victim and the murderer only hours before the crime.[9] Chapman was apparently ecstatic, boasting to Goresh, "John Lennon signed my album . . . nobody in Hawaii is going to believe me." After about two hours, Goresh told Chapman he was leaving. Chapman replied, "I'd wait . . . you never know if you'll see him again."[10] The veiled prophecy was, of course, self-fulfilling. Chapman was to address Lennon again after the limousine pulled up in front of the Dakota. As Lennon walked slightly ahead of Yoko, he was hailed in the darkness of the entryway by a voice calling, "Mr. Lennon." John turned around; from five feet away, in the shadows, Chapman dropped into a combat stance and unloaded his .38 revolver into his victim. He then dropped the revolver, took up his paperback novel and a cassette-recorder with 14 hours of Beatles tape and quietly waited for his arrest.[11]

Those are the facts. But how do we account more penetratingly for the senseless killing of the man who, for the past decades, had spoken so eloquently for love and peace—who gave even his mourners the memorable exhortation "Give Peace a Chance"? Various editorial writers and psychiatrists gave their explanations. Several stressed that Lennon was not murdered but assassinated, like a king or a political leader or a pope. As Jay Cocks

8. Paul L. Montgomery, "Police Trace Tangled Path to Lennon's Slaying at the Dakota," *The New York Times,* December 10, 1981, pp. 1, B6.

9. The picture was reproduced frequently by the media in the aftermath; see, for example, *Time,* December 22, 1981, p. 17.

10. Quotations from "Death of a Beatle," p. 34.

11. This narrative was put together from the following reports: "Death of a Beatle," pp. 32–35; Montgomery, "Police Trace Tangled Path," p. 1, B6; Jay Cocks, "The Last Day in the Life," *Time,* December 22, 1980, p. 19; Pete Hamill, "The Death and Life of John Lennon," *New York,* December 22, 1981, pp. 42–45.

put it in his excellent retrospective article in *Time,* it was "a ritual slaying of something that could hardly be named. Hope, perhaps; or idealism. Or time. Not only lost, but suddenly dislocated, fractured."[12] Some commentators went considerably further, suggesting in the irrationality of their shock a veiled preference for another victim. As the wife of one editorialist is reported to have asked: "Why is it always Bobby Kennedy or John Lennon? Why isn't it Richard Nixon or Paul McCartney?"[13] The answer, if we confine ourselves to the first, the sensible, question is that

> John Lennon held out hope. He imagined, and however quietistic he became he never lost the utopian identification. But when you hold out hope, people get real disappointed if you can't deliver. You're famous and they're not—that's the crux of the relationship. You command the power they crave—the power to make one's identity felt in the world, to be known.[14]

Probably, it was all a whole lot more complicated. Psychiatrists felt that Chapman had developed a deep pathological identification with Lennon, so much so that the murder was really an act of "psychological suicide." The signing by Chapman of Lennon's name, his marriage to a Japanese woman, his devotion to the Beatles music, his playing the guitar—all these, according to Dr. Stuart Berger, indicate "a psychotic loss of ego boundaries with the victim so that the murderer almost perceives himself as one with the victim, and ultimately he is the victim."[15] This confusion of identities, however, cuts two ways. On one level the murder eliminates the hated self. On another level, it eliminates the hero because he enjoyed the success that the aggressor could not. While the psychopathology is extremely complicated, there is finally no rational or acceptable explanation for the terrorism that cuts down our best and our most gifted.

John Lennon's gifts were not so much acquired as they were native. Actually, he was, by general consensus, not an outstanding technical musician: He couldn't read music and his guitar playing was in no way more accomplished than that of his own early rock heroes. So, then, what were his gifts? As Pete Hamill, who knew him well personally, put it,

> he was the leader of the Beatles for most of their time together; he was the driving force, the hard guy who helped shove McCartney, and

12. Cocks, "The Last Day in the Life," p. 18.
13. Robert Christgau, Editorial, *Village Voice,* 25 (December 10–16, 1980), p. 1.
14. Ibid.
15. See Edward Edelson, "Chapman May Have Lost Identity," *New York Daily News,* December 11, 1980, p. 7.

to a lesser degree George and Ringo, past the adolescent stereotypes into a kind of music that dragged all other pop music along behind it.[16]

His gifts were intellect, leadership, a deep understanding of human values in a world that had become hypnotized by television and had no genuine voices that communicated with the younger generation. He was "the bohemian, the artist, the intellectual."[17]

If environment rather than birth had anything to do with his remarkable career as a popular musician and media personality, it was a sensitivity to what was false and meaningless in his world—"he was . . . carrying around those things that, in Auden's phrase about Yeats, hurt him into art."[18]

The life of John Lennon is too well known to require more than a sketch here. He was born on October 9, 1940, in Liverpool, a place that never much appealed to him as he grew up. He once told Pete Hamill,

> I'm a Liverpudlian . . . I grew up there, I knew the streets and the people. And I wanted to get out of there. I wanted to get the hell out. I knew there was a world out there and I wanted it.[19]

He came from a home that disintegrated soon after his birth when his father, Alfred, a porter, enlisted in the Navy and abandoned his family. His mother, Julia, was unable to maintain her son, and, as a result, at 4½ years of age he came to live with his Aunt Mimi on Penny Lane in the outskirts of Liverpool. His relationship with his mother was nevertheless a profound one. Though she continued to live apart from him, she saw him often. She taught him the guitar, and she probably was his model for his sense of anarchy and his humor. As the obituary in *Newsweek* tells us, "She'd go for a walk with him wearing a pair of panties on her head and sporting spectacles without lenses through which she'd scratch her eyes to disconcert passers-by."[20] Her death, the result of a hit-and-run automobile accident, when John was 16, made an indelible mark on his consciousness and feelings. Songs like "Julia" and "Mother" have left a permanent expression of his anguish in boyhood—the mixture of sorrow, rage, and confusion—that he suffered by what he characterized as the double loss of his mother.[21]

Lennon was never much of a student in high school. From the start of his teen years, he was interested in music, particularly that of the earliest

16. Hamill, "Death and Life of John Lennon," p. 46.
17. Christgau, Editorial, p. 1.
18. Hamill, "Death and Life of John Lennon," p. 47.
19. Ibid., p. 45.
20. "Death of a Beatle," p. 42.
21. Cocks, "The Last Day in the Life," p. 21.

American rock-and-roll stars like Elvis Presley, Little Richard, and Jerry Lee Lewis, all of whom were popular among sailors in the seaport of Liverpool and engaged Lennon's rowdy and iconoclastic spirit. In 1956, at age 15, he formed his first rock-and-roll group, the Quarrymen, and he enlisted Paul McCartney as guitar player, thus creating "one of the great symbiotic collaborations of modern art."[22] Two unremarkable years passed for the Quarrymen, when the youngest of the eventual "Fab Four" joined them, George Harrison. Their reputation grew, and they accepted a date to play at the Top Ten Club in Hamburg, West Germany. It was here that the name "Beatles"— at first "Silver Beatles"—was coined by Lennon for the group. He had heard an American group known as Buddy Holly and the Crickets. "He decided on the Beatles, he told an interviewer later, because it incorporated the name of an insect with the word 'beat.' "[23]

The subsequent history of the Beatles is so well known, it can be recounted with a simple enumeration of facts. In 1961, Brian Epstein, an inspired promoter, became their manager. He obtained a recording contract for them that created a long string of Beatles hits in England. By then, of course, Ringo Starr had become the drummer to complete the foursome. Not until "I Want to Hold Your Hand" was released, on January 13, 1964, did the Beatles become a success in the United States, but when they did, they took the country by storm. Their appearances on "The Ed Sullivan Show" are a high point in the history of pop music. An audience of some 73 million saw those performances; over 50,000 people tried to obtain studio tickets when only 725 could be accommodated.[24] What followed were the golden years of the Beatles: They toured all over the world; together made three highly successful movies—*A Hard Day's Night, Help,* and *Yellow Submarine*—of which the first two were given Royal Premieres at the London Pavillion Theatre; they were awarded the MBE (Member of the Order of the British Empire), which they accepted, though later John returned his in protest against Britain's involvement in the Nigerian and Vietnamese wars; they were seen on television specials; they released a total of 24 albums in the United States alone, from "Meet the Beatles" on January 20, 1964, to "Love Songs" on October 24, 1977. Although gradually each became involved in separate projects, they were pulled together by their discipleship of the Maharishi Mahesh Yogi and by the death of their trusted friend and producer, Brian Epstein, in 1967. They also formed their own corporation, Apple Corps Ltd., which was to diversify their investments and multiply their wealth.[25]

22. "Death of a Beatle," p. 43.

23. Robert Palmer, "John Lennon: Guiding Force in Music and Culture of 60's," *The New York Times,* December 10, 1980, p. B7.

24. *John Lennon Tribute,* Premier Memorial Edition (New York: Woodhill Press, 1980), pp. 27–30.

25. Ibid., pp. 28–40.

While all four Beatles had been married, either before or during their whirlwind in the 1960s, John Lennon divorced his first wife, the former Cynthia Powell, by whom he had a son, Julian, born in 1963. His subsequent marriage to Yoko Ono was often blamed for the breakup of the Beatles in 1970. Yoko had been twice married and was herself a performer of sorts— a conceptual artist, who created "happenings." Yoko as well as John has denied that she was the cause of the breakup, though she felt she was "under heavy surveillance" by the other Beatles. "I sort of went to bed with this guy that I liked and suddenly the next morning I see these three in-laws standing there."[26] In a famous interview with *Playboy* (of both John and Yoko, two months before the assassination), John made clear that it was not Yoko but a change in his sensibility that caused the breakup, though the drift toward separation was clearly there already. Asked whether it was unthinkable for the Beatles to get back together again, John said, "Do you want to go back to high school?" He thought that the Beatles had something special once but that they had lost it. In the *Playboy* interview he said:

> When the Beatles played in America for the first time, they played pure craftsmanship. Meaning they were already old hands. The jism had gone out of the performances a long time ago. In the same respect, the songwriting creativity had left Paul and me in the mid-Sixties. When we wrote together in the early days, it was like the beginning of a relationship. Lots of energy. In the *Sgt. Pepper-Abbey Road* period, the relationship had matured. Maybe had we gone on together, more interesting things would have happened, but it couldn't have been the same.[27]

The perfectionist in him made him personally dissatisfied with every record the Beatles ever made and all his individual ones. He clearly was leaving one part of his artistic life behind him and was eager to explore new fields.

The 1970s were the years—both tempestuous and ultimately calm—of John Lennon's marriage to Yoko. His life clearly was changing, though he still composed and, by general acclaim released at least one great solo record, "Plastic Ono Band." In the early years of the decade, John and Yoko "lived in a series of elaborate post-hippie crash pads, became obsessed not only with artistic experimentation but with radical political flamboyance."[28] In this environment, the marriage was bound to be threatened, and, indeed,

26. Quoted by Cocks, "The Last Day in the Life," p. 23.
27. David Sheff, "John Lennon and Yoko Ono—Candid Conversation," *Playboy*, January 1981, p. 86. The interview in *Playboy* is an extremely useful source of firsthand information from Lennon and Yoko. It is especially informative about the inspiration behind many famous songs and about the Lennon-McCartney collaboration.
28. Cocks, "The Last Day in the Life," p. 24.

for eighteen months—months of agony and debauchery—John separated from Yoko. He almost drank himself to death. When reconciliation came, it clearly proved a step toward a new peaceful, satisfied, and most of all, isolated life. John had come out of his age of flamboyance, of being captive to his fans, and he now serenely accepted the role of what he called a "househusband," while Yoko went to the office to manage all the Ono-Lennon business interests, including the purchase of a large herd of Holstein cows. (Lennon was quoted as saying when Yoko sold one of the cows, "Only Yoko could sell a cow for $250,000.") On October 9, 1975, John's birthday, Yoko gave birth to Sean, and it was for Sean, as much as for Yoko and himself, that Lennon turned househusband. Of the shared birthday, he said, "We're like twins." From 1975 to 1980, Lennon "went private"; he granted virtually no interviews and stayed at home in the Dakota. Ironically, it was only a month before his assassination that he and Yoko reemerged before their public, completing the album "Double Fantasy" (not widely admired by the critics).[29]

It will take books in future years to explain and assess the role that John Lennon played not only as a composer-musician but also as an important leader in the cultural revolution that some think he led. As one reviewer has put it, the Beatles, and especially Lennon, their impudent and brilliant leader, were media guerrillas. They brought eye contact to a world hypnotized by the ubiquitous stare of the tube: "She looked at me," they sang, "And I could see. . . ." They brought a sense "of connection" to a whole generation.[30] They asked for people to come together, and they managed to remain themselves in spite of the media hype in which they were caught. They sang about love and peace and authenticity, and their songs, though considered by many as the expression of drug orgies, were often the product of very energetic and creative musical and even literary talents. The famous LSD song "Lucy in the Sky with Diamonds," according to Lennon, was based on a sketch of a girl named Lucy brought to him by his son Julian. The images, he carefully points out, were all from *Alice in Wonderland.*[31]

John Lennon, at the request of his wife, was quietly cremated. Crowds held a continuous vigil for John outside the Dakota. Yoko asked the world to express its grief on the following Sunday at 2:00 P.M., Eastern Standard Time. The largest crowd, estimated at 100,000, gathered in the Sheep Meadow in Central Park. Yoko remained in her apartment but had a clear view of the throng. The band shell contained only a picture of John Lennon draped by garlands and set within a wreath. Speakers played some of Lennon's

29. Ibid.
30. Nicholas Bromell, "John Lennon: 1940-1980," *New Boston Review,* 6 (February 1981) 30.
31. Sheff, "John Lennon and Yoko Ono," p. 105.

more subdued music, "In My Life," "You've Got to Hide Your Love Away," "Norwegian Wood," and "All You Need Is Love." In the gray setting of a December afternoon, the crowd sang along when they heard "Give Peace a Chance" over the speakers. At 2:00 P.M., all noise ceased. For ten minutes, New York's Central Park lay in quiet remembrance. The tribute ended with a playing of "Imagine," and as the crowd filtered out, snow began to fall quietly on the city.

Yoko took out a full-page ad in *The New York Times* of January 18, 1981. She wrote the message herself. It was entitled simply "In Gratitude." This paragraph appeared in her open letter:

I thank you for your feelings of anger for John's death. I share your anger. I am angry at myself for not having been able to protect John. I am angry at myself and at all of us for allowing our society to fall apart to this extent. The only "revenge" that would mean anything to us, is to turn the society around in time, to one that is based on love and trust as John felt it could be. The only solace is to show that it could be done, that we could create a world of peace on earth for each other and for our children.[32]

### Bibliography

Brownell, Nicholas. "John Lennon: 1940–1980." *New Boston Review* 6 (February 1981): 30.

Christgau, Robert. Editorial. *Village Voice* 25 (December 10–16, 1980): 1.

Cocks, Jay. "The Last Day in the Life." *Time,* December 22, 1980, pp. 18–24.

"Death of a Beatle." *Newsweek,* December 22, 1980, pp. 31–36.

Doyle, Patrick, et al. "John Lennon Slain Here." *New York Daily News,* December 9, 1980, p. 1 ff.

Edelson, Edward. "Chapman May Have Lost Identity." *New York Daily News,* December 11, 1980, p. 7.

Fagen, Cynthia R., and Leo Standora. "John Lennon Shot Dead." *New York Post,* December 9, 1980, p. 2.

Flippos, Chet. "Radio: Tribal Drum." *Rolling Stone,* January 22, 1981, p. 19.

Hamill, Pete. "The Death and Life of John Lennon," *New York,* December 22, 1981, pp. 34–48.

*John Lennon Tribute.* Premier Memorial Edition. New York: Woodhill Press, 1980.

Katz, Gregory. "Inside the Dakota." *Rolling Stone,* January 22, 1981, p. 17f.

Ledbetter, Les. "John Lennon of Beatles Is Killed." *The New York Times,* December 9, 1980, p. 1f.

Lennon, Yoko Ono. "In Gratitude." *The New York Times,* January 18, 1981, p. 24E.

32. Yoko Ono Lennon, "In Gratitude," *The New York Times,* January 18, 1981, p. 24E.

Montgomery, Paul L. "Police Trace Tangled Path to Lennon's Slaying at the Dakota." *The New York Times,* December 10, 1981, p. 1f.

Palmer, Robert. "John Lennon: Guiding Force in Music and Culture of the 60's." *The New York Times,* December 10, 1981, p. B7.

Sheff, David. "John Lennon and Yoko Ono—Candid Conversation." *Playboy,* January 1981, pp. 75–114f.

(Note: Bibliography differs from footnote form in two particulars: author's last name is given first, and page numbers are inclusive.)

## WRITING THE RESEARCH PAPER

If you have carefully read the preceding obituary of John Lennon, you will be aware that it is a report of reports. The point of such a report is to put together a coherent account of a topic based entirely on information collected from a variety of sources. The report of reports normally is not written in the first person. It is, after all, a compilation of facts and quotations from others. The writer's intrusion in such a paper is obviously out of place. Note, however, that a report need not necessarily exclude evaluative comments. If you find one particular source unusually interesting or informative, you are free to say so, as we did in describing Jay Cocks' obituary in *Time* magazine (see p. 124). Footnotes need not be mere source references. They are useful as well to include related but not essential facts (see notes 2 and 5). Sometimes, footnotes can help a reader in selecting further useful informational sources (see note 27). All direct quotations must, of course, be footnoted. At least some of the references should be to primary sources—either statements made by the subject or by someone who knew the subject (such as Pete Hamill, a friend of Lennon's, or Yoko Ono Lennon, both of whom we quoted in the paper). On occasion when the topic is a very well known event, it is useful to rely on several sources and write a composite footnote (see note 11). To assure coherence and adequate coverage, one is well advised to outline the major points of the report and to list under each heading the authors and page numbers of relevant citations. The first draft of the paper should strive to include action language where appropriate (see the first part of the Lennon paper describing his death) and to link major parts of the paper with effective transitions.

Footnote form varies in different fields of research. The important thing about footnoting is consistency. We recommend the following format as a general mode. Note that this format differs from that of the periodical indexes.

*Book*
John Jones, *Winston Churchill* (New York: Random House, 1965), p. 13.

If more than one page, use the abbreviation *pp.*

*Edition*
John Jones, ed., *The Speeches of Winston Churchill* (New York: Macmillan, 1960), pp. 55–68.

*Encyclopedia*
"Winston Churchill," *Encyclopedia Brittanica,* 1972 ed.

*Periodical*
John Jones, "Churchill in Parliament," *Current History* 22 (July 1963): 313–15 f.

NOTE: Titles of articles appear in quotation marks, names of journals are underlined, volume numbers are written in arabic numerals immediately after the name of the journal. You should be aware that most periodicals no longer list volume numbers on the cover or on page citations. The f. or ff. after page numbers indicates that the article continues after intervening pages.

As you can see in the Lennon paper, the word "Ibid.," followed by a comma, a page number, and a period is used when the immediately following footnote comes from the same source (see note 4). Ibid., an abbreviation of the Latin word *ibidem,* meaning "in the same place," is no longer italicized (or underlined in typescript) in most bibliographical guides. For repeated but not consecutive references to the same source, use the author's last name followed by the title of the work (shortened form suffices if title is long), followed by another comma, the page number and a period (see note 12).

## Assignment

Write a report of reports, the length to be decided by your instructor. The subject is to be the life, character, and accomplishments of some famous person, living or dead. Pretend to write an obituary—if the person is still living, an "advance obituary." You may, if you wish, select a name from the A.P. 470 list. You should obviously refer to as many sources as possible, consulting bibliographical guides, making notes, and assembling the paper in accordance with the instructions given above.

# UNIT III

# NARRATION

**A**s we move from descriptive writing to narration, we must realize that these two modes are not in any way mutually exclusive. You have no doubt noticed that several selections in the preceding unit, like the sketches of Cheryl Tiegs and Stan Dragoti or the portraits of Phyllis Schlafly, are also in a certain sense narratives. Conversely, many of the selections in this unit contain scenes that are essentially descriptive. We shall emphasize throughout this book that the various modes of writing that form our unit headings are interdependent. It is difficult to conceive of pure description, narration, exposition, persuasion, or criticism in any single piece of writing. In this unit we shall, therefore, highlight the process of narration as one mode of writing by examining its methods and structures and by observing some of its typical uses.

# 10

# THE NARRATIVE VOICE

In its most general sense narration is simply the act of telling. Thus, any rendering of an experience or of several experiences as recollected in the memory is an act of narration. Usually the source of narrative is either something that the narrator experienced or observed. Narrations can be written as first-person or as omniscient (meaning "all-seeing," "all-knowing") accounts. That is to say, writers may either be involved in the stories they tell, or they may stand, so to speak, in the wings of their narration, recounting what happened to others by use of the third person.

Narrative writing may be factual, fictional, or a combination of the two. In recent times it has become more and more difficult to make an absolute separation between factual and fictional narratives. Reporters of the so-called New Journalism often write in-depth, factual reports, some of which draw "composite" characterizations, made up of many persons who have shared similar experiences (e.g., prostitutes, mercenaries, loan sharks—the list is endless), with the result that fact cannot easily be sifted from fiction. So, too, novelists like Norman Mailer and Truman Capote have added a new classification to popular literature, the nonfiction or real-life novel, as exemplified by Mailer's *Executioner's Song* or Capote's *In Cold Blood.* What these instances show us is that effective narrative must be based on authentic human experience and feelings. In some instances, of course, narrative demands the re-creation of something that actually happened with as much objectivity as possible, as in newspaper reports of a current event, testimony in a trial, or documentation of a historical happening. But when the subject is a pure narrative, as is true of some of the reading selections in this chapter, the

**135**

truth of what happened is as much an imaginative as an objective reconstruction of events that may have occurred in the "real world."

All this is to say that even very simple narrations cannot be the equivalents of what actually happened. Take the following news account of a real event as reported in a lead paragraph by *Newsweek* magazine:

> On a sweltering morning last August, 3-year-old Kelly Keen wandered out of her home in Glendale, Calif., and camped on the curb, waiting to be taken swimming. When her father came looking for her ten minutes later, he found only her rubber sandals. Robert Keen then spotted a doglike animal moving off the sidewalk into the brush, holding the tiny girl by her neck in its jaws. He chased the animal, which fled, abandoning its prey. But four hours later Kelly died of a broken neck and severe internal injuries—by most accounts, the first death in the United States ever attributed to a coyote attack. ("Man Vs. Coyote in L.A.," *Newsweek,* October 26, 1981, p. 35.)

Undoubtedly we have here all the basic ingredients of a story. There is the setting of a sweltering day in Los Angeles; the heart-wrenching account of a coyote carrying off a three-year-old child; the conflict of the father chasing the animal; and the tragic conclusion of the death of the child. This event really happened, and *Newsweek* uses it as an instance to demonstrate that coyotes are becoming increasingly more brazen and that they are more and more a menace to outlying suburban communities. Yet for all the actuality of Kelly Keen's death, the *Newsweek* account does not really tell us more than a few salient facts. If we were to judge it as narrative—and that admittedly was not what the writer intended to stress—we could easily enumerate a vast variety of details and feelings that the *Newsweek* report does not tell us at all. We know nothing, for instance, of the layout of the setting—where the coyote came from, how it stalked the child, whether the child actually saw its attacker—and more important, we know nothing about the emotional turmoil, the grief, the shock, and the response of the family or the community to the event. It would be interesting to speculate what a reporter for a sensational newspaper or a fiction writer would stress in narrating this story.

Narration is of necessity an act of imaginative re-creation. It is an artistic (if not always artful) rendering of either a subjective or objective reality. It depends for its success on such a wide range of variables that to enumerate them here would be impossible. But one requirement for a successful narrative is that it speaks directly to its reader, that it renders its account through a consistent and believable voice. We said in Unit I that "the writer's voice is the device by which we discover the personality that the writer wishes to project on the written page" (see p. 27). In narration, especially first-person narration, we need to discover this voice, or, to use another metaphor, the mask with which the writer enters the world of narration. That mask becomes the writer's *persona*. Who is this persona, this other self of the writer? Is he or she an eccentric, an egoist, a disinterested reporter, a well-intentioned observer, a misanthropist, a curmudgeon, a philosopher, a masochist, a dreamer, a bully, a zealot? Unless we know, we will not be able to respond successfully to the narrative, the characters within it, or its ultimate significance. Narration depends for its success on the personality its speaker projects, even when that personality is that of the disembodied voice of the third person objective *persona*.

In this chapter, we concentrate on the first-person voice, or persona, of the writer. The intention is to demonstrate, through several reading selections, how writers manage to project themselves in their writings and how in consequence, they control the plot and characters they have created. These selections should help you, in turn, to develop a narrative persona of your own, for the first and most essential ingredient of all first-person narrative— no matter how trivial or important the subject—is that the writer projects a personality within any story that he or she has to tell.

## Reading Selection

The selection that follows appeared originally as an editorial column in the student newspaper of Columbia College, the *Columbia Daily Spectator*. Like most college newspapers, the *Spectator* usually includes columns that allow student reporters to express views, often with a humorous perspective, about college life or their private lives. This selection is a form of narrative—the musings of a student about the anxieties of being a senior. The narrative itself is simple and straightforward. Nothing earth-shattering happens. Rather, the central question that it ponders comes out of ordinary daily experience, the sort that each of us encounters in numerous shapes and forms. Read it by giving special attention to the way in which Ampolsk represents himself in his column. Try to discover the essential qualities of his persona.

### SO NOW YOU ARE A SENIOR

#### *Alan G. Ampolsk*

For years I have heard about being a Senior in College. Whenever I felt frustrated by the present my family would remind me about it. "Someday," they said, "You'll be a Senior in College." I knew what it meant, too. Immense freedom. The end of confinement. A future overflowing with possibilities. . . . Even last August, when I was adjusting to the idea that I'd spent the entire summer as a freelance writer (this is a polite way of saying, unemployed) the old formula worked. "You'll enjoy being a Senior in College." I felt better, knowing that that meant freedom . . . overflowing possibilities. . . .

"Welcome to your Senior year in College," said the letter from the Dean. . . .

He was enthusiastic. "I see you're a religion major. That's excellent, just excellent. You know we have so few Liberal Arts majors these days. . . ."

"I see."

"You realize that any medical school would be happy to have you. . . ."

"So," asked my family. "What's it like being a Senior in College?"

My advisor smiled. "What do you plan to be doing this time next year?"

"Ah . . . living . . . somehow. . . ."

"Nothing more specific?"

I thought quickly. "The trouble is, there's such immense freedom . . . such overwhelming possibilities. . . ."

"You ought to give some thought to where you want to wind up. . . ."

I thought again. "Something fulfilling . . . that I won't regret . . . fulfilling and just . . . and stimulating . . . and relatively prosperous. . . ."

"Well, law schools are glutted. Graduate schools aren't, but that's only because there's no work. . . ."

Little poisons started to drain the promise out of Senior year in College.

Research! The idea came out of nowhere. That might be fun. God knows I'm trained for it. . . .

Outside Kent Hall a conversation drifted past. "What languages do you know?"

"Latin, French, German . . . some Italian."

"No Urdu?"

"No."

"That's going to be a problem. . . ."

Two students walked in the opposite direction. "I don't see why you object to writing about Catalan sheep breeding. Think of the implications! Think of Medieval Sexuality. . . ."

Am I cut out for academe, then? If I'm forced to become mercantile. . . .

"What are you doing back here?" said a student on the steps of Low. "I thought you had a job."

"So did I," said the other. "Where's the GRE?"

I returned to my advisor. "The possibilities," I said, "aren't as immense as I thought they were."

"Welcome to the present day," he said.

My family began to avoid mentioning Senior Year in College.

On the steps of Low we talked it over. "We don't have any skills," said a friend of mine.

"Sure we do," said a friend of his. "We have bureaucratic skills. The trouble is, I don't want a bureaucratic job. . . ."

Classes began. In the smaller ones we introduced ourselves. "My name is . . . and I'm a senior. . . ."

"What are you going to be doing next year?"

"Ah . . . well . . . that's to say. . . ."

At home I started a notebook. It began with a list of ideal employment. Holy Roman Emperor was first (but it's hard to get investiture) . . . followed by the Papacy (but it's been done). I added a few small prayers ("Our Father which art in Heaven, canst thou spare a dime . . . ? or some other manner of social program?").

A letter arrived from my Army recruiter, offering me attractive benefits . . . and a pair of free Army tube socks. . . .

In the middle of being tempted by that I stopped. What was I coming to? Frankly, I'm not such a despairing man as I seem. Perhaps there are too many possibilities and too many of them are extinct. Nevertheless my optimism asserted itself. In spite of myself I began to visualize a promise of freedom . . . escape from confinement.

How to bring it about?

A little research, a few dropped points. Some small manipulation, and it just might work. . . .

With a little bit of luck, this time next year, I'll be a Senior in College.

From the *Columbia Daily Spectator,*
September 16, 1981, p. 4.

## Questions

*Content/Meaning*

1. Besides the immediate question of what the writer will be doing when his senior year is ended, what larger questions does his column pose indirectly?

2. It is clear with whom we side in this column. Who is the adversary? (Be as specific as possible.) Can you justify your answer?

*Style*

1. Characterize the persona of this essay. What three or four adjectives in your mind capture his personality?

2. What is the basis of the humor in this essay? How, for example, does Ampolsk characterize other people? What is his response to them? How seriously does he contemplate his prospects for employment?

3. The essay progresses from "then" to "now." In what way do these two times differ? What are the major stages in the narrative progression of the essay? At what time in the writer's career was this column written? Is it important to know that fact?

# Reading Selection

The following selection is clearly a piece of fiction, though no one would call it such. It is, like Ampolsk's essay, a humorous newspaper column—one designed to expose a particular piece of folly that the writer observes in his society. The first-person narrator in Buchwald's column is invariably a fictionalized version of the "real" Buchwald. This essay was written, as you will quickly discover, immediately after the election of Ronald Reagan in 1980. You will recall that the outcome of the election was an early landslide victory. Here Buchwald examines through a breezy humorous narrative, composed almost entirely of dialogue, the influence that modern communication, including the pollsters, can exert on the electorate.

## THE OLD THRILL IS GONE

### *Art Buchwald*

WASHINGTON—"Let's have an early dinner and then watch the election results," I said to my wife Tuesday night.

"That's a good idea." she agreed. "It's going to be a long evening but we'll get a head start."

We finished dinner at 8:15 p.m. and then went into the living room to sit back and watch what the pollsters had predicted would be one of the closest elections in history. I flipped on the set and heard either Tom Brokaw or John Chancellor announce: "NBC has projected that Ronald Reagan has won the election and will be the next president of the United States."

"What the hell is going on?" I asked my wife. "I haven't even finished my yogurt yet."

"Look at the map. The eastern part of it is all blue."

"It takes Archie Bunker longer to open a door than it does to decide a presidential election," I said.

"How do they know?" my wife said.

"I think they use an exit poll. They ask a black man in Buffalo, a Jewish man in Virginia, a housewife in Florida, a med student in Ohio and steelworker in Pennsylvania who they voted for, and then they start making the map all blue for Reagan. Would you care to play a game of Scrabble?"

"If we had known what was going to happen," my wife said, "we could have had an early dinner after the election results.

"I can't believe it," she said. "The polls aren't even closed in three-quarters of the states."

Since I had nothing to do I called my friend Bernheim in California. I got him at his office.

"Where are you going tonight to watch the election results?"

"To Phyllis and Don's," he said. "I have to go home and get cleaned up first, and then vote."

"I wouldn't do that if I were you, Alain."

"Why not?"

"Reagan won, and there isn't a thing anyone in California can do about it."

"What do you mean he won? It's only 4:15 p.m. here. How could he have won?

"He took Ohio, Michigan, New Jersey, Connecticut and Illinois."

"Where did you hear this?"

"It's all over television. NBC interviewed a senior citizen in Delaware and then gave the election to Reagan. Do you know what this means, Alain?"

"I'm not sure."

"The network polling methods have become so sophisticated we don't need anyone west of the Mississippi to decide a presidential election any more. You people are only wasting the nation's gasoline by going to the polls."

"But we're the most populous state in the union," Bernheim protested.

"Don't tell me your troubles. It's all over, Alain. As I talk to you Barbara Walters is trying to get to Nancy Reagan, and Walter Cronkite has just said, 'And that's the way it is November 4th, 1980.' Do you need any more evidence that you people are out of it?"

"Then you think I shouldn't vote?"

"Why not? It will kill some time when you get home. But if you think you're going to stop the landslide you're out of your gourd."

"I guess I'll call Phyllis and Don. Maybe they can cancel the caterer. Where's Ann?"

"She went to bed with a headache. She said she's not going to spend any more election nights with me. As far as our political life is concerned, she claims the thrill is gone."

From the *Los Angeles Times Syndicate,*
November 6, 1980.

## Questions

*Content/Meaning*

1. While this column is in general concerned with the speed of election coverage by the electronic media, what specific problems does Buchwald identify in his humorous dialogue? Since the outcome of the election proved the pollsters to be right, what solutions can you think of for the problems that Buchwald has dramatized in his column?

*Style*

1. Buchwald's column is technically a "literary burlesque," a mode in which a significant subject is treated frivolously. The literary burlesque

depends for its effectiveness on the contrast that the writer creates between the weightiness of the subject and the triviality of the style. How has Buchwald achieved his effect?

2. How does Buchwald characterize himself in this column? What appears to be the difference between this fictional Buchwald and the real Buchwald?

3. Compare Buchwald's persona with Ampolsk's. Would you say that they are essentially alike? How does the fictional "I" in each of the essays determine the point of view that the narrative of the column expresses?

# Reading Selection

The *persona* who tells the following narrative is not the author but the subject he interviewed. It thus differs from the literary voices of Ampolsk and Buchwald. In fact, one might say that Emma Knight's voice is not at all literary; it is colloquial (or conversational). To account for this fact, we need to know the characteristic method that Studs Terkel employs in his writings. In essence, Terkel is an interviewer. His subjects are usually common people who respond to various questions Terkel poses on preselected themes. For example, he has conducted a whole range of such interviews on the subject of "work." What attitudes do people have toward the work they do? Are they happy with their occupations? Bored? Do they take pride in their work? Does work play an important role in the image they project to others? These, and many other questions, are typical of his inquiries. Emma Knight was interviewed by Terkel as part of the project that led to his book *American Dreams: Lost and Found,* a collection of one hundred portraits told in the voice of the persons interviewed. While Terkel's book does not quite fit into the category of mass media, the source of most of our selections, he is very much a "media" author—one of our best popular interviewers and oral historians, as well as a radio personality in Chicago where his program is aired daily over WFMT. His earlier best-selling books featuring interviews include *Hard Times* and *Working.* In each of them he tested the aspirations of people against the realities of their lives and discovered in the process the enormous resources they possess to make the reality more powerful and often more attractive than their illusions and their dreams.

## MISS U.S.A.: EMMA KNIGHT

### Studs Terkel

*Miss U.S.A., 1973. She is twenty-nine.*

I wince when I'm called a former beauty queen or Miss U.S.A. I keep thinking they're talking about someone else. There are certain images that come to mind when people talk about beauty queens. It's mostly what's known as t and a, tits and ass. No talent. For many girls who enter the contest, it's part of the American Dream. It was never mine.

You used to sit around the TV and watch Miss America and it was exciting, we thought, glamorous. Fun, we thought. But by the time I was eight or nine, I didn't feel comfortable. Soon I'm hitting my adolescence, like fourteen, but I'm not doing any dating and I'm feeling awkward and ugly. I'm much taller than most of the people in my class. I don't feel I can compete the way I see girls competing for guys. I was very much of a loner. I felt intimidated by the amount of competition females were supposed to go through with each other. I didn't like being told by *Seventeen* magazine: Subvert your interests if you have a crush on a guy, get interested in what he's interested in. If you play cards, be sure not to beat him. I was very bad at these social games.

After I went to the University of Colorado for three and a half years, I had it. This was 1968 through '71. I came home for the summer. An agent met me and wanted me to audition for commercials, modeling, acting jobs. Okay. I started auditioning and winning some.

I did things actors do when they're starting out. You pass out literature at conventions, you do print ads, you pound the pavements, you send out your résumés. I had come to a model agency one cold day, and an agent came out and said: "I want you to enter a beauty contest." I said: "No, uh-uh, never, never, never. I'll lose, how humiliating." She said: "I want some girls to represent the agency, might do you good." So I filled out the application blank: hobbies, measurements, blah, blah, blah. I got a letter: "Congratulations. You have been accepted as an entrant into the Miss Illinois-Universe contest." Now what do I do? I'm stuck.

You have to have a sponsor. Or you're gonna have to pay several hundred dollars. So I called up the lady who was running it. Terribly sorry, I can't do this. I don't have the money. She calls back a couple of days later: "We found you a sponsor, it's a lumber company."

It was in Decatur. There were sixty-some contestants from all over the place. I went as a lumberjack: blue jeans, hiking boots, a flannel shirt, a pair of suspenders, and carrying an axe. You come out first in your costume and you introduce yourself and say your astrological sign or whatever it is they want you to say. You're wearing a banner that has the sponsor's name on it. Then you come out and do your pirouettes in your one-piece bathing suit, and the judges look at you a lot. They you come out in your evening gown and pirouette around for a while. That's the first night.

The second night, they're gonna pick fifteen people. In between, you had judges' interviews. For three minutes, they ask you anything they want. Can you answer questions? How do you handle yourself? Your poise, personality, blah, blah, blah. They're called personality judges.

I thought: This will soon be over, get on a plane tomorrow, and no one will be the wiser. Except that my name got called as one of the fifteen. You have to go through the whole thing all over again.

I'm thinking: I don't have a prayer. I'd come to feel a certain kind of distance, except that they called my name. I was the winner, Miss Illinois. All I could do was laugh. I'm twenty-two, standing up there in a borrowed evening gown, thinking: What am I doing here? This is like Tom Sawyer becomes an altar boy.

I was considered old for a beauty queen, which is a little horrifying when you're twenty-two. That's very much part of the beauty queen syndrome: the young, untouched, unthinking human being.

I had to go to this room and sign the Miss Illinois-Universe contract right away. Miss Universe, Incorporated, is the full name of the company. It's owned by Kaiser-Roth, Incorporated, which was bought out by Gulf & Western. Big business.

I'm sitting there with my glass of champagne and I'm reading over this contract. They said: "Oh, you don't have to read it." And I said: "I never sign anything that I don't read." They're all waiting to take pictures, and I'm sitting there reading this long document. So I signed it and the phone rang and the guy was from a Chicago paper and said: "Tell me, is it Miss or Ms.?" I said: "It's Ms." He said: "You're kidding." I said: "No, I'm not." He wrote an article the next day saying something like it finally happened: a beauty queen, a feminist. I thought I was feminist before I was a beauty queen, why should I stop now?

Then I got into the publicity and training and interviews. It was a throwback to another time where crossed ankles and white gloves and teacups were present. I was taught how to walk around with a book on my head, how to sit daintily, how to pose in a bathing suit, and how to frizz my hair. They wanted curly hair, which I hate.

One day the trainer asked me to shake hands. I shook hands. She said: "That's wrong. When you shake hands with a man, you always shake hands ring up." I said: "Like the pope? Where my hand is up, like he's gonna kiss it?" Right. I thought: Holy mackerel! It was a very long February and March and April and May.

I won the Miss U.S.A. pageant. I started to laugh. They tell me I'm the only beauty queen in history that didn't cry when she won. It was on network television. I said to myself: "You're kidding." Bob Barker, the host, said: "No, I'm not kidding." I didn't know what else to say at that moment. In the press releases, they call it the great American Dream. There she is, Miss America, your ideal. Well, not my ideal, kid.

The minute you're crowned, you become their property and subject to whatever they tell you. They wake you up at seven o'clock next morning and make you put on a negligee and serve you breakfast in bed, so that all the New York papers can come in and take your picture sitting in bed, while you're absolutely bleary-eyed from the night before. They put on the Kaiser-Roth negligee, hand you the tray, you take three bites. The photographers leave, you whip off the negligee, they take the breakfast away, and that's it. I never did get any breakfast that day. (Laughs.)

You immediately start making personal appearances. The Jaycees or the chamber of commerce says: "I want to book Miss U.S.A. for our Christmas Day parade." They pay, whatever it is, seven hundred fifty dollars a day, first-class air fare, round trip, expenses, so forth. If the United Fund calls and wants me to give a five-minute pitch on queens at a luncheon, they still have to pay a fee. Doesn't matter that it's a charity. It's one hundred percent to Miss Universe, Incorporated. You get your salary. That's your prize money for the year. I got fifteen thousand dollars, which is all taxed in New York. Maybe out of a check of three thousand dollars, I'd get fifteen hundred dollars.

From the day I won Miss U.S.A. to the day I left for Universe, almost two months, I got a day and a half off. I made about two hundred fifty appearances that year. Maybe three hundred. Parades, shopping centers, and things. Snip ribbons. What else do you do at a shopping center? Model clothes. The nice thing I got to do was public speaking. They said: "You want a ghost writer?" I said: "Hell, no, I know how to talk." I wrote my own speeches. They don't trust girls to go out and talk because most of them can't.

One of the big execs from General Motors asked me to do a speech in Washington, D.C., on the consumer and the energy crisis. It was the fiftieth anniversary of the National Management Association. The White House, for some reason, sent me some stuff on it. I read it over, it was nonsense. So I stood up and said: "The reason we have an energy crisis is because we are, industrially and personally, pigs. We have a short-term view of the resources available to us; and unless we wake up to what we're doing to our air and our water, we'll have a dearth, not just a crisis." Oh, they weren't real pleased. (Laughs.)

What I resent most is that a lot of people didn't expect me to live this version of the American Dream for myself. I was supposed to live it their way.

When it came out in a newspaper interview that I said Nixon should resign, that he was a crook, oh dear, the fur flew. They got very upset until I got an invitation to the White House. They wanted to shut me up. The Miss Universe corporation had been trying to establish some sort of liaison with the White House for several years. I make anti-Nixon speeches and get this invitation.

I figured they're either gonna take me down to the basement and beat me up with a rubber hose or they're gonna offer me a cabinet post. They had a list of fifteen or so people I was supposed to meet. I've never seen such a bunch of people with raw nerve endings. I was dying to bring a tape recorder but thought if you mention the word "Sony" in the Nixon White House, you're in trouble. They'd have cardiac arrest. But I'm gonna bring along a pad and paper. They were patronizing. And when one of 'em got me in his office and talked about all the journalists and television people being liberals, I brought up blacklisting, *Red Channels,* and the TV industry. He changed the subject.

Miss Universe took place in Athens, Greece. The junta was still in power. I saw a heck of a lot of jeeps and troops and machine guns. The Americans were supposed to keep a low profile. I had never been a great fan of the Greek junta, but I knew darn well I was gonna have to keep my mouth shut. I was still representing the United States, for better or for worse. Miss Philippines won. I ran second.

At the end of the year, you're run absolutely ragged. That final evening, they usually have several queens from past years come back. Before they crown the new Miss U.S.A., the current one is supposed to take what they call the farewell walk. They call over the PA: Time for the old queen's walk. I'm now twenty-three and I'm an old queen. And they have this idiot farewell speech playing over the airwaves as the old queen takes the walk. And you're sitting on the throne for about thirty seconds, then you come down and they announce the name of the new one and you put the crown on her head. And then you're out.

As the new one is crowned, the reporters and photographers rush on the stage. I've seen photographers shove the girl who has just given her reign up thirty seconds before, shove her physically. I was gone by that time. I had jumped off the stage in my evening gown. It is very difficult for girls who are terrified of this ending. All of a sudden (snaps fingers), you're out. Nobody gives a damn about the old one.

Miss U.S.A. and remnants thereof is the crown stored in the attic in my parents' home. I don't even know where the banners are. It wasn't me the fans of Miss U.S.A. thought was pretty. What they think is pretty is the banner and crown. If I could put the banner and crown on that lamp, I swear to God ten men would come in and ask it for a date. I'll think about committing an axe murder if I'm not called anything but a former beauty queen. I can't stand it any more.

Several times during my year as what's-her-face I had seen the movie *The Sting.* There's a gesture the characters use which means the con is on: they rub their nose. In my last fleeting moments as Miss U.S.A., as they were playing that silly farewell speech and I walked down the aisle and stood by the throne, I looked right into the camera and rubbed my finger across my nose. The next day, the pageant people spent all their time telling people that I hadn't done it. I spent the time telling them that, of course, I had. I simply meant: the con is on. (Laughs.)

Miss U.S.A. is in the same graveyard that Emma Knight the twelve-year-old is. Where the sixteen-year-old is. All the past selves. There comes a time when you have to bury those selves because you've grown into another one. You don't keep exhuming the corpses.

If I could sit down with every young girl in America for the next fifty years, I could tell them what I liked about the pageant, I could tell them what I hated. It wouldn't make any difference. There're always gonna be girls who want to enter the beauty pageant. That's the fantasy: the American Dream.

> From Studs Terkel, *American Dreams: Lost and Found* (New York: Pantheon, 1980), pp. 1–6.

### Questions

*Content/Meaning*
1. At one point in her account Knight says, "Miss U.S.A. is in the same graveyard that Emma Knight the twelve-year-old is." What does she mean by this statement? How are these two buried "selves" different?
2. What are the major criticisms (not just the anecdotes of experiences) that Emma Knight makes of the American beauty contest? What would you consider her most serious objection?
3. How does this interview relate to the general topic of "the American Dream"? With what particular dream does Emma Knight's experience deal? What is her attitude toward that dream? Was her attitude before she was Miss U.S.A. significantly different from what it was afterward?

*Style*
1. In the preface to this selection, we called Emma Knight's narrative voice "colloquial" rather than literary. Analyze Emma Knight's vocabulary. Can you find expressions that you would normally associate with informal conversation?
2. Would you agree that whereas Ampolsk and Buchwald use literary masks to cover their real selves, Emma Knight is concerned throughout her narrative to be totally authentic? How does the incident relating to the title of "Ms." and the White House experience add or detract from her desire to be authentic? Do you think that you have

met the true Emma Knight in this account? Do you know, for example, why she allowed herself to become involved in beauty contests even though she was critical of them? On the basis of everything that she reveals about herself, what would be your own portrait of Emma Knight?

## Reading Selection

The selection that follows was delivered as a speech at Airlie House, Virginia, by a Japanese doctor addressing the first Congress of International Physicians for the Prevention of Nuclear War. It is a narrative by a survivor of the atomic bomb dropped by the United States on Nagasaki in 1945, the event which, together with the dropping of the first atom bomb on Hiroshima, precipitated the unconditional surrender of Japan to end World War II. Read the account with a particular view toward Dr. Ichimaru's literary persona.

### NAGASAKI, AUGUST 9, 1945

#### *Michito Ichimaru*

In August 1945, I was a freshman at Nagasaki Medical College. The ninth of August was a clear, hot, beautiful, summer day. I left my lodging house, which was one and one half miles from the hypocenter, at eight in the morning, as usual, to catch a tram car. When I got to the tram stop I found that it had been derailed in an accident. I decided to return home. I was lucky. I never made it to school that day.

At 11 A.M., I was sitting in my room with a fellow student when I heard the sound of a B-29 passing overhead. A few minutes later, the air flashed a brilliant yellow and there was a huge blast of wind.

We were terrified and ran downstairs to the toilet to hide. Later, when I came to my senses, I noticed a hole had been blown in the roof, all the glass had been shattered, and that the glass had cut my shoulder and I was bleeding. When I went outside, the sky had turned from blue to black and the black rain started to fall. The stone walls between the houses were reduced to rubble.

After a short time, I tried to go to my medical school in Urakami which was 500 meters from the hypocenter. The air dose of radiation was more than 7000 rads at this distance, but I could not complete my journey because there were fires everywhere. I met many people coming back from Urakami. Their clothes were in rags, and shreds of skin hung from their bodies. They looked like ghosts with vacant stares. The next day, I was able to enter Urakami on foot, and all that I knew had disappeared. . . .

Only the concrete and iron skeletons of the buildings remained. There were dead bodies everywhere. On each street corner, we had tubs of water used for putting out fires after the air raids. In one of these small tubs, scarcely large enough for one person, was the body of a desperate man who sought cool water.

There was foam coming from his mouth, but he was not alive. I cannot get rid of the sounds of crying women, in the destroyed fields. As I got nearer to school, there were black charred bodies, with the white edges of bones showing in the arms and legs. A dead horse with a bloated belly lay by the side of the road. Only the skeleton of the medical hospital remained standing. . . . Because the school building was wood, it was completely destroyed. My classmates were in that building attending their physiology lecture. When I arrived some were still alive. They were unable to move their bodies. The strongest were so weak that they slumped over on the ground. I talked with them and they thought they would be okay, but all of them would eventually die within weeks. I cannot forget the way their eyes looked at me and their voices spoke to me forever. I went up to the small hill behind the medical school where all of the leaves of the trees were lost. The green mountain had changed to a bald mountain. There were many medical students, doctors, nurses, and some patients who escaped from the school and hospital. They were very weak and wanted water badly, crying out "give me water please." Their clothes were in rags, bloody and dirty. Their condition was very bad. I carried down several friends of mine on my back from this hill. I brought them to their houses using a cart hitched to my bicycle. All of them died in the next few days. Some friends died with high fever, talking deliriously. Some friends complained of general malaise and bloody diarrhea, caused by necrosis of the bowel mucous membrane by severe radiation.

One of my jobs was to contact the families of the survivors. In all the public schools I visited, there were many many survivors brought there by the healthy people. It is impossible to describe the horrors I saw. I heard many voices in pain, crying out, and there was a terrible stench. I remember it as an inferno. All of these people also died within several weeks.

One of my friends who was living in the same lodging houses cycled back from medical school by himself that day. He was a strong man doing Judo. That night he gradually became weak but he went back to his home in the country by himself the next day. I heard he died a few weeks later. I lost many friends. So many people died that disposing of the bodies was difficult. We burned the bodies of my friends in a pile of wood which we gathered, in a small open place. I clearly remember the movement of the bowels in the fire.

On August 15, 1945, I left Nagasaki by train to return to my home in the country. There were many survivors in the same car. Even now, I think of the grief of the parents of my friends who died. I cannot capture the magnitude of the misery and horror I saw. Never again should these terrible nuclear weapons be used, no matter what happens. Only when mankind renounces the use of these nuclear weapons will the souls of my friends rest in peace.

> Professor Michito Ichimaru, M.D., March 21, 1981, Airlie, Virginia.

### Questions

*Style*

1. Can you describe the voice of the narrator? To what extent is his account influenced by the fact that he has since become a doctor? (Comment especially about his use of medical terminology.) How does it and references to the "hypocenter" affect his first-person description as a survivor?
2. This narrative is written essentially in short, simple sentences. Does the style add to the effectiveness of the description? The language, moreover, contains several unidiomatic expressions, the sort that often occur in the language of nonnative speakers. Can you find any such expressions? How would you change them into idiomatic English? If you were to edit the speech for a newspaper column, would you make those changes?
3. Were you prepared by the essay for the direct appeal in the last few sentences? If so, indicate how.

## Exercises and Assignments

1. Skim the contents of a weekly newsmagazine or a daily newspaper and read carefully all first-person narratives. Make a list of the selections in which such narrations occur. Briefly describe two or three first-person narrators who have revealed personality facets that particularly interested you.

2. Write a 200- to 300-word essay in which you assume a first-person narrative voice. The subject matter should be a personal experience that aroused a strong emotion within you. Direct your remarks to a college readership. You might pretend that you are writing a personal column for your college newspaper.

3. Read some additional columns by Buchwald and other humorists, such as Russell Baker, the syndicated columnist of *The New York Times*.

Note what devices of humor they use to identify serious problems and expose the absurdities of modern life.

4. Using the Buchwald column as your model, choose a social or political problem and write a narrative, with you as a participant in the action, to expose an absurdity, illogicality, or injustice that you have observed or experienced. You might wish to concentrate on a college rule, a foolish law, or some aspect of etiquette or social role playing that you find ridiculous.

5. Comment about an American dream that in your mind does not match the reality you have encountered. Begin by describing the elements that constitute the typical dream and then examine the conditions of real life, as you know it, that stand in conflict with it.

6. Interview someone you know in depth. Choose a topic on which to focus (as Terkel did with "Work" or "the American Dream"). You might, for example, concentrate on "the college experience." Prepare a set of questions and take careful notes as your subject answers them. If you have access to a tape recorder, you could use it to good advantage here in place of taking notes. After concluding the interview, write a 300- to 500-word paper. Try to characterize the person through his or her own language. The essay should be written in the first person, as spoken by the person you interviewed. Aim for authenticity, as Terkel did in his portrait of Emma Knight.

7. Write a 200- or 300-word character sketch of yourself, emphasizing your reaction to a specific experience (as did Emma Knight and Dr. Ichimaru). The event can be light and amusing or serious. Be sure to decide what sort of persona you would like to assume.

8. Write another essay on the same subject as the one assigned in 7. This time adopt a different persona. For example, if the first finds you self-mocking, let the second be earnest and grave. Or if the first shows you to be naive, natural, and unsuspicious, let the second show you as wise, profound, and distrusting. Or if in the first you assumed a colloquial tone, now take on a literary voice.

# 11 THE STRUCTURE OF NARRATION

In the preceding chapter, with our focus on the narrative voice, we looked at relatively straight-forward and simply designed narrative accounts. In this chapter, we wish to take a closer look at the structure of narration, or the element that, in fiction especially, is known as plot. Actually, every narration, whether fictional or factual, needs to be plotted. We have already seen that the line between these two modes is not a distinct one, and, in fact, every successful narration requires some sort of planned arrangement of incidents and details.

While traditionally a narrative is said to require *plot, character,* and *theme,* many narrations may well slight one or another of these ingredients. *Plot* refers to a plan of action that customarily involves conflict between a protagonist and an antagonist. The *protagonist* is the main character on whom the action is centered; the *antagonist* is his or her adversary (if a person) or an opposing force (if some power of nature or an abstraction). The plot of a narrative may thus pit one individual against another or against any number of opposing forces—an overwhelming emotion, society at large, a natural disaster, or even an ideology. *Character* refers not simply to an individual person but also to the internal state of that person. A narration may, in essence, be a character study in which the reader learns about the emotional makeup and feelings of the protagonist. In such a study, plot is often negligible: What happens is subordinated to the understanding of a particular human nature or psyche. *Theme* refers to the meaning or motif of a narrative. While some narratives may well be superficial—they simply tell a story for escape and entertainment—every narrative, no matter how trivial, must finally have a point. If the narrative is superficial or inauthentic, its theme, or point, will lack significance for the serious reader.

As we have said, narration in its simplest terms is the act of telling. The sequencing of events in a narrative is essentially the result of the author's

**152**

choice. Here, for example, is a narrative response to the question, "What did you do yesterday?"

> Well, let's see. I went to my biology class, took a test in math. In the afternoon, Joe and I played handball. Oh, yes—I also went to McDonalds with Jill and asked her to go out with me Saturday night. And I played for a while with the pinball machines in the Union. What else? I jogged my usual two miles, washed some clothes, and wrote a paper for English. After dinner I saw *Star Wars* (I think for the tenth time) in the film series. Come to think of it, I sure had a busy day.

The narrative design of this rather prosaic paragraph is not very successful. It lacks a sense of progression and it rambles. Effective narration presupposes a more deliberate and purposeful design.

Note how the same paragraph can be organized into a coherent narrative simply by giving it a chronological time frame.

> After getting up at around eight, I jogged my usual two miles. Then I had breakfast and went to my ten o'clock bio class. Right afterward, I had math and took a test. For lunch, I went over to McDonalds with Jill and asked her for a date on Saturday night. What else? In the afternoon I first played handball for an hour or so with Joe, then went to the library and wrote my paper for English. Before dinner I washed out some clothes, and at night, after playing with the pinball machines in the Union, I saw *Star Wars* in the film series (I think for the tenth time). It sure was a busy day.

## SEQUENCED NARRATION

The important words and phrases added to the original in the above paragraph have to do with time sequence. Suddenly, we no longer have a random telling but a sequenced (if still prosaic) narration. We might call such a narration a *chronicle,* which, in simple terms, is the telling of an experience or experiences in a temporal frame. Chronicle implies chronological: Events are told in the order that they happened.

The chronicle, when executed with care and rigorous attention to detail, is the kind of narration that attempts most persistently to be objective. It tries to re-create in as natural a language as possible and in accurate chronological sequence the event or experience being reported. The farther we move away from such objectivity, the more, of course, we enter the realm of the imagination. In its least objective form—that which is farthest removed from the chaos of "real" experience—narration becomes story, the distinctive quality of which is to give a larger meaning, or universal design, to a segment of human experience. This kind of narration at its extreme is pure fiction. It implies a progressive ordering and imaginative rendering of experience as structured by the memory.

In this chapter we more or less disregard the first kind of narration, *random telling,* and are concerned only incidentally with the second, chronicling. The former of these, in a sense, enters into the stage of prewriting, for it is really not much more than the collection of facts and perceptions on which an ordered narrative will be based. The latter, while a time-honored and important means of recording objective reality, is more directly relevant to reporting. We concentrate here on narration as *story,* or *narrative.*

In the readings that follow you have an opportunity to study the structure of narrative by focusing on sports events. The reason for this choice of subject is apparent: Sports, in the abstract, are already structure in the mode of narrative. There is, at base, a conflict—protagonists and antagonists vying for victory. Yet, we should realize that sports, like games in general, are not in themselves narratives. They are the raw material from which narrative can easily be fashioned. Sports differ from narrative in that they have, by the rules of their games, no meaning beyond the event. Whether the sport involves teams or individuals, the object of competitive sport is to win, either over an immediate opponent or over the record of a previous opponent. Those who would attach larger meaning to the sports event—reporters, commentators, novelists—are writing narratives, for they not only impose their own imaginative design but also an interpretation on the event and its participants. When a competitor becomes a hero, he becomes the protagonist of a story.

Our particular focus in this chapter is on boxing. Of course, we might have selected virtually any other sport for purpose of illustration, but we chose boxing, not because it draws the most universal response (though it might well), but because it presents a dramatic confrontation that has lent itself often to wider interpretation. Moreover, boxing has the reputation of being physically more demanding and more dangerous than most sports. Consequently, it attracts a great deal of interest, for any activity that asks the maximum in effort is bound to engage our views of human potentiality. Boxing is also noted for its sheer violence and has, therefore, attracted much controversy. Boxing logically prompts us to ask, What sort of person will endure such hardship and punishment, and for what purpose? Or what kind of purpose can make a game of something so deadly? Unlike baseball, boxing requires no expertise for the layman's understanding, and therefore it communicates effectively across national boundaries and beyond technical analysis.

Although the reading matter in this chapter is limited to prizefighting, the exercises and assignments are designed for an exploration of other sports.

The daily newspaper or weekly newsmagazine can well serve as supplementary texts during your study of sports as narrative.

As a further narrowing down of our subject, we have decided to concentrate on the career of one prizefighter, Muhammad Ali, in four of the reading selections that follow. Before you read those accounts, however, we need to say something more about Ali not only as a controversial and immensely popular personality but also as a heavyweight champion. In the readings he will variously be shown as protagonist and antagonist, mostly for reasons that have less to do with his skill as a boxer than his political or social views. The structure of the sports reports will depend directly on how the writer perceives Ali vis-à-vis his opponents. For that reason, we must digress for a moment to talk about the myth of the heavyweight champion.

Boxing has always been prone to myth making. Somehow, the heavyweight championship has bestowed a special grace on its holder, and the press has tried, sometimes against all odds, to make the champion a symbol of all the traditional manly virtues associated with the Anglo-American hero. This was reasonably easy to do with personalities like Jack Dempsey, Joe Louis, Jersey Joe Walcott, Rocky Marciano, and Floyd Patterson. But, occasionally, a contender from the wrong side of the law succeeded, and then the myth of the Christian hero was a bit more difficult to uphold. Perhaps the most extreme example was that of Sonny Liston, the champion who had defeated Floyd Patterson and who was later to be dethroned by Muhammad Ali (or, as he was known then, Cassius Marcellus Clay). Liston was characterized by *Time* magazine as "semi-literate, surly and suspicious." Prior to winning the championship, Liston had been arrested nineteen times, had been convicted twice for armed robbery, and had spent three years in prison. He was widely associated with underworld figures, and his career as a boxer was assumed by many to have been supported by organized crime.

If Liston was a threat to the mythmakers, he was nevertheless a harmless departure from the stereotype compared to Ali. After all, Liston had only been a criminal, and even if he was owned by ganglords, as *Time* intimated, he was yet a "true blue American." He could be represented as a tough guy—a real-life George Raft or Jimmy Cagney. Other outlaws, like the James brothers of the Old West, had become folk heroes, so the possibility was at least there for Sonny Liston. But what do you do with a heavyweight champion who is a political and spiritual enemy of the American hero myth? That is what Muhammad Ali turned out to be. He started simply and plainly as a clown, an incredible braggart who had managed to win a gold medal in the Rome Olympics. He was an 8 to 1 underdog, and few reporters took him seriously. After he had completely overwhelmed Sonny Liston, it was hard for the press to believe that the fight was on the up and up. They thought Liston had quit, that he simply did not want to come out for the seventh round. Actually, he sat on his stool exhausted and in obvious pain, as the videotape of the fight later showed. Ali had won a masterful fight.

When Ali met the press the next day, he took on a whole new personality. Dropping the pose of the loudmouth (he was called "The Louisville Lip"), he spoke softly and said, "I'm through talking, all I have to do is be a nice, clean gentleman." For a moment, the press sighed with relief—America had another gentleman champion. But then almost as quickly, the spell was broken. Before the fight, Ali had been associating with the Black Muslims, a religious group considered at the time by middle-class America as a violent revolutionary sect. One reporter asked Ali whether he was a "card carrying member of the Black Muslims." Ali said he didn't know what "card carrying" meant, and he added, almost wistfully, "I don't have to be what you want me to be. I'm free to be who I want." With that declaration of independence from the hero myth, America had its first free-spoken heavyweight champion who was—to the abhorrence of the sports establishment—a Black Muslim.

He also refused induction into the armed services during the Vietnam war on religious grounds. The press was outraged. An American heavyweight champion a draft dodger who refused to fight for his country? Intolerable. Instantly he was stripped of his title by the World Boxing Association. Eventually, he was officially judged a conscientious objector by the Supreme Court of the United States, but because of this episode in his private life, he was deprived of being champion for three and a half years. Even after the Court decision, he did not gain back his title—he had to fight for it before a generally hostile press, which would not so much as allow him the right to his name (he was called "Clay" by many). But Ali had a huge following nevertheless— he had become the idol of the Third World and the symbol of the counterculture. Gradually he prevailed, and even the hardiest among his critics accepted him as one of the great boxers of his time.

## Reading Selection

Our first selection is a fairly straightforward account of the first title fight between Muhammad Ali and Joe Frazier, the man who had been crowned champion during Ali's enforced exile from the championship. It took place in Madison Square Garden in New York City on the evening of March 8, 1971. The round-by-round account that follows is fairly typical of the "factual" coverage given to important fights. Read it and note the extent to which this account presents a factual summary of the fight. We use the selection as an example of a *chronicle*.

## ALI VS. FRAZIER, ROUND-BY-ROUND ACCOUNT, MARCH 9, 1971

### *United Press International (UPI)*

ROUND ONE—Ali took the first round as he outboxed Frazier and landed most of the punches. Ali landed the first seven blows including two good left hooks as Frazier tried to get inside. When Joe landed one good body punch Ali tied him up and then mugged to the crowd that he wasn't hurt. Ali used his reach effectively and was landing both left hooks and left jabs consistently.

ROUND TWO—Ali did less dancing and more punching in the second round and also took that session. At the end of it he waved contemptuously at Frazier and motioned to the crowd that he didn't consider the champion very much.

ROUND THREE—Frazier took the third round by a narrow margin, when there was a very slight trickle of blood from his left nostril. Frazier got inside more often in the third and landed several thumping blows to the body and head. The round ended with Frazier pummelling a covered-up Ali in Ali's corner.

ROUND FOUR—Frazier also took the fourth round, and now he was getting inside and staying inside. Frazier landed three hard left hooks in the last minute of the round while most of Ali's shots in the session bounced off Joe's head.

ROUND FIVE—Ali took the fifth round when he went back to long-range boxing and bounced lefts and rights off the head of the oncoming Frazier.

ROUND SIX—Ali, using his left jab often like a long spear, had the edge in the sixth round. Frazier kept boring in, taking shots on his head in order to pound body blows that did not seem to upset Ali.

ROUND SEVEN—Ali's boxing skill and reach kept him in charge in the seventh round and once again he finished the session with a contemptuous wave toward Joe's corner. Near the end of the round Frazier backed Ali into a corner, pummelled him to the body and landed two shots to the head while Ali contented himself with jabs.

ROUND EIGHT—Frazier pressed the attack and took the eighth round, part of which Ali devoted to clowning. Twice Ali stood along the ropes and playfully pushed away Frazier's hands in patty-cake fashion.

ROUND NINE—Ali took the ninth round by counter-punching and in one stretch landed eight straight solid shots to Frazier's head. Joe shook up Ali once with a left hook sending him into the ropes just before that barrage. Frazier was bleeding slightly from the left nostril.

ROUND TEN—They fought on even terms in the 10th round. Frazier landing several powerful hooks to the head and Ali countering with lefts and rights to the head. Frazier had a slight swelling over his right eye.

ROUND ELEVEN—Frazier staggered Ali with a thundering left hook after two minutes of the 11th and Ali almost went down. He spun into the ropes and then on rubbery legs managed to elude Frazier for the rest of the round. In the first minute of the round, Ali went down but that was by a slip on the water in Frazier's corner.

ROUND TWELVE—Frazier staggered Ali again early in the 12th round with two left hooks but Ali, though dazed, fought back with jabs during the rest of the round. Frazier won the round by a wide margin. Frazier had a slight cut inside his mouth but he was the one landing the solid punches.

ROUND THIRTEEN—Frazier won the 13th round by a solid margin, shaking off Ali's long punches and crowding him into the corners. Frazier took a few punches to the head and landed solid shots to the body and once snapped Ali's head back with a left hook. There was no bounce in Ali's legs as he went to his corner.

ROUND FOURTEEN—Frazier moved in and walked into two light lefts and rights from Ali.

Ali got over a left to the head but Frazier came back with a good left to the body.

Ali opened up with another volley of four punches to the head and then repeated it before tying up the swollen-faced Frazier.

ROUND FIFTEEN—Frazier floored Ali with a left hook to the jaw in the first minute of the 15th round. Ali went down on his back, rolled over and took the eight count. Frazier pressed the attack the rest of the round. Ali spent most of the round hanging on, his right jaw swollen out of shape, and he took a bad battering. Ali's eyes were glazed and he was just going the distance at the end and Frazier laughed at him at the final bell.

### Questions

*Content/Meaning*
1. The foregoing account is meant to be a chronicle, hence an objective rendering of the fight. Do you think it avoids taking sides? If so, which of the two fighters does the UPI seem to favor and make into a protagonist?
2. Is there any point at which any (or all) of the individual rounds violate strict chronological order? Explain.

*Style:*
1. In each of the rounds described, what words, phrases, or sentences do not directly relate the action of the fight? How much of the account finally is straightforward chronicle and how much is interpretation?

2. If you were to write a narrative or story of the fight, which actions would you highlight? Which were the least eventful rounds?
3. How lively is the language describing the action of the fight? Does the writer overuse any particular words or phrases? Does he use any figures of speech? Does he use multiple-concept verbs?

## Exercises and Assignments

1. Find some examples of straightforward chronicles. Bring to class a copy of the one that in your mind is the most objective. You need not restrict yourself to sports. (Your textbooks might contain good examples.)

2. Write a chronicle of a sporting event—either one that you have observed in person or that you have seen on TV.

## Reading Selection

The following is a narrative, not a round-by-round chronicle, of the fight chronicled in the previous selection. The account that follows has a decided point of view toward the two principals and especially toward Ali. Read it, first, bearing in mind the round-by-round chronicle, and determine how and where this account differs. Then read it as narrative. How is it structured? Who is the protagonist? What sort of characterizations do we get of the two fighters? Besides giving a report of the fight, what point or commentary does Montgomery's account make?

### ALI VS. FRAZIER: MARCH 9, 1971

#### *Jim Montgomery*

NEW YORK—In what was more of a non-fight than The Fight for much of 14 rounds, Joe Frazier grimly chased Cassius Clay around the Madison Square Garden ring Monday night and kept his World Heavyweight Championship by unanimous decision.

Frazier, the aggressor throughout, dropped Clay for a mandatory eight count in the 15th round to secure the victory. It was one of only two really telling punches landed, and Frazier was on the shipping end of both.

Referee Arthur Mercante scored it closer than anyone, giving Frazier an 8-6-1 advantage. The judges' votes were 9-6 and 11-4.

Clay's speed of hand and foot were not in evidence. He spent most of the fight leaning on the ropes while Frazier whaled away—not too effectively— at the body. The crowd booed from time to time as the two fighters played pattycake in this fashion.

Occasionally, with a flash of the old Clay bravado, Cassius would look down at the hardworking Frazier and flick his head with lefts and rights, much like a boxer drills on the speed bag.

Cassius also periodically tried another of his contemptuous maneuvers, laying his left hand atop Frazier's head just to show he could do it and keep it there.

What fight there was came from Frazier. He seemed to have Clay in trouble briefly in the 11th round after another of those unproductive sessions with Clay on the ropes, almost passive.

Joe got across a good left hand to the head about 2:15 into the round. It either buckled Clay's knees or else Cassius made it look that way. He wobbled through the rest of the round though, and if he was hurt it didn't last long. He came back to win the 13th round on The Enquirer Scorecard.

There was no shamming on the 15th-round knockdown, though.

Although well ahead on points by then, Frazier continued to pursue Clay as the round began. He chased Cassius into a neutral corner and drove home the left hook, almost a semi-uppercut.

Clay hit the floor instantly with a heavy thump. He was up before the count reached five, took the required eight-count and looked dazed.

Frazier clubbed home two more good punches, both lefts, but Cassius was able to tie him up after each and simply held on for the last 15 seconds of the fight with no blows thrown.

Clay had predicted on closed-circuit television that "all the Frazier fans and boxing experts will be shocked at how easily I will beat Joe Frazier . . . Frazier falls in six."

The Clay of five years ago might have made that come true, but this time it wasn't even a particularly good fight for the millions who watched.

Cassius, however, inflicted more damage than he received. He cuffed the flesh around Frazier's eyes, drew blood from Joe's nose in the ninth round and twice had Frazier bleeding from the mouth.

The puzzling part was Clay's willingness throughout to lean on the ropes, cover up and let Joe swing away. Frazier wasn't doing much damage, but Clay was doing none.

Cassius did keep flicking his left into Frazier's face when the two were at long range, but when Joe kept coming Clay would jab and then miss with the second half of his combinations.

There was no preliminary to the knock-down punch. The two had clinched briefly, they broke apart, and Frazier slammed home a left hook to Clay's jaw.

That was what the evening offered to offset those periods of tedium on the ropes. Clay's beloved Ali Shuffle . . . he even wore special tasseled boots to show it off . . . was never in evidence.

The sixth round was Clay's best. He spatted Frazier midway through the round with a series of rights and lefts. Joe fought back, undamaged, then Cassius got through with another flurry. Assistant trainer Bundini Brown grinned at Clay, showering him at mid-ring with water as the round ended.

It didn't seem that Frazier was scoring to any great extent with the body punches which were supposed to drain Clay's vitality and take away his speed. The 11th round was perhaps the key when Frazier knocked Cassius wobbly-legged.

Something sent Cassius into neutral gear and cost him the first loss in his professional career. There will be a rematch one of these days. Perhaps that one will be The Fight.

From the *Cincinnati Enquirer,* March 9, 1971, p. 31.

### Questions

*Content/Meaning*
1. What point of view does this account take toward Muhammad Ali? How does the writer convey his attitude? Is there reason to believe that Ali's image as the antihero bothers the writer? Is he enthusiastic about Frazier? What is his total attitude toward the fight? Does this attitude square with the round-by-round description rendered by UPI?
2. At one point in the account, Montgomery says: "Frazier wasn't doing much damage, but Clay was doing none." Does his own account support this statement? Do you find inconsistencies in the report?
3. How does the account work as narrative? Can you comment on its structure, sense of conflict, narrative voice, and apparent main point?
4. To what extent does the following comment by Arthur Daley, then the sports editor of *The New York Times,* summarize what has been said here about the first Ali-Frazier encounter:

   It was a thriller all the way, jam-packed with suspense and tingling from start to finish with the special brand of drama inherent in all heavyweight championship bouts. Not until the last third of the fight—it is proper to partition it that way—did Frazier's thumping hooks carry him definitely into the lead. (March 9, 1971)

   You might wish to read *The New York Times* coverage of the fight to get a fuller view both of Daley's opinion and of the paper's general coverage.

*Style*
1. Is the Montgomery article well written? Examine it from the point of view of organization, sentence structure, and word choice.

# Reading Selection

We include the following selection describing the Ali/Frazier rematch in 1975 in Manila to provide a comparison and contrast with the preceding accounts. Ali had finally regained the championship in 1974 by beating George Foreman in Zaire. The fight in Manila is considered by many one of the greatest championship matches ever fought. Ali, in his inimitable style, "created" atmosphere for this much-sought-after encounter by labeling it "The Thrilla in Manila." Read the account closely and then answer the questions that follow it.

## THE THRILLA IN MANILA

### Champ Ali Stops Joe After 14th in Manila

*Associated Press (AP)*

MANILA (AP)—Muhammad Ali stopped Joe Frazier's strength-sapping body attack, pounding Frazier's head lopsided with powerful blows that stopped the challenger after the 14th round here Wednesday morning to retain his world heavyweight championship.

It was a war and Ali fired the most accurate and telling shots as he pounded and pounded rights and lefts to Frazier's head in the 13th and 14th rounds that closed the challenger's eyes and had him reeling.

After Frazier groped to his corner after the 14th, trainer Eddie Futch signaled to referee Eddie Padilla Jr. that the game challenger could not continue. And the fight was stopped.

At the end Frazier's face was a mask of lumps. His eyes looked like glass and they were nearly swollen shut. The 31-year-old man simply was finished.

But for a time it looked as if Smokin' Joe might become the third man in history to regain the heavyweight championship.

From the fifth to the 11th rounds, Frazier had the best of it, jolting Ali with lefts and rights to the body and occasional bombs to the head.

Ali desperately tried to find a solution to the relentless pursuit of the man he lost to in the first of their three fights. But Frazier kept charging.

Then, with his title seemingly slipping away, Ali, who has risen so many times in his spectacular and controversial career, went for Frazier's head. And it worked.

At the opening of the 12th round, the 33-year-old champion, who had looked every bit his age in the six previous rounds, drilled six shots to Frazier's head. Then, after Frazier drove him into the ropes, Ali ripped eight more clean shots to Frazier's head and Joe was on his way to his last hurrah.

In the 13th round, Frazier opened with a body attack, but by now his punches were lacking their earlier steam. Ali seemed to sense it.

The champion fired a one-two to Frazier's head and another hard right to the head and then came back with a series of five straight head punches. After a brief pause, Ali buckled Frazier's knees with a left-right to the head.

Ali might have done more damage then, but he slipped and briefly lost the initiative.

But in the 14th round, it was all Ali. Like this: A left-right to the head, a right to the head, a one-two, and after a body punch by Frazier, there was a series of head shots fired with lightning speed that had the challenger reeling around the ring.

It seemed as if Frazier was about to go down. The bell, ending the 14th, saved him from further punishment and at the same time sent the former champion into retirement.

Ali stayed alive to fight another day, as he has so many times before when it looked as if he would be beat. The next one probably will be against George Foreman, from whom he regained the title 11 months ago with a stunning eight-round knockout in Zaire.

Or it could be against Ken Norton, the only man besides Frazier to beat Ali, who has never lost while he held the championship.

Immediately after the fight, Ali told the worldwide audience watching on closed circuit television that he intends to fight Foreman although he earlier had said he would prefer to fight the winner of a Foreman-Norton match.

Then he said, "I want to retire. It's too much work; too painful. I might have a heart attack. I want everyone to know that I'm the greatest fighter of all time."

Ali had to be great on this Philippine morning before a crowd of more than 20,000 at the indoor Philippine Coliseum.

It was the third meeting between Ali and Frazier, and it was every bit as good as the first two and every bit as intense between these bitter rivals. The first two were split—Frazier winning a 15-round decision as champion in 1971 and Ali winning a 12-round non-title decision on Jan. 28, 1974.

At the end of 14 rounds, the Associated Press had it 63-63 with Frazier doing most of his damage from the fifth through the 11th when it appeared that Ali might succumb to the body attack.

The champion's corner was clearly worried during those middle rounds and there wasn't a trace of a smile until Ali found the way to come back.

The three officials did not see the fight as closely as some of the working press. Referee Padilla had it 66-60 for Ali. Judge Alfredo Quiazon had it 67-62 and Larry Nadayag had 66-62, both for Ali. Quite a bit of that margin was built in the last three rounds.

Report 1, AP account, October 1, 1975, p. 17.

**Questions**

*Content/Meaning*

1. Examine the structure of this sports report. Is it arranged essentially into the beginning-middle-end order of a chronicle? What stage of the fight receives the most emphasis? the least?
2. Is there a clear-cut protagonist in this fight story?
3. What is the essential function of paragraph 5? Do you find other paragraphs with a similar function in the story?
4. Do you get the sense, from this report, that more than a heavyweight championship was at stake?
5. Does the reporter at any time treat either fighter as an antihero? Is there a difference in his attitude from that of Montgomery in the preceding report?

*Style*

1. In the second paragraph, the report tells us that this fight "was a war." What sort of figure is the writer using here? Does he elaborate on this figure or return to it elsewhere in the report?


# Reading Selection

Red Smith was universally admired as a sportswriter. He started writing his column in 1945 for the *New York Herald Tribune.* In 1971 he joined *The New York Times*, and his column was syndicated for nationwide distribution. Smith was a stylist; his prose was sparse and muscular. He had the remarkable talent of writing with precision and literary awareness even under the pressure of headlines. The column reprinted here is an admirable example of the Smith style—it is terse, clear, crisp, and direct. He often wrote passages made up of simple, short words ("he walked into the blows that beat him stupid"), though he could also marshall polysyllabic words ("with abandoned, almost joyous, ferocity") and, for yet another change of pace, highly colloquial language ("this swaggering, preening, play-acting slice of theatrical ham"). He was, moreover, the unusual sportswriter: He was not addicted to overstatement. Hence, when he used even such simple adjectives as "good," they had strong force.

## JOE WAS STILL COMING IN

### *Red Smith*

MANILA, Wednesday, Oct. 1—When time has cooled the violent passions of the sweltering day and the definitive history is written of the five-year war between Muhammad Ali and Joe Frazier, the objective historian will remember that Joe was still coming in at the finish. For more than 40 minutes, the former heavyweight champion of the world, who was now the challenger, attacked the two-time champion with abandoned, almost joyous, ferocity. For seven rounds in a row he bludgeoned his man with hooks, hounding him into corners, nailing him to the ropes. And then, when Ali seemed hopelessly beaten, he came on like the good champion he is. In the 12th round, the 13th and all through a cruel 14th, Ali punched the shapeless, grinning mask that pursued him until Eddie Futch could take no more.

After 14 rounds of one of the roughest matches ever fought for the heavyweight championship, Frazier's trainer, Futch, gave up. At his signal, the referee stopped the fight with Ali still champion.

All three Filipino officials had Ali leading on points at the end, but in The New York Times book, Futch snatched defeat from the jaws of victory. On the Times' two scorecards, Frazier had won eight of the first 13 rounds when he walked into the blows that beat him stupid. He lost while winning, yet little Eddie was right to negotiate the surrender. Frazier's $2 million guarantee wasn't enough to compensate him for another round like the last.

So now the saga ended. It began on March 8, 1971, when Ali and Frazier met for the first time, both undefeated as professionals, both with valid claims to the championship, both in the glory and strength of youth. That time Frazier won it all. They fought again on Jan. 28, 1974, when both were ex-champions and Ali got a debatable decision. Today's might have been debatable, too, if a decision had been needed.

It has been a series both men can remember with pride—and pride has been the spur for both. All three meetings were happenings, memorable chapters in the annals of the ring, and in many respects this was the best of the three. It will be some time before anybody knows whether the gross revenue from the live gate, closed-circuit and home television around the world will equal the $20 million drawn for their first encounter, but this day's business in the Philippine Coliseum may have broken all records for an indoor fight. Attendance was estimated at 25,000, with a gate of something like $1.5 million at $333 tops.

If a price can be put on the suffering of brave men, this returned a dollar in pain for every dollar involved. Curiously, the winner's suffering was the greater. Not many men could have stood up under the punishment Ali took from the fifth round through the 11th.

Yet Ali not only endured when he had taken all that Frazier could deliver, but he also had enough to win. Say what one will about this noisy extrovert, this swaggering, preening, play-acting slice of theatrical ham: the man is a gladiator. He was a callow braggart of 22 when Sonny Liston surrendered the title to him 11 years ago. At the ripe age of 33, he is a champion of genuine quality.

He has been saying he would have one more fight, probably with George Foreman, and then retire as the greatest of all time. It is not wise to accept his promises on faith, but he must take his leave some day. When he does, he will be remembered as one of the good ones.

Whatever can be said to Ali's credit must be said with equal emphasis about Joe Frazier. This man was a good champion in his own right. He is the best man Ali ever fought, an opponent who searched Ali's inner depths and brought out qualities Ali never had to reveal to any other man.

It was Joe, rather than Muhammad, who made this a great fight. In the early rounds, Ali made half-hearted attempts to strut the posture the way he has done against men like Joe Bugner and Chuck Wepner, but Frazier's persistent advance brooked no such nonsense. Ali's faster hands and circling retreat held Joe off for a while. Joe was remorseless, though, and single-minded.

He brushed pawing gloves aside, rolled in under punches, bore straight ahead and slugged, and by the fifth round he was getting the message across. It was hook, hook, hook—into the belly to draw Ali's hands down, then up to the head against the ropes.

He beat the everlasting whey out of Ali. His attack would have reduced another man to putty. The guy in the white trunks was not another man. He was the champion, and this time he proved it.

From *The New York Times,* October 1, 1975.

## Questions

*Content/Meaning*
1. Compare and contrast Red Smith's account of "The Thrilla in Manila" with the AP report. Do they essentially provide the same emphasis?
2. Is there a protagonist in Smith's account? Does he seem to like one fighter better than the other?

*Style*
1. Sportswriters have a reputation for the use of *clichés,* worn-out, over-used, and hackneyed expressions like "twin bill," "throwing in the towel," or "splitting the uprights." Even Red Smith was not immune from writing the cliché: e.g. "the annals of the ring" (paragraph 5). In paragraph 12, Smith uses the phrase "beat the everlasting whey out of Ali." Do you consider that phrase a cliché? Have you heard it or a variant of it before? Is Smith here using the expression for humorous effect? How about the phrase "would have reduced another man to putty"? How effective, considering the cliché, is the last paragraph?

2. At the end of the first paragraph, Smith comments, "Ali punched the shapeless, grinning mask that pursued him until Eddie Futch could take no more." In plainer language, this sentence says, "Ali punched Frazier, who was stalking him, until Frazier's trainer surrendered." Do you consider Smith's sentence more effective than our paraphrase? If so, why? How effective are other sentences or passages in the column?

# Reading Selection

We include the selection that follows because it extends the subject of prizefighting beyond the sports columns. It is, in many respects, a more complex narrative than any we have read so far, both in treatment of subject and in mode of presentation.

The welterweight championship fight between Emile Griffith and Benny Paret is probably not one that most people remember, not even fairly committed sports fans. Yet it was a notable fight for reasons you will discover as you read Norman Mailer's brilliant account of it. Mailer, one of the outstanding prose writers of our times, has often antagonized readers because he is passionately opinionated. Boxing, which allows him latitude to express his *macho* views, is a favorite topic of his; yet he is by no means uncritical of it. He is a great admirer of Muhammad Ali—an interest he pursued in his book *The Fight,* covering the Ali-Foreman championship match in Zaire in 1974.

As you read the following selection, note how effectively Mailer has set up his account to give it maximum suspense. Note also that this is far more a commentary about the brutalities of boxing, both psychologically and physically, than any other piece you have read in this chapter. Mailer is seriously concerned here with a number of important issues that transcend sports and have to do with human nature in general.

## GRIFFITH VS. PARET

### *Norman Mailer*

On the afternoon of the night Emile Griffith and Benny Paret were to fight a third time for the welterweight championship, there was murder in both camps. "I hate that kind of guy," Paret had said earlier to Pete Hamill about Griffith. "A fighter's got to look and talk and act like a man." One of the Broadway gossip columnists had run an item about Griffith a few days before. His girl friend saw it and said to Griffith, "Emile, I didn't know about you being that way." So Griffith hit her. So he said. Now at the weigh-in that morning, Paret had insulted Griffith irrevocably, touching him on the buttocks, while making a few more remarks about his manhood. They almost had their fight on the scales.

The accusation of homosexuality arouses a major passion in many men; they spend their lives resisting it with a biological force. There is a kind of man who spends every night of his life getting drunk in a bar, he rants, he brawls, he ends in a small rumble on the street; women say, "For God's sakes, he's homosexual. Why doesn't he just turn queer and get his suffering over with." Yet men protect him. It is because he is choosing not to become homosexual. It was put best by Sartre who said that a homosexual is a man who practices homosexuality. A man who does not, is not homosexual— he is entitled to the dignity of his choice. He is entitled to the fact that he chose not to become homosexual, and is paying presumably his price.

The rage in Emile Griffith was extreme. I was at the fight that night. I had never seen a fight like it. It was scheduled for fifteen rounds, but they fought without stopping from the bell which began the round to the bell which ended it, and then they fought after the bell, sometimes for as much as fifteen seconds before the referee could force them apart.

Paret was a Cuban, a proud club fighter who had become welterweight champion because of his unusual ability to take a punch. His style of fighting was to take three punches to the head in order to give back two. At the end of ten rounds, he would still be bouncing, his opponent would have a headache. But in the last two years, over the fifteen-round fights, he had started to take some bad maulings.

This fight had its turns. Griffith won most of the early rounds, but Paret knocked Griffith down in the sixth. Griffith had trouble getting up, but made it, came alive and was dominating Paret again before the round was over. Then Paret began to wilt. In the middle of the eighth round, after a clubbing punch had turned his back to Griffith, Paret walked three disgusted steps away, showing his hindquarters. For a champion, he took much too long to turn back around. It was the first hint of weakness Paret had ever shown, and it must have inspired a particular shame, because he fought the rest of the fight as if he were seeking to demonstrate that he could take more punishment than any man alive. In the twelfth, Griffith caught him. Paret got trapped in a corner. Trying to duck away, his left arm and his head became tangled on the wrong side of the top rope. Griffith was in like a cat ready to rip the life out of a huge boxed rat. He hit him eighteen right hands in a row, an act which took perhaps three or four seconds, Griffith making a pent-up whimpering sound all the while he attacked, the right hand whipping like a piston rod which had broken through the crankcase, or like a baseball bat demolishing a pumpkin. I was sitting in the second row of that corner—they were not ten feet away from me, and like everybody else, I was hypnotized. I had never seen one man hit another so hard and so many times. Over the referee's face came a look of woe as if some spasm had passed its way through him, and then he leaped on Griffith to pull him away. It was the act of a brave man. Griffith was uncontrollable. His trainer leaped into the ring, his manager, his cut man, there were four people holding Griffith, but he was off on an orgy, he had left the Garden, he was back on a hoodlum's street. If he had been able to break loose from his handlers and the referee, he would have jumped Paret to the floor and whaled on him there.

And Paret? Paret died on his feet. As he took those eighteen punches something happened to everyone who was in psychic range of the event. Some part of his death reached out to us. One felt it hover in the air. He was still standing in the ropes, trapped as he had been before, he gave some little half-smile of regret, as if he were saying, "I didn't know I was going to die just yet," and then, his head leaning back but still erect, his death came to breathe about him. He began to pass away. As he passed, so his limbs descended beneath him, and he sank slowly to the floor. He went down more slowly than any fighter had ever gone down, he went down like a large ship which turns on end and slides second by second into its grave. As he went down, the sound of Griffith's punches echoed in the mind like a heavy ax in the distance chopping into a wet log.

Paret lay on the ground, quivering gently, a small froth on his mouth. The house doctor jumped into the ring. He knelt. He pried Paret's eyelid open. He looked at the eyeball staring out. He let the lid snap shut. He reached into his satchel, took out a needle, jabbed Paret with a stimulant. Paret's back rose in a high arch. He writhed in real agony. They were calling him back from death. One wanted to cry out, "Leave the man alone. Let him die." But they saved Paret long enough to take him to a hospital where he lingered for days. He was in coma. He never came out of it. If he lived, he would have been a vegetable. His brain was smashed. But they held him in life for a week, they fed him chemicals, and made exploratory operations into his skull, and fed details of his condition to The Goat. And The Goat kicked clods of mud all over the place, and spoke harshly of prohibiting boxing. There was shock in the land. Children had seen the fight on television. There were editorials, gloomy forecasts that the Game was dead. The managers and the prizefighters got together. Gently, in thick, depressed hypocrisies, they tried to defend their sport.

From Norman Mailer, *The Presidential
Papers* (Baltimore: Penguin, 1968), pp.
263-65.

## Questions

*Content/Meaning*
1. The account by Mailer has a good deal to say about rage and about pride, though the latter is never mentioned. There is the sort of pride that is good, as pride in one's workmanship, and the sort that is bad because it isolates us and makes us defensive, angry, unreasonable.

Obviously, Mailer was concerned with the latter sort. How does it come up? How important is it as a way of explaining the death of Benny Paret?

2. One gets the sense that there is something inhuman about Emile Griffith in Mailer's account of him. Are we meant to hate him for what he did? to regard him as a madman? to see him as an ordinary human being who, being goaded, went berserk? or to respond to him as a dehumanized fighting machine?

3. Does Mailer use this incident as an argument for the abolition of boxing?

*Style*

1. Mailer is masterful in his use of figures of speech. What are the most prominent metaphors and similes he uses in this selection? What is their impact?

2. Speaking of the slumping figure of Benny Paret, Mailer observes, "some part of his death reached out to us." How does Mailer develop this phrase?

3. Examine closely the sentence structure of the last paragraph. How would you describe it and evaluate its effectiveness?

## Exercises and Assignments

1. Using the two reports of the March 9, 1971 Ali vs. Frazier fight printed in this chapter, write your own narrative account of the fight in approximately 300 words. Set out deliberately to make one or the other fighter your protagonist. You may embellish the story in whatever way you please as long as you hold to the basic facts you now know about the fight (i.e., you cannot make Ali the winner).

2. Choose a live sports event other than boxing—either an event on television or one that you can watch in person—and write a narrative report of it in less than 500 words. In a short paragraph accompanying the report, indicate for what audience and what specific newspaper or magazine your story is intended.

3. Choose a sports story from a magazine or local paper that has a heavy slant toward one or another of the competitors or teams. You may, if you wish, go back in time and select an article from *The New York Times* (or any other newspaper for which your library has a backlog) of an event from the past. Xerox the article. Then rewrite it, slanting it toward one or the other of the competitors or teams. To complete this assignment you may need to gain some additional background information. You should, therefore, read other articles and columns related to the event you have chosen.

4. Select a sporting event from the past in which a violent, unexpected outcome occurred, as in the fight between Griffith and Paret. Take notes on newspaper and magazine reports of the event, and write your own account. At the end of the paper list articles you consulted by giving the name of the author, the title in quotation marks, the name of the journal or newspaper underlined, volume number of any periodicals, date of publication, and page number(s). You should bear in mind that these are background readings; they should not be used as direct sources. The writing must be all your own, but you are free to rely on the articles for facts about the event. You may give your account whatever emphasis you like.

5. Using the last Ali-Frazier fight, the "thrilla in Manilla," as an example, research the background of a sports story. You may choose a sporting event that is about to happen or one that has already taken place. Try to focus on one or more important background issues that, when known in detail, will add either suspense or depth of understanding to the unfolding of the contest proper. Read about the event in various appropriate sources such as *The New York Times,* the news weeklies, or the sports magazines, and take notes of relevant information. Then write a 500-word analysis with a clearly developed thesis and relevant supporting paragraphs, concluding with a paragraph that directly relates the issue to the contest.

6. Sports reporting often develops a special angle. For example, the *Sports Illustrated* story of the fight between Ali and Patterson begins by stating its angle: "He was seeking to humiliate Floyd Patterson, but Cassius Clay, known to his fellow Black Muslims as Muhammad Ali, only succeeded in ennobling him." It is clear from this introductory sentence that the sports report we are about to read will not be satisfied in giving simply a straightforward account of the fight. Virtually every sports story has an angle. Select a major sports story from your local or college newspaper, describe the angle, and demonstrate how it was developed. Turn in a xerox copy of the sports story with your paper, which should not exceed 500 words.

7. Choose one sports columnist either from a newspaper or a magazine and read from five to ten of his columns. Take notes or make xerox copies and mark them up with your reactions. After having absorbed the columnist's approach and style, write an essay on his narrative voice, the audience he seems to be addressing, and his techniques as a "storyteller." Be sure to support your generalizations with facts and quotations.

# 12 THE USES OF NARRATION

In the preceding chapter we focused on narrative structure, including the development of conflict between the protagonist and antagonist and the importance of design in telling a story. In this chapter we look at a small sampling of narratives to see how writers use various forms of narratives to make a point or bring enlightenment to their readers. The selections in this chapter, excluding Grace Paley's short story, essentially use narrative as a means to an end; that is, they do not simply tell a story to engage the reader's interest but make use of narrative to explain an event or support an opinion.

Narrative is embedded in many different forms of writing. A straightforward news report can either be a story or contain one. Story can be used as illustration or as substance in practically any kind of expository writing. It can be found in editorial columns, historical essays, biography or autobiography, satire, and background reports within a newspaper or a magazine. By extension, narrative is also an important element in all kinds of reading and writing that you do in the college classroom. Textbooks in such diverse fields as art, philosophy, history, religion, sociology, psychology, among many others, frequently rely on narrative to cover their subjects. So, inevitably, will you as a writer, whether in the composition classroom or in others, to illustrate points or lend interest to your development of a subject.

We have chosen the following illustrations of narrative for their inherent interest, their diversity in form, and the specific statements they make about society or life in general. Thus, while Chapter 10, the first chapter in this unit, concentrated on characterization (especially of the first-person narrator), and Chapter 11 focused on plot, the point of emphasis here is the theme or general point that a story may support or develop. The selections in this chapter provide you with examples of narrative and its various uses. They should also serve to guide you in the discovery of narrative in your daily reading.

# Reading Selection

What follows is the opening of an article by Nat Hentoff in the *Village Voice*, a weekly tabloid published in New York City. The "Village" in the title refers to Greenwich (pronounced "Grenitch") Village, a section of lower Manhattan noted for its population of artists and intellectuals. The *Village Voice* is consequently a most unusual newspaper: It puts emphasis on criticism of political and social issues and events and on reviews of the arts. It contains very little neighborhood news, though it does contain many local ads, and it is read widely not only in New York City but nationally. Its point of view is often that of minorities and the counterculture. Nat Hentoff is a weekly commentator in the paper.

## RUSSELL, THE BEE EXPERT

### *Nat Hentoff*

*In every child who is born, under no matter what
circumstances, and of no matter what parents,
the potentiality of the human race is born again.*

James Agee, *Let Us Now Praise Famous Men*

In 1966, while reporting on an elementary school on the Upper West Side, I got to know a fair number of the kids, the majority of whom were black and variously Hispanic. To say that one of them, a black fifth-grader, was a slow reader was to stretch euphemism to its outer limits. Yet he was one hell of a talker, and, in an argument, could reveal a lethally logical mind.

Other assignments kept me away from the school for about a year and a half, but I came by a week before summer vacation to check out the scholars' progress. The principal, long since retired, was actually fond of children, which is why he held them, as best he could, to high standards. I asked him about the slow reader.

"No more," the principal said. "He found an interest. He found an obsession. Bees. Russell knows more about bees than anyone in this school and, I'm willing to bet, more than anyone on the whole West Side." Russell had seen something on television about bees, and, the next morning, had charged into the school library which in those days had an honest-to-God professional librarian, who gave Russell everything she had on those assiduous hymenopterous insects.

Having soon exhausted the resources of the school library, Russell became a regular patron of the branch public library six blocks from his home. It was open six days and four nights a week then, and Russell, when not in school, was more often there than not. When he had absorbed the branch's entire store of beesworks, a librarian, fearful that he might get overwhelmed by the complexities of the research caverns in the main library downtown, enabled Russell to get books from the main library sent to him at his neighbor-hood branch.

Russell was not only becoming one hell of a reader, but the eclat he received in school as an expert on bees gave him the confidence to branch out. The confidence to know, at last, that he was not dumb.

We have deliberately refrained from using the actual title of the article in order not to give away the subject that Hentoff introduced with this illustration. What point, do you suppose, he will go on to make? Are there several possibilities? Try to sketch out in your mind what use you could make of the story.

Here is how Hentoff continues:

Russell is lucky he was not born later. There is no professional librarian in that elementary school now. Although a library is technically required by law in each elementary school, a professional librarian is not. And so, in a good many districts, that "luxury" was one of the first dispensed with when, in the mid-1970s, budget cuts began to land disproportionately on city services for children. There is a teacher in that library now, sometimes, and the collection has stagnated. Books, after all, are more and more expensive these days.

If he were in the sixth grade at his old school now, Russell could still, of course, go to his branch library. But he would not be likely to find it open. Most of the branches are open three or four days a week, if that, and often at hours that would not fit Russell's availability. Some are only open *12 hours a week*. And staff cuts have been so severe—at least a third are gone—that Russell might well not find a librarian with the time to nurture his interest in bees and, not incidentally, in reading.

From "Our Vanishing Libraries," *Village Voice*, February 4, 1981, p. 8.

## Exercise and Assignment

1. Choose an issue of a mass-circulation magazine like *Esquire, Saturday Review, Harper's, New Republic, Atlantic Monthly, New York Magazine, Playboy,* or *The New Yorker* and glance through the openings of feature articles. Look for one that begins with a narrative illustration. Then read the article and be prepared to discuss how the illustration relates to the rest of the article.

2. Write an expository paper on a topic of your choice using an illustration as your introduction.

## Reading Selection

The essay that follows is filled with narratives. It appeared originally in *The New Yorker,* probably the most literate and sophisticated mass-market popular magazine published in America. Over the years, *The New Yorker* has assembled a group of exceptional staff writers who contribute articles irregularly but often. John McPhee is one of these writers, and he is considered by many to rank among the most talented of our contemporary essayists. He has a special knack for finding interesting and unusual topics to write about, including oranges in Florida, the pine barrens of south-central New Jersey, profiles of the headmaster of an eastern prep school or a former director of the Metropolitan Museum, and the semifinals in a world tennis match. What is especially unusual and refreshing in McPhee's style is his arrangement of facts, observations, and historical narratives into multitiered and deeply introspective essays. Many of his magazine articles have been reprinted as books.

In "The Search for Marvin Gardens," McPhee examines a deteriorating seaside resort, Atlantic City, in the framework of the game Monopoly, whose inventor borrowed the street names of Atlantic City to identify the properties that must be bought by players in the game. The result is a finely woven fabric of game and reality, as well as fiction and fact, forming an essay that makes some trenchant observations about the history and decay of an American resort city. Bear in mind that McPhee wrote this essay in 1972 before New Jersey legalized gambling in Atlantic City and before the construction of luxury hotels and casinos. The poverty and decay linger on, however, and McPhee's essay may be even more appropriate and meaningful now than it was when he wrote it. When you read it, pay particular attention to the uses to which McPhee puts narrative.

### THE SEARCH FOR MARVIN GARDENS

#### *John McPhee*

Go. I roll the dice—a six and a two. Through the air I move my token, the flatiron, to Vermont Avenue, where dog packs range.

The dogs are moving (some are limping) through ruins, rubble, fire damage, open garbage. Doorways are gone. Lath is visible in the crumbling walls of the buildings. The street sparkles with shattered glass. I have never seen, anywhere, so many broken windows. A sign—"Slow, Children at Play"—has been bent backward by an automobile. At the lighthouse, the dogs turn up Pacific and disappear. George Meade, Army engineer, built the lighthouse—brick upon brick, six hundred thousand bricks, to reach up high enough to throw a beam twenty miles over the sea. Meade, seven years later, saved the Union at Gettysburg.

I buy Vermont Avenue for $100. My opponent is a tall, shadowy figure, across from me, but I know him well, and I know his game like a favorite tune. If he can, he will always go for the quick kill. And when it is foolish to go for the quick kill he will be foolish. On the whole, though, he is a master assessor of percentages. It is a mistake to underestimate him. His eleven carries his top hat to St. Charles Place, which he buys for $140.

The sidewalks of St. Charles Place have been cracked to shards by through-growing weeds. There are no buildings. Mansions, hotels once stood here. A few street lamps now drop cones of light on broken glass and vacant space behind a chain-link fence that some great machine has in places bent to the ground. Five plane trees—in full summer leaf, flecking the light— are all that live on St. Charles Place.

Block upon block, gradually, we are cancelling each other out—in the blues, the lavenders, the oranges, the greens. My opponent follows a plan of his own devising. I use the Hornblower & Weeks opening and the Zuricher defense. The first game draws tight, will soon finish. In 1971, a group of people in Racine, Wisconsin, played for seven hundred and sixty-eight hours. A game begun a month later in Danville, California, lasted eight hundred and twenty hours. These are official records, and they stun us. We have been playing for eight minutes. It amazes us that Monopoly is thought of as a long game. It is possible to play to a complete, absolute, and final conclusion in less than fifteen minutes, all within the rules as written. My opponent and I have done so thousands of times. No wonder we are sitting across from each other now in this best-of-seven series for the international singles championship of the world.

On Illinois Avenue, three men lean out from second-story windows. A girl is coming down the street. She wears dungarees and a bright-red shirt, has ample breasts and a Hadendoan Afro, a black halo, two feet in diameter. Ice rattles in the glasses in the hands of the men.
"Hey, sister!"
"Come on up!"
She looks up, looks from one to another to the other, looks them flat in the eye.
"What for?" she says, and she walks on.

I buy Illinois for $240. It solidifies my chances, for I already own Kentucky and Indiana. My opponent pales. If he had landed first on Illinois, the game would have been over then and there, for he has houses built on Boardwalk and Park Place, we share the railroads equally, and we have cancelled each other everywhere else. We never trade.

In 1852, R. B. Osborne, an immigrant Englishman, civil engineer, surveyed the route of a railroad line that would run from Camden to Absecon
Island, in New Jersey, traversing the state from the Delaware River to the
barrier beaches of the sea. He then sketched in the plan of a "bathing village"
that would surround the eastern terminus of the line. His pen flew glibly,
framing and naming spacious avenues parallel to the shore—Mediterranean,
Baltic, Oriental, Ventnor—and narrower transsecting avenues: North Carolina, Pennsylvania, Vermont, Connecticut, States, Virginia, Tennessee, New
York, Kentucky, Indiana, Illinois. The place as a whole had no name, so
when he had completed the plan Osborne wrote in large letters over the
ocean, "Atlantic City." No one ever challenged the name, or the names of
Osborne's streets. Monopoly was invented in the early nineteen-thirties by
Charles B. Darrow, but Darrow was only transliterating what Osborne had
created. The railroads, crucial to any player, were the making of Atlantic
City. After the rails were down, houses and hotels burgeoned from Mediterranean and Baltic to New York and Kentucky. Properties—building lots—
sold for as little as six dollars apiece and as much as a thousand dollars.
The original investors in the railroads and the real estate called themselves
the Camden & Atlantic Land Company. Reverently, I repeat their names:
Dwight Bell, William Coffin, John DaCosta, Daniel Deal, William Fleming,
Andrew Hay, Joseph Porter, Jonathan Pitney, Samuel Richards—founders,
fathers, forerunners, archetypical masters of the quick kill.

My opponent and I are now in a deep situation of classical Monopoly.
The torsion is almost perfect—Boardwalk and Park Place versus the brilliant
reds. His cash position is weak, though, and if I escape him now he may
fade. I land on Luxury Tax, contiguous to but in sanctuary from his power.
I have four houses on Indiana. He lands there. He concedes.

Indiana Avenue was the address of the Brighton Hotel, gone now. The
Brighton was exclusive—a word that no longer has retail value in the city.
If you arrived by automobile and tried to register at the Brighton, you were
sent away. Brighton-class people came in private railroad cars. Brighton-
class people had other private railroad cars for their horses—dawn rides
on the firm sand at water's edge, skirts flying. Colonel Anthony J. Drexel
Biddle—the sort of name that would constrict throats in Philadelphia—lived,
much of the year, in the Brighton.

Colonel Sanders' fried chicken is on Kentucky Avenue. So is Clifton's
Club Harlem, with the Sepia Revue and the Sepia Follies, featuring the Honey
Bees, the Fashions, and the Lords.

My opponent and I, many years ago, played 2,428 games of Monopoly in a single season. He was then a recent graduate of the Harvard Law School, and he was working for a downtown firm, looking up law. Two people we knew—one from Chase Manhattan, the other from Morgan, Stanley—tried to get into the game, but after a few rounds we found that they were not in the conversation and we sent them home. Monopoly should always be *mano a mano* anyway. My opponent won 1,199 games, and so did I. Thirty were ties. He was called into the Army, and we stopped just there. Now, in Game 2 of the series, I go immediately to jail, and again to jail while my opponent seines property. He is dumbfoundingly lucky. He wins in twelve minutes.

Visiting hours are daily, eleven to two; Sunday, eleven to one; evenings, six to nine. "NO MINORS, NO FOOD, Immediate Family Only Allowed in Jail." All this above a blue steel door in a blue cement wall in the windowless interior of the basement of the city hall. The desk sergeant sits opposite the door to the jail. In a cigar box in front of him are pills in every color, a banquet of fruit salad an inch and a half deep—leapers, co-pilots, footballs, truck drivers, peanuts, blue angels, yellow jackets, redbirds, rainbows. Near the desk are two soldiers, waiting to go through the blue door. They are about eighteen years old. One of them is trying hard to light a cigarette. His wrists are in steel cuffs. A military policeman waits, too. He is a year or so older than the soldiers, taller, studious in appearance, gentle, fat. On a bench against a wall sits a good-looking girl in slacks. The blue door rattles, swings heavily open. A turnkey stands in the doorway. "Don't you guys kill yourselves back there now," says the sergeant to the soldiers.
"One kid, he overdosed himself about ten and a half hours ago," says the M.P.
The M.P., the soldiers, the turnkey, and the girl on the bench are white. The sergeant is black. "If you take off the handcuffs, take off the belts," says the sergeant to the M.P. "I don't want them hanging themselves back there." The door shuts and its tumblers move. When it opens again, five minutes later, a young white man in sandals and dungarees and a blue polo shirt emerges. His hair is in a ponytail. He has no beard. He grins at the good-looking girl. She rises, joins him. The sergeant hands him a manila envelope. From it he removes his belt and a small notebook. He borrows a pencil, makes an entry in the notebook. He is out of jail, free. What did he do? He offended Atlantic City in some way. He spent a night in the jail. In the nineteen-thirties, men visiting Atlantic City went to jail, directly to jail, did not pass Go, for appearing in topless bathing suits on the beach. A city statute requiring all men to wear full-length bathing suits was not

seriously challenged until 1937, and the first year in which a man could legally go bare-chested on the beach was 1940.

Game 3. After seventeen minutes, I am ready to begin construction on overpriced and sluggish Pacific, North Carolina, and Pennsylvania. Nothing else being open, opponent concedes.

The physical profile of streets perpendicular to the shore is something like a playground slide. It begins in the high skyline of Boardwalk hotels, plummets into warrens of "side-avenue" motels, crosses Pacific, slopes through church missions, convalescent homes, burlesque houses, rooming houses, and liquor stores, crosses Atlantic, and runs level through the bombed-out ghetto as far—Baltic, Mediterranean—as the eye can see. North Carolina Avenue, for example, is flanked at its beach end by the Chalfonte and the Haddon Hall (908 rooms, air-conditioned), where, according to one biographer, John Philip Sousa (1854–1932) first played when he was twenty-two, insisting, even then, that everyone call him by his entire name. Behind these big hotels, motels—Barbizon, Catalina—crouch. Between Pacific and Atlantic is an occasional house from 1910—wooden porch, wooden mullions, old yellow paint—and two churches, a package store, a strip show, a dealer in fruits and vegetables. Then, beyond Atlantic Avenue, North Carolina moves on into the vast ghetto, the bulk of the city, and it looks like Metz in 1919, Cologne in 1944. Nothing has actually exploded. It is not bomb damage. It is deep and complex decay. Roofs are off. Bricks are scattered in the street. People sit on porches, six deep, at nine on a Monday morning. When they go off to wait in unemployment lines, they wait sometimes two hours. Between Mediterranean and Baltic runs a chain-link fence, enclosing rubble. A patrol car sits idling by the curb. In the back seat is a German shepherd. A sign on the fence says, "Beware of Bad Dogs."

Mediterranean and Baltic are the principal avenues of the ghetto. Dogs are everywhere. A pack of seven passes me. Block after block, there are three-story brick row houses. Whole segments of them are abandoned, a thousand broken windows. Some parts are intact, occupied. A mattress lies in the street, soaking in a pool of water. Wet stuffing is coming out of the mattress. A postman is having a rye and a beer in the Plantation Bar at nine-fifteen in the morning. I ask him idly if he knows where Marvin Gardens is. He does not. "HOOKED AND NEED HELP? CONTACT N.A.R.C.O." "REVIVAL NOW GOING ON, CONDUCTED BY REVEREND H. HENDERSON OF TEXAS." These are signboards on Mediterranean and Baltic. The second one is upside down and leans against a boarded-up window of the Faith Temple Church of God in Christ. There is an old peeling poster on a warehouse wall showing a figure in an electric chair. "The Black Panther Manifesto" is the title of the poster, and its message is, or was, that "the fascists have already decided in advance to murder Chairman Bobby Seale in the electric chair." I pass an old woman who carries a bucket. She wears blue sneakers, worn through. Her feet spill out. She wears red socks, rolled at the knees. A white handkerchief, spread over her head, is knotted at the corners. Does she know where Marvin Gardens is? "I sure don't know," she says, setting down the bucket. "I sure don't know. I've heard of it somewhere, but I just can't say where." I walk on, through a block of shattered glass. The glass crunches underfoot like coarse sand. I remember when I first came here—a long train ride from Trenton, long ago, games of poker in the train—to play basketball against Atlantic City. We were half black, they were all black. We scored forty points, they scored eighty, or something like it. What I remember most is that they had glass backboards—glittering, pendent, expensive glass backboards, a rarity then in high schools, even in colleges, the only ones we played on all year.

I turn on Pennsylvania, and start back toward the sea. The windows of the Hotel Astoria, on Pennsylvania near Baltic, are boarded up. A sheet of unpainted plywood is the door, and in it is a triangular peephole that now frames an eye. The plywood door opens. A man answers my question. Rooms there are six, seven, and ten dollars a week. I thank him for the information and move on, emerging from the ghetto at the Catholic Daughters of America Women's Guest House, between Atlantic and Pacific. Between Pacific and the Boardwalk are the blinking vacancy signs of the Aristocrat and Colton Manor motels. Pennsylvania terminates at the Sheraton-Seaside— thirty-two dollars a day, ocean corner. I take a walk on the Boardwalk and into the Holiday Inn (twenty-three stories). A guest is registering. "You reserved for Wednesday, and this is Monday," the clerk tells him. "But that's all right. We have *plenty* of rooms." The clerk is very young, female, and has soft brown hair that hangs below her waist. Her superior kicks her.

He is a middle-aged man with red spiderwebs in his face. He is jacketed and tied. He takes her aside. "Don't say 'plenty,' " he says. "Say 'You are fortunate, sir. We have room available.' "

The face of the young woman turns sour. "We have all the rooms you need," she says to the customer, and, to her superior, "How's that?"

Game 4. My opponent's luck has become abrasive. He has Boardwalk and Park Place, and has sealed the board.

Darrow was a plumber. He was, specifically, a radiator repairman who lived in Germantown, Pennsylvania. His first Monopoly board was a sheet of linoleum. On it he placed houses and hotels that he had carved from blocks of wood. The game he thus invented was brilliantly conceived, for it was an uncannily exact reflection of the business milieu at large. In its depth, range, and subtlety, in its luck-skill ratio, in its sense of infrastructure and socio-economic parameters, in its philosophical characteristics, it reached to the profundity of the financial community. It was as scientific as the stock market. It suggested the manner and means through which an underdeveloped world had been developed. It was chess at Wall Street level. "Advance token to the nearest Railroad and pay owner twice the rental to which he is otherwise entitled. If Railroad is unowned, you may buy it from the Bank. Get out of Jail, free. Advance token to nearest Utility. If unowned, you may buy it from Bank. If owned, throw dice and pay owner a total ten times the amount thrown. You are assessed for street repairs: $40 per house, $115 per hotel. Pay poor tax of $15. Go to Jail. Go directly to Jail. Do not pass Go. Do not collect $200."

The turnkey opens the blue door. The turnkey is known to the inmates as Sidney K. Above his desk are ten closed-circuit-TV screens—assorted viewpoints of the jail. There are three cellblocks—men, women, juvenile boys. Six days is the average stay. Showers twice a week. The steel doors and the equipment that operates them were made in San Antonio. The prisoners sleep on bunks of butcher block. There are no mattresses. There are three prisoners to a cell. In winter, it is cold in here. Prisoners burn newspapers to keep warm. Cell corners are black with smudge. The jail is three years old. The men's block echoes with chatter. The man in the cell nearest Sidney K. is pacing. His shirt is covered with broad stains of blood. The block for juvenile boys is, by contrast, utterly silent—empty corridor, empty cells. There is only one prisoner. He is small and black and appears to be thirteen. He says he is sixteen and that he has been alone in here for three days.

"Why are you here? What did you do?"

"I hit a jitney driver."

The series stands at three all. We have split the fifth and sixth games. We are scrambling for property. Around the board we fairly fly. We move so fast because we do our own banking and search our own deeds. My opponent grows tense.

Ventnor Avenue, a street of delicatessens and doctors' offices, is leafy with plane trees and hydrangeas, the city flower. Water Works is on the mainland. The water comes over in submarine pipes. Electric Company gets power from across the state, on the Delaware River, in Deepwater. States Avenue, now a wasteland like St. Charles, once had gardens running down the middle of the street, a horse-drawn trolley, private homes. States Avenue was as exclusive as the Brighton. Only an apartment house, a small motel, and the All Wars Memorial Building—monadnocks spaced widely apart— stand along States Avenue now. Pawnshops, convalescent homes, and the Paradise Soul Saving Station are on Virginia Avenue. The soul-saving station is pink, orange, and yellow. In the windows flanking the door of the Virginia Money Loan Office are Nikons, Polaroids, Yashicas, Sony TVs, Underwood typewriters, Singer sewing machines, and pictures of Christ. On the far side of town, beside a single track and locked up most of the time, is the new railroad station, a small hut made of glazed firebrick, all that is left of the lines that built the city. An authentic phrenologist works on New York Avenue close to Frank's Extra Dry Bar and a church where the sermon today is "Death in the Pot." The church is of pink brick, has blue and amber windows and two red doors. St. James Place, narrow and twisting, is lined with boarding houses that have wooden porches on each of three stories, suggesting a New Orleans made of salt-bleached pine. In a vacant lot on Tennessee is a white Ford station wagon stripped to the chassis. The windows are smashed. A plastic Clorox bottle sits on the driver's seat. The wind has pressed newspaper against the chain-link fence around the lot. Atlantic Avenue, the city's principal thoroughfare, could be seventeen American Main Streets placed end to end—discount vitamins and Vienna Corset shops, movie theatres, shoe stores, and funeral homes. The Boardwalk is made of yellow pine and Douglas fir, soaked in pentachlorophenol. Down-beach, it reaches far beyond the city. Signs everywhere—on windows, lamp-posts, trash baskets—proclaim "Bienvenue Canadiens!" The salt air is full of Canadian French. In the Claridge Hotel, on Park Place, I ask a clerk if she knows where Marvin Gardens is. She says, "Is it a floral shop?" I ask a cabdriver, parked outside. He says, "Never heard of it." Park Place is one block long, Pacific to Boardwalk. On the roof of the Claridge is the Solarium, the highest point in town—panoramic view of the ocean, the bay, the saltwater ghetto. I look down at the rooftops of the side-avenue motels and into swimming pools. There are hundreds of people around the rooftop pools, sunbathing, reading—many more people than are on the beach. Walls, windows, and a block of sky are all that is visible from these pools—no sand, no sea. The pools are craters, and with the people around them they are countersunk into the motels.

The seventh, and final, game is ten minutes old and I have hotels on Oriental, Vermont, and Connecticut. I have Tennessee and St. James. I have North Carolina and Pacific. I have Boardwalk, Atlantic, Ventnor, Illinois, Indiana. My fingers are forming a "V." I have mortgaged most of these properties in order to pay for others, and I have mortgaged the others to pay for the hotels. I have seven dollars. I will pay off the mortgages and build my reserves with income from the three hotels. My cash position may be low, but I feel like a rocket in an underground silo. Meanwhile, if I could just go to jail for a time I could pause there, wait there, until my opponent, in his inescapable rounds, pays the rates of my hotels. Jail, at times, is the strategic place to be. I roll boxcars from the Reading and move the flatiron to Community Chest. "Go to Jail. Go directly to Jail."

The prisoners, of course, have no pens and no pencils. They take paper napkins, roll them tight as crayons, char the ends with matches, and write on the walls. The things they write are not entirely idiomatic; for example, "In God We Trust." All is in carbon. Time is required in the writing. "Only humanity could know of such pain." "God So Loved the World." "There is no greater pain than life itself." In the women's block now, there are six blacks, giggling, and a white asleep in red shoes. She is drunk. The others are pushers, prostitutes, an auto thief, a burglar caught with pistol in purse. A sixteen-year-old accused of murder was in here last week. These words are written on the wall of a now empty cell: "Laying here I see two bunks about six inches thick, not counting the one I'm laying on, which is hard as brick. No cushion for my back. No pillow for my head. Just a couple scratchy blankets which is best to use it's said. I wake up in the morning so shivery and cold, waiting and waiting till I am told the food is coming. It's on its way. It's not worth waiting for, but I eat it anyway. I know one thing when they set me free I'm gonna be good if it kills me."

How many years must a game be played to produce an Anthony J. Drexel Biddle and chestnut geldings on the beach? About half a century was the original answer, from the first railroad to Biddle at his peak. Biddle, at his peak, hit an Atlantic City streetcar conductor with his fist, laid him out with one punch. This increased Biddle's legend. He did not go to jail. While John Philip Sousa led his band along the Boardwalk playing "The Stars and Stripes Forever" and Jack Dempsey ran up and down in training for his fight with Gene Tunney, the city crossed the high curve of its parabola. Al Capone held conventions here—upstairs with his sleeves rolled, apportioning among his lieutenant governors the states of the Eastern seaboard. The natural history of an American resort proceeds from Indians to French Canadians via Biddles and Capones. French Canadians, whatever they may be at home, are Visigoths here. Bienvenue Visigoths!

My opponent plods along incredibly well. He has got his fourth railroad, and patiently, unbelievably, he has picked up my potential winners until he has blocked me everywhere but Marvin Gardens. He has avoided, in the fifty-dollar zoning, my increasingly petty hotels. His cash flow swells. His railroads are costing me two hundred dollars a minute. He is building hotels on States, Virginia, and St. Charles. He has temporarily reversed the current. With the yellow monopolies and my blue monopolies, I could probably defeat his lavenders and his railroads. I have Atlantic and Ventnor. I need Marvin Gardens. My only hope is Marvin Gardens.

There is a plaque at Boardwalk and Park Place, and on it in relief is the leonine profile of a man who looks like an officer in a metropolitan bank—"Charles B. Darrow, 1889–1967, inventor of the game of Monopoly." "Darrow," I address him, aloud. "Where is Marvin Gardens?" There is, of course, no answer. Bronze, impassive, Darrow looks south down the Boardwalk. "Mr. Darrow, please, where is Marvin Gardens?" Nothing. Not a sign. He just looks south down the Boardwalk.

My opponent accepts the trophy with his natural ease, and I make, from notes, remarks that are even less graceful than his.

Marvin Gardens is the one color-block Monopoly property that is not in Atlantic City. It is a suburb within a suburb, secluded. It is a planned compound of seventy-two handsome houses set on curvilinear private streets under yews and cedars, poplars and willows. The compound was built around 1920, in Margate, New Jersey, and consists of solid buildings of stucco, brick, and wood, with slate roofs, tile roofs, multimullioned porches, Giraldic towers, and Spanish grilles. Marvin Gardens, the ultimate outwash of Monopoly, is a citadel and sanctuary of the middle class. "We're heavily patrolled by police here. We don't take no chances. Me? I'm living here nine years. I paid seventeen thousand dollars and I've been offered thirty. Number one, I don't want to move. Number two, I don't need the money. I have four bedrooms, two and a half baths, front den, back den. No basement. The Atlantic is down there. Six feet down and you float. A lot of people have a hard time finding this place. People that lived in Atlantic City all their life don't know how to find it. They don't know where the hell they're going. They just know it's south, down the Boardwalk."

From The New Yorker, September 9,<br>1972, pp. 45–62.

## Questions

*Content/Meaning*
1. While there are many narratives in the McPhee essay, two are especially prominent. What are they and how does he interweave them?

2. What is the significance of the title? Why is Marvin Gardens especially important to the fiction and fact of McPhee's essay?
3. What sort of commentary does McPhee make of Atlantic City and its history? Who were P. B. Osborne, Anthony J. D. Biddle, and John Philip Sousa, and what part did each play in the history of the city? Why does McPhee give so much attention to the jail? Does he imply that the economics of Monopoly is in some way reflective of the forces that destroyed Atlantic City?

*Style*
1. Can you comment on the narrative structure of the Monopoly tournament that frames the essay? Does McPhee create a protagonist and antagonist in this narrative? How important is the result of the tournament in the final analysis?
2. Choose one of the paragraphs describing the streets or other important locations of Atlantic City. Can you analyze McPhee's skill in descriptive writing, paying particular attention to the choice of language and details?

# Reading Selection

The following selection was originally a newspaper column in the *San Francisco Examiner*. Its author is Paul Hemphill, a southerner who, after a failed Class-D baseball career (of five days), decided to become a writer. He has written books entitled *The Nashville Sound* and *Long Gone*, a description of life in the minor leagues, and has for some years contributed articles, mostly of the human interest variety, to *Life, The New York Times Magazine, Sport*, the *Atlanta Journal-Constitution*, and the *San Francisco Examiner*. While much of his reporting has to do with the life style of "good ol' boy-ism," a southern equivalent to the values of the tough-guy writers of the North, he has written sensitively and observantly about many aspects of the American scene including sports heroes, the Vietnam war, life on the road, San Francisco society, circus performers, and most important, his own life including a divorce and a remarriage. His latest book, *Too Old to Cry*, contains the essay reprinted here and some fifty more, all or most of which are concerned with the expectations of youth and the realities of later years. He has been praised as a reporter for his storytelling gift and his sense of drama, qualities that clearly emerge in "Starting Over." Indeed, of all the selections in this chapter, it comes closest in its tone, introspection, and imaginative design to being a short story.

## STARTING OVER

### Paul Hemphill

Because my life seems to feed off impulses rather than cool logic, it came as no surprise when I found myself looking up from the absolute bottom of the mine one Halloween. This was around 1974, getting toward midnight in a Laundromat on the seedy fringes of downtown Montgomery. Much earlier that day I had left a note for my wife of fourteen years and slammed some books and clothes into a two-hundred dollar junker station wagon and said farewell to my first life. Now, at an hour when Lisa and David and Molly would be out terrorizing the citizens of our little island on the coast of Georgia, I found myself watching my clothes dry in the presence of a hunched-over old black man, four hundred miles to the west.

"You ain't out spookin' tonight?" he said, wearily smiling after reading the *Montgomery Advertiser* one more time. He sat next to the wide plate-glass window in hopes of catching a neighborhood kid soaping obscenities in the window.

"Did that this morning," I told him.

"Morning? Spookin' this morning?"

"Ran away from home. Scared my kids."

The old man blinked. What he saw was a forty-year-old man with a load of clothes spinning in the dryer, and the man was telling him he had already celebrated Halloween by frightening his own children. "Ran away from home, you say," the old man said.

"This morning. Yes, sir."

"No costume, nothin' like that? For Halloween?"

"Pair of jeans, boots, T-shirt."

"Humph." The old man snapped open the *Advertiser*. "See what the gov'nor had to say yesterday?"

You cry. God knows, you cry, and you curse the dream you had of a picket-fenced house and a shiny Chevrolet and a lush green front yard and a Sears swing set in the backyard and three or four children to call you Daddy. You were programmed to believe that if you studied and stayed out of what they called "trouble" and minded your manners and went to church, you were entitled to all of these things. More important, you were convinced that these things were worth having. Ike was president. The Korean War was over. Music was provided by Elvis Presley and Patti Page, scenery by Robert Young and Fred MacMurray and Doris Day, and you were given no hints that Hollywood was presenting anything less than a true picture of marriage.

So we went into it, we products of the fifties, with every promise that all of it was right. I was a very young twenty-five, she a very young twenty, when I proposed (on my knees, of course, while she sat on the sofa in a dress that told me she knew this was the day it would happen). I had been accepted for a new job in a new line of work. She said yes, we kissed passionately, the phone rang, I said yes to the job, we sketched out our new life, and her mother began preparing for the wedding. Now I look back and see how fervently we wanted to hang on to the memory of that time and believe it could blot out the rest.

We simply grew apart. Three children couldn't keep it together. I went one way, she another, and the kids got caught in the middle. It was a foolish way to marry. Not only did we not know each other; we didn't know ourselves. Neither party should be blamed. You blame the American Dream—the one being perpetuated then by Fred Astaire and all of those sappy pop singers and shellacked movie stars—but you don't blame the principals. We were only doing what, in our time, came naturally.

On a Saturday morning some two years after my divorce I was kicked awake by the woman who would, that very afternoon, become the second Mrs. Paul Hemphill. We had been together for nearly a year. Her first marriage had gone much like mine, except that there were no children involved in hers, and now we found that if we didn't know what we wanted, at least we knew what we *didn't* want. She and I had been sharing things—an apartment, underarm deodorant, bed, comb, TV, books, car—for three months. It was a fine old apartment building overlooking the Bay, loaded with saucy old blue-haired dowagers ("Well," they would invariably prod the resident manager as he ferried them up the elevator shaft, "have they married *yet?*"), and it was in that apartment building, so far away from what we Southerners knew as home, that we learned to know each other and ourselves. But now I was being kicked awake at dawn, on my second wedding day, by the bride-to-be. "Okay, Hemphill," she said, "your ninety-day free-home-demonstration period is up. Either pay up or return the merchandise." So we went off to get married.

We had found ourselves humming that sappiest of sappy wedding songs, "The Second Time Around," but with fervor, as we went through the details of getting blood tests and securing a license and arranging for the ceremony. It would be held in the backyard of *San Francisco Examiner* sports columnist Wells Twombly and his wife, Peggy, officiated by a Carolina-born rabbi-turned-Superior Court judge, attended by fifty-odd friends at poolside in the calm of a northern California suburban town. Hemphill even bought a velvet coat to go with his faded jeans and halfway promised to wear a tie. Susan—Susan Farran Percy, thirty-two, Phi Beta Kappa, reporter—bought a special suit. There would be dinner and an obligatory "wedding night" in Monterey.

Of course we would refer to it as the Wedding of the Year. Enough whiskey to float the aircraft carrier *Coral Sea.* Photographers everywhere, naturally, when the principals are journalists. A veteran three-year-old ring bearer. A sometime rabbi marrying a redneck atheist and a backsliding Catholic, all three from the south, before fifty cynical journalists at poolside in California is what Herb Caen, the columnist, would call an "item." Wedding cake topped by the Twomblys' original bride-and-groom statue. Men taking their billfolds out of their pockets in case an impromptu swimming orgy might ensue. Happy tears, at the end, when the history of the rings was revealed: The groom's belonged to her late father; it was a silver, cowboyish ring made thirty-five years earlier on Fifth Avenue in New York. The bride's was part of the loot involved when his parents were married for free in a "Perfect Couple" wedding on the stage of a movie house in Birmingham during the Depression. And off they went, these by-products of the fifties, trying to forget the Dream and to start over as adults; off they went to see if there really is a second life after a first death.

"The wedding announcement," she said as she picked the grains of rice from her hair and shoes and cleavage (there had been no rice that season in northern California) and the car sped southward toward Steinbeck Country.

"Wedding announcement," he said.

"I want my picture in the paper. 'New Bride.' "

"It'd be embarrassing."

"Embarrassing. What do you mean by that?"

"They can't say 'The bride wore white.' "

"Well," she said, "at least they can give our address."

"Address? I don't want people knowing our address."

"Something like, 'Following the ceremony the couple will be at home. Where they have been for the past ninety days.' "

From Paul Hemphill, *Too Old to Cry*
(New York: Viking, 1980), pp. 178–81.

## Questions

*Content/Meaning*

1. As you know, Hemphill wrote this self-revealing narrative as a news-paper column. His purpose, apparently, was therefore not simply to tell a real-life story. What issues do you suppose he meant to raise in writing this piece?

2. What is Hemphill's attitude toward his first marriage? What was the cause of its breakup? In what ways does his first marriage contrast with his second?

3. Would anyone you know find Hemphill's column objectionable?

*Style*

1. Can you describe Hemphill's style? Does he use more than one voice as he progresses in his narration? (Consider the scenes with the old

black man, the sketch of his proposal to his first wife, and the "report" of his second wedding.)

2. What sort of person is Hemphill's second wife? What are the stylistic devices through which we get to know her?

3. How would you describe the organization of the essay? Is it arranged essentially in chronological order? To what extent is comparison and contrast an organizational device in it?

# Reading Selection

The short story that follows was first published in *The Atlantic*. Later it was incorporated in a collection of short fiction, the second such published by the author, Grace Paley, whose other book is entitled *The Little Disturbances of Man*. This story, as several others by Paley, has much to say about the art of fiction and the act of writing it. We need not know whether the conversation recorded in the story between the narrator and her father actually took place. We do not even need to know whether Ms. Paley's father lived to be an old man who was once a doctor, had been an artist, and craved for his daughter to write understandable stories. In a sense that is what the story is all about—our not having to know those real-life details. (As a matter of fact, do we even know that the narrator is a woman, or is that an inference we make because the writer is a woman? Think about that as you read the story.) You should pay special attention to the stories within the story and what points they are designed to make. Also think about the function of the conversation itself as a framework for the story.

## A CONVERSATION WITH MY FATHER

### *Grace Paley*

My father is eighty-six years old and in bed. His heart, that bloody motor, is equally old and will not do certain jobs any more. It still floods his head with brainy light. But it won't let his legs carry the weight of his body around the house. Despite my metaphors, this muscle failure is not due to his old heart, he says, but to a potassium shortage. Sitting on one pillow, leaning on three, he offers last-minute advice and makes a request.

"I would like you to write a simple story just once more," he says, "the kind de Maupassant wrote, or Chekhov, the kind you used to write. Just recognizable people and then write down what happened to them next."

I say, "Yes, why not? That's possible." I want to please him, though I don't remember writing that way. I *would* like to try to tell such a story, if he means the kind that begins: "There was a woman . . ." followed by plot, the absolute line between two points which I've always despised. Not for literary reasons, but because it takes all hope away. Everyone, real or invented, deserves the open destiny of life.

Finally I thought of a story that had been happening for a couple of years right across the street. I wrote it down, then read it aloud. "Pa," I said, "how about this? Do you mean something like this?"

> Once in my time there was a woman and she had a son. They lived nicely, in a small apartment in Manhattan. This boy at about fifteen became a junkie, which is not unusual in our neighborhood. In order to maintain her close friendship with him, she became a junkie too. She said it was part of the youth culture, with which she felt very much at home. After a while, for a number or reasons, the boy gave it all up and left the city and his mother in disgust. Hopeless and alone, she grieved. We all visit her.

"O.K., Pa, that's it," I said, "an unadorned and miserable tale."

"But that's not what I mean," my father said. "You misunderstood me on purpose. You know there's a lot more to it. You know that. You left everything out. Turgenev wouldn't do that. Chekhov wouldn't do that. There are in fact Russian writers you never heard of, you don't have an inkling of, as good as anyone, who can write a plain ordinary story, who would not leave out what you have left out. I object not to facts but to people sitting in trees talking senselessly, voices from who knows where . . ."

"Forget that one, Pa, what have I left out now? In this one?"

"Her looks, for instance."

"Oh. Quite handsome, I think. Yes."

"Her hair?"

"Dark, with heavy braids, as though she were a girl or a foreigner."

"What were her parents like, her stock? That she became such a person. It's interesting, you know."

"From out of town. Professional people. The first to be divorced in their county. How's that? Enough?" I asked.

"With you, it's all a joke," he said. "What about the boy's father? Why didn't you mention him? Who was he? Or was the boy born out of wedlock?"

"Yes," I said. "He was born out of wedlock."

"For Godsakes, doesn't anyone in your stories get married? Doesn't anyone have the time to run down to City Hall before they jump into bed?"

"No," I said. "In real life, yes. But in my stories, no."

"Why do you answer me like that?"

"Oh, Pa, this is a simple story about a smart woman who came to N.Y.C. full of interest love trust excitement very up to date, and about her son, what a hard time she had in this world. Married or not, it's of small consequence."

"It is of great consequence," he said.

"O.K.," I said.

"O.K. O.K. yourself," he said, "but listen. I believe you that she's good-looking, but I don't think she was so smart."

"That's true," I said. "Actually that's the trouble with stories. People start out fantastic. You think they're extraordinary, but it turns out as the work goes along, they're just average with a good education. Sometimes the other way around, the person's a kind of dumb innocent, but he outwits you and you can't even think of an ending good enough."

"What do you do then?" he asked. He had been a doctor for a couple of decades and then an artist for a couple of decades and he's still interested in details, craft, technique.

"Well, you just have to let the story lie around till some agreement can be reached between you and the stubborn hero."

"Aren't you talking silly, now?" he asked. "Start again," he said. "It so happens I'm not going out this evening. Tell the story again. See what you can do this time."

"O.K.," I said. "But it's not a five-minute job." Second attempt:

Once, across the street from us, there was a fine handsome woman, our neighbor. She had a son whom she loved because she'd known him since birth (in helpless chubby infancy, and in the wrestling, hugging ages, seven to ten, as well as earlier and later). This boy, when he fell into the fist of adolescence, became a junkie. He was not a hopeless one. He was in fact hopeful, an ideologue and successful converter. With his busy brilliance, he wrote persuasive articles for his high-school newspaper. Seeking a wider audience, using important connections, he drummed into Lower Manhattan newsstand distribution a periodical called *Oh! Golden Horse!*

In order to keep him from feeling guilty (because guilt is the stony heart of nine tenths of all clinically diagnosed cancers in America today, she said), and because she had always believed in giving bad habits room at home where one could keep an eye on them, she too became a junkie. Her kitchen was famous for a while—a center for intellectual addicts who knew what they were doing. A few felt artistic like Coleridge and others were scientific and revolutionary like Leary. Although she was often high herself, certain good mothering reflexes remained, and she saw to it that there was lots of orange juice around and honey and milk and vitamin pills. However, she never cooked anything but chili, and that no more than once a week. She explained, when we talked to her, seriously, with neighborly concern, that it was her part in the youth culture and she would rather be with the young, it was an honor, than with her own generation.

One week, while nodding through an Antonioni film, this boy was

severely jabbed by the elbow of a stern and proselytizing girl, sitting
beside him. She offered immediate apricots and nuts for his sugar level,
spoke to him sharply, and took him home.

She had heard of him and his work and she herself published,
edited, and wrote a competitive journal called *Man Does Live By Bread
Alone.* In the organic heat of her continuous presence he could not
help but become interested once more in his muscles, his arteries, and
nerve connections. In fact he began to love them, treasure them, praise
them with funny little songs in *Man Does Live . . .*

> *the fingers of my flesh transcend*
> *my transcendental soul*
> *the tightness in my shoulders end*
> *my teeth have made me whole*

To the mouth of his head (that glory of will and determination)
he brought hard apples, nuts, wheat germ, and soybean oil. He said to
his old friends, From now on, I guess I'll keep my wits about me. I'm
going on the natch. He said he was about to begin a spiritual
deep-breathing journey. How about you too, Mom? he asked kindly.

His conversion was so radiant, splendid, that neighborhood kids
his age began to say that he had never been a real addict at all, only
a journalist along for the smell of the story. The mother tried several
times to give up what had become without her son and his friends a
lonely habit. This effort only brought it to supportable levels. The boy
and his girl took their electronic mimeograph and moved to the bushy
edge of another borough. They were very strict. They said they would
not see her again until she had been off drugs for sixty days.

At home alone in the evening, weeping, the mother read and reread
the seven issues of *Oh! Golden Horse!* They seemed to her as truthful
as ever. We often crossed the street to visit and console. But if we
mentioned any of our children who were at college or in the hospital
or dropouts at home, she would cry out, My baby! My baby! and burst
into terrible, face-scarring, time-consuming tears. The End.

First my father was silent, then he said, "Number One: You have a
nice sense of humor. Number Two: I see you can't tell a plain story. So
don't waste time." Then he said sadly, "Number Three: I suppose that means
she was alone, she was left like that, his mother. Alone. Probably sick?"

I said, "Yes."

"Poor woman. Poor girl, to be born in a time of fools, to live among
fools. The end. The end. You were right to put down. The end."

I didn't want to argue, but I had to say, "Well, it is not necessarily
the end, Pa."

"Yes," he said, "what a tragedy. The end of a person."

"No, Pa," I begged him. "It doesn't have to be. She's only about forty. She could be a hundred different things in this world as time goes on. A teacher or a social worker. An ex-junkie! Sometimes it's better than having a master's in education."

"Jokes," he said. "As a writer that's your main trouble. You don't want to recognize it. Tragedy! Plain tragedy! Historical tragedy! No hope. The end."

"Oh, Pa," I said. "She could change."

"In your own life, too, you have to look it in the face." He took a couple of nitroglycerin. "Turn to five," he said, pointing to the dial on the oxygen tank. He inserted the tubes into his nostrils and breathed deep. He closed his eyes and said, "No."

I had promised the family to always let him have the last word when arguing, but in this case I had a different responsibility. That woman lives across the street. She's my knowledge and my invention. I'm sorry for her. I'm not going to leave her there in that house crying. (Actually neither would Life, which unlike me has no pity.)

Therefore: She did change. Of course her son never came home again. But right now, she's the receptionist in a storefront community clinic in the East Village. Most of the customers are young people, some old friends. The head doctor has said to her, "If we only had three people in this clinic with your experiences . . ."

"The doctor said that?" My father took the oxygen tubes out of his nostrils and said, "Jokes. Jokes again."

"No, Pa, it could really happen that way, it's a funny world nowadays."

"No," he said. "Truth first. She will slide back. A person must have character. She does not."

"No, Pa," I said. "That's it. She's got a job. Forget it. She's in that storefront working."

"How long will it be?" he asked. "Tragedy! You too. When will you look it in the face?"

From Grace Paley, Enormous Changes at<br>the Last Minute (New York: Farrar,<br>Straus, Giroux, 1960), pp. 161–167.

### Questions

*Content/Meaning*

1. Does the narrator give her father the simple story he requests with her first version about the woman across the street? Do either the narrator or the father like the story? What sort of detail did the father want when he said, "You left everything out"? Does he seem

to characterize people by what they look like, where they come from, how well they conform?

2. At one point, the narrator responds to her father that people get married in "real life" but not in her stories. She sets up an important distinction here, one on which she elaborates when she says that she can never seem to control what becomes of her characters after she starts to give them fictional life. Who or what controls those characters? Does the second version of the story about the woman across the street demonstrate her point about the growth of characters?

3. Is the second version a good story? Does the father seem to like it? Why or why not? Why does the narrator disagree with him about his interpretation of "the end"? Is he guilty of confusing fiction with reality? If so, how?

4. The father comments in response to the second version, "You have a nice sense of humor." Do you agree? Is the second version comic? What role does reversal or irony play in the second story?

5. Would Paley's father consider Hemphill's "Starting Over" a satisfactory story? Would Paley? What distinctions does she draw between fact and fiction? Do they coincide with yours?

*Style*

1. What are the differences in vocabulary and sentence structure between the story within the story (both versions) and the story told by Paley about her father? Is one more literary than the other? To what extent does the first paragraph prepare us for the differences in style we will experience in the rest of story?

## Exercises and Assignments

1. Grace Paley's father objects to her first version of the story about the woman and her son because she had "left everything out." Find a short news story that, similar to Paley's first version, simply gives a skeletal narrative report. Then, using your imagination, write a longer version to fill in some of the details that the old man asks for.

2. Write an essay on one of the following subjects. You are free to agree or disagree with the statement you choose. Use for illustration any of the readings or discussions in this chapter and/or supporting examples from your own experience, from television programs, films, books, newspapers, or magazines.

   *a.* Truth is stranger than fiction.
   *b.* Any figure who appears in a written account is to some degree fictional.

*c.* Fiction is a making up of imaginative happenings.

3. Select a problem that interests you and on which you have a decided point of view, such as women's liberation, pot smoking, divorce, nuclear power, racism, teenage rebellion, authoritarianism, modern fashions, or brutality in sports. Then find two or three articles in current newspapers or magazines and write an essay in which:

*a.* You state your point of view.
*b.* You choose two or three narrative examples to support that view.

4. As an alternative to assignment 3, write a paper on a subject of your choice using your own experience, as Hemphill did, to explain your point of view. Report your experience as a carefully structured narrative, preferably including dialogue.

5. Historical events, as in McPhee's essay, are likely to contain interesting and little-known narratives. Choose an event that interests you and read a number of reports of it. Select a minor narrative within the larger event and develop it into a story. *The New York Times Index* may help you to locate a subject. Here is a list of suggestions:

The Wreckage of the Dirigible *Roma,* February 22, 1922
The Arrest of Mahatma Gandhi in London, March 11, 1922
The Opening of Tut-Ankh-Amen's Inner Tomb, February 17, 1923
Byrd's Flight over the North Pole, May 12, 1926
Six Men Found Alive in Sunken Sub S-4, December 19, 1927
Dillinger Slain in Chicago, July 23, 1934
French Liner *Normandie* Keels Over in New York Harbor, February 10, 1942
Assassination Attempt on President Truman, November 2, 1950
Rosenbergs Executed as Atom Spies, June 20, 1953
Eisenhower Sends Troops to Little Rock, September 25, 1957
127 Die as Two Airliners Collide Over New York City, February 17, 1960
Trujillo Shot Dead by Assassins, June 1, 1961
Power Failure Snarls Northeast, November 10, 1965
1,000 State Troopers Storm Attica Prison, September 14, 1971
Nine Israelis on Olympic Team Killed, September 6, 1972

# EXPOSITION AND ANALYSIS

**H**ere at the midpoint of the book we study two kinds of writing that are central to all others. *Exposition* is writing to inform, to make an object, idea, or process clear to a reader. Starting with such a broad definition, we assert that almost all writing is to some degree expository. Descriptive and narrative writing intend to make things clear. Criticism relies in part on simply informing readers about what the critic has seen, on providing a context for evaluation, and on analyzing the parts of an object or performance. Argument must include some factual information in order to be persuasive. Indeed, some rhetorics classify all these kinds of writing as exposition.

As we noted at the beginning of the book, rhetorical categories overlap, and so it is perhaps pointless to spend much time deciding whether a particular passage is "descriptive analysis" or "argumentative analysis" or is using description in the service of argument. The categories are useful as teaching devices and as means of imposing some order on the subject, but the distinctions are artificial; published writing presents few "pure," "textbook" examples of each rhetorical type.

Exposition as a pure form of discourse is supposed to be "objective" and detached in its intentions. The writer has no bias to inflict and is aiming only to make the subject as clear as possible. Similarly, *analysis* denotes taking something apart, dividing it into its constituent parts and examining each piece carefully and closely: dissecting a frog to observe its organs and their interrelationships, testing blood for the presence or absence of various substances, examining a car's electrical and fuel systems to determine why it will not start are all acts of analysis. But such objective analysis is easier to do when the subject is an object or a process. Analyzing a poem or a play, or an idea or a social issue, is usually much more complicated and frustrating than our examples of biological, medical, or mechanical analysis: You either find the frog's heart or you do not, the white blood count is at a certain level or it is not, you dry the spark plugs and the car starts or it does not. But no single analysis is going to have the last word on subjects like the influence of television programming on people's attitudes or the roles of women in culture or the acceptance of minorities in society. With these issues there is likely to be little agreement even about what constitutes the "parts" of the problem.

# 13 ORGANIZING EXPLANATIONS

**T**here are many strategies and devices for setting forth information, and most expository writing uses a variety of them. This chapter introduces you to seven of the most common methods and suggests ways of using them to develop your writing. How you organize expository writing of your own will depend, of course, on your subject and your intentions. Informational writing is often used either to help someone understand a subject or to enable someone to do something. In both cases effective explanations depend on the quality and extent of the supporting details and the means by which those details are organized and presented.

The most straightforward means of telling someone how to do something—assemble a bicycle or bake a cake—is simply to list the steps necessary to accomplish the task. These instructions or directions can be called *process descriptions,* and most such descriptions use *chronological* order: They take up the steps in the process in sequence from beginning to end.

The following paragraph is taken from an article titled "How to Make Sure Your Water Is Fit to Drink." It comes near the end of the article and is offered as a "homemade alternative" to buying bottled water or using a commercial home filter unit.

Put a coffee filter paper in a large funnel. Wash enough granular activated carbon to fill one-quarter of the funnel. . . . (To wash carbon, put it in a jar, fill it with water, cover and shake. Let the carbon settle and pour off the water at the top. Repeat until the water you pour off is clear.) Now set the funnel in a large clean jar, add the carbon and slowly pour your tap water through the funnel. Change the carbon every three weeks, or after 20 gallons of water have been filtered through it.

This paragraph is simple, clear, and direct, if a little uninspiring; it is written in the unadorned, imperative style typical of recipes.

Such process descriptions should be triumphs of clarity, but they will seldom be interesting by themselves unless a particular reader needs to have the information; few people read repair manuals unless they are trying to fix something. A greater challenge to the writer's skill is to provide an appropriate setting for the information or to explain its significance in order to compel our interest and attention. The paragraph on filtering water depends for its urgency on the 1,500-word article of which it is a part. The "recipe" for home filtering is, in fact, a solution to the problem of water contamination that the writer details in the rest of the article.

As you read that article now, consider how the writer attempts to engage our interest by establishing a setting and by explaining the significance of her subject.

## Reading Selection

### HOW TO MAKE SURE YOUR WATER IS FIT TO DRINK

*Jane E. Brody*

For many decades, Americans have taken the healthfulness of their water supply for granted. And undoubtedly many—perhaps most—people still do. After all, you rarely if ever hear these days of oubreaks of typhoid, cholera, dysentery and other waterborne diseases once common before the advent of chlorinated community water supplies and restrictions on the placement of wells and cesspools.

But sales of bottled water have zoomed in recent years, as millions of Americans have become concerned about their health and the safety of that liquid that comes out of their taps. Others have purchased various filtering devices to purify their home water supplies. Studies suggest that their concern may be justified, but that the alternatives they've chosen are often no better than the tap water they spurn. Stronger, community-based action may be needed to clean up our water.

Not only do infectious diseases transmitted through tap water still occur—afflicting at least 10,000 Americans a year (and probably many more since most cases of illnesses like intestinal "flu" go unrecognized as attributable to water)—but a far more serious threat may exist. Studies have shown that the nation's 50,000 water supplies are liberally laced with potentially harmful substances—including asbestos, pesticides, heavy metals like lead and cadmium, arsenic, nitrates, sodium, viruses and organic chemicals that are known to cause cancer.

Ironically, the very process by which we cleanse our water of infectious organisms—chlorination—is responsible for creating cancer-causing substances, or carcinogens, from otherwise innocent chemicals in water. The chlorine can combine with other pollutants in water to form such carcinogens as chloroform, carbon tetrachloride and bis-chloroethane and other chemicals collectively called trihalomethanes.

In the mid-1970's, the Environmental Protection Agency, the Federal unit responsible for the purity of our water, made two surveys of municipal water supplies around the country and found chlorinated organic chemicals in significant amounts virtually everywhere.

To date, more than 300 different organic chemicals have been identified in American drinking water; most have not yet been tested for their ability to cause cancer. Even though these chemicals may be present in only minuscule amounts, the average person consumes one and a half or more quarts of water every day of life. Chronic exposure to small amounts of carcinogens can add up to a significant hazard.

Indeed, in at least 51 studies carried out so far, a real hazard has been suggested. In New Orleans, where the Mississippi drains agricultural chemicals into the water supply and where the hazard of chlorinated carcinogens was first noted, cancers of the kidney, bladder and urinary tract are more common than in most other American cities.

A study of 88 counties in Ohio showed that death rates for cancer of the stomach and bladder were more common in those served by surface water supplies (from rivers and lakes) than in those with ground water (from wells). The E.P.A. surveys revealed that the concentration of organic chemicals was considerably higher in surface water supplies. Another nationwide study showed a relationship between the levels of trihalomethanes in the drinking water and deaths from cancers of the bladder, brain, kidney and lymph glands.

While none of the studies so far proves that a waterborne cancer hazard exists, they all suggest there's cause for concern. The hazard can be greatly reduced by filtering the water through activated carbon granules prior to chlorination. However, only a few water systems currently do this, and then only to remove foul odors and tastes. Another approach involves the use of ozone instead of chlorine to purify the water.

Other substances in water that are worrisome include the following:

**Nitrates.** These chemicals, present in both surface and well water from agricultural runoff and seepage from septic tanks, are a direct hazard to infants, causing methemoglobinemia or blue-baby syndrome. In persons of all ages, they may contribute to the formation of potent carcinogens called nitrosamines in the digestive tract. Nitrates can be removed from the water supply by treatment through an ion exchanger.

**Sodium.** The Environmental Defense Fund, which has petitioned the E.P.A. for stronger water safety rules, notes that water supplies may contain up to 500 parts of sodium per million parts of water.

In some sections of the country, such as the Northeast and Middle West, the problem is seasonal, the result of runoff from highways that have been salted in winter. In others, the water is naturally high in sodium.

This may have no effect on most people, but for the 10 percent who are predisposed to high blood pressure and the 25 million Americans who already have this disease, the high sodium content of drinking water could be a hazard. While sodium is hard to remove from water, the fund suggested that the sodium content be monitored regularly and the public be warned when high levels occur in the water supply.

**Heavy metals.** In communities where the water is "soft"—that is, the water is corrosive because it contains relatively few dissolved minerals and salts—toxic metals from water pipes may leach into the tap water. For reasons not yet known, studies have shown that in soft water areas the death rates from cardiovascular diseases are considerably higher than they are in areas where the water is hard.

This may result from higher levels of cadmium (leached from galvanized pipes) and sodium in soft water. Some communities, like Boston, where many homes have lead pipes, now add lime and carbonates to the water supply to reduce its corrosive action.

**Asbestos.** Asbestos fibers enter the water supply primarily through erosion of asbestos-containing rocks and asbestos cement water pipes and runoff from sanded roads. Several years ago, persons drinking water from Lake Superior were shown to be consuming large amounts of asbestos fibers dumped in the lake by a mining company.

Although the hazards of asbestos in water are not known, asbestos workers exposed to the persistent fibers of this mineral have high rates of cancers of the lung and gastrointestinal tract and an otherwise rare fatal cancer called mesothelioma. Asbestos levels in water can be reduced by hardening the water to make it less corrosive, and the fibers can be removed by conventional filtration techniques.

What can you, the consumer, do about making sure your water is fit to drink? Aside from being costly, bottled water is not necessarily better than that which comes out of your tap. Some is just processed tap water to which minerals, with or without carbonation, have been added.

Dr. Robert Harris, water specialist at the Environmental Defense Fund, suggests that before you make a major investment in bottled water, check with the manufacturer as to its source, the type of processing and results of tests of its content and purity. Most nationally sold brands are probably free of organic carcinogens. However, an E.P.A. survey showed that many bottling plants had sanitary deficiencies and some bottled water was contaminated with intestinal bacteria.

In general, Dr. Harris suggests you choose natural spring water derived from a protected watershed, that is, one in a nonindustrial area. The addition of minerals or carbonation by the processor does not compromise the safety of the water. However, carbonation can be a problem for persons with hiatus hernia or other digestive disorders.

As for home water purifiers, the E.P.A. has completed tests on seven of the more than three dozen now available. The results ranged from "totally useless" for a $12 model that fits on your faucet to "as effective as filtration at a water treatment plant" for a $300 unit that's attached to your main water source.

The main problem, however, is that even the expensive units permitted the growth of bacteria on the intake side of the unit; the bacteria can then contaminate the water that comes out of your tap. Home filter units can magnify the bacterial content of tap water by tens of thousands of times.

The Environmental Defense Fund suggests an inexpensive and safer homemade alternative:

Put a coffee filter paper in a large funnel. Wash enough granular activated carbon (it can be purchased in one-pound bags from Walnut Acres, Penns Creek, Pa. 17862) to fill one-quarter of the funnel. (To wash carbon, put it in a jar, fill it with water, cover and shake. Let the carbon settle and pour off the water at the top. Repeat until the water you pour off is clear.) Now set the funnel in a large clean jar, add the carbon and slowly pour your tap water through the funnel. Change the carbon every three weeks, or after 20 gallons of water have been filtered through it. Store the filtered water in the refrigerator.

For further purification, you might boil your tap water gently for 15 to 20 minutes, which would evaporate off many of the carcinogens. After boiling, bottle it and store closed in the refrigerator. Certainly, any water that appears turbid (cloudy, indicating possible contamination by sewage) should be boiled for at least 10 minutes if you have no choice but to use it.

An alternative is to add liquid chlorine laundry bleach or tincture of iodide. Use two drops bleach per quart of clear water or four drops per quart of cloudy water. Mix thoroughly and let stand for 30 minutes. You should detect a slight chlorine odor. If not, repeat the treatment and let stand an additional 15 minutes. For iodide, use five drops per quart of clear water, 10 per quart of cloudy water, mix and let stand for 30 minutes.

If your water is soft, first thing in the morning or after hours of nonuse, let the cold water run for a few minutes before you draw it for drinking or cooking. Don't use hot water from the tap for these purposes, since it's likely to have a higher metal content.

The article is accompanied by a "sidebar" that provides a "how to" for people who want to pursue the issue in their own communities:

### Turning On The Pressure

For citizens interested in knowing what's in their water and doing something to improve it, Consumers Union recommends that they organize a community group and start by familiarizing themselves with the facts about drinking water.

A useful pamphlet for individuals or groups—"Safe Drinking Water for All: What You Can Do"—may be obtained for 25 cents from the League of Women Voters Education Fund, 1730 M Street N.W., Washington, D.C. 20036.

Citizens' groups might also find useful the "Manual for Evaluating Public Drinking Water Supplies." Single copies are available free from the Water Supply Division, Environmental Protection Agency, Washington, D.C. 20460.

Then get in touch with the local water superintendent and ask for the results of water-sampling tests and sanitary surveys. Consumer Reports suggests that if you get no cooperation, inform the local media—they might be interested in finding out what the water officials are trying to hide.

Compare the test results with the Public Health Service standards in the E.P.A. manual. Was the water tested at the tap as well as in the plant? If the Federal standards are being met, broach the matter of further purification or alternative methods of purification. Many improvements can be made for just pennies a day per family.

From *The New York Times,* November 14, 1979.

Though this "how to" article is 28 paragraphs long, only 3 paragraphs actually include process descriptions. Overall, the article is organized into two parts, following a problem-solution format: Paragraphs 1 through 18 state the problem, and paragraphs 19 through 28 discuss solutions. The first three paragraphs are introductory, and as is typical of journalistic writing, the writer finds a setting in something topical: The rising sales of bottled water and home water filtration devices suggest wide concern about the purity of home tap water. The writer has investigated these concerns, and having researched various unspecified studies of drinking water, she then presents her findings: There is a significant problem. Infectious diseases are still transmitted through tap water, it contains many harmful substances, and only a few of the more than 300 chemicals found in water have been tested for their potential to cause cancer. Why are these findings significant? Since drinking water is a lifelong daily routine, the sustained exposure to even small quantities of harmful agents must eventually cause health problems.

After reviewing four of the better-known substances that can be present in water, the writer turns to solutions to the problem she has presented. She advises caution in choosing bottled water, dismisses home purifiers, and endorses the homemade process.

The tone of the article is interesting to note also. As is true of most journalistic writing, and as should be true of strictly expository writing as well, the article is written in an "objective" style: A serious threat "may" exist; pesticides, arsenic, and viruses are only "potentially" harmful; the studies do not prove anything, they "suggest . . . concern." The writer, though, manages to have it both ways, simultaneously qualifying the hazard and providing readers with the information necessary to do something about it.

# Reading Selection

Another important method of developing explanations is to supply the reader with essential background information. The following newspaper article depends almost completely on history and context to make sense out of the news being reported. The report concerns the reevaluation of the research and conclusions of a major figure in psychology. The writer establishes the importance of this reevaluation by explaining the context surrounding the research: The findings of Cyril Burt, the discredited psychologist, have been used for years as major evidence in the controversy over the precedence of heredity or environment in the development of the human being. More specifically, his findings have been said to support those who argue that blacks are intellectually inferior to whites. The article also reviews the major research studies by Burt that are the subject of the reevaluation.

### BRITON'S CLASSIC I.Q. DATA NOW VIEWED AS FRAUDULENT

*Boyce Rensberger*

The classic reports of the late Cyril Burt, the eminent British psychologist, whose research had long been accepted by many as evidence that differences in intelligence were hereditary, are now widely considered to be without scientific value.

Because Dr. Burt's writings had been a major buttress of the view that blacks have inherited inferior brains, his discrediting is regarded as a significant blow to the school of thought espoused by such persons as Arthur Jensen of the University of California, Richard Herrn-Stein of Harvard and William Shockley of Stanford.

Dr. Jensen, a leading proponent of the view that blacks have inherently lower I.Q.'s than whites do, but who has helped to expose Dr. Burt's errors, said that there remained ample valid evidence to support his beliefs.

Richard Lewontin, a Harvard geneticist who has long been a leader of the countervailing and dominant school of thought that intelligence levels are chiefly determined by environmental factors, said that Dr. Burt's data had been considered the most persuasive evidence put forth by the hereditarians. He added that its loss was "no trivial problem for the heritability people."

Dr. Burt's research, unquestioned and highly influential before his death in 1971, has been criticized in psychological circles since 1972, when it was found to contain a number of virtual impossibilities.

In recent weeks, however, the basis for criticism has widened as a result of a report in The Sunday Times of London that Dr. Burt's two collaborators, cited in his published articles, may never have existed.

Further investigations by The Sunday Times and by Leon Kamin, a Princeton University psychologist, suggest many additional instances of questionable scientific thought, including biased language, favorably reviewing his own books, using pseudonyms in his own journal and fabricating data.

While such allegations might seem unremarkable if aimed at a young and ambitious researcher, Cyril Burt was a major figure in British and American psychology. He was the first psychologist to work for a school system, London's, and, through his research and pioneering analyses of the problems of backward children, he came to be regarded as the father of educational psychology.

His view that intelligence was predetermined at birth and largely unchangeable helped to shape a rigid, three-tier school system in England based on an I.Q. test given to children at the age of 11.

Dr. Burt was the first psychologist to be knighted, and shortly before his death, he won the American Psychological Association's Thorndike Prize.

The scientific articles being questioned now were presented as having been based on studies of the I.Q.'s of identical twins reared in separate homes. They had been considered landmarks in psychology because they appeared to be models of scientific rigor.

Twin studies of the sort that Dr. Burt made, or said he made, are considered a valid method for estimating the relative strength of the influences of heredity and environment on some outcome. Since identical twins have the same heredity, any differences between them are presumed to be attributable to environmental differences.

In 1955, Dr. Burt published a report on 21 pairs of identical twins who had been separated after birth and reared in different adoptive homes. He said that the statistical correlation between the I.Q. scores of the separated twins was 0.771.

Such correlations are a measure of how much one member of a pair is linked, for any measurable trait, to the other member of the pair. A calculated correlation of 1.0 indicates 100 percent linkage. A correlation of zero indicates that the members of the pair are no more alike in that trait than would be the case if the members of the pair were randomly chosen.

Three years later, Dr. Burt published again when his collection of twins had grown to "over 30" pairs. Against odds of millions to one, the calculated correlation came out to be 0.771 again.

In 1966, he published his final report, with the group then standing at 53 pairs. Again, against even stiffer mathematical odds, the correlation was reported as 0.771.

In each of the three reports, the correlation among the group of twins that had not been separated remained unchanged at 0.944, a similarly improbable event.

The curious consistency went unnoticed for years, and the numbers were taken as strong evidence that I.Q. was heavily determined by genetics. They were especially valued because Dr. Burt's studies were the only ones purporting to show that the separated twins were reared in different socioeconomic levels.

This is a crucial point, because the opponents of the Burttian view contend that the high correlation in I.Q. is the result not of genetic similarity but of the fact that both twins were adopted into similar environments.

In 1972, Dr. Kamin, the Princeton psychologist, read Dr. Burt's papers for the first time.

"It didn't take more than 10 minutes of reading to begin to suspect that it was fraudulent," he said.

Dr. Kamin said that he had discovered many inconsistencies, methodological errors and omissions of crucial information such as the ages of the people tested. Many of Dr. Burt's references in his papers were to unpublished reports, making it impossible for others to verify information.

At about the same time that Dr. Kamin became interested in Dr. Burt, Dr. Jensen also began a review of the Briton's publications. In a 1974 article, Dr. Jensen reported 20 instances of implausible statistical coincidences and, for all practical purposes, declared Dr. Burt's writings useless as scientific documents.

However, Dr. Jensen said recently: "This doesn't change my position at all. We now have a considerable amount of other data that support the heritability of I.Q."

In any event, Dr. Jensen added, people who believe as he does now put less stock in the kind of study Dr. Burt described and have developed methods of studying other kinship patterns and measuring heritability in them.

"The evidence indicates that 60 to 80 percent of the variability in I.Q. is genetic," Dr. Jensen said, "and the evidence is still overwhelming."

By contrast, Dr. Kamin contends that the loss of the Burt data is crucial.

"The heredity people relied very heavily on Burt," Dr. Kamin said, "because his was the only study of separated twins that claimed to have evidence that the twins went into [homes of] different socioeconomic levels. And Burt was the only man who claimed to have used the same I.Q. test on all of his population and to have drawn all of his population from the same place."

Dr. Kamin, who said that he might be the only person to have read everything that Dr. Burt published, reported that he had detected in some of the psychologist's early writings additional evidence of "fakery."

"Even back in 1912, he did a paper purporting to have tested over a thousand children," Dr. Kamin said, "and there are things in it that clearly suggest fakery."

Dr. Kamin said that Dr. Burt asserted that he had determined that not only were slum children less intelligent than upper-class children, but that Jews and Irish people were less intelligent than English, and that, across the board, men were smarter than women.

Dr. Kamin asserted that what he called Dr. Burt's prejudice against all classes but his own was repeatedly evident in his choice of language for his formal reports.

In a report on a child for whom Dr. Burt was responsible as a school psychologist, for example, the child is described as "a typical slum monkey with the muzzle of a paleface chimpanzee."

From *The New York Times*, November 28, 1976, p. 26.

### Questions

*Content/Meaning*

1. After reading this article, can you state the basic question underlying the "nature or nurture," heredity or environment, controversy? What are the implications for education of favoring one influence over the other?
2. Why are "twin studies" so important scientifically to this controversy?
3. What is the evidence reported in the article that discredits Dr. Burt's conclusions? What, in your opinion, is the most devastating evidence against him?

*Style*

1. Has the writer drawn any conclusions in the nature or nurture controversy? If he has, which side is he on? How, specifically, do you know?

2. Why has the final paragraph been included? Is it necessary? If so, should it have come sooner in the story?

## Reading Selection

The selection that follows is a feature article from the journal *Mother Jones*. The magazine is named after a social activist who lived from 1830 to 1930 and became involved in a variety of social causes. It carries many investigative and interpretive reports, and its editorial policy calls for exhaustive analyses on a wide variety of subjects, especially in the consumer and environmental fields. The article reprinted here was co-authored by Marlene Cimons, a consumer reporter for the *Los Angeles Times*, and Michael Jacobson, director of the Center for Science in the Public Interest and author of *Eater's Digest*, a guide to food additives. The writers use investigative analysis in the service of extended exposition and their article approaches being a college research paper based on secondary sources. While the writers did research on food labeling, they did not do any tests of their own, nor did they uncover any new information. A part of the article concentrates on passing on consumer information using the "how to" formula, though here we see it in a much longer format.

As an aid to reading the piece, you might wish to observe the organizational scheme: The first part of the article (paragraphs 1–21) defines the problem; the second part (paragraphs 22–27) gives advice on how to cope with the problem; the third part (paragraphs 28–49) presents solutions.

The article basically presents a *problem-solution* plan: In the first part the problem is analyzed, and before the end a solution to remedy the problem is synthesized. One obvious question that must be asked of such an article is whether the proposed solutions will eliminate the problem or create new ones. Other, more basic questions include whether the problem is clearly defined, whether a remedy is possible, and if so, whether the writer has found the best available solution. Keep these questions in mind as you read the article.

### HOW TO DECODE A FOOD LABEL

#### Marlene Cimons and Michael Jacobson

A ten-year-old Boston boy with chronic allergies was given an unfamiliar brand of ice cream at a friend's house. Several hours later, he was dead. The child had suffered a hypersensitive reaction called anaphylactic shock, triggered by eating peanuts, a food he was not supposed to have. He knew peanuts were forbidden. But he could not have known they were in the ice cream. The ingredients were not listed on the label.

Rep. Benjamin S. Rosenthal (D-N.Y.), sponsor of comprehensive food-labeling legislation pending in Congress, calls the contents of the boxes, cans and jars we heap into our supermarket carts "the best kept secrets in America today." Rosenthal is right. We have food-labeling laws now, but they are inadequate, deceptive and sometimes even ignored. "All of us have a right to know what we are eating, ingredient by ingredient," Rosenthal says. "Concealing such information clearly violates the public interest."

It clearly does not violate corporate interests, however, to keep silent about what is in the products we eat. The food industry has no desire to reveal trade secrets or give consumers the opportunity to make economic or nutritional judgments by comparison shopping.

Most foods must list their ingredients in fine print in order of their predominance in the product—that is, by weight. Here is how the industry gets tricky: have you looked at a cereal box lately? Instead of putting sugar where it really belongs—at the top—producers break it down into white sugar, brown sugar, corn syrup and corn sugar, so that each item appears farther down in the list, each by a separate weight. Don't call it breakfast food anymore. Call it candy. Or cookies. Ralston Purina, in fact, has done so, marketing a cereal known as "Cookie Crisp," which is about 47 percent sugar.

Although most food labels have to list ingredients (there are many exceptions, and we'll get to them later), colors, flavors and spices do not have to be listed by their specific names. A food whose label says "artificial color" or "artificial flavor" may contain a dozen different chemicals.

Very few artificial flavors have been well tested, but because most are identical to the flavoring chemicals that occur in natural foods, they are probably not dangerous. Colors, however, are another story—probably the most suspect category of food additives. A history of artificial colors would read like the guest register of a transient hotel. Butter Yellow and Sudan No. 1 were banned in 1919. Orange No. 1, Orange No. 2, Red No. 1 and

Honesty: Packages should carry notices when sugar or fat content is high.

Yellow Nos. 1, 2 and 3 were all outlawed by late 1960. Green No. 1 was banned in 1965. Violet No. 1 was banned in 1973. Red No. 2 was banned in 1976. Currently, questions have been raised about Red No. 40—one of the two most widely-used colorings (more than a million pounds per year)—Orange B and several others. Most of the banned dyes caused cancer or organ damage to laboratory animals when fed at high dosages. These coal-tar dyes do not occur in nature; and the human liver metabolizes many of them as toxic substances.

Who needs them? Manufacturers use them mainly for cosmetic—or economic—reasons. Food sells better if it looks pretty. The presence of an artificial color or flavor, however, usually means something has been left out of the food, like fruit. It's certainly cheaper to color something red than make it with real cherries. You can almost always assume that such a food will be junk—high in sugar or fat, low in nutrition.

If an artificial color has been used, the label will usually say so. (The exceptions, however, a gift from Congress to the dairy industry, are butter, cheese and ice cream.) But the label won't name the specific color. The Food and Drug Administration (FDA), in a partial remedy, has proposed a labeling requirement for one color only—Yellow No. 5, or tartrazine. Yellow No. 5, the FDA estimates, causes allergic reactions in 50,000 to 100,000 Americans. Symptoms include wheezing and difficulty in breathing, hives and stuffy and runny noses. But why label only products with Yellow No. 5? It would be easy to list all colors; there are only nine left on the market.

The largest category of foods not subject to ingredient labeling laws are those known as "standardized foods." There are some 350 products, including such common items as enriched white bread, soda pop and mayonnaise, that are not required to disclose ingredients because the basic ones can all be found in the Code of Federal Regulations. Just drop by any law library on your way to the grocery if you want to find the ingredients in these.

But, even then, you may be missing some information. The Code's "standards of identity," a classic example of good intentions gone awry, were created to require—thus guarantee—the presence of certain ingredients. But there are also permissible options—thickening agents, emulsifiers, even caffeine—that may be added, if the manufacturer chooses. But they won't be in the Code. So they might be in the food, or they might not. You have no way of knowing.

What other labeling requirements can be found in our hodgepodge of laws? The Department of Agriculture, which shares jurisdiction with the FDA in certain areas, has standards for some meat-containing products. Hot dogs, for example, may contain no more than 30 percent fat. Chicken noodle soup must contain a minimum of two percent chicken.

If a product does not meet the standard, it cannot be called by the "standard" name. For instance, if the chicken soup contains only one percent chicken, manufacturers would have to call it something like "noodle soup with chicken."

Following a successful court battle with the frozen-food industry, the FDA has effected a similar regulation. Under the "common or usual names" rules, manufacturers of a few foods (frozen shrimp cocktail, for example) are required to list the percentage of the "valuable ingredient" (shrimp) on the label.

Alcoholic beverages have also fallen into the labeling loopholes. But this may be temporary. Recently, the White House called upon two federal agencies to draft a proposal requiring partial ingredient labeling of all alcoholic beverages, both domestic and imported. The White House asked both agencies to move quickly. The labels will have to list such additives as artificial colors, flavors, preservatives and clarifiers.

The compromise is an attempt to end several years of bickering between the FDA—which sought labeling of all ingredients—and the Treasury Department's Bureau of Alcohol, Tobacco and Firearms, which sided with the liquor industry in wanting none. In early 1975, the FDA and the Bureau jointly issued a proposed regulation for full ingredient labeling. The next November, however, after a series of hearings, the Bureau withdrew its support.

"We felt the cost (to manufacturers) was excessive in relationship to the benefit to be received," a Bureau official said. The liquor industry, in fact, exerted tremendous pressure against the proposal, claiming that it would cost too much and that it would force them to disclose trade secrets.

Thirteen days after the Bureau pulled out, the FDA reissued the proposal, insisting it had the authority to do so. Eight distilleries and three trade associations filed suit, contending that the Bureau had exclusive jurisdiction over the labeling of alcoholic beverages. A federal judge in Louisville, Kentucky, agreed, ruling against the FDA.

The FDA asked the Department of Justice to appeal the judgment. The Bureau asked the Justice Department to let it stand. The Solicitor General, not knowing who his "client" was, turned the matter over to the White House for a policy decision. And the White House decided in behalf of the consumer, asking the two agencies to draft a labeling proposal.

Nutritional labeling, another area of the law, is required by the FDA when nutrients are added to a food ("fortified" cereals, for example) or when nutritional claims are made on the label or in advertising. But nutritional labeling also can be extremely deceptive. The very presence of such labeling (which includes calories, protein, carbohydrates, vitamins, fats and number of servings) may lead people to assume a product is nutritious, simply because it's labeled. It may not be.

Most of the space of nutritional labeling is given to protein and a series of vitamins and minerals. Considering the dietary problems of Americans, what should be glaringly obvious are the levels of added sugar (which causes tooth decay, a $3-billion-a-year problem), sodium (which contributes to high blood pressure, hypertension and strokes) and saturated fat (which contributes to the number one killer—heart disease). The government doesn't require that sodium be listed on a label, but it should be for those who must limit their intake of salt. Sugar added by the manufacturer is often included with starch, fiber and naturally occurring sugars as "grams of carbohydrate per serving." Saturated fat can be found with other fats under "grams of fat per serving."

Kellogg's "Cocoa Krispies" now lists sugar as "13 grams per ounce." A more easily understood description would be "46 per cent sugar." Many hot dog labels list fat in grams. They should say, instead: "X percent of the calories come from fat."

Another major problem with the current nutritional labeling is that most people (except, perhaps, nutritionists) ignore it. The jumble of figures is "information overkill." The FDA, concerned about this and other difficulties with nutritional labeling, has begun to study the subject. This means that substantial changes are probably at least five years in coming.

As deficient as the laws are, we can still learn some things from labels now. And we can protect ourselves from certain dangers by reading them carefully.

Avoid artificial colors and flavors. The colors are particularly questionable. Furthermore, many parents and physicians—most notably Dr. Ben Feingold of the Kaiser/Permanente Medical Center in San Francisco—believe that artificial colors and flavors (also BHT and BHA) contribute to hyperkinesis, or hyperactivity, in some sensitive children. Though reliable studies are difficult to perform, some have lent scientific support to more informal observations.

Feingold, a pediatrician and allergist, first connected hyperkinesis with synthetic food colorings and flavorings in 1965. He began experimenting with hyperactive children, eliminating artificial additives from their diets—as well as natural salicylates, found in many fruits and vegetables—and saw remarkable changes in behavior and personality. His diet has not worked in all cases, however. He told a Senate health subcommittee a few years ago that his success rate has been about 50 percent—but, he says, that still translates into several million children.

Stay away from products high in sugar and fat. Avoid caffeine, especially

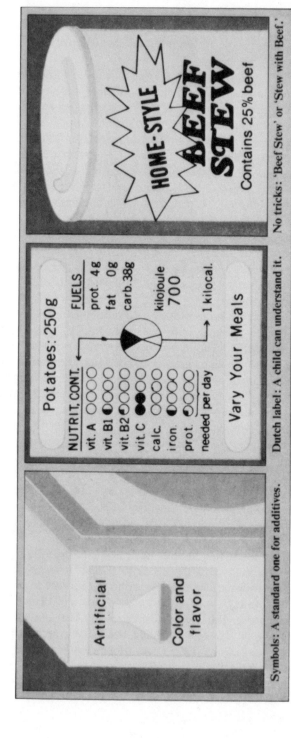

Symbols: A standard one for additives.

Dutch label: A child can understand it.

No tricks: 'Beef Stew' or 'Stew with Beef'.

in the first trimester of pregnancy, since it has been associated with birth defects in animals. (You know caffeine is in coffee, but did you know it is also in chocolate, cola, tea and "stay-awake" pills?)

Do not buy products containing sodium nitrite, especially bacon. The substance—also found in ham, nearly all luncheon meats, hot dogs and smoked fish—is added to retain color, enhance flavor and, according to the industry, prevent botulism. It can combine with substances in food or drugs called amines to form nitrosamines—one of the most potent families of carcinogens known. There is an increased danger with bacon: frying bacon produces nitrosamines before it is even eaten. Sodium nitrite will be listed on labels, unless you buy meat unpackaged at the butcher or delicatessen. Even the Department of Agriculture has acknowledged that nitrosamines cause cancer—and has advised the industry that, unless nitrosamines can be prevented from forming in bacon and other foods, it will ban nitrite. Meanwhile, you can either search for nitrite-free meats (often frozen) at natural food or health food stores, or give them up entirely.

There are some chemicals with foreign-sounding names that are safe. Among the harmless are calcium propionate, a bread preservative; citric acid, which is already found in every cell of the body; carboxy methyl cellulose, one thickening agent that runs right through the human system; and carotene, a coloring agent (often found in margarine) that is used by the body as Vitamin A—and is actually nutritious.

What can we do to improve labels? First, we can make them more honest. How many times have you purchased a name-brand product (more expensive) over a supermarket brand because you believed the name brand to be of better quality? Often, they are manufactured by the same company. It should say so on the label.

If it's true that consumers risk botulism without sodium nitrite, shouldn't they know they risk cancer with it? A proposed label warning for bacon: "Contains sodium nitrite. When this product is cooked, chemicals are formed that may increase the risk of cancer."

The most important way to improve food labeling, however, would be to require prominent notices on the front of food packages when the sugar or fat content is above a certain level. Candy, cupcakes, sugared breakfast cereals and other high-sugar foods should be labeled: "This product contains ———— per cent sugar. Frequent use contributes to tooth decay and other health problems."

Hot dogs, vegetable oil, mayonnaise and other high-fat foods should bear a similar warning, listing the percentage of fat.

America's high-sugar, high-fat, high-sodium and high-calorie diet contributes to some of the most prevalent, painful and costly health problems in this country, including—but not limited to—tooth decay, obesity, constipa-

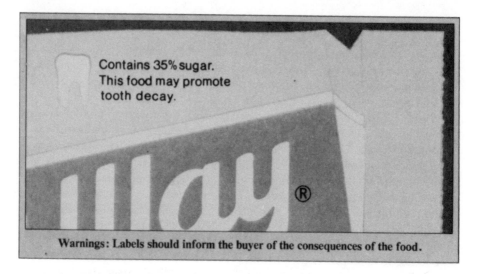

Contains 35% sugar.
This food may promote
tooth decay.

Warnings: Labels should inform the buyer of the consequences of the food.

tion, diabetes, stroke and heart disease. Educating the public through labels could go a long way toward reducing those health costs and prolonging lives.

We can learn something from the Dutch. A supermarket chain in the Netherlands recently began using nutritional labels using graphics so simple that even children can understand the information. A circle indicates the useful nutritional components in the upper segment and the calories in the lower segment. Anyone who wants a wholesome, low-calorie food will buy the "top-heavy" products. The labels also show vitamin and mineral content, grams of fat, protein and carbohydrates and the number of calories per serving.

Another good idea is placing an easily recognizable symbol on all products containing artificial colors and flavors, so that when shoppers see it on an item, they will leave it on the shelf.

An additional approach could be the "Nutrition Scoreboard" grading system, which evaluates a food's overall nutrition. A serving of orange juice, for example, would have a score of "62", while a bottle of soda pop would score a "−91."

The Consumer Food Labeling Act (H.R.2180), proposed by Benjamin Rosenthal, would do much, as Rosenthal says, to close the "still widening gap between the ability of government to protect consumers and the ability of some segments of the business community to abuse them."

The measure would require:

- That food makers show on their labels all ingredients by percentage, including all additives and preservatives, by their common or usual names.

- Nutritional statements, including fat content, vitamin and protein value, fats and fatty acids, calories and other nutritional data.
- Listing the net weight and drained weight of canned or frozen products packed in a liquid medium.
- Listing the major ingredients by percentage weight of any combination food item (existing food labels fail to show the exact proportion of one ingredient to another). Some brands of combination food items contain more of the major ingredients than others—for instance, some brands of beef stew contain more meat, vegetables, etc. than others.
- Labeling of all packaged perishable and semi-perishable foods to show clearly the date beyond which it should not be sold and the optimum storage conditions at home. It also provides that overage products can be sold—but only if they are safe, separated from other items and clearly identified as being beyond the expiration date.
- A uniform system of retail quality-grade designations for consumer food products based upon quality, condition and nutritional value, since there is currently no such system. As it is now, one product may be graded A, B, C and D, while another is AAAA, AAA, AA and A; hence the two A grades are opposites—not equals—but there is no way for the consumer to know.
- Labels on foods, drugs and cosmetics to contain the name and place of business of the true manufacturer, packer and distributor. This would aid in the event of a recall—now difficult because hundreds of private labels and private-brand products do not bear this information. (According to Rosenthal, Bon Vivant vichyssoise was packed under more than 30 different private labels, without Bon Vivant's name appearing on one of them.) Secondly, private label products tend to be lower priced than their nationally advertised counterparts—although there is frequently no difference between them, and they are often made by the same company.
- Disclosure by retailers (those with sales below $250,000 a year are exempted) of the unit price of packaged consumer commodities and that retailers mark the actual selling price on the product itself, regardless of the presence of computerized checkout systems.
- That notices be printed by manufacturers, alerting consumers to ingredient changes.
- Prohibition of the use of misleading product brand names.

Although the Senate has passed two food labeling bills in recent years, anti-consumer lobbying has grown intense on the House side, and the fate of the measure there is uncertain.

The Food and Drug Administration plans to hold public hearings on nutritional and ingredient labeling this winter. FDA Commissioner Donald

Kennedy wants to see what he calls "a comprehensive strategy" set for increasing nutritional information available to consumers.

In the meantime, perhaps the best kinds of foods for consumers to buy are the ones that come without any labels at all—they're called fresh fruits and vegetables.

From *Mother Jones,* February/March
1978, pp. 32–35.

### Questions

*Content/Meaning*
1. What is the main point of the article? Is there a clear "thesis statement" of the point?
2. What facts are cited to support the article's main point? Which are the most and least convincing?
3. In paragraph 3 the authors state that labeling abuses serve "corporate interests." How is this assertion supported in the article?
4. Is it possible to remedy the problems the article analyzes?
5. Are the solutions proposed in the article the best ones? Will they cause other problems? Are the graphics on the Dutch label "so simple that even children can understand" them?
6. What values do the writers (and the magazine) hold that prompted the investigation, its conclusions, and the recommendations? What do the writers believe is right and wrong, good and bad?

*Style*
1. Why do the writers put the story of the Boston boy in the first paragraph? Is it an effective opening or cheap sensationalism?
2. The authors use sarcasm in paragraph 9. Is it justified or offensive?
3. How would you characterize the voice of the article? What specific words, phrases, and other details disclose this voice to you?

## Exercises and Assignments

1. Look in one of your textbooks or in a magazine for "how to" instructions and consider how they might be improved; then rewrite the instructions.

2. In one or two paragraphs (less than 300 words) write a brief article explaining how to do something. Choose something that you know well, something in which you have an interest, and something worth knowing about. Address your article to a reader inexperienced with or uninformed about your subject. Develop your piece using chronological order, a problem-solution format, or any organizational structure that seems to fit your subject.

3. In 500 to 750 words, write a "how to" article that includes a process description of the instructions or directions plus an extended introduction that establishes the purpose, setting, or significance of the process you describe. You may look to the "how to" article by Brody as a model, but your organization and development should grow out of your subject.

4. A "how to" article can produce dull, mechanical writing unless you are interested in your subject and can establish that interest. Robert M. Pirsig in *Zen and the Art of Motorcycle Maintenance* at one point describes the attitude of some mechanics who had carelessly botched a repair job as being "uninvolved. They were like spectators." Hence the poor work. Later in the book he contrasts their work with the behavior of true mechanics:

> They have patience, care and attentiveness to what they're doing, but more than this—there's a kind of inner peace of mind that isn't contrived but results from a kind of harmony with the work. . . . The material and the craftsman's thoughts change together in a progression of smooth, even changes until his mind is at rest at the exact instant the material is right. . . .
> So the thing to do when working on a motorcycle, as in any other task, is to cultivate the peace of mind which does not separate one's self from one's surroundings. When that is done successfully then everything else follows naturally. . . .
> The real cycle you're working on is a cycle called yourself. The machine that appears to be "out there" and the person that appears to be "in here" are not two separate things. They grow toward Quality or fall away from Quality together.

Write a 500- to 750-word "how to" article with Pirsig's point of view in mind. That is, write about your task by establishing your relationship to it. Don't think simply of how you were taught to perform a certain task or how you might be able to get someone else to go through the same mechanical procedures; instead, think with a broader perspective. Report not only on your external behavior, but also on your internal behavior, your attitude or state of mind in relation to the task and its materials.

6. Follow up on the *Mother Jones* food labeling article by performing your own investigative analysis: Investigate the ingredients and label listings for several supermarket foods that are regularly eaten by you and your family. Which labels are honest according to the standards presented in the article and in the proposed Consumer Food Labeling Act? Which are still deceptive? Which are easy or difficult to read and understand? You might consider, for example, if cereal labels still list various sugars separately or express quantities indirectly.

You might also consult Michael Jacobson's *Eater's Digest*, Nikki and

David Goldbeck's *Supermarket Handbook,* or other sources on processed foods and their contents.

Write up the results of your investigation in 500 to 750 words. The focus of your analysis will be to decide which, if any, labels are inadequate or deceptive.

# 14

## DEFINITION

anguage is an abstraction; it *refers* us to objects and ideas. The word "chair" is a word, not an object. Definition is the process by which a word is linked with its *referent* (that which it stands for, that to which it refers). One of the simplest forms of definition, and the least complete, is the use of synonyms or short phrases to restate the meaning of a word. This method is especially important to explanations that rely on technical vocabulary, on the slang of a particular group, or on the jargon of a particular job or profession. The parentheses two sentences above contain two statements that attempt to define "referent" quickly, without lingering over the concept. Similarly, the how-to article on water purity used the phrase "cancer-causing substances" to define "carcinogens" and the synonym "cloudy" to define the unfamiliar "turbid." The quick translation of difficult or unfamiliar words into simpler, more common ones frees the writer to use the vocabulary natural to the subject.

## EXTENDED DEFINITIONS

This method is only satisfactory, however, where the object or idea is not central to the explanation. These quick restatements leave out more than they contain: What makes the water cloudy? How do these substances cause cancer? Longer definitions of objects and ideas that are central to an explanation must draw on various kinds of information to "re-create" the referent with clarity.

Extended definitions often try to explain things by describing them, by naming their parts, and by showing them in operation. Here is a definition that uses this strategy.

The hamburger maker is a variation of an old, familiar design—the electric waffle iron. Instead of having two waffled plates, the typical hamburger maker has a flat-surfaced top plate and a bottom plate with two "wells" for hamburgers (there are single-burger models, but we didn't test them). The bottom plate can be reversed to give a flat grilling surface. The hamburger maker's hinged, detachable halves come together, clam-fashion, for cooking burgers or sandwiches, but the appliance can also be used for open grilling. It has long handles that lock together, during closed grilling, to put pressure on the food inside. It has no temperature control, but it does have a thermostat to prevent overheating. ("Who Needs a Hamburger Maker," copyright 1978 by Consumers Union of the United States, Mount Vernon, N.Y. 10550. Reprinted/excerpted by permission from *Consumer Reports,* July 1978, p. 408.)

The definition begins by comparing the unfamiliar hamburger maker with the familiar waffle iron and then contrasts them. As the definition develops, it includes description and the naming of parts ("a flat-surfaced top plate and a bottom plate with two 'wells' "; "it has no temperature control"), and it shows how the appliance operates ("hinged, detachable halves come together, clam-fashion, for cooking"; "long handles . . . lock together, during closed grilling, to put pressure on the food inside").

In addition to describing the parts, functions, or unique features of an object or idea, a definition may also tell us something about origin. Here is an extended definition recounting the invention of a unique structural device to serve as the "armoring" outer layer of a harbor breakwater. "Merrifield" in the passage is Eric M. Merrifield, the harbor engineer of East London, South Africa, who invented the *dolosse* breakwater.

The idea was to cover the breakwater with objects of branching shape— like children's jacks—that would engage with one another, clinging together while absorbing and dissipating the power of waves. There had been similar attempts. The French had tried a four-legged concrete form, a tetrapod, and it had worked well enough but had required an expensive preciseness in construction, because each one had to be carefully set in place in relation to others. Merrifield wanted something that could almost literally be sprinkled on the breakwater core. Eventually he thought of *dolosse.*

*Dolosse*—the singular is *dolos*—were crude toys that had been used by South African white children since the eighteen-thirties, when they acquired them from tribal children in the course of the eponymous trek, the overland march of the *voortrekkers* from the Cape Colony to the Transvaal. A *dolos* was the knucklebone of a goat or a sheep, and might be described as a corruption of the letter "H" with one leg turned ninety degrees. The game that had been played with *dolosse* by *voortrekker* children, and by South African children ever since, was called knucklebone. As crude toys, *dolosse* were also thought of as imaginary oxen. Witch doctors had used them as instruments of magic power.

Merrifield replicated them on a grand scale in concrete, making *dolosse* that weighed twenty tons apiece, and with these he armored his breakwater. When high seas hit them, the water all but disappeared— no slaps of thunder, no geysers in the air. The revised breakwater seemed to blot up the waves after breaking them into thousands of pieces. (John McPhee, "The Atlantic Generating Station," *The New Yorker*, May 12, 1975, p. 68.)

**Questions**

*Content/Meaning*
1. What is a "tetrapod"? What does "eponymous" mean? *"Voortrekker"?*
2. In this explanation McPhee seems to return frequently to words associated with childhood ("imaginary oxen," "game," "crude toys") and magic ("magic power," "all but disappeared"). Are these words there just to remind us of the origin of *dolosse,* or is McPhee implying something more?

*Style*
1. Note the use of phrases like "slaps of thunder," "blot up the waves," "like children's jacks," and "geysers in the air." What effects does McPhee achieve with these phrases and others like them?
2. McPhee uses both simple language ("sprinkled," "knucklebone," "blot up") and more elevated language ("dissipating," "eponymous," "replicated"). Is this just verbal virtuosity, or is there some point to the mixing of simple and sophisticated language?

## DEFINING ABSTRACTIONS

The most difficult words to define are those that stand for abstract qualities. For such words there are no referents in the world of objects, and thus definitions for them depend entirely on language. High-level abstractions like *honor, friendship, free enterprise* are difficult to define because there can be a great deal of variation in their individual uses, and often they register highly personal, emotional, subjective meanings. Such connotative meanings (see p. 30) cannot be disregarded in any extended definition. That is to say, dictionary definitions emphasizing strict denotation are not enough for words in this category.

While words that describe complex feelings cannot be defined objectively, we must not therefore neglect to define them at all. Finally, all that we can insist on is that we do define our terms. And while we are not free to define them anyway we like—we do have to put them in an appropriate class (*love* is an emotion or feeling of affection)—we are free to give them personal interpretations. Difficulties are likely to arise much more often when we do not define our terms than when we define them idiosyncratically. We are all familiar with the use of abstract words as slogans that cause misunderstanding and can lead to conflict—words like *patriotism, terrorism, racism.* When exposition depends on an understanding of abstract words, it is important that they be defined specifically and clearly.

## Reading Selection

The following article, which is part book review, part exposition, depends on the definition of the high-level abstraction "the criminal mind." There has been little agreement, even among experts, as to what a criminal is, to say nothing of what constitutes "the criminal mind," a phrase that some experts do not recognize at all.

### A COLD NEW LOOK AT THE CRIMINAL MIND

#### *Michael S. Serrill*

Scholars, physicians, scientists, and pseudoscientists have been investigating the "criminal mind" for more than 400 years. Much of the early thinking postulated that criminals were innately evil people who could only be stopped by maiming or execution. Barely 100 years ago, the Italian criminologist Cesare Lombroso was taken very seriously when he asserted that criminality was a trait inherited from degenerate ancestors. He spent much of his professional career measuring the skulls and other anatomical parts of dead criminals in an effort to discover their typical dimensions.

More recently, legions of social scientists have devoted millions of hours and billions of dollars to more sophisticated studies. They have concluded, overwhelmingly, that criminals are victims. The sociologists say those who break the laws are victims of urbanization, family disintegration, poverty, discrimination, poor schooling, unemployment, and the pressure of peers. Psychologists and psychiatrists say criminals are victims of alcohol abuse, drug abuse, child abuse, and a variety of mental illnesses, from the all-purpose "character disorder" to psychopathy. All three professions also cite a pervasive rage of the poor against the social conditions they are forced to endure.

To suggest that individuals who commit criminal acts or adopt criminal careers are not simply responding to their environment would deny all of the insights of modern sociology and psychiatry. Yet that is just what Samuel Yochelson and Stanton Samenow do in a recently published two-volume study called *The Criminal Personality,* which has caused considerable controversy in psychiatric and correctional circles. . . . They argue that habitual criminals possess "thinking patterns" that distinguish them from noncriminals, and that the development of these criminal thinking patterns has little or nothing to do with either social status or mental illness. . . .

Perhaps the most controversial assertion in *The Criminal Personality* is that there *is* a criminal personality. The authors contend that there were certain deviant thinking patterns present to an extreme degree in every one of the criminals they studied. The habitual criminal, they write, is a liar and a deceiver; he has little capacity for love, friendship, or companionship; he can commit brutal acts without a twinge of conscience and yet continue to believe that he is a "good" person. He "finds the restraints of responsible living unacceptable and even contemptible," the authors write. "The criminal disregards other people's right to live safely, but demands that others show him the utmost respect and consideration. . . . It does not bother him to injure others. . . . Untrustworthy himself, he demands that others trust him. If he happens to earn others' trust, he exploits it."

From *Psychology Today,* February 1978, p. 86.

### Questions

*Content/Meaning*
1. What do "postulated," "innately," and "deviant" mean? What are their basic etymological roots? To what other words are they related?
2. The author discusses "early thinking" about the criminal mind, more recent sociological and psychological thinking, and the thinking in the book under review. Are there three rival definitions of the "criminal mind" here, or does the new book return to and justify the early theory?
3. What implications for society's treatment of criminals are suggested by the various definitions?

*Style*
1. Can you characterize the voice and language of this excerpt?
2. Does the absence of figurative language make this excerpt difficult or uninteresting to read? Why has the writer chosen to avoid colorful description?

# Reading Selection

The following article is a response to outbreaks of violence and vandalism against blacks that occurred in the New York metropolitan area in 1979. Is there a clear point or central idea to this article? How is it supported?

## WHITE PROGRESS

### *Joel Dreyfuss*

In another era, H. Rap Brown would have observed that it was as American as apple pie: a rush of feet down a darkened street, the smell of gasoline, a sudden burst of fire, the squeal of automobile tires. But former revolutionaries now tend health-food stores or their own brand of designer sportswear. We are closing in on the next decade. Such rituals as cross burnings on the lawns of blacks who move into white neighborhoods are supposed to be behind us.

To those who have grown weary of racial issues, the photograph of a black corporate executive being comforted before the charred ruins of his home by a black magazine publisher presents certain difficulties. Since the mainstream political consensus is that class has superseded race among our major social problems, such a scene—reported on the front page of the *Times* because the victim is, after all, *a corporate executive*—suggests that all is not as well as some would like to believe.

The same newspaper of record tells us there have been 15 cross burnings in Suffolk county so far this year, along with similar incidents in Queens, Nassau, and Westchester. The FBI has been asked to join the investigation by local law-enforcement agencies. Much of the violence has taken place where blacks have moved into previously all-white areas and are seen as a threat to social order and property values. The reaction is part of the American tradition, and so is the speech by the spokesman for the resistance movement. "They have destroyed 'their' neighborhoods and 'we' don't want them doing the same in 'our' neighborhood." Beyond the irony of possession based on color is the fact that most whites don't differentiate between classes of blacks. Because of inflation and because blacks pay more for decent housing, those moving in often surpass their white neighbors in income, education, and achievement. But the idea that black people could actually upgrade a neighborhood is beyond the imagination of a large number of Americans.

Logic has little to do with fire bombings, cross burnings, and other ultra-Americanisms. These incidents on Long Island are the Bakke cases of the mindless: blind resistance against an enemy determined by skin color or culture. In a world of increasing complexity, many can take comfort in an analysis of a problem that is literally black and white. It's "us" against "them" and the rituals of nighttime can be traced back to the most provocative events of our own American Revolution. The lighting of the cross, with its Christian implications, can meld into the righteousness of the Boston Tea Party. "The blacks are coming!" "The blacks are coming!" is still the cry of bigots, speculators, and the suburban ignorant, but instead of lanterns we get crosses and firebombs.

My Uncle Ferdinand has never set foot in America. During the American occupation of Haiti he took an oath never to touch the soil of this country, and now that he is 89 years old it is unlikely that he will change his mind. When I visited him during the turmoil of the civil rights era, he would invariably ask: "Have those white people up there made any progress?" His question was a valuable counterpoint to the prevalent concept of the "first black." The definition implies that black people (and other minorities) have somehow evolved to a point where they can perform functions once reserved for whites. The "first black" label obscures the fact that such achievements are primarily the result of white progress.

In looking back on the 1970s, there is evidence that blacks have changed more than whites in their perception of themselves and others. Our national obsession with statistics manifests itself in the definition of racial progress through income figures. But the most revolutionary gain that blacks have made has been psychological: a movement toward the concept of entitlement, that they deserve to reap the rewards of their labor as fully as their white counterparts and that they should be unwilling to settle for anything less.

As I followed the recent reports of racial violence, I realized that they differed markedly from similar reports of a decade or two ago. In virtually all the stories I read, there was little mention of fear. The outrage of the IBM executive came out of his disappointment that his neighbors could not recognize him for what he was: an extremely successful American who had overcome all sorts of obstacles that his attackers could not imagine. When the victims are West Indians, they assure the reporter they come from hardy stock and that they have no intention of surrendering to terror. "This is what America is about," they say of their determination to better themselves by moving to a more desirable area. Two Haitian women who have crossed the line from Queens to Nassau county are bewildered, as immigrants tend to be when their illusions are forcibly removed. But they, too, intend to stay where they are. There's no going back.

The most significant advances made by blacks in the last decade are the result of laws and court decisions that banished legalized racism. The disappointment of that period has been the inadequacy of those laws. Equality turned out to be much more complex than a piece of legislation. The struggle to redistribute opportunities became a bureaucratic tangle symbolized by affirmative action.

As the economy winds down into recession, the scramble for opportunities has been used to pit blacks and whites against each other. In the new consciousness, race becomes the reverse scapegoat. Personnel officers find it easier to say, "we're looking for a black" when they really don't want to hire a white applicant. Despite the fact that the economic gap between blacks and whites grows wider each year, more than a few whites have come to

believe that "blacks are getting everything." Even in some of the most hal-
lowed liberal circles, the presumption of black incompetence has become
fashionable.

Those who have little power must concern themselves with the whims
of the powerful. As blacks engage this new white resistance, it is evident
there have been more accommodations than conversions in the last decade.
All too often blacks run into a negativism that implies a discomfort with
the roles they would play rather [than] a difference over substantive issues.
Attitudes progress more slowly than courts and laws, and there are signs
of a lapse.

In another time, acts of violence against blacks had the tacit endorsement
of the white power structure. Now, those whites who turn to violence find
themselves strangely isolated. They may find individuals in the police or
among the ranks of politicians who sympathize secretly. But the bombing
and cross burnings will provoke no groundswell of white support. Whites
no longer find it necessary to do those kinds of things. There are other
avenues of resistance. White progress, therefore, must be measured by the
degree of acceptance of black entitlement. The response of white politicians
and institutions is a crucial test of that progress.

The loss of fear may be the most crucial change in the relationship
between blacks and whites in this country. Its most negative manifestation
is in the young men who have been discarded by society and who are willing
to confront the loaded guns of police officers in violent and frequently suicidal
affirmations of their manhood. The violence they resort to is a clear reaction
to their own despair. But the black middle class remains curiously optimistic
about its future. Those who work in white institutions know that—despite
the rhetoric of complaints about affirmative action—the double standard begins among those who hold power. When black middle-management executives were polled, they said they had to work twice as hard and be twice
as good to acquire the rewards freely given to their white counterparts; but
the black managers also believed they would succeed. The strains of "We
Shall Overcome" move subliminally in corporate boardrooms, where the civil
rights struggle is being fought in its most subtle form.

The general tone of reportage about the issue has been to dismiss the
incidents as isolated pranks by children who do not know the full meaning
of what they do. There are suggestions that television has encouraged more
such acts. But television has been meticulous in reporting the outrage of
responsible officials. Ed Koch puts his arm around a black victim. A group
of business and community leaders offers a reward. Police officials beef up
their patrols. If the children have seen the news, they have also seen the
unanimous abhorrence of such acts.

If the kids are doing it, we have good reason to be pessimistic. One of our expectations over the last 25 years was that somehow children could grow up and not repeat the sins of their parents. A casual trip through the lunchroom of any public high-school cafeteria in New York shows clearly that the racial divisions in our society transcend age groups. We should not be surprised, but it gets more difficult to remain optimistic.

The white middle class has seen its budget stretched tight by inflation and recession. It has heard all the propaganda about affirmative action and has come to believe those who say that blacks are getting everything. Its children run into the unexplained hostility of black children who have been cast about by an educational system whose last concern is their education.

"I was always told it took time," says James Baldwin, "but I'm 54 years old. You took my time. Do you want theirs, too? You want their children's time and their grandchildren's?" The problem remains with us—and the solution. And the alienation of blacks and whites is passed down from father to son, mother to daughter, changing, twisting, altering with the times. The burning cross remains the symbol. In another decade or two, we will once again blame the kids.

"It's always the kids," says a journalist who went into his newspaper's files and found reports of incidents going back 30 years. The young move faster than the old and they are sensitive to the currents generated by their elders. In writing about young southerners and the Klan in her new book, *The Rock Cried Out,* Ellen Douglas observes: "I think it was a game for them, too. They did it like they did the football and baseball, because it was what they were expected to do. And then it turned into something else and some of them were bewildered and ashamed. But their daddies had said: this is true. Do this. And how could they turn their backs and shame their daddies and call them sinners and criminals? They had to go on."

As we move toward a national culture and a common experience, both the good and the bad travel in the North-South exchange. The Klan's revival in the North and West responds to a deeply felt but inarticulate concern that the problems of the South have come up to haunt us. The condescension once held by whites here toward whites on the other side of Mason-Dixon has faded. Here and there, acts of violence have always been perpetrated by a handful—those most daring, most angry, most frightened. But the response of the majority provides a true test of its intentions. And the response of the majority toward these incidents of racial violence will tell us much about what progress whites will make in the 1980s.

Dear Uncle Ferdinand, they're making progress, but not enough, soon enough.

From *Village Voice* October 1, 1979, pp. 16–17.

**Questions**

*Content/Meaning*
1. What is the "Bakke case"? How will you find out?
2. In paragraph 4 Dreyfuss calls fire bombings and cross burnings "ultra-Americanisms." What does he mean by that?
3. How does Dreyfuss define "white progress"? How is it measured? What slows it down? What is its relationship to the "concept of the 'first black' "?
4. How does Dreyfuss define "entitlement"? What is the relationship between entitlement and white progress?
5. Is there a clear point here? Is it expressed in a thesis sentence?

*Style*
1. In paragraphs 3, 4, 7, 9, and elsewhere Dreyfuss takes on the voice of other people. Is this an effective expository device? Why or why not?
2. Why does Dreyfuss bring his Uncle Ferdinand into the piece? What does it add or subtract from his essay?
3. What is the tone of Dreyfuss's voice? How does it contribute to the point of the essay?
4. Is there a clear organizational structure to this essay? What is the structure? How does it contribute to the meaning of the piece?

## Exercises and Assignments

1. In one or two paragraphs write a definition for a familiar object by describing it, naming its parts, showing it in operation, and including its unique features.

2. Using John McPhee's definition of *dolosse* as a model, write a definition for a word that you are interested in or curious about, taking into account the word's origin and history. Your definition should go beyond merely stating what you can find out in a dictionary. Here, for example, is the entry for "bowdlerize" in the *American Heritage Dictionary.*

> **bowd·ler·ize** (bod′ləriz′, boud′-) *tr.v.* **-ized, -izing, -izes.** To expurgate prudishly. [After Thomas *Bowdler* (1754–1825), English editor who published an expurgated edition of Shakespeare's works.]—**bowd′ler·ism′** *n.*—**bowd′ler·i·za′tion** *n.*

After the pronunciation, the verb forms, and the definition, the word's origin is explained inside the brackets. Usually the origin is traced through earlier stages of English or other modern languages down to its source, as far as that can be known, in even older languages such as Latin or Greek. In this case, however, the word is traced to the name of a man who died in 1825. You will find more information about the word in *The Oxford English Dictionary* (*OED*), a monumental 12-volume work that took 45 years to compile. The *OED* is very thorough and includes with its definitions extensive citations of the usages of a word throughout its history in English, often reaching back to A.D. 1000 or earlier. Here is the entry in the *OED* for "bowdlerize":

> **Bowdlerize** (bau·dlərəiz), *v.* [f. the name of *Dr. T. Bowdler,* who in 1818 published an edition of Shakspere, 'in which those words and expressions are omitted which cannot with propriety be read aloud in a family': see-IZE.] *trans.* To expurgate (a book or writing), by omitting or modifying words or passages considered indelicate or offensive; to castrate.
>     **1836** GEN. P. THOMPSON *Let.* in *Exerc.* (1842) IV. 124 Among the names . . are many, like Hermes, Nereus . . which modern ultra-christians would have thought formidably heathenish; while Epaphroditus and Narcissus they would probably have *Bowdler*ized. **1869** *Westm. Rev.* Jan., It is gratifying to add that Mr. Dallas has resisted the temptation to Bowdlerize. **1881** SAINTSBURY *Dryden* 9 Evil counsellors who wished him to bowdlerise glorious John. **1883** *Ch. Times* 703/4 It [Henry IV] is Bowdlerized, to be sure, but that is no evil for school purposes.
>     Hence **Bow·dlerism, Bow:dleriza·tion, Bow· dlerized** *ppl. a.,* **Bow·dlerizer, Bow·dlerizing,** *vbl. sb.* and *ppl. a.*
>     **1869** *Pall Mall G.* 4 Aug. 12 We doubt whether Juvenal . . can be read with advantage at the age when Bowdlerism, as a moral precaution, would be desirable. **1878** *Athenæum* 6 Apr., False squeamishness or inclination to Bowdlerism. **1882** *Westm. Rev.* Apr. 583 The bowdlerization . . is done in an exceedingly awkward and clumsy fashion. **1879** F. HARRISON *Choice Bks.* (1886) 63 A Bowdlerised version of it would be hardly intelligible as a tale. **1886** HUXLEY in 19*th Cent.* Apr. 489 We may fairly inquire whether editorial Bowdlerising has not prevailed over historic truth.

In addition to the further information on Bowdler's edition of Shakespeare and the meaning "to castrate," there are nine instances of the use of the word between 1836 and 1886. Since all these usages cast bowdlerizing in a negative light, we might infer that the practice of this form of censorship has not been popular.

For this exercise you would find out who Bowdler was, what exactly he did to Shakespeare's plays, and why, as well as asking and answering any other questions that seem important or pertinent to you.

If you can't find a word of your own to research, try "shrapnel," "boy-cott," "sandwich," "chauvinism," or "Welsh rabbit." While you are in the library consulting the *OED,* you might also want to consult Eric Partridge's *Name into Word,* George H. McKnight's *English Words and Their Back-ground,* or James Bradstreet Greenough and George Lyman Kittredge's *Words and Their Ways in English Speech.* Partridge also has interesting collections of words in his *Dictionary of Slang and Unconventional English* and his *Dictionary of the Underworld,* as does Isaac Asimov in his *Words of Science and the History Behind Them.*

3. Attempt to define an abstract concept or quality concretely by showing it in operation instead of relying on further abstract words (love is a feel-ing . . .). You might use as a model the way Dreyfuss uses dialogue and narration to sketch the attitudes of those prejudiced against blacks in para-graphs 3 and 4 of "White Progress."

# 15 ILLUSTRATION, EXAMPLE, AND ANALOGY

**W**hile the words "illustration" and "example" are often used interchangeably, we differentiate them here on the basis of their functions. An illustration is usually hypothetical; its purpose is *to make something clear.* An example is a typical instance or detail; it is used both to make clear and *to demonstrate the truth* of a general assertion. An illustration, therefore, is not proof, while a well-chosen example, one that is truly typical, can be. Ideally, an exposition will include both illustrations and examples, but to provide logical support for its central ideas, it cannot rely solely on illustrations.

The following paragraph of exposition is taken from the analytic news article in Chapter 13 about the reevaluation of the psychological research of Cyril Burt, "the father of educational psychology." The reevaluation and the news article turn on the statistical correlations between the IQ scores of separated twins that Burt reported in his research. The paragraph begins with a brief definition, which it then makes clear with an illustration.

> Such correlations are a measure of how much one member of a pair is linked, for any measurable trait, to the other member of the pair. A calculated correlation of 1.0 indicates 100 percent linkage. A correlation of zero indicates that the members of the pair are no more alike in that trait than would be the case if the members of the pair were randomly chosen.

Examples differ from illustrations in that they are actual instances, and their territory is, therefore, factual. If we were to make the statement that Shakespearean tragedy always ends in the death of the tragic hero (a statement

**233**

that can be proved to be true), we could point to the four major tragedies, *Hamlet, Othello, King Lear,* and *Macbeth,* to demonstrate the truth of our assertion, since in each of those plays the title character, who is also the tragic hero, does indeed die at the end of the play. By citing examples we do not necessarily prove our case, but we give it factual support.

## Reading Selection

The following is an example taken from an article entitled "Trouble with Antibiotics." Specifically, it is meant to support the statement that "sometimes . . . side effects of antibiotics are unexpected and reporting them can be vitally important." It is worth noting that this example is an extended one, incorporating a central idea of its own ("the antibiotic clindamycin proved to have unexpected side effects"), and it is developed, in turn, by the citation of its own supporting examples.

### *From* TROUBLE WITH ANTIBIOTICS

#### *Jack S. Remington*

The most recent example of an unexpected reaction to antibiotics is the case of clindamycin. First marketed in the 1960s, clindamycin had passed the tests for safety and effectiveness required by the Food and Drug Administration. The FDA approved the drug for treatment of infections caused by three common bacteria: pneumococcus, streptococcus, and staphylococcus. Antibiotics against these organisms were already plentiful, but a drug does not need to be a significant improvement over existing drugs to be approved for sale. One side effect of clindamycin was diarrhea, but investigators did not consider it serious particularly because intestinal upset so often accompanies antibiotic therapy. As the antibiotic went into wide use, sporadic reports in medical journals described patients treated with it who developed alarmingly severe, indeed occasionally fatal, diarrhea and intestinal bleeding.

The new drug was a chemical derivative of another antibiotic that investigators had already recognized as a cause of severe diarrhea. Many practicing physicians, however, were unaware of the new drug's pedigree or of the increasing concern surrounding its use. Reliable information about untoward reactions to new drugs takes a long time to reach the family doctor. By the time data appear in medical journals, they may be six months to a year old, and isolated reports of complications that develop after a drug is put on sale can easily go unnoticed. Pharmaceutical houses are usually the first to become aware of side effects, and physicians depend on them for early information.

When clindamycin was approved for physicians to prescribe to their patients, the side effects seemed mild enough. Besides, continued research on the drug showed that its spectrum of action was broader than first realized: It was effective against a common cause of fatal abscesses (accumulations of pus) in the abdomen without the threat of anemia posed by the antibiotic then in use.

But disturbing reports continued until the potential danger was seen to be more serious than unpleasant diarrhea: The drug was causing destruction of the lining of the intestine. The result, a form of colitis, sometimes did not appear until after the required week or two of drug therapy had been completed and it was too late to change the drug. Milder cases of the colitis healed on their own, but some patients required intravenous feeding and anti-inflammatory drugs or surgical removal of parts of their bowel. For some infections, the risk of colitis was clearly worth taking, but clindamycin was still being prescribed to treat infections that would have responded to less hazardous antibiotics.

In 1974 and 1975, after we had seen 14 cases of the colitis in the Palo Alto area, John Swartzberg, Rosemary Maresca, and I conducted a local survey that showed that despite reports of the potentially life-threatening side effect of clindamycin, approximately 50 percent of people receiving the antibiotic were suffering from conditions no more serious than acne. The drug is still available, although the FDA requires it to carry a warning to restrict its use to certain conditions in which it is highly effective and often saves lives.

From *Human Nature* I (June 1978): 68–69.

### Questions

*Content/Meaning*
1. What examples support Remington's central point?
2. In paragraph 2 Remington gives support to the assertion that many physicians were unaware of the problems associated with using clindamycin. What are the supporting points, and are they illustrations or examples?

*Style*
1. In the final paragraph Remington reports on a local survey that discovered that "50 percent of people receiving the antibiotic were suffering from conditions no more serious than acne." Why does he choose to report only about this half of the survey?
2. Is Remington in favor of or against the use of clindamycin? How do you know?

When comparison is used alone to establish similarity between two objects or ideas, we have analogy. An example of this can be seen in the excerpt in the next chapter, where Robert E. Cole uses two analogies to contrast attitudes of Japanese and U.S. firms: "Japanese managers treat their employees as resources that, if cultivated, will yield economic returns to the firm." Whereas in the United States "the term 'quality control' accurately suggests the image of police monitoring others' performance." The manager to employee relationship in Japan is characterized as similar to the relationship between gardener and crop; if the crop is properly tended, the analogy implies, there will be a great harvest. The manager to employee relationship in the United States is likened to the police monitoring the potentially unruly or misbehaving, suggesting that "quality control" sounds like a variation of "crowd control." These analogies add much to the exposition, providing a pointed contrast and suggesting a difference in tone that would be difficult to describe directly.

Most often, analogy is used as a clarifying device that concentrates on using a familiar situation to introduce one that is less familiar. Here is one example.

> The visitor should begin with an understanding that every medieval church is a book, in which the story of God's creation and the human condition is told. A small church may contain only a few chapters—a capital here, an altarpiece there, a painted window, a tomb. But in Bourges, as in other great cathedrals, there are literally thousands of chapters. Nothing of importance is omitted, since the cathedral must be a *speculum majus,* or what we would now call an encyclopedia.
>
> Like an encyclopedia, a great cathedral cannot be read at a glance. If one's time is limited, it is best to concentrate on a few particularly glorious chapters. At Bourges, these are the center portal of the west facade and the windows. These should be read slowly, with the aid of good binoculars. (Alice Mary Hilton, "How to Read the Great Cathedrals of Europe," *The New York Times,* April 19, 1981, Section 10, pp. 1 *f.*)

Often analogies are extended to clarify an idea in some detail. The following is an extended analogy from an essay printed in *Freshman English News* and addressed to teachers of composition. The writer speaks from the point of view of a writing student dissatisfied with the standard essay and with traditional teaching.

> What I have been taught to construct is: the well-made box. I have been taught to put "what I have to say" into a container that is always remarkably the same, that—in spite of varying decorations—keeps to

a basically conventional form: a solid bottom, four upright sides, a fine-fitting lid. Indeed, I may be free to put "what I have to say" in the plain box, or the ornate box, in the large box or the small box, in the fragile box or the sturdy box. But always *the box*—squarish or rectangular. And I begin to wonder if there isn't somewhere a round box or oval box or tubular box, if somewhere there isn't some sort of a container (1) that will allow me to package "what I have to say" without trimming my "contents" to fit into a particular compositional mode, (2) that will actually encourage me to discover new "things to say" because of the very opportunity a newly-shaped container gives me, (3) that will be more suitable perhaps to my own mental processes, and (4) that will provide me with a greater rhetorical flexibility, allowing me to package what I have to say in more ways than one and thus reach more audiences than one. (Winston Weathers, *An Alternate Style: Options in Composition,* Montclair, N.J.: Boynton/Cook, 1980.)

**Questions**

*Content/Meaning*
1. Can you state the analogy simply and directly? What are the terms of the comparison?
2. Do you think Weathers' implied disapproval is just?

*Style*
1. Keeping in mind Weathers' audience, why do you think he uses analogy to make his point?
2. Can you characterize the voice and tone of the paragraph? How is the tone established? Do you think it persuaded anyone in its intended audience?

# Exercises

1. Find examples of writing that use illustration, example, or analogy to make their points and comment on them in your journal. Note the terms of the comparison for any analogies you notice.

2. Think of a process or an activity that you know well and write a 100–200 word explanation of it using analogy to make the explanation clear.

3. Think of an idea, situation, or conclusion that you have had difficulty explaining to someone. Then think of an illustration, a series of examples, or an analogy that would make the idea clear or help demonstrate the truth of your conclusion.

# 16

# COMPARISON AND CONTRAST

Sometimes we can develop a point best by showing how one detail compares and contrasts with another. Comparison involves showing similarities, while contrast shows differences. Comparisons must be made before we can make contrasts. Usually when we wish to make a contrast between two objects or ideas, we need to see, first, in what ways the two are alike.

If we return to the article on the hamburger maker (p. 221), we find that the three paragraphs following the definition depend essentially on contrast; it is their primary form of support and development. Note that the first paragraph concentrates on the contrast between the hamburger maker and the waffle iron, the similarities between which were discussed in the previous paragraph. The last two paragraphs report that all but one of the models failed to cook their hamburgers evenly on both sides.

This article contrasts two mansions designed as official residences for governors of California. As it happens, neither of them is currently (1982) occupied. As you read through this piece, note the points of contrast on which Didion focuses. Notice also how Didion uses both major organizational devices common to extended comparison and contrast:

1. first one thing, then the other: the new official residence (paragraphs 1 to 3), then the old residence (paragraphs 4 to 6);

and, briefly,

2. one thing and the other thing alternatively: "The bathrooms are big and airy and they do not have bidets" and "In the kitchen there is no trash compactor and there is no 'island' with the appliances built in but there are two pantries, and a nice old table with a marble top for rolling out pastry" (paragraph 6).

**238**

# Reading Selection

## MANY MANSIONS

### *Joan Didion*

The new official residence for governors of California, unlandscaped, unfurnished, and unoccupied since the day construction stopped in 1975, stands on eleven acres of oaks and olives on a bluff overlooking the American River outside Sacramento. This is the twelve-thousand-square-foot house that Ronald and Nancy Reagan built. This is the sixteen-room house in which Jerry Brown declined to live. This is the vacant house which cost the State of California one-million-four, not including the property, which was purchased in 1969 and donated to the state by such friends of the Reagans as Leonard K. Firestone of Firestone Tire and Rubber and Taft Schreiber of the Music Corporation of America and Holmes Tuttle, the Los Angeles Ford dealer. All day at this empty house three maintenance men try to keep the bulletproof windows clean and the cobwebs swept and the wild grass green and the rattlesnakes down by the river and away from the thirty-five exterior wood and glass doors. All night at this empty house the lights stay on behind the eight-foot chain-link fence and the guard dogs lie at bay and the telephone, when it rings, startles by the fact that it works. "Governor's Residence," the guards answer, their voices laconic, matter-of-fact, quite as if there were some phantom governor to connect. Wild grass grows where the tennis court was to have been. Wild grass grows where the pool and sauna were to have been. The American is the river in which gold was discovered in 1848, and it once ran fast and full past here, but lately there have been upstream dams and dry years. Much of the bed is exposed. The far bank has been dredged and graded. That the river is running low is of no real account, however, since one of the many peculiarities of the new Governor's Residence is that it is so situated as to have no clear view of the river.

It is an altogether curious structure, this one-story one-million-four dream house of Ronald and Nancy Reagan's. Were the house on the market (which it will probably not be, since, at the time it was costing a million-four, local real estate agents seemed to agree on $300,000 as the top price ever paid for a house in Sacramento County), the words used to describe it would be "open" and "contemporary," although technically it is neither. "Flow" is a word that crops up quite a bit when one is walking through the place, and so is "resemble." The walls "resemble" local adobe, but they are not: they are the same concrete blocks, plastered and painted a rather stale yellowed cream, used in so many supermarkets and housing projects and Coca-Cola bottling plants. The door frames and the exposed beams "resemble" native redwood, but they are not: they are construction-grade lumber of indeterminate quality, stained brown. If anyone ever moves in, the concrete floors will be carpeted, wall to wall. If anyone ever moves in, the thirty-five exterior wood and glass doors, possibly the single distinctive feature in the house, will be, according to plan, "draped." The bathrooms are small and standard. The family bedrooms open directly onto the nonexistent swimming pool, with all its potential for noise and distraction. To one side of the fireplace in the formal living room there is what is known in the trade as a "wet bar," a cabinet for bottles and glasses with a sink and a long vinyl-topped counter. (This vinyl "resembles" slate.) In the entire house there are only enough bookshelves for a set of the World Book and some Books of the Month, plus maybe three Royal Doulton figurines and a back file of *Connoisseur,* but there is $90,000 worth of other teak cabinetry, including the "refreshment center" in the "recreation room." There is that most ubiquitous of all "luxury features," a bidet in the master bedroom. There is one of those kitchens which seem designed exclusively for defrosting by microwave and compacting trash. It is a house built for a family of snackers.

And yet, appliances notwithstanding, it is hard to see where the million-four went. The place has been called, by Jerry Brown, a "Taj Mahal." It has been called a "white elephant," a "resort," a "monument to the colossal ego of our former governor." It is not exactly any of these things. It is simply and rather astonishingly an enlarged version of a very common kind of California tract house, a monument not to colossal ego but to a weird absence of ego, a case study in the architecture of limited possibilities, insistently and malevolently "democratic," flattened out, mediocre and "open" and as devoid of privacy or personal eccentricity as the lobby area in a Ramada Inn. It is the architecture of "background music," decorators, "good taste." I recall once interviewing Nancy Reagan, at a time when her husband was governor and the construction on this house had not yet begun. We drove down to the State Capitol Building that day, and Mrs. Reagan showed me how she had lightened and brightened offices there by replacing the old burnished leather on the walls with the kind of beige burlap then favored in new office buildings. I mention this because it was on my mind as I walked through the empty house on the American River outside Sacramento.

From 1903 until Ronald Reagan, who lived in a rented house in Sacramento while he was governor ($1,200 a month, payable by the state to a group of Reagan's friends), the governors of California lived in a large white Victorian Gothic house at 16th and H Streets in Sacramento. This extremely individual house, three stories and a cupola and the face of Columbia the Gem of the Ocean worked into the molding over every door, was built in

1877 by a Sacramento hardware merchant named Albert Gallatin. The state paid $32,500 for it in 1903 and my father was born in a house a block away in 1908. This part of town has since run to seed and small business, the kind of place where both Squeaky Fromme and Patricia Hearst could and probably did go about their business unnoticed, but the Governor's Mansion, unoccupied and open to the public as State Historical Landmark Number 823, remains Sacramento's premier example of eccentric domestic architecture.

As it happens I used to go there once in a while, when Earl Warren was governor and his daughter Nina was a year ahead of me at C. K. McClatchy Senior High School. Nina was always called "Honey Bear" in the papers and in *Life* Magazine but she was called "Nina" at C. K. McClatchy Senior High School and she was called "Nina" (or sometimes "Warren") at weekly meetings of the Mañana Club, a local institution to which we both belonged. I recall being initiated into the Mañana Club one night at the old Governor's Mansion, in a ceremony which involved being blindfolded and standing around Nina's bedroom in a state of high apprehension about secret rites which never materialized. It was the custom for the members to hurl mild insults at the initiates, and I remember being dumbfounded to hear Nina, by my fourteen-year-old lights the most glamorous and unapproachable fifteen-year-old in America, characterize me as "stuck on herself." There in the Governor's Mansion that night I learned for the first time that my face to the world was not necessarily the face in my mirror. "No smoking on the third floor," everyone kept saying. "Mrs. Warren *said.* No smoking on the third floor *or else.*"

Firetrap or not, the old Governor's Mansion was at that time my favorite house in the world, and probably still is. The morning after I was shown the new "Residence" I visited the old "Mansion," took the public tour with a group of perhaps twenty people, none of whom seemed to find it as ideal as I did. "All those stairs," they murmured, as if stairs could no longer be tolerated by human physiology. "All those stairs," and "all that waste space." The old Governor's Mansion does have stairs and waste space, which is precisely why it remains the kind of house in which sixty adolescent girls might gather and never interrupt the real life of the household. The bedrooms are big and private and high-ceilinged and they do not open on the swimming pool and one can imagine reading in one of them, or writing a book, or closing the door and crying until dinner. The bathrooms are big and airy and they do not have bidets but they do have room for hampers, and dressing tables, and chairs on which to sit and read a story to a child in the bathtub. There are hallways wide and narrow, stairs front and back, sewing rooms, ironing rooms, secret rooms. On the gilt mirror in the library there is worked a bust of Shakespeare, a pretty fancy for a hardware merchant in a California farm town in 1877. In the kitchen there is no trash compactor and there is no "island" with the appliances built in but there are two pantries, and a nice old table with a marble top for rolling out pastry and making divinity fudge and chocolate leaves. The morning I took the tour our guide asked if anyone could think why the old table had a marble top. There were a dozen or so other women in the group, each of an age to have cooked unnumbered meals, but not one of them could think of a single use for a slab of marble in the kitchen. It occurred to me that we had finally evolved a society in which knowledge of a pastry marble, like a taste for stairs and closed doors, could be construed as "elitist," and as I left the Governor's Mansion I felt very like the heroine of Mary McCarthy's *Birds of America,* the one who located America's moral decline in the disappearance of the first course.

A guard sleeps at night in the old mansion, which has been condemned as a dwelling by the state fire marshal. It costs about $85,000 a year to keep guards at the new official residence. Meanwhile the current governor of California, Edmund G. Brown, Jr., sleeps on a mattress on the floor in the famous apartment for which he pays $275 a month out of his own $49,100 annual salary. This has considerable and potent symbolic value, as do the two empty houses themselves, most particularly the house the Reagans built on the river. It is a great point around the Capitol these days to have "never seen" the house on the river. The governor himself has "never seen" it. The governor's press secretary, Elisabeth Coleman, has "never seen" it. The governor's chief of staff, Gray Davis, admits to having seen it, but only once, when "Mary McGrory wanted to see it." This unseen house on the river is, Jerry Brown has said, "not my style."

As a matter of fact this is precisely the point about the house on the river—the house is not Jerry Brown's style, not Mary McGrory's style, *not our style*—and it is a point which presents a certain problem, since the house so clearly *is* the style not only of Jerry Brown's predecessor but of millions of Jerry Brown's constituents. Words are chosen carefully. Reasonable objections are framed. One hears about how the house is too far from the Capitol, too far from Legislature. One hears about the folly of running such a lavish establishment for an unmarried governor and one hears about the governor's temperamental austerity. One hears every possible reason for not living in the house except the one that counts: it is the kind of house that has a wet bar in the living room. It is the kind of house that has a refreshment center. It is the kind of house in which one does not live, but there is no way to say this without getting into touchy and evanescent and finally inadmissible questions of taste, and ultimately of class. I have seldom seen a house so evocative of the unspeakable.

From Joan Didion, *The White Album*
(New York: Pocket Books, 1979), pp. 67–
73.

**Questions**

*Content/Meaning*
1. Is there a single, essential contrast between the mansions that includes all others?
2. Contrast paragraphs 2 and 6. To what is the new residence compared in paragraph 2? How is the old mansion described in paragraph 6?
3. Is it unfair of Didion to furnish the empty bookcases in paragraph 2? Why does she choose the objects she names?
4. What is wrong with having a wet bar in the living room or not knowing what a "pastry marble" is? What is Didion getting at in the last paragraph?

*Style*
1. How is the opening paragraph organized? (Look for patterns of repetition and contrast.)
2. How would you describe the tone of the piece and the sound of the writer's voice? Does this tone of voice help give you clear pictures of the mansions, or does it interfere?
3. Didion is very explicit and concrete in comparing and contrasting concrete details until the last paragraph. Is the last paragraph vague or evasive? What does she mean by "the unspeakable"?

# Reading Selection

Here is a piece that develops an extended contrast between the approaches of Japanese and U.S. industrial organizations to the problem of managing product quality. As you read, look for instances of specific points of contrast as well as for other methods of developing the exposition, such as definition, illustration, and example.

### *From* THE JAPANESE LESSON IN QUALITY

#### *Robert E. Cole*

Organization of quality control is critical. Japanese line managers and production employees, rather than staff specialists, are primarily responsible for quality assurance. Training in quality assurance is company-wide, including statistical problem-solving methods for top management, which actively directs quality-control activities. Middle management is largely responsible for interdepartmental planning and coordination of quality activities, while staff quality-assurance specialists have only a limited role as consultants and trainers. Production managers and supervisors assume an important role in product and process planning, quality control, shop improvements, and quality-improvement programs for workers. Finally, production workers themselves, through "quality-control circles," are encouraged to inspect their own work and are trained to identify and solve shop problems.

At Toyota, workers who spot quality problems can halt assembly without consulting superiors, helping to pinpoint the exact cause. Doing the job right the first time is more than a slogan—it is built into the organizational structure. Reliance on worker self-inspection encourages attention to detail and preventive problem solving, reducing the costs of hiring full-time inspectors.

Thus, Japanese managers treat their employees as resources that, if cultivated, will yield economic returns to the firm. Firms invest in training for all employees and emphasize development of a labor force skilled in a variety of jobs. All workers are assumed to be capable and desirous of contributing to the firm and are made to feel like fully contributing members: production workers, for instance, are on monthly salary rather than hourly wage.

By comparison, U.S. automotive firms maintain separate and large staffs of quality specialists, including quality-control inspectors and reliability engineers with major responsibility for achieving quality. Indeed, the term "quality control" accurately suggests the image of police monitoring others' performance. This approach greatly emphasizes continuous training for managers and staff specialists and is quite effective in establishing a formal system of quality planning and practices. But there are also significant costs. In particular, available human resources are not fully utilized. As one senior U.S. automotive executive says, "We wrote off the workers as contributors to the organization in the 1930s when they unionized."

U.S. automobile assembly plants employ approximately one full-time inspector for every twenty production workers. By comparison, Toyota and Nissan employ one full-time inspector for every thirty production workers, resulting in significant savings and increased productivity. In U.S. plants, the inspectors do in fact find a great deal of substandard production, but reliance on inspectors causes other employees to be less concerned about quality, which in turn leads management to hire even more inspectors. Indeed, problems are often passed on to the dealer, who receives large "dealer preparation fees" to make final adjustments and corrections. The consumer often ends up with a costlier, poorer-quality product. This cycle reveals the disadvantages of separating quality assurance from its execution.

Perhaps the most publicized Japanese innovation in quality control is the effort to involve production employees in quality assurance through the so-called "quality circles." Developed in the early 1960s, this practice has become standard at most large manufacturing firms. For example, at Toyota there are 4,200 quality-control circles for 47,000 employees, and at Nissan, 99 percent of eligible employees participate in 4,162 quality-controlled circles. The circles are in principle voluntary and autonomous study groups, though in practice there is company pressure to participate.

Circles averaging ten workers apiece, usually led by the supervisor or a senior worker, meet every week or two for an hour to analyze and solve shop problems. Participants are taught elementary techniques in problem solving, including statistical methods. In principle, workers select their own problems to work on, including not only reduction of defects and scrap but also broader problems such as cost reduction, safety, absenteeism, and energy conservation.

The circles are geared to small-scale but continuous improvements, and the overall results are impressive. Consider the following: General Motors receives an average of .84 suggestion per eligible employee each year, of which it adopts about 23 percent. Nissan Motors reported in 1979 a total of 9 suggestions per employee and an adoption rate of 85.7 percent, with more than 70 percent of these suggestions made by groups, most originating in the quality-control circles. In 1980, Toyota Motors reported 17.8 suggestions per employee, of which it adopted close to 90 percent. Thus, not only are these firms getting more suggestions, they are getting better ones. The adoption of quality-control circles over the last decade and the rapid rise in the number of Japanese employee suggestions are closely correlated with the rapid increase in Japanese automotive quality and productivity.

Suggestion systems in the U.S. firms are notably different. Managers implicitly assume that individual workers have enough information about operations to generate constructive suggestions. In contrast, the assumption behind Japanese quality-control circles is that joint efforts are needed to determine causes of a problem and to arrive at solutions. A corollary is that workers must be provided with the tools—training and access to information—to identify and solve these problems.

From *Technology Review,* July 1981, pp. 36, 38, 40.

### Questions

*Content/Meaning*
1. What is being compared and contrasted in this excerpt? What is the main point of the contrasts? What supports the point?
2. What contrasts in philosophy and attitude underlie the differing Japanese and U.S. approaches to managing product quality?

*Style*
1. How is this excerpt organized? Does Cole discuss first the Japanese system, then the U.S., or does he treat the two systems alternately? Or does he, like Didion, do both? Point to some specific paragraphs.
2. Can you characterize the voice and tone of this piece? To whom is it addressed?

3. Does the writer prefer the Japanese or the U.S. system? How do you know? What are his reasons? his values?

## Reading Selection

The following article is from a journal that specializes in book reviewing and in printing excerpts from forthcoming books; this is an excerpt from Susan Griffin's *Pornography and Silence: Culture's Revenge Against Nature.* The article is a subtle and difficult analysis of the place of the sex goddess in the minds of females and males in our culture. To help you read the piece, consider the following divisions:

- Part 1 introduces us to the themes and ideas of the excerpt: the culture of pornography, the pressures on the powerless to impersonate false images, the similarities between the film star and the ordinary woman (paragraphs 1–10).
- Part 2 takes up the life of Marilyn Monroe; how and why she became a sex goddess (paragraphs 11–31).
- Part 3 brings us to a conclusion: pornographic culture first annihilates a woman's real self and then annihilates the false self that had been erected in its place (paragraphs 32–37).

### MARILYN MONROE

### The Sex Goddess as Scapegoat

#### Susan Griffin

Like the men and women who lived in slavery, women have become talented at seeming to be what we are not. Within the institution of slavery, and even outliving this institution, the racist mind of the slave owner required that the men and women he enslaved resemble the image which he had of them. Because he imagined that blacks were stupid and slow, he required of his slaves that they appear to be stupid and slow. And because they wished to survive, men and women of quick intelligence learned to mime a slow and stupid manner. . . . Because their masters needed to believe them happy, they mimed happiness. Thus we have a whole panoply of "black" characters: Jim Crow, Aunt Jemima, Uncle Tom, all of whom were created by a white racist mind, and in turn were only acted out by black slaves.

This acting out, however, does not belong to a particular class or race; it belongs to a situation. Survival forces all people to learn to perform, and women are no exception. For the same situation which created and is still creating the black actor also makes a woman into an actor. Just as the slave master required the slaves to imitate the image he had of them, so women, who live in a relatively powerless position, politically and economically, feel obliged by a kind of implicit force to live up to culture's image of what is female. Thus we learn to impersonate pornography's idea of a woman.

Nowhere is this impersonation so clear as in the woman whom culture has chosen to be a symbol for female sexuality. Just as the black comedian Bert Williams wore blackface so that he could more easily resemble the stereotyped Negro, the female "sex symbol" never appears simply as herself. Such women even have artificial bodies. We know, for instance, that Jean Harlow dyed her hair. We know that Carol Doda had her breasts enlarged with silicone. That Marilyn Monroe had her nose shortened.

But this artificiality and this illusory history were not created by these performers. Rather, these women were impersonating the pornographic idea of a female, and of female sexuality. Marilyn Monroe actually created a character, whom she called "Marilyn," and who she knew was not her*self*. The actress Simone Signoret tells us that in Monroe's private life she rarely dressed anything like the self we know as "Marilyn." Signoret refers to the costume required to create Monroe's illusory self as her "Marilyn getup." She spent hours applying makeup, teasing a lock of hair to drop "casually" over her forehead, choosing the proper tight and exposing dress. We learn from Signoret that in the actress's private life she wore loose and comfortable clothing. Moreover, the personality which she presented to the public was not hers. Signoret tells us that Monroe would suddenly assume a "simpering and sighing" attitude when she became "Marilyn" for the public.

Pornographic culture does not entirely ignore the fact of this false persona. Norman Mailer writes of Marilyn Monroe: "She is a mirror of the pleasure of those who stare at her." Yet, knowing that her symbolic existence was a mask, he refuses to look behind this mask. All he hypothesizes about a self behind this mask is that this first self must have felt a need to create a false self. Beyond that, he records no being, no will, no intelligence, no *self.* And in this we sense the attitude of a whole culture toward the "sex symbol." Beneath the extravagant worship of the sex goddess we can hear the echo of Otto Weininger's words: "Woman is nothing."

And yet, had another self not existed, a self to be lost and a self to be violated, the life of this actress would not have been a tragedy. In an interview before her death, she said: "I used to get the feeling, and sometimes I still get it, that sometimes I was fooling somebody, I don't know who or what— maybe myself." But this *is* the *experience* of loss. When one has lost one's *self,* one does not say, I am one way but I behave another. Rather, one has forgotten that the lost self ever existed. Only a feeling of falsity remains, and a sense of grief, and of anger.

Although these feelings arise out of absence, they should be taken as evidence for a self which cries out to be recognized and which will inevitably turn its rage upon the false self that has destroyed her. And because pornographic culture attaches this false self to her body, she confuses this false self with her own body. It is thus that a woman angry with pornography's false image of herself tries to destroy her own body.

But in this, the extraordinary film star is not so different from an ordinary woman. Rather, she is emblematic of culture's expectations of us. Ordinary women wear makeup. Ordinary women attempt to change our bodies to resemble a pornographic ideal. Ordinary women construct a false self and come to hate this self. And yet the film star who represents to culture the perfection of a false image of women can represent a danger and a threat to an ordinary woman's life. For the image of the film star is held up to her both as what she must imitate and to show her how she has failed to live up to the pornographic ideal. Moreover, the ordinary woman can choose to project her hatred of her own false self upon the "sex symbol." It is always easier for a woman within pornographic culture to take out her rage over her silence and her powerlessness on another woman than on that culture itself. Therefore, certain ordinary women come to hate the woman who has become culture's sex symbol. We cast her away, we become almost violent in our effort to remove her and all memory of her from our sight. We tell ourselves we despise her. We deny that this image of her has anything to do with ourselves. And yet this image has entered us. And now we are no longer free. For in another layer of our minds, we are convinced that we are like this woman, indeed identical to her. Thus, just as we have lost her, the possibility of knowing her, of resonating with her being, we have lost ourselves.

And too, when we do this, we participate ultimately in a cruelty to ourselves. We become instruments of pornography's sadism against women. . . .

But if we move to *know* this being, we are taking back an aspect of ourselves which has been stolen. We refuse to hate another woman. We refuse to enter this drama that pornography has asked us to act.

If we enter the life of Marilyn Monroe, we find that behind a facade of glamour is the life of an ordinary woman. Let us begin with a simple recital of facts (some of which seem ordinary and others extraordinary). When she is a baby, her mother is abandoned by her father. And soon her mother abandons her to the care of a foster mother, who lives across the street from the child's grandmother. This foster mother is a traditional woman, who gives all her life to the care of children and a husband and who is, moreover, a Christian fundamentalist.

This child begins as a kind of tomboy, physically strong and tough. She is often admonished for overpowering her half-brother. Her mother will not allow her to be adopted by her foster mother. But her "brother" is adopted. In her early years in school she is described as a bright student, but after a few years, her efforts as a student suffer a sudden decline.

Now her mother, who works in the film industry, takes her child to live with her. But soon after, she breaks down and is incarcerated in a mental institution. Thus the child is sent to foster homes and to an orphanage. In one foster home, she tells us, she is molested by her foster father. In the orphanage she is given special attention by a teacher who tells her she is pretty and allows her to wear makeup. As she is growing up, she is happy to receive attention from boys and men who admire her body.

She marries conventionally, and very early, partly so that she will be able to leave her foster home. But this marriage fails. Then she begins work as a model. She comes to the attention of the film industry when she models for a pornographic photograph. She changes her name to Marilyn Monroe. Later she becomes one of the most famous actresses of her time or any other time. She is, in Mailer's words, society's "sex goddess." At the pinnacle of her career, she takes her own life.

Now we know that the circumstances of Marilyn Monroe's childhood were extreme. And yet her suffering is not wholly unfamiliar to the ordinary woman with an ordinary childhood. For there is a sense in which all women are motherless. The classic social idea of what it is to be "a mother" is that one is in effect a nonbeing. The mother's name has been erased and substituted with a man's name. She exists to please her husband and her children. She serves and organizes herself about other needs. Therefore, her decisions have no meaning for herself, and her intelligence has no independent life.

To look back into childhood, in the place occupied by one's mother, and find nothing, this is a desolation. Every moment of adult fear is colored by this backward glance into invisibility. No image for courage exists, none of the mind's ways of creating courage. But it is precisely great courage which a woman needs if she is to step out of her pornographic role and to cease impersonating the female.

And to this absence of a female model of courage we must add the cultural idea of female destructiveness. We find this idea manifest in the childhood of Marilyn Monroe and in the lives of ordinary women. Here is the bright and tough little girl who slowly transforms herself into a simpering and sighing creature. Statistics have recorded that at a certain age, a girl's performance in school declines. The little girl decides not to be a "tomboy." But why? Let us make a conjecture about Marilyn Monroe's decision to become "feminine," for this decision may be emblematic of every female decision to give up the self in favor of a pornographic self.

First, we must recall that children are given to feeling guilty about events over which they really have no control. Indeed, guilt is one way in which they might pretend to themselves they can control an overpowering world. And in this light, let us suppose that Marilyn Monroe felt guilty about the fact that her father abandoned her mother. Thus, from guilt, she would look at her own character to find what might have caused this abandonment. And this is why she becomes extremely sensitive to those criticisms which are made of her, and which society makes of women. She learns that it is wrong for her to be stronger than her brother, Lester. She learns that men like pliable, submissive, quiet, and not too intelligent women. She imagines that her strength, her intelligence, the very power of her beingness, drove her father away, and therefore she becomes afraid of the destructiveness of her authentic self. *Her own erotic energy is set against her need to be loved.*

But this is not so far from an ordinary woman's experience. Even if she is not abandoned by her father, over and over again culture tells her that men abandon women who speak too loudly, or who are too *present.* And her very survival in the world depends on her being able to find a man to marry. Therefore, she gives up being a tomboy and learns "femininity."

But now let us, from an "ordinary" woman's knowledge of female sexuality, reconstruct another explanation for why Monroe became the seductive "sex goddess." To begin with, let us take note of the rather extraordinary suggestion made by Norman Mailer, which he tells us was based on "private," "reliable" male sources, that Monroe was almost "frigid." (She herself tells us that she did not understand what it was that made young men so "urgent.")

We do not know if Mailer's observation is truthful. But let us conjecture that there is some truth in it. And let us try to discover the meaning of that by translating a male word for female experience into female language. For a women never experiences herself as being *frigid.* Rather, she feels *numb.*

Now inside numbness, or behind numbness, is the capacity for feeling. Numbness does not signify an absence of feeling, but rather an arrest. And certainly in the early life of the child who was to become Marilyn Monroe we can find much cause for an arrest of feeling. Yet, too, in this early life we discover a bright and energetic child, a child of much power, who must also have been very feeling. One can still sense this strong feeling even through the pornographic mask of the adult Marilyn Monroe.

Here is the classic condition of the female self: the experience of numbness and the burial of feeling. Yet this lost and feeling self, in Marilyn Monroe, must have been crying to be known. We imagine that she must have mourned this "erotic" self, this lost self. Indeed she is not content at all with numbness or nonbeingness. She refuses to submit to this female condition. She would have nothing less than her own capacity to feel returned to her, her own eros returned to her.

But she is numb. To be well again, she needs to find a way back to her original self. And that way is blocked to her. Therefore, in order to find herself, she turns to culture for some model of female sexuality to imitate.

But an ideal is so much more elusive, so much harder to follow than a real human being. To follow such a dream takes very large acting talents. Monroe must learn to impersonate not only a "woman," but she must impersonate culture's *ideal* of a "sexual" woman.

We read that Laurence Olivier described her as "being able to suggest one moment that she is the naughtiest little thing and the next that she's perfectly innocent . . ." But this is pornographic culture's idea of female sexuality. The virgin and the whore. Justine and Juliette. Complete innocence, or a destructive depravity. Paradoxically, this is an imagery which when combined expresses Monroe's dilemma perfectly. The quality she has of "lostness" and of grief becomes "virginal." That she is afraid of her own power, that her guilt causes her to repress her own intelligence, all this contributes to the sense of her "innocence." In her uncertainty over who she is, she whispers. (Like the black slave, she must appear to be incapable of learning.) Therefore, she exhibits carnal knowledge, but she does not dare to have carnal knowledge.

And again, nowhere can she find models of feminine protest against this pornographic imagery. For any attempt which a woman makes to protest this falsity is described by the pornographic culture as prudery. Finally, those women who would protest this imagery even take up the language of prudery, because for them no other language exists. They worry that their daughters will be exploited and made into things. But they can only express this worry by asserting that certain behavior is not "proper." For they have no way to say that such behavior is dangerous to a woman's body and soul.

Thus Marilyn Monroe could find only one kind of image to express the female eros she wanted to reclaim for herself. Here is the essence of her tragedy. We sense that because she wished to reclaim her own eros, she was moved to impersonate a pornographic image of female sexuality. But if she was trying to escape emptiness, she unwittingly took upon herself an image of emptiness. For hidden beneath every pornographic image of female glamour is the conviction that a woman does not really exist. Even the studio where she worked told her that they had created her. "Marilyn" did not belong to her. Indeed, the narcissist in this dramatic scene composed of film star and audience turns out to be not the star at all, but clearly the audience, for when they see her, they see a part of themselves. Like all pornographic heroines, the image which Marilyn Monroe impersonated was a projection of the male psyche.

Think of the ironic progress of her life. Increasingly, as she felt empty, she must have decided that if only she could improve her impersonation of a sex symbol, she might finally find her real *self*. All her life, she had been led to believe that it was herself and not the pornographic ideal who was deficient. That she felt herself to be a fraud, that is, to be in reality unlike the image she copied, only made her try harder and harder to perfect her impersonation. Finally, she became the sex goddess of her age. Now she was the very image she had hoped . . . desperately to imitate. Yet, even *being* this image, she still *felt* empty. Inside this perfection was the same nothingness and the same numbness she feared.

But the ordinary woman suffers a similar dilemma. All her life she tries to be the star, or to be like her. And all her life she fails. Or she decides that she is so deficient she cannot even try to become this ideal. (Or if she sees through this ideal and rejects it, all her life she senses that society measures her against an alien idea of what it is to be a woman.) Thus an ordinary woman has the same sense of inner failure as does the "star." And if this "ordinary" woman achieves some degree of extraordinariness, if she is perceived as very attractive, if she is sought after by men, if she is "loved," she will eventually discover this adulation, and the role she plays, to be empty too.

But, like Monroe, she has escaped into an image of glamour so that she will not share the fate of the ordinary woman. For everywhere in society we see that the "ordinary" woman is subjected to a subtle derision. At the same time that a woman is encouraged to be a wife and a mother, a woman who takes on this role says of herself, "I'm just a housewife." And we come to accept as common knowledge that a man will be more attracted to an extraordinary woman than to his wife. Everything that is exciting about the sex goddess speaks of a corresponding dullness in the wife and mother. For in the pornographic idea of sexuality, passion is opposed to the material necessities of daily life. Therefore, like Marilyn Monroe, all women within this culture find ourselves caught between the Scylla and Charibdis of ordinariness and extraordinariness. We are afraid of "becoming our mothers."

Now we are at the heart of a female tragedy within pornographic culture. For within this culture, when a woman expresses her real power, this power can only be expressed through images which transform female power into an image of submissiveness. Marilyn Monroe's "charisma"—a word used often about her (which means a "gift of grace")—was clothed in an image of "simpering and sighing."

And yet pornographic rage against female power does not stop with this diminishment and degradation. For pornographic culture has the same relationship of ambivalence with and ultimate hatred for its "sex goddesses" as does the pornographic hero for the pornographic heroine. Therefore, Monroe was aware of a continual current of hostility against her. She tells us that people see her as a commodity. She complains that she is "always running into people's unconscious." And finally, knowing from her own experience that the sexual object becomes the object of violence, she tells us, ". . . everybody is always tugging at you. They'd all like . . . a chunk of you. They kind of take pieces out of you."

But the ritual sacrifice of the female sex goddess is not new to us. We are accustomed to thinking of her as dying young. We are not so shocked to learn she lives an unhappy life. Our image of her includes self-destructive behavior. We expect that she takes drugs and drinks too much and attempts suicide. For we know that the women who take the pornographic image of female sexuality upon themselves live out the tragedy of the female condition within pornographic culture. This is the culture which Mailer accurately describes as "drawing a rifle sight on an open vagina," a culture that even within its worship of the female sex goddess hates female sexuality.

And ironically, just as she becomes more extraordinary, as she is made into a supernatural being, a goddess, the pornographic star ceases to be a creature for whom one has compassion. She exists in the imagination, outside human identity and identification. Culture can imagine her destroying her body as easily as in the 1950s Hungarian protesters destroyed a statue of the head of Stalin. For she becomes a pornographic symbol in pornographic culture and is no longer real.

Indeed, Marilyn Monroe's death has actually become a pornographic fantasy. In an "expose" of her death in *Hustler* magazine, one reads that she was murdered. And, the prose of this expose reminds one of the classic pornographic account of the murder of the pornographic heroine. Here is the same cold cruelty of language. Of her autopsy, for example, one reads that with "practised precision Dr. Noguchi eased a razor sharp scalpel in Marilyn's lower abdomen, slicing open the skin as he moved the blade up toward her sternum." Now the culture relishes the destruction of this body which it has said it worships.

In both image and event, fact and fantasy, pornographic culture annihilates the female sex. Pornography begins by annihilating the real female self and replacing this self with a false self. But this false self is finally only a projection which belongs to the pornographic hero. Therefore, the false self, too, must be annihilated. Thus along with the feeling of emptiness, a woman inherits from culture a continual experience of fear. For the image of a woman's body must be replaced with an image of her absence.

From New Boston Review, March/April<br>1981, pp. 20-23.

### Questions

*Content/Meaning*
1. This piece begins with a series of comparisons between the institution of slavery and the position of women in a pornographic culture. What are the comparisons?

2. A major point in this analysis is that the lives of ordinary women are similar to the life of Marilyn Monroe. How is this assertion supported?

3. Does Griffin provide a clear definition of "pornographic culture"? How would you define it?

4. What is the "female tragedy within pornographic culture" (paragraph 32)?

5. The central segment of this article is a reconstruction of Marilyn Monroe's life, including very intimate and psychologically subtle decisions and feelings. What supports these reconstructions? Are they believable?

6. Much of this article analyzes how our culture destroys women. Does Griffin propose any solution to this problem?

*Style*

1. Is this excerpt difficult to read? If so, why?

2. Is there a clear voice or tone to this piece? To whom is it addressed?

## Exercises and Assignments

1. Think of two similar but contrasting objects, products, ideas, activities, events, or people from your experience and write an essay exploring their differences. Remember, there must be a basis of similarity before a contrast can work. Try to think of a single basic contrast that might organize all the others.

2. In the second paragraph Griffin suggests that all women "learn to impersonate pornography's idea of a woman." Write the story of a situation where this impersonation takes place.

3. In paragraph 21 Griffin translates "a male word for female experience into female language," changing *frigid* to *numb*. Can you think of other example, of what males and females mean by phrases like "be a tease," "play hard to get," or "be after only one thing."

Write a paper where you make the need for translation clear by placing the words in their proper context: that is, define the words operationally by referring to specific situations, actions, and dialogue and by focusing on the contrast between male and female perceptions. You might think, for example, of what males and females mean by phrases like "be a tease," "play hard to get," or "be after only one thing."

# 17

## CAUSES AND EFFECTS

One way to develop explanations is to trace causes and effects. Statements about causes and effects are common in exposition but do not always occur with supporting evidence. In the article on water purity in Chapter 13 the writer stated that "turbid," or cloudy, water (the effect) could indicate possible contamination by sewage (the cause). We are not let in on why this may be true, but we trust that the writer has done her homework and are warned not to drink cloudy water without boiling it.

Cause-and-effect exposition is also present in the article evaluating the hamburger maker (Chapter 14). Most of these devices have a heating element on only one side. The article investigates the effect of this design and finds that the burgers come out browned on one side and grayish brown on the other. The one exception is the model with two heating elements, neatly proving that the design is the cause of the uneven cooking.

Life rarely provides the occasion for such sure testing, and most exposition is not primarily concerned with proving or disproving the truth of assertions. In the unit on argument and persuasion, we take up questions of how to evaluate cause-and-effect relationships. In this chapter we focus on cause-and-effect statements in the service of the clear explanation of things known to be true or believed to be true by the writer. For example, consider this sentence from the excerpt on Japanese quality assurance practices in Chapter 16: "Reliance on worker self-inspection [a cause] encourages attention to detail and preventive problem solving, reducing the costs of hiring full-time inspectors [some effects]." No evidence is given for this statement. It may be the observation or conclusion of the writer, or he may be repeating the explanation of Japanese managers commenting on their program. As stated, however, the conclusion is a theory, not a fact, though it does explain the rationale for using "worker self-inspection."

**255**

Some cause-and-effect statements are, perhaps, unprovable. Consider this sentence from the same article: "The adoption of quality-control circles over the last decade and the rapid rise in the number of Japanese employee suggestions are closely correlated with the rapid increase in Japanese automotive quality and productivity." This statement may stop just short of asserting a cause-and-effect relationship between the quality circles and Japanese productivity; what exactly does "closely correlated" mean? Correlated by whom? The author? The Japanese? The U.S. firms who are studying and adapting Japanese methods? And how correlated? Is there a causal relationship or not? Are the quality circles just one of a number of factors? Though the situation may be too complicated ever to prove such a relationship with certainty, the writer might have offered some more information on the point. While the statement fails as proof and is not as precise as it could be, it may go a long way toward explaining the interest of U.S. firms and U.S. publications like *Technology Review* (which published the article) in the business practices of a country widely recognized as a major competitor of the United States.

## Reading Selection

In accepting cause-and-effect statements in exposition, we rely on the knowledge and experience of the writer to know what he or she is talking about. Here is a writer on a specialized topic writing in a specialized magazine, *Money*. This passage examines the failure of Real Estate Investment Trusts at a time when individuals could sell real estate at very high profits. It is developed using an effect-to-cause organization. We begin by examining a general effect: Publicly owned companies have not been profitable in real estate transactions when individuals have. The rest of the explanation examines multiple causes for this paradoxical situation.

### From BUYING A PIECE OF SOMEONE ELSE'S ACTION

#### Charles J. Rolo

It seems paradoxical that publicly owned companies should have done so badly in real estate while so many individuals have profited from investments in their own homes, as well as from rental properties and even from vacant land. But the paradox isn't hard to explain. To begin with, real estate is not a single market but several different ones—houses, apartments, commercial and industrial property and different types of land. In land, for example, the profits made by individuals were mostly reaped in the path of development, in farmland and in residential lots in suburbs or resorts. By contrast, the big land companies typically bought the cheapest sort of land—often desert and sometimes swamp. They marketed small lots at exorbitant prices, using high-pressure sales tactics and bringing upon themselves tighter government regulation, court actions and bad publicity. Their sales and profits suffered as a result, knocking down their stock prices.

Furthermore, the real estate industry is unusually sensitive to business cycles. It is exceptionally highly leveraged—that is, it operates largely on borrowed money. When highly leveraged companies are hit by a recession, their profits fall precipitously or turn into losses, causing their stock prices to plunge. From 1971 to 1976, according to a recent nationwide survey by the research firm of Norman B. Ture Inc., the annual growth rate of the real estate industry was substantially less than that of the rest of American business. Because of overexpansion in the early 1970s, the industry was highly vulnerable to the soaring costs and interest rates of 1973-74 and the recession that followed. The result was the worst slump in real estate since the 1920s.

From *Money,* February 1978, pp. 74-75.

### Questions

*Content/Meaning*
1. What causes does Rolo name for the poor showing of publicly owned companies in the real estate market?
2. Is there a single, most important cause for the effect he is analyzing?

*Style*
1. What expository device besides cause and effect does Rolo use?
2. Can you characterize the voice in the excerpt? Is it well matched to the audience being addressed?

## Reading Selection

In this essay the analysis of certain observations leads Ben Stein to synthesize explanations. In his introduction to the book from which this essay is taken, Stein explains that he began studying television the way he had been taught to study film: for the political and social messages they contained. He concluded from this study that TV programming transmitted many similar messages.

"Businessmen on Television" is the first chapter in Stein's book that attempts to account for one of the "social messages" he observes. The chapter falls into two parts: (1) In paragraphs 1–17, Stein observes one of TV's social messages; (2) in paragraphs 18–53, he attempts to account for his observations.

The chapter has, thus, an effect-to-cause organization. As you read you will first want to ask yourself if and how Stein has demonstrated the presence of the social message "businessmen are bad people." In the second part of the article you will want to decide if he has provided plausible reasons to account for this social message.

## BUSINESSMEN ON TELEVISION

*Ben Stein*

In the summer of 1977, a play entitled *The Quadrangle* was presented at a small theatre in Beverly Hills. The author of the play was Arthur Ross, writer of over one hundred teleplays and over twenty screenplays. The plot was about relations between psychiatrists and their patients and about the relation of predators to their prey. A fundamental theme, expressed in several different ways, was that the world is run by hardened, beastly people without consciences who torture and kill those weaker than they. In America, the play said, those stronger, more vicious people take the form of big business-men. To further demonstrate the point, *The Quadrangle* had as a crucial plot element a giant multinational company's takeover of the Mafia, which was to be used as a muscle arm for the company. The small audience (which filled the small theatre) roared with approval at those sentiments.

Indeed, it would have been foolish to expect anything else, because one of the clearest messages of television is that businessmen are bad, evil people, and that big businessmen are the worst of all. This concept is shared by a distinct majority of the writers and producers I spoke with. Since this attitude is so interesting and so clear, it bears being the first social and cultural message and attitude to be examined.

In TV comedies, businessmen play several different roles, all highly un-flattering. Often they are con men. Appearing unannounced, they promise the money-starved regular characters a way out of their poverty. Then, having bilked our lovable favorites, they disappear without a trace. Sometimes they simply appear as pompous fools, bullying and overbearing our regulars until a devastating joke blows them off the set. Some examples follow.

On a recent episode of "Good Times," a banker approached J. J., the teenage son in the poverty-stricken black family, and asked him to paint a mural for a new bank branch. After J. J. had painted it, putting his heart, soul, and hopes into it, the banker refused to pay him.

On "The Mary Tyler Moore Show," in the valedictory episode, a hard-headed businessman was brought in to salvage the ratings of WJM, the fic-tional station where the most appealing human beings on earth worked and played. He fired Mary and all her friends. In an earlier episode, a fast-talking businessman convinced Ted Baxter, the newscaster on the station, to back a "famous broadcasters' school." Ted, a buffoon, was broken-hearted when the con man fled with the students' money, leaving Ted to make up the loss.

On "Laverne and Shirley," a wealthy, fat entrepreneur tried to make Laverne a star. But he told her that she would have to stop hanging around with her soulmate, Shirley. Otherwise, the rich man of business said, Laverne would simply remain a yokel forever.

On "Maude," Maude's harassed husband, Walter, went bankrupt in the retail home appliance business. When he announced his loss to his fellow businessmen, they threw rotten eggs and vegetables at him at a Chamber of Commerce dinner. In another episode, Maude sought a donation for her campaign for office from a wealthy businessman, who demanded that she change her position on a number of issues and then deprived her of the contribution.

On the short-lived "All's Fair," a businessman with extremely right-wing ideas was revealed to be a hypocritical sex fiend.

And on it goes. The most succinct summary of the way businessmen are shown in TV comedies came from a producer at a successful comedy production company. A writer approached him with an idea: How about a comedy with businessmen who were good guys? The producer's answer was, "Impossible."

But businessmen are positively glorified on sitcoms compared to their appearance in adventure shows. There, they are almost always criminals in disguise—and murderers more likely than not. Behind the three-piece pin-stripe suit, the inevitable badge of crime, lurks the heart of a Bluebeard. The depths of depravity of these fictional characters is truly impressive.

One of my favorite examples appeared on the now-defunct "Harry O," about an eccentric private eye, Harry Orwell. A girl had been murdered. Among the suspects were her boyfriend, a junkie, a hired killer, and her employer, who owned an architectural business. As it happened, the killer was the businessman.

On a show aired in the summer of 1977, "Baretta," a teenage girl was killed by an overdose of heroin. After an excursion through New York's netherworld, the detective, Tony Baretta, found that the man who had supplied the heroin was not a pimp—not a murdering dope dealer—but a banker who, behind the scenes, was the kingpin of a dope empire.

On a recent "Hawaii Five-O" episode, a rotund nursing home operator was compelling his elderly wards to swindle the government of millions of dollars. When one of the patients balked, he was rubbed out by the jolly nursing home entrepreneur.

On a recent "Starsky and Hutch," an art collector and dealer used his connections and position to import and sell heroin.

Not even the smallest of businessmen is exempt from the mark of Cain. In a recent episode of "Kojak," a local candy store owner in New York was, in reality, fencing stolen goods and giving the teenage suppliers heroin. In an extremely similar episode, Kojak discovered that a businessman and a dentist who sponsored a little league team forced the youngsters on the team to steal for their fencing operation.

On almost every episode of "Columbo," a rich businessman has killed someone and seeks to bully Columbo into leaving him alone because of his high status. (Needless to say, he never succeeds.)

The well-dressed businessman who pays for his kids' orthodontia by selling heroin to teenagers and the manufacturer who has murdered his go-go dancer girlfriend are staples of TV adventure shows. Of course, there are many staple plots, and even a few original ones, so that the evil businessman does not dominate the airwaves. However, the murderous, duplicitous, cynical businessman is about the only kind of businessman there is on TV adventure shows, just as the cunning, trickster businessman shares the stage with the pompous buffoon businessman in situation comedies.

If one grants that businessmen are not held in high esteem by the population generally—as one must—television's treatment is still harsh. In fact, few businessmen in three-piece suits commit violent crimes, and even a nodding acquaintance with the drug trade is sufficient to show that drug dealers do not often wear three-piece suits or work as bankers or stock brokers during the day.

What, then, is the point of reference for all the fictional businessmen who kill go-go dancers and rob the poor? Among other possible sources is the feeling of TV writers and producers towards businessmen—a feeling of animosity.

To start with a relatively sanguine comment, a major adventure-show producer who asked for anonymity said that "business controls our lives far more than we'll ever know."

Still in the vein of moderation, Gary Marshall, the fabulously successful producer of "Laverne and Shirley" and "Happy Days," sees big business behind the government. "When the government says something, I'm never sure whether the government is telling the truth, or whether it's big business talking." If big business is talking, Marshall does not generally believe them. "They're always hyping people," he says.

One of the most interesting comments on businessmen came from Jerry Thorpe, the former producer of "Harry O" and a man with years of credentials in TV production, starting as far back as "Playhouse 90." Thorpe sees businessmen as "ambitious, driven, and self-destructive." Businessmen, as Thorpe sees them, are so repressed that they have powerful violence locked up within them. Thorpe adds that the idea of businessmen as killers is pitched to him by writers so often that he has to restrain them.

Stanley Kramer, a world-famous producer of both movies and TV shows, sees business as "part of a very great power structure which wields enormous power over the people."

Meta Rosenberg, producer of "The Rockford Files," sees businessmen themselves as individuals. But she also sees them as part of a "dangerous concentration of power."

Jim Brooks, one of the most gifted writers in television and the producer of "The Mary Tyler Moore Show," has more specific comments on businessmen: "They're all sons of bitches. They're all cannibals. I think of them as eating their own, like in the GE price-fixing scandal. They commit fraud when they say they are interested in anything but profit. They distrust people who are brilliant."

Allen Burns, partner of Brooks and also a brilliant writer and a producer of "The Mary Tyler Moore Show," agrees that he is "pretty unsympathetic toward businessmen." He distrusts and dislikes big business because of its "bigness." He believes that large companies have private armies, which frightens him.

Bob Schiller, a classy name in TV comedy production who wrote for Red Skelton and for Lucille Ball (for thirteen years) and also wrote and produced "Maude" and the ill-starred "All's Fair," said of businessmen, "I don't judge. I think there are good lepers and bad lepers. By and large, because of the structure of our laws, I think that most business is amoral." Schiller cites as examples the "constant outcroppings of bribery, extortion, attempts to bend laws to their own use, interlocking directorates, and so forth."

While the negative view of businessmen was predominant, it was not completely unanimous. Indeed, a few of the comments were highly favorable. Mort Lachman, a producer-writer with long experience writing for Bob Hope and other major comedians and now in charge of "All in the Family," notes that business is "in some ways terrifically inventive and effective." He is fond of one company in particular: "IBM has led the way." He believes that competition is the essence of making business act decently. But even Lachman, whose views were unusually favorable, believes that all too often business behaves the way it did in *Network*, a popular movie of 1976 and 1977 whose central theme was that the world is run by huge businesses with the sole aim of expansion and profit.

An answer on business and businessmen which contained an unusual amount of social criticism as well as predictive content came from Douglas Benton, who has written or produced for "Police Woman," "Columbo," "Ironside," "The Name of the Game," and many others. "Leftists have made 'big business' the 'heavy,' " he said, "the culprit for what's wrong with everything. People on the right, the capitalists, are saying it's the answer because it's the only way creative enterprise can flourish." (Benton, like many others, used "business" and "free enterprise" or "market economy" synonymously.) "It's economic democracy at work. It's the strong smart people who get all the money and the weak dumb people who suffer. That's economic democracy? It's like what Winston Churchill said about democracy, that it's one of the worst systems ever put together. Very little can be said about it that's good or worthwhile. The only thing that can be said about it is that it's better than anything else.

"Big business is not very efficient. It tends to rob people of creativity. It tends to stultify them. . . . The big corporations like GM and IBM are dinosaurs. They will die out after my lifetime. We are inevitably moving toward socialism. It's been happening ever since the democracy was set up. Ultimately it will come to socialism, because it's the only governmental organization which attempts to take care of the dumb and the weak and the helpless. The free enterprise system is set up to reward your energy."

Perhaps the most unusually detailed and sympathetic view of businessmen came from Charlie Hauck, producer of "Maude." Hauck has an unusual background for a TV producer. He was a producer of a children's TV show on the Public Broadcasting Service, and before that he wrote for *Business Week*. His response to a question about his feelings towards big business is worth quoting at length.

Hauck believes he is "more sympathetic to business than are most people in TV . . . more sympathetic than I should be." He also believes he is more privy to its operations than are most people in television because of his work at *Business Week*. "I met very few executives I didn't like or respect," Hauck says, "even when I was at odds with them. Executives in any given corporation tend to collectively make mistakes that they don't view as mistakes. They are like small towns in that respect. They are narrow-minded. They sincerely don't understand why welfare mothers are picketing the lobby of their bank if they don't distribute food stamps.

"The bank and the mothers see themselves differently. The bank wants to maximize profits. The welfare mothers want the bank to do something for the community. The mothers don't put themselves in the position of the bankers and no one expects them to. The bankers don't put themselves in the position of the mothers, but everyone expects them to."

(Another positive view of businessmen came from David Begelman, then president of Columbia Pictures, which includes Columbia Pictures Television. Interestingly enough, I interviewed Begelman in the erroneous belief that he was a former writer and producer. Instead, as I should have known, he is a former lawyer and talent agent. At that time, he was a businessman and head of a large corporation. His views were not only positive but enthusiastic. Begelman saw businessmen as uncommonly intelligent, hardworking, honest, socially committed, patriotic, and devoted to their families.)

Despite the views of Lachman, Benton, and Hauck, however, the predominant view of businessmen is extremely negative, and the conclusion one is left with was well, if scatalogically, summarized by a writer who said that when he thought of businessmen running the country, he got a "clong," which he described as a rush of fecal matter to the heart.

It is important to realize that people who have reached the stage of being writers for or producers of TV shows are similar to businessmen in a number of outward respects. For one thing, they are all in business, trying to produce a product or service and sell it for more than it cost to make it. Also, both groups share in the success of their enterprise by making more money (in the case of producers, far more) if the product is successful than if it is not. And both groups share the uncertainties of life in a highly competitive world.

A dimension of the TV writers' image of business, and of big business in particular, is the writers' insistence that it is closely connected with the Mafia. That concept was entirely new to me. It first surfaced spontaneously at an interview. When I included a question about the link between business and the Mafia as part of my questionnaire, and even when I specifically mentioned businesses on the scale of U.S. Steel, I found near unanimity on the answer.

A producer who had worked for many years on adventure shows set all over the country (and recently on two shows set in the Depression in different locales) laid out the matter most baldly: "If you don't believe that the Mafia is running big business, you must be blind."

The late Bruce Geller, a writer and executive producer on "Mission Impossible," "Mannix," "Have Gun Will Travel," and "Bronk," among many others, and then an executive in charge of production at Twentieth Century-Fox, got down to cases:

"Of course the two are connected. It's a very shady area. Organized crime has massive amounts of money that is put in extremely legitimate enterprises." Geller pointed out that, in his opinion, many parts of show business are financed by underworld money. "It's understandable in my business where financing is difficult. . . . In any circumstance people tend to take money where they can find it."

Gary Marshall saw the connection plainly. "There's definitely a link between big business and organized crime. There has to be a link to make big business work."

Bob Schiller gave the most popular answer to the question about big business and the Mafia when he said that he saw a link not only between big business and the Mafia but also between government and the Mafia, and between labor and the Mafia.

Again, however, there was less than total unanimity about the situation. Mort Lachman, for one, saw a link but said it was nothing to feel paranoid about. Several people who preferred to remain anonymous simply could not be made to respond to the question as it was asked. They read it as, "Do you personally receive money from the Mafia?" and all denied receiving any.

Not everyone saw the Mafia in bed with IBM, and William Blinn, one of the biggest guns in TV writing and author of one or more episodes of "Roots," "Starsky and Hutch," "The New Land," "The Rookies," "Bonanza," and "The Interns," gave a unique and unequivocal answer: "There is a conscious, deliberate un-relationship [*sic*] between big business and organized crime. They tend to leave each other alone. It's mutually understood that they have their own territory. By not competing, they actually help each other. They allow each other to thrive in their separate fields." But the comment of Stanley Kramer that "the Mafia is part of the entire corporate entity now" is far more representative than Blinn's.

To some extent, the allegation that the Mafia is linked with business explains why businessmen are shown to be such bad people on television. If the businessman is really a Mafioso, then we could hardly expect him to be anything but a bad man. Even if the businessman is a silent partner of the Mafia, he is still a different person from Horatio Alger's businessman. But that leads to another question. Why is there such widespread belief in the link between the Mafia and the business world? The belief itself is a phenomenon I had never encountered before.

Part of the answer may be that it is true—the Mafia might be an integral part of the corporate structure. It may be that TV writers have simply discovered something I did not know. Certainly they have often led fuller lives than I have where business is concerned. But a larger part of the reason why so many people think the Mafia is linked to business comes, in my opinion, from the prevailing conspiracy theory of history. In Hollywood, almost nothing is explained except on the basis of conspiracies and cabals. It is here, for example, that serious, intelligent people believe that the world is run by a consortium of former Nazis and executives of multinational corporations.

Why Hollywood should be wedded to the conspiracy explanation of human events is beyond my knowing for certain. It probably has something to do with the unpredictability and randomness of human life in Hollywood, especially in terms of success and failure. It is difficult for people to come to grips with the randomness of events, and rather than do so, they often invent complex reasons for phenomena. Perhaps my reasoning in itself is an example of the prevalence of conspiracy explanations. At any rate, for some reason, people who write for television believe that there is a definite link between the Mafia and business, especially big business.

A further explanation of the animosity TV writers feel toward businessmen is that TV writers know something about business. The writer aiming to make a great deal of money in Hollywood is quite different from most intellectuals or academic writers. The latter usually deal with business and businessmen as abstractions, either good or bad. If they deal with real businessmen besides the ones who fix their cars, those businessmen tend to be elderstatesmen types or public relations men. Academics and editorial writers do not conduct business with businessmen except for the occasional purchase of a speech or an article.

The Hollywood TV writer, on the other hand, is actually in a business, selling his labor to brutally callous businessmen. One actually has to go through the experience of writing for money in Hollywood or anywhere else to realize just how unpleasant it is. Most of the pain comes from dealings with business people, such as agents or business affairs officers of production companies and networks. The number of calamities that can and do happen can hardly be believed unless they are experienced. The TV writer is not an honored guest at a meeting of businessmen at the Greenbriar. He is actually down there in the pit with the clawing agents and businessmen, and he often has reason to feel that he has been shortchanged, to say the least. It was fascinating to notice that those who were the most positive toward businessmen were those whose experiences with them were not adversary but rather collegial or reportorial. On the other hand, those who had been writers all their lives usually felt the most anger toward businessmen, and with good reason.

There are yet other explanations for why the businessman comes off so badly in Hollywood. The key one is that businessmen, especially big businessmen, are perceived as coming from a different class from that of the TV writers and producers—and an adversary one at that. Although not one producer or writer said so for the record, a number of writers with whom I became familiar spoke of businessmen from AT&T or IBM in terms that contrasted their Gentile, Ivy League backgrounds with the more ethnic, "school-of-hard-knocks" backgrounds of the TV writers.

There was a distinct feeling that, despite the high pay and the access to powerful media that TV writers and producers enjoy, they are still part of a despised underclass, oppressed psychologically and (potentially) physically by an Aryan ruling class of businessmen and others. This feeling was by no means confined to Jews.

The belief in a ruling class of white, East Coast Protestants meeting occasionally in corporate board rooms to give its orders to whoever happens to be elected to office is so strong that no amount of argument to the contrary makes a dent. And hostility to that real or imagined class is just as strong.

But whatever the reasons for the situation, the net result of it is that on prime-time TV shows, businessmen and business are despised. And that portrayal fits well with the general, although not unanimous, vision of businessmen and business in the community of Hollywood TV writers.

From Ben Stein, *The View from Sunset Boulevard: America as Brought to You by the People Who Make Television* (New York: Basic Books, 1979), pp. 15–28.

### Questions

*Content/Meaning*

1. Does Stein's evidence—the examples of the treatment and behavior of businessmen on some comedy and adventure shows—support his conclusion that one of television's clearest messages is that businessmen are evil?
2. What, according to Stein, is the source of this social message; what causes this effect?
3. Are Stein's explanations of the causes for this social message convincing? What support does he offer for his explanations? Does he give all his explanations equal emphasis? Are all his explanations equally convincing? If not, what makes some explanations stronger or weaker?
4. Does Stein's chapter support the assertion that writers and producers of television programs have a "unified, idiosyncratic view of life" when it comes to businessmen?

*Style*

1. Is the lead paragraph a strong opening to this article? Why does Stein use it?
2. Is the voice in this essay appealing? believable?
3. What is Stein's "view of life" as it pertains to businessmen? Is Stein a disinterested viewer, or does he have ideas and feelings about how businessmen should be portrayed on television but aren't? What is his attitude toward television? television writers and producers? businessmen?

## Reading Selection

This excerpt is from an essay published in a small-circulation journal called *Christianity and Crisis.* Michael Harrington chairs the Democratic Socialist Organizing Committee. His book *The Other America* is credited with helping launch the "war on poverty" of the 1960s. This excerpt focuses on what Harrington sees as a major cause of the "malfunctioning" of the U.S. economy.

## SOLVING POVERTY WITH STATISTICS

### *Michael Harrington*

Why is the economy malfunctioning? There are a number of causes, none of them having to do with the costs of welfare, food stamps, Medicaid or other social programs.

One is the ability of corporations to fix prices by their control over the market. Another is the nature of our energy system, one of the most wasteful and most heavily subsidized by government anywhere in the world. A third is the high and always rising cost of medical care in this country, the only advanced industrial nation without a national health system. (Why do we spend 9.5 percent of GNP on medicine? Because we have private, fee-for-service medical care paid for by third-party insurers, a system in which nobody has to worry about cost or quality.)

A fourth reason, one that I will develop a little more fully, is the near-absence of social control over investment. Last year the chairman of the Securities and Exchange Commission testified before a Senate committee that some $100 billion was spent by corporations over the final three years of the 70's for the purpose of acquiring other corporations—an enormous expenditure that did not create a single new job or add anything to productivity. As the research director of the Federal Trade Commission points out in *The New Republic* for February 21, we in the U.S. do not invest less than the West Germans and the Japanese, we just invest in different ways. Whereas they invest in productivity, we invest much more for corporate takeovers and in commodity speculation. Until recently the steel industry has been investing its cash flow in buying up the chemical industry. That does not make either steel or chemical more productive, it simply means that a lot of money changes hands. So also with the recent spate of multi-billion-dollar takeover bids by the oil corporations, which will do nothing for productivity, nothing for jobs, nothing for the poor. All this *may* increase short-term profits for investors; it will certainly create millions of dollars in new income for accountants, lawyers and brokers.

What is Ronald Reagan doing about this situation, which has become so obvious that even the business press and business-oriented academics are talking about it? He is aiding and abetting it. At the same time that he is scapegoating the poor, holding them responsible for inflation, he is enormously increasing welfare for the rich. His tax program would give approximately 75 percent of its benefits to the wealthiest 27 percent of the American people. A single new tax write-off, the so-called 10-5-3 program, would allow depreciation of structures in 10 years, machines in five years and vehicles in three years. On the Administration's own projections, that would cost the Treasury approximately $60 billion in one year, 1986. That single write-off for the corporate rich is worth more than all the cuts imposed on the poor.

What is the rationale for slanting the tax cuts in favor of the wealthy? The theory is that the rich will not do what they in fact are doing—spending their excess on speculation, on corporate acquisitions, on third and fourth homes and other forms of conspicuous consumption—but will invest their newest gains wisely for socially useful purposes. That contention flies in the face of enormous continuing evidence to the contrary. What will actually happen, to the extent Reagan prevails, is that the poor will get soaked, the rich will get richer, inflation will continue and the economy will go on floundering.

What are the alternatives for the economy? And what political strategy must we forge to achieve them?

To deal with the problems that now afflict this nation, I believe we must go beyond the old liberalism that ruled America from Roosevelt to Carter. The old liberalism is incapable of dealing with stagflation. It rested on an assumption that is no longer true (and was never wholly true): that the fundamental corporate infrastructure and our system for allocating resources was fundamentally sound, so that all government had to do was to manipulate the fiscal and monetary levers to help the corporations do their benign work. Anyone who believes in the automatic wisdom or benevolence of corporate decision-making has not looked at the automobile industry, the steel industry, the railroad industry and other major, dominant segments of the American economy.

The only way we are going to achieve full employment and reduce inflation is through democratic planning leading to social investment, investment intended precisely to put people to work, increase productivity and thereby fight inflation. It can be done. Imagine, for one example, the multiple returns on investment that could be achieved by putting people to work in the Northeast and the Midwest building a decent rail system. One of the great stupidities and tragedies of the past quarter-century, now being repeated in the subways of New York City, is that we destroyed one of the most efficient, energy-conserving, environmentally benign forms of transportation, railroads, and put tens of billions of dollars of government subsidies into private automobiles, with all the consequences we know—from the decline of the cities to the fouling of the air, from profligate wasting of petroleum to the resegregation of the races, from the carnage on the highways to the privatizing of life. Stupidity on such a scale is hard to reverse—not, however, because it is hard to see or to document, but because the interests that still profit by it have even greater power now than when the process began. Witness the tepidity of Congressional interest in sustaining, not to speak of rebuilding, the rail system.

One could give other examples of how democratically arrived at investment for social purposes would change the orientation of our economy, at once putting people to work in socially relevant projects and combatting inflation. The need we see for creating alternative energy systems, for greater conservation, for cleaning up our air and water, for fighting the erosion of our land need not be, must not be understood as, drags on the economy, any more than the original investment of labor and capital in our rail system in the last century hindered growth.

Consider, for example, how governmental statistics define productivity in the segment of industry that produces antipollution devices. In these statistics, believe it or not, such devices are defined not as benefits but as costs. Plants producing catalytic converters in the U.S. are deemed to have *negative* productivity. The underlying assumption is that we are not to regard equipment that helps save people from premature death by cancer as a benefit that can be quantified. When that assumption is turned into numbers, it obviously will affect policy: The more antipollution efforts we make, the worse off the economy will be. Observe that the same assumption is not made in measuring the output of the arms industry. Planes, missiles, tanks, guns—equipment that has no use outside of war, that nobody but the armed forces wants to buy—are seen by the statisticians as benefits, as contributions to the Gross National Product.

All that we need is the shared understanding among enough of our citizens that the economy exists for the people, not the people for the sake of the economy. I am not talking about socialism—I'm afraid that's not in the cards, even though I am a Socialist. But we do need to go on to a much more radical liberalism than has been talked about in this country for a long time, a liberalism that will assert democratic control in a variety of ways over at least some corporate power and that will insist on full employment as the first priority for the economy.

From *Christianity and Crisis,* April 27,
1981, pp. 121–24.

### Questions

*Content/Meaning*
1. What, according to Harrington, are the consequences of the "near-absence of social control over investment"?
2. What evidence does Harrington offer to support his conclusions about the negative impact of current corporate investments?
3. What is "social investment"? What does Harrington think would be the effects of "democratically arrived at investment for social purposes"? What support does he offer for his solution to the problems of the economy?

4. What might a representative from a major corporation or from the Reagan administration say about the effects of "social investment"?

*Style*
1. Harrington tells us in the last paragraph that he is a socialist. Does knowing that change your opinion of the essay? What do you expect of a socialist and his arguments?
2. Is there specific language that you would characterize as the voice of a socialist?
3. Do you find Harrington persuasive in explaining his position? Why or why not?

## Exercises and Assignments

1. Choose an activity, process, or situation that you know well and that involves cause-and-effect relationships: how to make something, achieve something, solve a problem, and so forth. Focus your paper, not on how to accomplish some goal, but on *why* the goal can be accomplished by the means you specify.

2. In *The View from Sunset Boulevard* Ben Stein analyzes crime, the police, the military, the government, small towns, big cities, the rich, the poor, and the clergy—in addition to businessmen—as they are portrayed on television.

Take one of these groups, categories, or subjects, or think of another— doctors, families, working—and perform your own cause-and-effect analysis. Watch several current or past (on reruns) prime-time television shows involving the group or subject you have chosen.

Do you find common characteristics among members of your group, examples of your subject? How do members of your group behave? How do others treat them? What happens to them during the programs? Can you generalize from your observations (the effects) to any social messages (causes) in the programming? What can you infer about the attitudes of writers, producers, or society at large toward your group or subject?

You may begin your analysis with no particular hypothesis in mind, or you may start—as Stein did—with the idea of investigating whether a casual observation is true: Are businessmen usually depicted as evil? Are doctors always selfless heroes who never charge fees? Can all family problems be cheerfully resolved in 30 or 60 minutes? And so forth.

In 500 to 750 words present the results of your analysis. State the social message, if any, you observe in the treatment of your subject on television. Cite and describe examples from your viewing that support your conclusions.

3. Stein's analysis focuses on prime-time comedy and adventure entertainment programs. Undertake a similar investigation and analysis focusing on the social messages contained in other kinds of programming: afternoon "soap operas," quiz shows, news shows, children's shows, and the like. Present the results of your analysis in 500 to 750 words.

# ARGUMENT
# AND
# PERSUASION

In turning from exposition and analysis to argument and persuasion we move from writing intended to inform to writing intended to convince. Just as we looked in the last unit at support for assertions, we look in this unit at evidence for conclusions and at the pseudoevidence so common in commercial and political persuasion. Since persuasive writing tries to change (or reinforce) beliefs and behavior, many selections here are presented in pairs or groups where opinions conflict. Your challenge, as critical readers and writers, is to analyze the evidence and reasoning and come to some conclusions about the truth and validity of those opinions.

There is a popular notion, perhaps growing out of the democratically inspired sentiment "everyone is entitled to his opinion," that all opinions are equal. But opinions are not equal: Some opinions are carefully considered and precisely stated, but many are uninformed or prejudiced; other opinions are based on faulty logic or unreliable evidence; still others are deliberately designed to deceive. This unit does not let you casually coexist with conflicting opinions, but keeps asking you to judge which conclusions are reliable, which are not, and which require further information.

All discussion of argument and persuasion should start with Aristotle, who identified three basic appeals necessary to convince an audience: *logos* is the appeal to reason and the mind with logic and evidence. It is concerned with the *subject* of the persuasion, and we focus on it in Chapters 18 and 19. *Pathos* is the appeal to the emotions using feelings, needs, and desires. It is concerned with the *audience* to whom the persuasion is addressed and we focus on it in Chapters 20 and 21. *Ethos* is based on the appeal of the writer's character, on the reliability of the *source* of the persuasion. Since *ethos* is closely tied to the voice of the writer, we consider it throughout this unit.

It is important to note that these three kinds of appeals do not have to be genuine. According to Aristotle, the mere *appearance* of logic is as good as a truly logical argument; a source seeming to be trustworthy is as good as one that actually is reliable; persuaders can as easily appeal to base emotions as to praiseworthy ones, to greed as easily as to love, to irrational fears as to justifiable ones, to perceived wants as to real needs.

Since appearances are, unfortunately, often sufficient to persuade us, we must, as critical readers, be alert in what follows to separate the false from the genuine.

# 18    REASONING

**F**ormal logic is complicated and can be intimidating. In modern Western culture it has become increasingly the study of mathematical and grammatical rules, a branch of philosophy that is now more science than art. To the untrained and unappreciative mind it can even seem impractical because it is possible for an argument to be logically valid but untrue, or to be true but not logically valid. We are not concerned here with formal logic, but with the principles of logic; they are valuable instruments for analyzing and understanding arguments and for constructing arguments of our own.

An argument is a group of statements designed to make and support a point. In formal logic the "point" is called the *conclusion,* and the supporting statements are known as *premises.* Arguments are constructed from *evidence* (facts, data, details, statistics, and testimony that form the premises of the argument) and *reasoning* (means of demonstrating the relationship between the evidence and the conclusions). The practical point of studying and analyzing arguments is to decide whether or not to accept an argument's conclusions.

Our culture values logical reasoning highly; the university has been called "the Church of Reason" in recognition of its avowed quest for truth. As a result, our culture and the university especially have tended to discount such things as intuition and emotion and to see them as contrary to reason. Enforcing such a division is not a prescription for psychic health. It is important to acknowledge that reasoning is not the only way to arrive at truth. No one should think *with* his or her emotions, but one should certainly think *about* them. Emotions can be evidence every bit as valid and useful as other information about the world around us. The love of logic and reasoning is itself an emotion as powerful as many others.

We should not, then, be intimidated by logic; it is not a magic formula that determines right and wrong, good and bad absolutely. Confronted by logical arguments, we still have the obligation to decide which are most persuasive, which are most likely to be true. Consider that lawyers make a living out of manufacturing reasonable arguments on any side of any issue; it is still up to someone, judge or jury, to choose a side and determine which logical case is closer to the truth. This limitation to pure reason was long ago noted by the satirist Jonathan Swift, who, in his *Gulliver's Travels*, has his hero visit the floating island of scientists, which is named *La Puta*, Spanish for "whore." Reason is, indeed, promiscuous. It can be used by anyone, not just seekers after truth. All the more reason to become familiar with logic so that it cannot be used against us by the unscrupulous.

Logic is not evidence, but a method, a tool, that can be useful in thinking through problems and issues too subtle for emotion and too complicated for common sense to follow. Reasoning can help us find a path through the world's jungles of conflicting values, opinions, and facts.

## DEDUCTIVE REASONING

Reasoning can be classified as either *deductive* or *inductive*. In textbooks on logic both kinds of arguments are usually cast in the form of the syllogism, a three-statement formula made up of two premises and a conclusion. Unfortunately, life is rarely so obliging, and writers making arguments do not ordinarily produce clear syllogisms. We can often reconstruct the latent formula in an argument, however. Consider this statement from an editorial in the *Manchester* (New Hampshire) *Union Leader:* ". . . it is an established fact that women cannot play chess because chess requires a logical mind and women do not possess logical minds."

This argument can be recast as a syllogism:

> PREMISE:   *Only those with logical minds can play chess.*
> PREMISE:   *Women do not possess logical minds.*
> CONCLUSION:   *Therefore, women cannot play chess.*

It is perhaps astonishing to learn that this is a perfectly valid argument. Which is not to say that it is true.

The argument is a deduction, and it is valid because the conclusion follows logically from the premises. A major characteristic of a deductive argument is precisely that if its premises are true, then its conclusion must be true. A second major characteristic—really a way of restating the first—is that a deductive argument never introduces new knowledge; its conclusion must be contained in its premises.

But a valid argument does not guarantee a truthful argument. Validity and truth are separate conditions in logic. One way to attack a deductively valid argument is to question its premises. In the example above, few people would object to the premise that chess requires a logical mind. The second premise is highly doubtful, however, calling into question the truth of the conclusion. Before accepting any deductive conclusion as true, we must be assured of both the *truth* of the premises and the *validity* of the argument. The argument above, while valid, contains a highly questionable premise; the phrase "it is an established fact that" is a rhetorical flourish, neither argument nor evidence.

We may also observe about this argument that it moves, as most deductive arguments move, from general premises or principles to a specific conclusion, or, more precisely in this case, to a specific application of the general principles.

## INDUCTIVE ARGUMENTS

Inductive reasoning is much more common in everyday life than deductive reasoning; inductive reasoning is also more complicated, more controversial, and less certain than deductive reasoning. An inductive argument moves from particular observations or experience and reasons to a general conclusion.

> PREMISE: *All my friends have been smoking at least a pack of cigarettes a day for years.*
> PREMISE: *None of us has lung cancer.*
> CONCLUSION: *Therefore, smoking is safe.*

In an inductive argument the premises may be true, but that does not guarantee the truth of the conclusion because the claim in the conclusion goes beyond what is contained in the premises.

Sometimes the conclusion goes far beyond the premises, and we have a very weak argument, such as the one above. First, the informality and small size of the sample cannot support such a sweeping conclusion. Second, the premises do not rule out other health effects besides lung cancer that might be attributable to smoking and that would invalidate the conclusion. A third objection might be that cancer has a latency period; lung cancer may well yet appear over a longer period of time. The evidence here is obviously too weak to support the inductive leap to this conclusion.

Stronger inductive arguments have more precise data than our first example and reach more modest conclusions.

> PREMISE: *A diet pill was tested on 3,000 women between the ages of 20 and 40 who had no serious health problems.*
> PREMISE: *During a two-year period, none of them developed a serious health problem.*
> CONCLUSION: *This pill produces no serious health problems in healthy women between the ages of 20 and 40 during a two-year period.*

The data here are more specific, the sample is larger, and the conclusion is less sweeping. Though this is a strong argument, it is not certain proof that the pill is safe. Over a longer period of time or with a larger sample, ill effects might occur. All inductive arguments carry with them this uncertainty.

In order to increase the probability that an inductive conclusion is in fact true, we must study closely the evidence presented in the premises, we must be alert for a variety of errors and abuses to which inductive reasoning is especially vulnerable, and we must make certain that the distance between the evidence and the conclusion is short enough to ensure the success of the inductive leap.

## INDUCTIVE FALLACIES

There are many categories of logical fallacy, but learning the proper label is not so important as developing a questioning and critical habit of mind when confronting evidence in arguments. In addition to becoming aware of the fallacies discussed in the rest of this chapter, you also have your own native intelligence to help you evaluate evidence and reasoning. Your personal experiences, though perhaps limited and seldom conclusive, can help you assess premises, as can your "common sense," though that, too, has its limits: Someone once defined common sense as the thing that tells you the world is flat. There is no easy method, no mechanical system, that will do your thinking for you. Most of the time it is difficult to be certain about anything.

### Questionable Premises

Questionable premises are any assertions of fact that are open to doubt. Consider the following argument, a paragraph from an article called "Abortion and Teen-age Pregnancy" by Joseph L. Bernardin. The writer is addressing the problem of "teen-age pregnancy, which is reaching epidemic proportions in the United States." A key point in his argument is that contraception has failed to solve this problem.

There is good reason to doubt that more and better contraceptive information and services will make major inroads in the number of teen-age pregnancies. We already live—and have lived for many years—in a contraceptive culture: one, that is, in which contraception is taken for granted. Contraceptive information is widely disseminated and readily available. So are contraceptives. If sexually active teen-agers do not practice contraception, it is not because they lack opportunity.

Two conclusions are reached in this paragraph: (1) that more and better contraceptive information and services will not reduce teenage pregnancy; and (2) that if teenagers do not now practice contraception, it is not from lack of opportunity. These conclusions are supported by three premises: that we live in a "contraceptive culture," and that both contraceptive information and contraceptives themselves are widely available.

Calling our society a "contraceptive culture" is not by itself evidence since there is no precise meaning that can be ascribed to the phrase. Insofar as Bernardin defines the phrase as a culture "in which contraception is taken for granted," it seems to work against his conclusion. Does he mean by "taken for granted" that everyone practices contraception? He cannot mean this, or there would be no problem of a pregnancy "epidemic." If he means by "taken for granted" that people do not think about contraception very much, he also argues against his own conclusion. The phrase could suggest—though this is undoubtedly far from the writer's intended meaning—that people take for granted that they are safe from pregnancy, confusing knowledge of contraception with protection by contraceptives. Even granting that contraceptive information is widely and readily available, is the same true of contraceptive devices? Perhaps for males this is true, but female contraception involves several appointments with a physician or at a clinic and not a little expense, precisely the kinds of problems that might be addressed by "more and better contraceptive . . . services." And there are the further difficulties of risking possible parental shock, embarrassment, or disapproval that might, subjectively at least, reduce a teenager's opportunity to practice contraception. Two of Bernardin's three premises are open to doubts that he does not dispel. His evidence cannot support his conclusions.

### Hidden Assumptions

Assumptions are statements we accept as true without proof. In our everyday life they are the things we take for granted and do not bother thinking about: a flame will cause paper to burn; water flows down, not up. We could not get through a day if we constantly threw our basic assumptions into question, but some of these assumptions can be dangerous: We should not assume that traffic will stop just because the light is red. Some assumptions about the world at large are equally dangerous. Unwarranted assumptions often underlie racial, ethnic, and sexual stereotyping: Women are illogical, Poles are slow-witted, Orientals are "inscrutable." One problem with assumptions is that they are often unstated and are very difficult to detect when they are shared between writer and reader. If we assume that the United States is basically a just and moral force in international affairs and always acts or intends to act well, we find it difficult as a nation to accept blame for problems in the world that may be created by our policies.

## Reading Selection

The following editorial has so many logical flaws that it is difficult to name them all or to cite all the examples. For now, let us focus on assumptions both stated and hidden. How many can you find?

### YOUNG JACKASSES

Talk about young jackasses! The students at Brandeis University are protesting and urging the board of trustees of Brandeis to divest itself of stock holdings in American firms that do business with South Africa. This is the latest thing for the young kooks on campus. They always have to appear holier-than-thou about something, and now they are holier-than-thou about South Africa.

Just how foolish these uneducated protesters are can be noted from the following:

Brandeis is known largely as a college where many young Jewish people attend. It so happens to be that these ignorant kids apparently do not realize that Israel is the second largest exporter of cut diamonds. Israel is now next to Amsterdam as the greatest diamond cutting center in the world and probably will soon surpass in volume even historic Amsterdam.

Where do these diamonds come from? They come from South Africa.

This explains the fact that Israel has always had close relations with South Africa. Israel has helped South Africa, and South Africa has helped Israel.

If these Jewish students at Brandeis want to go on attacking South Africa, that is their privilege. This is a free country, but they are injuring the State of Israel by so doing.

One would have assumed that they would have done a little thinking before they let their emotions and their desire to be oh-so-pure-and-so-virtuous get the better of them.

From the *Manchester Union Leader,*
April 29, 1978, p. 17.

There is an interesting strain of illogic to be observed by following the identification given to the student protesters. They begin as "young jackasses" (an example of an *ad hominem* attack, to be discussed later in the chapter), and end as "these Jewish students" through the logically insufficient assertion "Brandeis is known largely as a college where many young Jewish people attend." The stated assumptions in this editorial thus include that all the protesters are Jewish and that the protesters do not know about the financial connections between South Africa and Israel. Two of the most prominent unstated assumptions are, first, that attacking a country that supports and is in turn supported by Israel is equivalent to attacking Israel itself, and second, that all Jews should and do support Israel. This second assumption is a kind of stereotyping that assumes that all members of a group hold the same opinions. The hidden assumption that no Jew would knowingly attack Israel, even indirectly, is the basis for this rather intemperate editorial outburst.

### Ambiguity and Unclear Definitions

We discussed definition in Chapter 14 where the purpose was to be clear and precise. In many arguments or statements that resemble arguments, the intent is to be as vague as possible while creating in the reader or listener the impression that a clear meaning has been communicated. George Orwell pointed out in his famous 1946 essay "Politics and the English Language" that many abstract words are used in this consciously dishonest way:

> In the case of a word like *democracy,* not only is there no agreed
> definition, but the attempt to make one is resisted from all sides. It is
> almost universally felt that when we call a country democratic we are
> praising it: consequently the defenders of every kind of regime claim
> that it is a democracy, and fear that they might have to stop using
> the word if it were tied down to any one meaning.

But politics is not the only source of deliberately vague language. Observe how the words "owns" and "owners" are used in the following excerpt from a corporate ad titled, "Who really owns Standard Oil (Indiana)?"

> It's easy to picture an oil company as greedy and impersonal. But that
> image fades fast when you understand that it is millions of individuals
> like you who really own it. It is people who own the refineries, the
> pipelines, the tank trucks. It is people who risk their money on exploring
> for energy and drilling the wells that may or may not pay off. This is
> free enterprise. . . .
> We feel that this investment in American energy is the best we
> can make. For America. For you. And for the millions of people like
> you who are the real owners.

The intention of the ad is clear in the first sentence: to create a favorable image of an oil company. The means used is to encourage readers to think of "the real owners" as small or indirect investors in the company, instead of the board of directors, the corporate management, or the owners of large blocks of stock who actually control the workings of the enterprise. While it is true that individuals own stock in the company, that is ownership in a sense quite different from the way in which one might own a car, or a house, or a business that is truly one's own.

### Begging the Question

A logical fallacy often closely related to ambiguous definitions is begging the question. This fallacy occurs especially where unclear or unstated definitions are used as persuasive devices that assume as true the argument at issue. To argue that increased military expenditures are necessary to "national security" without defining that term begs the question what makes a nation secure and, more specifically, the question whether increased military spending will make it secure. Similarly, in the abortion debate, to argue that abortion is wrong because the procedure kills babies is to assert without argument that the fetus is a human being, a major point of controversy. In the next chapter we read an essay by columnist George Will about the case of Walter Polovchak, a twelve-year-old boy who refused to return to the Soviet Union with his parents after an eight-month stay in the United States. When Will calls Walter "the littlest defector," he is openly begging the question of how to deal with the boy's status: Is he a political refugee or a boy running away from his parents? Unless Will goes on to argue that Walter is indeed entitled to status as a defector, he is guilty of begging the question at issue (see p. 297).

### Hasty Conclusions

Hasty conclusions are arrived at with insufficient evidence in the premises. This fallacy occurs especially often in statistical arguments where the sample may be too small or biased in some direction, a topic to which we will soon turn. For now, let us examine two nonstatistical examples.

The first comes from an opinion article titled "No Risk, No Energy" written by Herbert Jaffe, who identifies himself as "a member of the executive board of the Association of Investors in New York Utilities." The article argues in favor of nuclear power and contains the following paragraph on radioactive waste:

> In any event, three professors at the Catholic University of America have recently been awarded patent No. 4,224,177 for the permanent storage of radioactive waste. First, the waste is immobilized by being absorbed in liquid form into the pores of a special glass matrix. After drying, the pores are fused at a high temperature and the radioactive atoms become part of the glass structure. According to the patent, "Such techniques produce a highly durable glass similar to tektite, a somewhat rounded, glassy body of probably meteoric origin which is said to have

survived under the ocean for more than 35 million years." So much for nuclear waste disposal. (*The New York Times,* November 16, 1980, Long Island Section, p. 26.)

The conclusion is that nuclear waste disposal, perhaps the most vexing technical issue associated with nuclear power, is no problem. The evidence is, first, that a patent has been issued for a process that vitrifies nuclear waste and, second, that the resulting glass is "similar to" tektite, which in turn is "said to have" lasted 35 million years under the ocean. If we are reading critically, we should notice that a patent for a unique process is no guarantee that the process will accomplish some larger task, in this case safely isolating hazardous material indefinitely. Suspending nuclear waste in glass does not address the problem of what to do with the radioactive glass, nor does this argument address how long the wastes may remain so suspended. Though the argument tries to suggest that the glass will last 35 million years, we should be careful to note that it is tektite, not radioactive glass, that "is said" (by whom?—a questionable premise) to last this long. We might also notice the ways in which words and meanings shift in the paragraph: waste "storage" in the first sentence becomes waste "disposal" in the last; Jaffe's "permanent" in the first sentence is reduced to "highly durable" in the patent itself. We must be especially critical of arguments written by passionate and convinced writers; often, as here, their evidence fails to support the conclusions in whose truth they already believe. They succeed in convincing themselves before they can logically claim to have formulated valid arguments.

As another example, consider this paragraph from a letter to the editor written by James Stewart who identifies himself as president of Smokers United, Inc. Stewart is arguing that smokers are persecuted by the government and the press:

> Heart specialist Christiaan Barnard recently proclaimed that "jogging is a dangerous mania," pointing out that roads and highways are "a sewer of noxious gases from car exhaust dragged into your lungs with every straining breath." Why not an all-out war against jogging, obviously more lethal than tobacco smoking?

It is fallacious to conclude so hastily that tobacco smoking is less dangerous than jogging. We should notice that no comparisons are made between the health effects of jogging and smoking; jogging is judged by the writer to be "obviously more lethal" on the basis of a partial quotation from a famous heart surgeon. The conclusion, besides being hasty, relies for evidence on the reputation of a presumably expert witness and so commits the further logical error known as the appeal to authority.

### Appeal to Authority

Someone once remarked that for every Ph.D. there is an equal and opposite Ph.D. This mocking paraphrase of Newton's Third Law of Motion highlights the major problem with experts: whom to believe. One standard for judging the pronouncements of alleged authorities is their qualifications for making the pronouncement. Christiaan Barnard is used in the last example for his comments on jogging, an area outside his professional expertise. An expert's apparent qualifications are an uncertain standard, however, since nonexperts can often become knowledgeable in a field within their interest but outside their professional training. The successful personal injury lawyer, Louis Nizer, for example, was famous for demolishing the expert testimony of opposing physicians.

The challenging, though perhaps disconcerting, fact is that we must not accept blindly the opinions and conclusions of experts based solely on their reputation as experts. We commit or accept the fallacy of appeal to authority when we believe without evidence expert opinions. When experts disagree, we must seek out the *evidence* and *arguments* that support their opinions and come to conclusions of our own.

### Ad Hominem Argument (Argument to the Individual)

The fallacy of the *ad hominem* argument is the opposite of the appeal to authority fallacy. The appeal to authority attempts to support a conclusion by associating it with a reputable source; an *ad hominem* attack attempts to discredit a conclusion by associating it with a disreputable source or by attempting to make the source seem disreputable. Both fallacies avoid evidence and argument and focus instead on the reputations (either for expertise or villainy) of those holding particular opinions. To say that full employment is a bad idea because Adolf Hitler favored it is an *ad hominem* fallacy. If Bella Abzug owned a handgun, that would not invalidate her arguments against handgun ownership, though it would make her guilty of hyprocrisy.

The editorial that attacked Brandeis students as "young jackasses" and "young kooks" is low level *ad hominem* name-calling. More subtle is the *ad hominem* attacks found in many Mobil ads. The following is taken from an ad in which Mobil objects to a CBS news broadcast that reported on oil company profits. This is how Mobil replied in the ad to a critic quoted during the broadcast:

The American "expert" interviewed was from the Washington-based Energy Action Educational Foundation, a virulent anti-oil group that can often be found, as here, quoting fantasy as fact. What is Energy

Action? Who are the private individuals who provide its funds? What kind of changes are they really trying to bring about in America through their repeated attacks on our country's energy industry?

The attack is brilliant for its vagueness. Mobil's series of questions attempts without any evidence to suggest that there is something sinister about its critics. Even "private individuals" are made to sound questionable. Attacking oil companies is equated by insinuation with being un-American. The charge of subversion lies very close to the surface of this ad, whose rhetorical questioning imitates the charges once hurled in the same way during the anticommunist "red scare" in the 1950s.

*Ad hominem* attacks are irrelevant arguments designed to persuade without evidence by appealing to fear and prejudice. We must always reject them as logically insufficient by themselves to prove anything.

### Statistical Fallacies

Statistical reasoning is inductive; it counts a number of individual instances, organizes them in various ways as percentages, averages, ratios and the like, and then uses the results to support general conclusions. Even though we have the familiar sayings "Figures never lie, but liars can figure" and "There are three kinds of lies: lies, damn lies, and statistics," we still are often easy prey for authoritative-sounding numbers. They seem so definite, so "scientific." It is far beyond the scope of this section to survey all types of statistical fallacy, but we will introduce the subject.

*Irrelevant statistics* can be used as easily as irrelevant arguments to support shaky conclusions. Consider this statement in an ad by Mobil written to counter an article by Senator Howard Metzenbaum attacking the oil industry:

> Senator Metzenbaum takes the industry to task for spending "only 8.6 percent of its profits on research and development." Come now; that's rhetorical sleight of hand. Mobil's research expenditures in 1978 amounted to $86 million, no paltry sum. But beyond this Mobil risked $1.1 *billion* last year in finding and developing new oil and gas.

The careful reader should notice that the sleight of hand is Mobil's. Eighty-six million dollars may be no paltry sum, but it may still be only 8.6 percent of profits. The charge leveled by Senator Metzenbaum stands unchallenged.

Irrelevant arguments can also result from *faulty comparisons,* what is also called "comparing apples and oranges." Consider this claim, part of an eight-page advertising insert sponsored by the Can Manufacturers Institute that appeared in the *Columbia Journalism Review:*

### Do Deposit Laws Help Conserve Our Resources?

Yes, but other methods are cheaper and more effective. *In Milwaukee, a new resource recovery system called Americology can economically recover up to 90% of the city's garbage for new uses.*

The system recovers more than 90% of the steel cans in Milwaukee's garbage and almost as high a percentage of aluminum cans. This compares to a return rate of less than 75% for cans in the deposit states of Vermont and Oregon.

Do the figures 90 percent and 75 percent compare? The 90 percent figure covers only those cans deposited in city garbage, whereas the 75 percent figure refers to the return rate of *all* cans. We do not know in the first figure how many cans are never put in the garbage to become part of the recycling system, a crucial point since one argument in favor of deposit legislation is that it reduces litter. Until we know what percent of *all* cans the recycling system recovers, we cannot compare that system to deposit legislation; even then, we will not have addressed differences that may exist between the city of Milwaukee and the states of Vermont and Oregon that would also tend to make the comparison faulty.

Besides faulty comparison, we may also be able to accuse the Can Manufacturers Institute of suppressing evidence because it presumably could have produced the necessary missing figures.

Another common problem with statistics is *overgeneralizing*, a flaw often found in informal polls and surveys. Invalid conclusions can result from not considering the limitations of polls. Polls may be biased by a number of factors, including the bias of the poll taker or those writing the questions. Two examples of statistical bias are the use of a small sample population or the use of one that is unrepresentative of the larger population the poll is trying to characterize.

The classic case of the unrepresentative sample involved the presidential poll of 1936 carried out by the now-defunct *Literary Digest.* The *Digest* mailed out millions of ballots to voters throughout the country, a very large sample. The results showed a landslide victory for Republican Alf Landon. When Franklin D. Roosevelt gathered 60.7 percent of the vote, the *Digest's* statistical methods were studied closely. Among other errors, the *Digest's* mailing list had been compiled from directories of automobile owners and telephone subscribers who, in 1936, were disproportionately prosperous and Republican. While the sample was large and probably represented those it sampled, it did not represent the total voting population in the country that year. Similarly faulty conclusions can result from generalizing with polls taken in only one geographical area, among only a single economic class, or social or cultural group, unless, of course, the poll is designed narrowly to consider only a single group or area.

The charge of generalizing from too small a sample is one that can be made against many treatments of large social issues in the popular press. A recent *New York Times* front-page survey concluded in its headline, "Many Young Women Now Say They'd Pick Family Over Career." The conclusion was supported mostly by "dozens of interviews" in four schools, three in New York and one in New Jersey. The amount of personal detail in such an article tends to obsure the fact that such "anecdotal" evidence is too small to draw any solid conclusions from. This same charge is continually lodged against the A. C. Nielsen Company, for example, because its influential television rating service uses only 1,200 families to project the viewing preferences of the entire country. How, one might ask, can so few be said to stand for so many?

### Causation

The close juxtaposition of two sets of events or occurrences frequently leads us to assume that these events or occurrences are causally related. And, in many cases, the causal connection can be proved to exist, though absolute certainty about the causal relationship between two concurrent events is rarely possible outside the scientific laboratory and is often questioned within it. Doctors have for years relied on statistics to prove that cigarette smoking causes lung cancer. Since the immediate biochemical cause of cancer is not known, the medical profession has had to rely on the coincidence of the exterior phenomenon, smoking, with the organic symptom, lung cancer. While members of the tobacco industry still insist that this coincidence has no causal validity, laboratory experiments that have linked nicotine tars with cancer in mice and the sheer weight of the statistical correlations give credence to the conclusion that smoking causes lung cancer in human beings. At the same time it is clear that smoking is not the only cause of lung cancer, nor is it a certain cause: Nonsmokers contract the disease, and heavy smokers die in their sleep at the age of ninety.

Outside the laboratory, the best we can do is to establish a reasonable case that one set of circumstances causes another, bearing in mind that we cannot offer as proof what is, finally, an imperfect generalization. It would, for example, be hazardous to prove that there is a general causal connection between the increased incidence of realistic crime drama on television and increased instances of crime in the streets. But a causal assumption could well be made if statistics, examples, and testimonials exist to support it. If there were a sufficient number of such instances, one would have to be satisfied with the statement that TV drama may well be a *contributing cause* of an increase in crime, but not a sole cause (other causes might as easily exist: a heat wave, economic depression, a decrease in police patrols, and so on).

Finally, we must recognize that the world is complicated and not always knowable. Sometimes it is just impossible to separate causes and effects (the chicken-or-the-egg question) or to state cause-and-effect relationships adequately: Some causes produce multiple effects; many interrelated causes may contribute to a single effect.

Two common causal flaws result from trying to simplify complex processes. The *post hoc, ergo propter hoc* fallacy (Latin for "after this, therefore because of this"), mistakes sequence for cause. Spring follows winter, but winter does not, therefore, cause spring. Other evidence beyond mere sequence is necessary to prove a causal relationship.

A second fallacy has been given the name *"slippery slope"* because it pushes the reasonable mind over a precipice arguing that step A (a cause) will eventually and inevitably lead to a particularly horrible end at the bottom of the conceptual cliff (the effect). So the "domino theory" of the Vietnam war argued that if communism were not "stopped" in Asia, it would soon be invading our home towns. Such reasoning is fallacious unless all the supporting links in the causal chain are forged and found to be strong.

With this introduction as your background, see how well you can analyze the reasoning in the following selections.

## Reading Selection

### IN DEFENSE OF SMOKING

#### *Ross R. Millhiser*

The 60 million American adults who smoke are hard put these days to find a sympathetic word of approval for a practice that provides them with a certain sense of personal satisfaction, relaxation, and even pleasure.

So it is notable that the Carter Administration has brought an enlightened voice of reason to their harassed world of health warnings, induced guilt, and threatened social ostracism. That voice was heard recently as President Carter's top adviser on health, Dr. Peter G. Bourne, addressed the Tobacco and Smoking Research Committee of the American Cancer Society on the issue of smoking and health.

It is too bad the American people were not fully exposed to these reasonable observations. Because Dr. Bourne, who obviously is not in favor of smoking *per se,* had the political and professional courage to place in full view of his peers the whole gamut of unanswered questions about smoking and health—a subject that has been relentlessly probed by world scientists for more than 25 years.

Dr. Bourne is not alone in posing the tough questions that scientists must answer before coming to any conclusion that the smoking cigarette is also the "smoking gun."

By daring to suggest that there are known, and may be many unknown, benefits in tobacco components and smoking, Dr. Bourne's position is hardly radical. He is joined in his opinion by many eminent scientists.

The Surgeon General's well-known report notes a list of psychological and physical benefits—for example, "The significant beneficial effects of smoking occur primarily in the area of mental health and the habit originates in a search for contentment."

Prof. Ulf von Euler, a winner of the Nobel Prize in Medicine or Physiology, decries the lack of research on the benefits of smoking: "Nobody would believe that so many people would use tobacco or products containing substances similar to nicotine unless it had positive effects."

The eminent Dr. Walter Menninger, clinical director of Topeka State Hospital, flatly states that smoking relieves tension in certain types of individuals. And Dr. Hans Selye, one of the world's foremost authorities on stress, says it is "frightening" that no one mentions the benefits of tobacco.

As for the lack of research on the "harmful" effects of smoking, the fact is there is good reason to doubt the culpability of cigarette smoking in coronary heart disease. That point is buttressed by an exhaustive, seven-country study of coronary heart disease coordinated by the renowned Dr. Amcel Keys, director of physiological hygiene at the University of Minnesota. In the summary of the study, Dr. Keys said: "Examination . . . of the so-called risk factors shows that most of these factors, whatever may be their influence . . . cannot explain the observed difference in the incidence of coronary heart disease . . . cigarette smoking cannot be involved as an explanation."

Harvard anthropologist Dr. Carl Seltzer stated in testimony before Congress: "The situation demands not special pleading but scientific truth, namely what is reasonably established. And, certainly, it has not been reasonably established that cigarette smoking causes coronary heart disease."

The inability of scientific probers to reach a verdict on cigarette smoking and lung cancer or respiratory disease is summed up by Dr. Philip Burch of Britain's University of Leeds. He says: "Studies that purport to show a causal connection between cigarette smoking and various cancers—particular lung cancer—fail when examined critically to establish the causal claim."

But, as significant as Dr. Bourne's remarks on the purely scientific side, his courage in expanding the scope of the debate to include the equally important social aspects of the tobacco issue sets a new high in official Washington candor.

His call for a Federal strategy that deals realistically with the industry and the social fabric which has built up around tobacco use over the past

300 years is one that is rarely heard in the scientific debate. We support his belief that the scientific community should come up with some facts on the health hazards—if indeed any—of other people's cigarettes before it recommends issuing orders to a very large segment of the public.

It is not likely that anybody would see an endorsement of cigarettes in Dr. Bourne's forthright statement.

Nevertheless, we heartily endorse Dr. Bourne's endorsement of *reason*. It's such a rare commodity these days—and particularly in the Great Tobacco Debate.

From *The New York Times,* January 12, 1978, p. A19.

### Questions

*Content/Meaning*
1. What are the major conclusions of this essay?
2. What evidence and reasoning support the conclusions? What evidence is provided by authorities?
3. Can you express any of the arguments as a syllogism? Is the reasoning inductive or deductive?
4. Can you find and explain any logical flaws in this essay?

*Style:*
1. How would you characterize the voice of the writer? Is it reasonable? emotional? authoritative? How does the language establish the voice?
2. When Ross R. Millhiser wrote this article, he was president of Philip Morris, a manufacturer of several brands of cigarettes. Are you surprised to learn his identity? Does the article sound as if it were written by a tobacco company president? Specifically, why or why not? Does knowing his identity change your evaluation of the essay?

## Reading Selection

### ABORTION AND TEEN-AGE PREGNANCY

*Joseph L. Bernardin*

In seeking common ground on the divisive issue of abortion, most people seem able to agree at least on this: Abortion is not desirable in and of itself. Even those who are generally favorable to abortion tend to present it as an unattractive but sometimes necessary solution to problems.

Therefore, it is worth asking what problems abortion is seen as solving and what other, possibly better solutions might be available. High on everyone's list of such problems is teen-age pregnancy, which is reaching epidemic proportions in the United States. What, if anything, can be done to reduce teen-age pregnancies?

The answer seems obvious to pragmatic minds. Pregnancies are prevented by contraception. If we increase contraceptive information and services for teen-agers, we shall be well on the way to cutting down on the number of pregnancies and so reducing the need for teen-age abortions.

Is a dissent in order? In speaking to this issue, a Catholic bishop is likely to be accused of special pleading. I am not making an argument here about the morality of contraception. My point is that the case made by those who argue for more contraception as a solution to teen-age pregnancies (and so, to that degree, to abortion) is faulty on its own pragmatic terms.

There is good reason to doubt that more and better contraceptive information and services will make major inroads in the number of teen-age pregnancies. We already live—and have lived for many years—in a contraceptive culture: one, that is, in which contraception is taken for granted. Contraceptive information is widely disseminated and readily available. So are contraceptives. If sexually active teen-agers do not practice contraception, it is not because they lack opportunity.

But, the counterargument goes, we haven't been getting through to them. Despite our best efforts, teen-agers in increasing numbers are getting pregnant. What to do? Obviously, more of the same.

So now the push is on for massive contraceptive indoctrination of the nation's teen-age population. Through the schools. Through television and radio advertising (if the rules and customs of the broadcasting industry can be breached). Thus, the twin problems of teen-age pregnancy and teen-age abortion will be solved.

Perhaps. But it does not seem very likely. More contraceptive indoctrination of teen-agers seems at least as likely (more likely, I would say) to have the same result that the contraceptive indoctrination of recent decades has had: It will motivate them to precocious sexual activity but by no means to the practice of contraception. In which case the "solution" will merely have made the problem worse.

What is the alternative? I believe there is one, but I do not think it is easy. It certainly does not have the attractive but delusory simplicity of more and better contraception. It amounts to turning things around and, instead of telling teen-agers that they can have sex without consequences, telling them the truth: There is no such thing as sex without consequences, whether these be emotional, physical, social—or all three.

It amounts, in other words, to telling them early what they need to know anyway. Sex is not merely for fun or for the expression of transitory affection. It is an enriching and serious business between mature people who are emotionally, socially, and even economically able to accept the consequences, of which pregnancy is hardly the only one.

I agree that more education of teen-agers—indoctrination, if you will—is needed. But I believe it should be education in such things as family values, a healthy and integrated acceptance of sexuality, stability in marital relationships, a sense of obligation toward other persons, and willingness to accept the consequences of one's actions. In other words, it should seek to help them grow up as sexually mature adults.

There is no reason to think more and better contraception will do this. This approach is a formula for short-changing young people, truncating the development of their emotional—and, yes, their sexual—lives. It is a cheap solution that will not work and that, if it did work, would not meet the real developmental needs of teen-agers searching for their sexual identity.

What I am suggesting, admittedly in the most general terms, is a very large order. It would not be easy at any time. It is particularly difficult at a time when the fruits of our contraceptive culture, bitter as they are, are widely accepted as staple fare. So much so that conventional wisdom's proposed solution to the conspicuous failure of more-and-better-contraception is—more and better contraception.

Abortion is a very serious problem. But from a certain perspective it is only the tip of the iceberg, beneath which lie some very strange ideas about sex and sexual responsibility.

If the apparent consensus that abortion, whatever else it may be, is not a good thing leads us to address these matters seriously, it is possible that we shall begin to find authentic solutions, not only to abortion and its causes but to other elements of our present cultural malaise. If we seek solutions instead in more of what has helped bring our problems to their present dimensions, we are likely to find our last state worse than our first.

From The New York Times, January 22, 1978, Section IV, p. 19.

### Questions

*Content/Meaning*
1. Is there one central point to this essay? Can you point to a thesis statement?
2. What evidence, reasoning, and assumptions support Bernardin's conclusions?
3. Can you find and explain any logical flaws in this essay?

*Style:*
1. What expository devices does Bernardin use to organize and develop his essay?

2. How would you characterize Bernardin's voice? Does Bernardin's being a Catholic bishop influence your evaluation of his reasoning and conclusions? Do you feel differently about Bernardin, who identifies himself in his essay, than about Millhiser in the last reading selection, who does not?

## Exercises and Assignments

1. From your outside reading, collect examples of the logical fallacies discussed in this chapter.

2. Find an argument from your outside reading that you think is flawed. In 500 to 750 words, specify the fallacies in the argument by analyzing the premises, assumptions, and reasoning.

# 19    PRESENTING ARGUMENTS

**W**e consider in this chapter the organization and development of extended arguments. Argumentation, as we define it here, is the application of solid evidence and logical reasoning to the task of reaching valid and true conclusions.

Good arguments usually include straightforward exposition: There must be some explanation of the case being argued, or the appropriate context or background must be established. After such an introduction, argumentation uses the same organizational devices as exposition: definition; illustration, example, and analogy; comparison and contrast; and cause and effect. As careful readers and writers, we should notice that many logical fallacies are the misuse or faulty use of those devices: ambiguity, hidden assumptions, and begging the question can all be examples of failing to define key terms clearly and openly; faulty comparison is the illogical application of comparison and contrast; hasty conclusions, overgeneralizing, and the slippery slope all offer false cause-and-effect relationships; some statistical fallacies involve the misuse of examples.

The reading selections that follow are grouped to show arguments in conflict. Most are addressed to a general audience, not to a particular, well-defined one. As you prepare for writing your own arguments, you should pay special attention to what makes some of these essays more convincing than others.

One factor should certainly be the quality of the evidence and reasoning. The facts must be accurate, not misleading, and they must be logically presented. A second factor is the tone of the writing voice. Good arguments *sound* reasonable; they establish the writer as a reliable and informed source of information. The tone of the editorial "Young Jackasses" in the last chapter is all wrong. Calling people names is likely to influence only those who already share your point of view and conclusions. A reasonable tone might

**294**

include giving some time in your argument to the other side, explaining what is wrong with those conclusions with which you disagree. Those rebuttals should be logical and factual. A third factor is the arrangement of your arguments. The poet Donald Hall has remarked that organizing an argument is comparable to organizing a relay team: The second fastest runner goes first, the slowest second, the third fastest third, and the speediest last, for an order of 2, 4, 3, 1. The idea here is to start "fast," or persuasively. Your strongest arguments are used at the beginning and the end to draw your readers into the controversy and leave them convinced. Your weakest arguments or your refutations, where you deal with the opposition's points, should be sandwiched in the middle. You might look to see if any of the articles you find particularly convincing follow this order.

# Reading Selections

The two articles that follow discuss the case of Walter Polovchak, a twelve-year-old boy who sought asylum in the United States when his parents, who had emigrated to this country from the Ukraine, decided to return to their native land.

## THE STATE'S NOSE IN FAMILY LIFE

### Ellen Goodman

Imagine that you, a parent of sound mind and body, are moving cross-country. You've had enough of California and want to try New England.

The children, however, don't want to move. They like the weather, their friends, the school, the usual.

You argue about it, of course; that's what families do. Eventually, you decide that the 17-year-old has a right to stay with her aunt and uncle because she is, after all, one year away from being on her own. But the 12-year-old must come along.

Rebelling, the boy runs away. But when the state finds him, they do not return him. Instead, they grant your son asylum in California.

Asylum from you.

Or maybe it wasn't California. Perhaps you have emigrated to a socialist country and seven months later, disillusioned, want to come home. But this time the state grants your 12-year-old political asylum to save him from a lifetime of materialism, capitalism—who knows what?—in the United States.

If you can imagine these situations, you can feel what has happened to the Polovchak family of Chicago and the Ukraine. The Polovchaks, five of them, emigrated to this country, apparently encouraged by a family member who promised them a leg up into American life. Now, disappointed, the parents want to go back, taking Walter and his younger brother with them.

But the U.S. government has offered Walter asylum and a lawyer and the temporary custody of the state. Two parents, who have neither abused nor neglected their son, have temporarily lost their right to make decisions for their boy, for reasons that are blatantly political.

If it happened to an American family, it would be an outrage. If it happened to an American family in the Soviet Union, it would make furious headlines. It goes against the basic American principle of keeping the state—whenever possible—out of family life.

"There is nothing that any of us would find in the current situation to justify the state entertaining this case," says Yale Law School's Joseph Goldstein, who has written extensively about parents' and childrens' rights. "We don't put someone else in the place of the parents unless they are disqualified. These parents did not abuse or neglect their children."

Psychiatrist Allen Stone, who teaches family law at Harvard, had very much the same reaction: "This is totally outside the range of what family law and family courts ought to be doing. The notion that they would interfere in an ongoing, intact family boggles the mind. It just boggles the mind."

The fact is that we have given much more weight to this Ukrainian boy's testimony than to any American boy of the same age. We have given his parents' views much less weight, because they want him to return with them to the Soviet Union.

But it is almost impossible to assess the boy's own frame of mind and values. Is he a 12-year-old who merely likes the ice cream and bicycles of America? "There is lots of food here," he said. "You can buy many things and I liked school."

Is he, like so many his age, testing the limits, tasting his first tidbits of rebellion? Or can he be mature enough to choose political freedom above family?

It is equally difficult to determine what is best for the boy. There are psychological terrors as well as exhilarations for a child who "wins" such an early and terminal battle with his parents. There are also troubles ahead for a child who returns unwillingly, an embarrassment, to the Ukraine.

But our laws assume (except in rare instances) that the parent is the best judge of the state of mind, the needs and the future of the child. Whether we approve or not, we do not interfere unless they have been proven unfit.

No matter what fantasies we have about rescuing Walter Polovchak, no matter how certain we are that his parents are wrong, we can't have two standards of law—one for Americans and one for Soviet immigrants.

In a Chicago courtroom on Aug. 4, Judge Joseph Mooney ruled that the boy should remain in the custody of the state, and the care of his aunt and uncle, for five more weeks. But his intention is clearly to reunite this family, "whatever the political consequences." And he is right.

The irony is that we criticize, even denounce, the power of the state in the Soviet Union, the way it interferes in private lives. We pride ourselves on being different, pride ourselves on protecting the integrity of the family from the state. But in the case of Walter Polovchak we very nearly lost that difference.

From Newsday, August 8, 1980, p. 59,<br>supplied by The Boston Globe.

## "THE LITTLEST DEFECTOR" DESERVES ASYLUM

### *George Will*

WASHINGTON—The case of Walter Polovchak, "the littlest defector," dramatizes the difficulties, logical and political, that occur when people do not take seriously the radical evil of totalitarian states. Americans who oppose Walter's plea for political asylum are disregarding the premise of the United States, or the manifest nature of the USSR, or both.

Eight months ago Walter, 12, and his family emigrated from the Soviet Union to Chicago. The father is unhappy and wants to return with his wife, Walter, and another son, 6. His daughter, 17, has her own visa and has no intention of leaving the United States. She and Walter are staying with relatives in Chicago, pending disposition of Walter's case.

People opposed to the Illinois court's intervention say the case is "political." Usually that adjective is used to imply that there are no legal standards to control judgment, or that the Constitution commits disposition of such matters to another branch of government. Whatever constitutional problem, if any, lurks here, most of those who complain that Walter's case is "political" seem to mean something else.

They seem to mean only that if Walter were resisting return to, say, Denmark rather than to a closed, totalitarian society, the court probably would not have given Walter a hearing. To which, the answer is: Of course. Justice cannot be done here without taking cognizance of the two regimes, under one of which Walter will live.

Many who oppose granting asylum say Walter is not "mature enough" to choose freedom above family. And they stress American respect for parental authority.

But the fundamental question pertains to claims that are being made to rights that are not contingent upon maturity: Should Walter's parents have the right to choose for him a future in which the possibility of freedom is foreclosed? A nation that asserts that fundamental rights are "inalienable" should not spurn the pleas of a boy whose parents are asserting a right to alienate his fundamental rights, permanently.

No serious person believes parents should exercise absolute sovereignty over their children. American law impinges upon parental authority reluctantly and not always wisely, but impinge it must.

Until the middle of the 19th Century, children were simply property of their parents. Restrictions on child labor were resisted in the name of parental sovereignty. Today, while insisting on the primary role of parents in rearing children, American law requires parents to provide children with specified levels of schooling; it sets varying limits on parental discretion in denying various sorts of medical treatment; in cases of abuse or neglect, it can deprive parents of custody of their children.

It is odd to argue, as Walter's opponents must, that as long as his parents are here, the law can compel them to treat, or refrain from treating, him in various ways, yet the law is deaf, dumb and paralyzed if they choose to confine him, against his pleas, forever in a society the horrors of which have been amply documented.

It is irrational to argue that American law can take Walter from his parents if they abuse him here, but cannot prevent them from turning him over to an abusive state that tries to stifle the spirits of all its captive subjects, and physically threatens those who will not be stifled.

It is bizarre to argue that American law should protect Walter from working in an American factory, but should not interfere with his being sent against his will, to a society in which the Gulag awaits the recalcitrant.

Walter's lawyer, who has experience dealing with the problems of Soviet dissidents, says Walter already qualifies as a dissident and probably would be denied a right to higher education in the Soviet Union. Walter's sister says: "I am so scared for my brother. If he is forced to go back with my parents, he will be punished there. He will be followed for the rest of his life for speaking out against the Soviet Union this way."

One of Walter's teachers says, "Walter has changed from a robot to a kid learning to laugh, cry and have a good time." Walter says, "The children in school here smile a lot—and they don't at home." Walter was raised by his grandmother, and his father has never taken his children on a vacation, or even to a movie, and has never attended a school event. He says, "That is for the state to provide."

Perhaps that's one reason the father wants to live under communism. It certainly is one reason why Walter should not be compelled to.

From *Newsday*, Sept. 4, 1980.

### Questions

*Content/Meaning*

1. Is the reasoning in these two essays inductive or deductive? What evidence or assumptions support the authors' conclusions?

2. Are any logical fallacies present? Is Goodman guilty of appealing to authority? Does Will beg the question of whether Walter Polovchak is a defector?

3. Which arguments are both valid and true? What issues remain in dispute and need to be resolved before any valid conclusions can be reached? How would you attempt to resolve those disputes?

4. Do Goodman (paragraphs 8 and 10) and Will (paragraph 10) use the word "abuse" in the same way?

5. How do Goodman and Will use illustration, example, and analogy? Do they make valid points using these devices?

6. Are any factual details omitted from one article that are included in the other? Are any such omissions crucial to the arguments?

*Style:*

1. At the beginning of arguments there is usually a statement or explanation of the case. How would you contrast Goodman's and Will's explanations? Which is more effective?

2. How do the voices of the two writers distinguish themselves? Do you find one more appealing or convincing than the other?

3. What major expository devices are used in these two essays?

4. How are the arguments organized? Do both have strong openings and endings?

5. How well does each writer answer the arguments of the opposition? Will's article appeared almost one month after Goodman's. Do you think Will read Goodman's article? What makes you think that he did or did not?

# Reading Selections

The two articles that follow are on the "Persian psyche." The first article is by L. Bruce Laingen, the top American diplomat among the 52 hostages held by the Iranians in Teheran. The second article, which comments on Laingen's "memo," is by Edward Said, a professor of English at Columbia University and the author of *Orientalism: The Question of Palestine* and *Covering Islam*.

## MESSAGE FROM IRAN: AUG. 13, '79

### L. Bruce Laingen

*Following are excerpts from a confidential cable sent Aug. 13, 1979, to Cyrus R. Vance, then the Secretary of State, and signed by L. Bruce Laingen, chargé d'affaires at the United States Embassy in Teheran, which was seized by militants on Nov. 4, 1979. Mr. Laingen, the top American diplomat in Teheran after the exile of Shah Mohammed Riza Pahlevi, was at the Foreign Ministry when the embassy was overrun, and remained there until after last Christmas. The cable was made available to* The New York Times *on Jan. 26, 1980, by Dale Van Atta, a reporter with the syndicated columnist Jack Anderson, and was held by* The Times *for publication until the 52 hostages were freed.*

Subject: Negotiations

Recent negotiations in which the embassy has been involved here, ranging from compound security to visa operations . . . highlight several special features of conducting business in the Persian environment. In some instances the difficulties we have encountered are a partial reflection of the effects of the Iranian revolution, but we believe the underlying cultural and psychological qualities that account for the nature of these difficulties are and will remain relatively constant. Therefore, we suggest that the following analysis be used to brief both USG [United States Government] personnel and private sector representatives who are required to do business with and in this country.

Perhaps the single dominant aspect of the Persian psyche is an overriding egoism. Its antecedents lie in the long Iranian history of instability and insecurity which put a premium on self-preservation. The practical effect of it is an almost total Persian preoccupation with self and leaves little room for understanding points of view other than one's own. Thus, for example, it is incomprehensible to an Iranian that U.S. immigration law may prohibit issuing him a tourist visa when he has determined that he wants to live in California. Similarly, the Iranian central bank sees no inconsistency in claiming *force majeure* to avoid penalties for late payment of interest due on outstanding loans while the Government of which it is a part is denying the validity of the very grounds upon which the claim is made when confronted by similar claims from foreign firms forced to cease operations during the Iranian revolution.

The reverse of this particular psychological coin, and having the same historical roots as Persian egoism, is a pervasive unease about the nature of the world in which one lives. The Persian experience has been that nothing is permanent and it is commonly perceived that hostile forces abound. In such an environment each individual must be constantly alert for opportunities to protect himself against the malevolent forces that would otherwise be his undoing. He is obviously justified in using almost any means available to exploit such opportunities. This approach underlies the so-called "bazaar mentality" so common among Persians, a mind-set that often ignores longer term interests in favor of immediately obtainable advantages and countenances practices that are regarded as unethical by other norms.

Coupled with these psychological limitations is a general incomprehension of causality. Islam, with its emphasis on the omnipotence of God, appears to account at least in major part for this phenomenon. Somewhat surprisingly, even those Iranians educated in the Western style and perhaps with long experience outside Iran itself frequently have difficulty grasping the interrelationship of events. Witness a Yazdi [Ibrahim Yazdi, who was Foreign Minister when the embassy was seized] resisting the idea that Iranian behavior has consequences on the perception of Iran in the U.S. or that this perception is somehow related to American policies regarding Iran. This same quality also helps explain Persian aversion to accepting responsibility for one's own actions. The *deus ex machina* is always at work.

The Persian proclivity for assuming that to say something is to do it further complicates matters. Again, Yazdi can express surprise when informed that the irregular security forces assigned to the embassy remain in place. "But the central committee told me they would go by Monday," he says. There is no recognition that instructions must be followed up, that commitments must be accompanied by action and results.

Finally, there are the Persian concepts of influence and obligation. Everyone pays obeisance to the former and the latter is usually honored in the breach. Persians are consumed with developing *parti bazi*—the influence that will help get things done—while favors are only grudgingly bestowed and then just to the extent that a tangible *quid pro quo* is immediately perceptible. Forget about assistance proferred last year or even last week; what can be offered today?

There are several lessons for those who would negotiate with Persians in all this:

First, one should never assume that his side of the issue will be recognized, let alone that it will be conceded to have merits. Persian preoccupation with self precludes this. A negotiator must force recognition of his position upon his Persian opposite number.

Second, one should not expect an Iranian readily to perceive the advantages of a long-term relationship based on trust. He will assume that his opposite number is essentially an adversary. In dealing with him he will attempt to maximize the benefits to himself that are immediately obtainable. He will be prepared to go to great lengths to achieve this goal, including running the risk of so alienating whoever he is dealing with that future business would be unthinkable, at least to the latter.

Third, interlocking relationships of all aspects of an issue must be painstakingly, forcefully and repeatedly developed. Linkages will be neither readily comprehended nor accepted by Persian negotiators.

Fourth, one should insist on performance as the *sine qua non* at each stage of negotiations. Statements of intention count for almost nothing.

Fifth, cultivation of good will for good will's sake is a waste of effort. The overriding objective at all times should be impressing upon the Persian across the table the mutuality of the proposed undertakings. He must be made to know that a *quid pro quo* is involved on both sides.

Finally, one should be prepared for the threat of breakdown in negotiations at any given moment and not be cowed by the possibility. Given the Persian negotiator's cultural and psychological limitations, he is going to resist the very concept of a rational (from the Western point of view) negotiating process.

From *The New York Times,* January 27, 1981.

## INNOCENCE ABROAD

### Bruce Laingen's Memo on "the Persian Psyche"

#### *Edward W. Said*

At one point during the recent ABC special on the secret negotiations leading to the hostage release, Christian Bourguet describes his late March 1980 meeting with Jimmy Carter at the White House. Bourguet, a French lawyer with ties to the Iranians, acted as an intermediary between the U.S. and Iran; he had come to Washington because, despite an arrangement worked out with the Panamanians to arrest the Shah, the deposed ruler had left suddenly for Egypt. So they were back to square one:

**Bourguet:** At a given moment [Carter] spoke of the hostages, saying, you understand that these are Americans. These are innocents. I said to him, yes, Mr. President, I understand that you say they are innocent. But I believe you have to understand that for the Iranians they aren't innocent. Even if personally none of them has committed an act, they are not innocent because they are diplomats who represent a country that has done a number of things in Iran.

You must understand that it is not against their person that the action is being taken. Of course, you can see that. They have not been harmed. They have not been hurt. No attempt has been made to kill them. You must understand that it is a symbol, that it is on the plane of symbols that we have to think about this matter.

In fact Carter seems to have viewed the embassy seizure very much in symbolic terms, but, unlike the Frenchman, he had his own frame of reference. From Carter's perspective, Americans were by definition innocent and somehow outside history; Iran's grievances against the U.S., he would say on another occasion, were ancient history. What mattered now was that Iranians were terrorists, and perhaps had always potentially been a terrorist nation. Indeed, anyone who disliked America and held it captive was dangerous and sick, beyond rationality, beyond humanity, beyond common decency.

Carter's inability to connect America's longstanding support for local dictators with what was happening to the Americans held unlawfully in Tehran is extraordinarily symptomatic. Even if one completely opposes the hostage taking, even if one has only positive feelings about the hostages' return, there are alarming lessons to be learned from what seems like the official national tendency to be oblivious to certain realities. All relationships between people and nations involve two sides. Nothing at all enjoins "us" to like or approve of "them," but we must at least recognize (*a*) that "they" are there, and (*b*) that so far as "they" are concerned "we" are, at least in part, what "they" have experienced of us. Neither side in a conflict has such command of reality as to disregard totally the other viewpoint. Unless of course we believe as Americans that whereas the other side is ontologically guilty, we are innocent.

Consider now the confidential cable sent from Tehran by Bruce Laingen to Secretary of State Vance on August 13, 1979—a document entirely consistent with President Carter's attitudes in his conversation with Bourguet. The cable was published on *The New York Times* Op Ed page January 27, 1981, perhaps to explain what Iranians are really like, perhaps only as an ironic footnote to the crisis. Yet Laingen's message is not a scientific account of "the Persian psyche," despite the author's pretense to calm objectivity and expert knowledge of the culture. The text is, rather, an ideological statement designed, I think, to turn "Persia" into a timeless, acutely disturbed essence, thereby enhancing the superior morality and national sanity of America. Each assertion about "Persia" *adds* damaging evidence to the profile, while shielding "America" from scrutiny and analysis.

This self-blinding is accomplished rhetorically in two ways. First, history is eliminated unilaterally: "the effects of the Iranian revolution" are set aside in the interests of the "relatively constant . . . cultural and psychological qualities" underlying "the Persian psyche." Hence modern Iran becomes ageless Persia. The unscientific equivalent of this would have Italians becoming dagos, Jews yids, blacks niggers, etc. (How refreshingly honest is the street-fighter compared to the polite diplomat!) Second, the Iranian national character is portrayed only with reference to their imagined (i.e., paranoid) sense of reality. Laingen neither allows that the Iranians may have experienced real treachery and suffering, nor that they may have arrived at a view of the United States based on their understanding of U.S. actions in Iran. This is not to say that Laingen implies the U.S. did *not* do anything in Iran: only that the U.S. is entitled to do what it pleases, without irrelevant complaints or reactions from Iranians. The only thing that counts for Laingen is the *constant* "Persian psyche" that overrides all other realities.

Most readers of the Laingen message will accept, as doubtless he does too, that one should not reduce other people or societies to such a simple and stereotypical core. We do not today allow that public discourse should treat blacks and Jews that way, just as we laugh off Iranian portrayals of America as the Great Satan. Too simple, too ideological, too racist. But for this particular enemy—Persia—the reduction serves. The question is what exactly does it serve if, as I shall argue, it neither taught us anything about Iran nor, given the existing tension between the U.S. and Iran after the Revolution, did it help to guide our actions there.

Laingen's argument is that no matter what happens, there is a "Persian proclivity" to resist "the very concept of a rational (from the Western point of view) negotiating process." We can be rational: Persians cannot be. Why? Because, he says, they are overridingly egoistical; reality for them is malevolent; the "bazaar mentality" urges immediate advantage over long-term gain; the omnipotent god of Islam makes it impossible for them to understand causality; and words and reality, in their world, are not connected to each other. In sum, according to the five lessons he abstracts from his analysis, Laingen's "Persian" is an unreliable negotiator, having neither a sense of "the other side," nor a capacity for trust, good will, or character enough to carry out what his words promise.

The irony of this cliché is that literally everything imputed to the Persian or Muslim without any evidence at all can be applied to "the American," that quasi-fictional, unnamed author behind the message. Who but "the American" denies history and reality in saying unilaterally that these don't mean anything to the "Persian." Now play the following parlor game: find a major Judeo-Christian cultural and social equivalent for the traits that Laingen ascribes to "the Persian." Overriding egoism? Rousseau. Malevolence of reality? Kafka. Omnipotence of God? Old and New Testaments. Lack of causal sense? Beckett. Bazaar mentality? New York Stock Exchange. The confusion between words and reality? Austin and Searle. But few people would construct a portrait of the essential West using only Christopher Lasch on narcissism, the words of a fundamentalist preacher, Plato's *Cratylus*, an advertising jingle or two and (as a case of the West's inability to believe in a stable or beneficient reality) Ovid's *Metamorphoses* laced with choice verses from *Leviticus*.

Laingen's message is a functional equivalent of such a portrait. In a different context it would be a caricature at best, a crude though not particularly damaging attack at worst. It is not even effective as a bit of psy-war, since it reveals the writer's weaknesses more than its opponent's. It shows, for example, that the author is extremely nervous about his opposite number; and that he cannot see others except as a mirror image of himself. Where is his capacity for understanding the *Iranian* point of view or for that matter the Islamic Revolution itself, which one supposed had been the result of intolerable *Persian* tyranny and the need to overthrow it?

And as for good will and trust in the rationality of the negotiating process, even if the events of 1953 and U.S. support for the Shah were not mentioned, much could be said about the attempted army coup against the Revolution, directly encouraged by the U.S.'s General Huyser in later January 1979. Then too there was the action of various U.S. banks (unusually compliant in bending the rules to suit the Shah) who during 1979 were prepared to cancel Iranian loans contracted in 1977 on the grounds that Iran had not paid the interest on time. (*Le Monde's* Eric Rouleau reported on November 25–26, 1979, that he had seen proof that Iran had actually paid the interest *ahead* of time.) No wonder that "the Persian" assumes his opposite number is an adversary. He *is* an adversary, and an insecure one at that: Laingen says it plainly.

Let us concede that accuracy, not fairness, is the issue. The U.S. man on the spot is advising Washington. What does he rely on? A handful of Orientalist clichés that could have been taken verbatim from Sir Alfred Lyall's description of the Eastern mind, or from Lord Cromer's account of dealing with the natives in Egypt. If poor Ibrahim Yazdi, then foreign minister of Iran, resists the idea that "Iranian behavior has consequences on the perception of Iran in the United States," which U.S. decision-maker was prepared to accept in advance that U.S. behavior had consequences on the perception of the U.S. in Iran? Why then was the Shah admitted here? Or do we, like the Persians, have an "aversion to accepting responsibility for one's own action"?

Laingen's message is the product of uninformed, unintelligent power, and certainly adds little to our understanding of other societies. As an instance of how we confront the world it does not inspire confidence. As an inadvertent *American* self-portrait it is frankly insulting. What use is it then? It tells us how our representatives created a reality that corresponded neither to our world nor to Iran's. But if it does not also demonstrate that such misrepresentations had better be thrown away forever, then we are in for more international troubles and, alas, our innocence will again be uselessly offended.

From *Village Voice,* February 4–10, 1981,
pp. 11 *f.*

## Questions

*Content/Meaning*
1. What is the major conclusion or point of each article?
2. What does Laingen say are the characteristics of the "Persian psyche"? How does he support his conclusions? Are they logically sufficient? Is the reasoning inductive or deductive?
3. Do you agree with all of Said's characterizations of Laingen's memo?

For example, is Laingen guilty of rhetorical "self-blinding" by referring to "Persia" instead of to "Iran"? Is the use of "Persia" comparable to a racial epithet? Does Laingen say plainly that he is an insecure adversary of Iran's?

4. What are Said's conclusions about Laingen's memo? How does he support his conclusions? Is the reasoning inductive or deductive?

5. Even if you don't know who Sir Alfred Lyall or Lord Cromer are (paragraph 13), do you understand the point Said is making?

*Style*

1. Keeping in mind the different intentions and audiences of the two pieces—Laingen's memo meant for internal State Department use, Said's a critique meant for publication—how would you characterize the voice of each piece? If Laingen knew his memo was going to be published, what changes, if any, do you think he would have made?

2. What expository devices does each writer use to develop his essay?

3. Laingen's position as an important embassy official would, normally, qualify him as a reliable and informed source of information. But it is precisely his reliability that Said calls into question. Is Said successful in undermining Laingen's credibility? Who emerges from this exchange as the more reliable source of information?

## Exercises and Assignments

1. In 750 to 1000 words analyze the premises, assumptions, and reasoning of the arguments in one of the groups from the reading selections. Choose one position to defend and support. Your analysis should state why you think certain arguments are convincing, why they have withstood counterargument, why they seem both valid and true. If you cannot decide an issue on the basis of the information given in the selections, state what information you need to know. Attempt to find the necessary material and add it to your analysis.

2. Find a letter to the editor, an editorial, or an opinion column with which you disagree and write a reply that effectively sets forth your opinions and your objections.

3. Choose an issue with which you are familiar, either through study or experience, and construct valid and truthful arguments about the issue, taking care that your evidence is unquestionable, your reasoning is valid, and your conclusions are strongly supported. You need not attempt to argue the most general formulation of the issue you have chosen; instead, take only a part of a larger issue: Instead of "abortion is murder," try "abortion

is not justifiable as an alternative to birth control"; instead of "shut down all nuclear power plants," try "government supports and subsidies should be removed from the nuclear industry." You will have more success by carefully narrowing the terms of your argument down to a size you can manage in 500 to 1000 words.

# 20      PERSUASION

**S**ome have said that all writing is basically persuasive: To describe an object is to attempt to convince you that the object indeed exists as the writer says it does; to narrate an action is to claim that events happened the way the writer put them down; to criticize or evaluate is to recommend the writer's judgments, often simply that you see the film, read the book, eat in the restaurant, or not. And once more we repeat, the traditional rhetorical categories are more conveniences of analysis and instruction than precise descriptions of how language functions in the world.

We discuss in this chapter writing whose primary purpose is not necessarily the discovery or presentation of truth, but which instead intends to convince an audience to agree with the conclusions of the writer. The writing here is in large part defined by the open self-interest of the writer or sponsor. It is also defined by the open attempt to appeal to its audience. The distinction we draw between argument and persuasion is, then, one of focus and emphasis: Arguments address subjects and apply logic with the aim of discovering truth; persuasion addresses audiences and applies any and all devices and techniques toward the end of convincing people to buy, believe, or do something.

According to Aristotle, people are persuaded by appeals to reason and logic (*logos*), by the appeal of the character or personality of the persuader (*ethos*), and by appeals to their emotions and feelings (*pathos*). Persuasion thus uses the familiar devices of exposition and argument, but in a new way. Being logical, for example, is not as important as *appearing* logical; being an informed and reliable source is not as important as *seeming* to be so. Being right is not as important as being able to move people. Persuasion relies especially on appeals to emotions and feelings, both our best and our worst ones. With persuasion we leave reason for psychology and travel over distinctly nonlogical terrain.

## PROPAGANDA DEVICES

Because the word has such negative connotations and is in our society quickly associated with communism, it is perhaps startling to know the origin of "propaganda." The word is part of the title *Congregatio de Propaganda fide*, "Congregation for Propagating the Faith," the name of the committee of Roman Catholic cardinals founded in 1622 to oversee the church's foreign missions. The root verb in propaganda is "propagate"; the root noun refers to the slips or shoots—what are sometimes called "cuttings"—used by gardeners to grow new plants. Propaganda, thus, seeks to breed or multiply adherents to particular beliefs or causes in the way plants are cultivated. But this benign metaphor has in our own day come to mean the false information spread by sinister and underhanded forces.

The negative connotations to the word come from its close association with totalitarianism, especially with the political or agitation propaganda of V. I. Lenin, the Russian revolutionary, and of Adolf Hitler. In the 1930s the Institute for Propaganda Analysis produced a list of devices synthesized from a study of Hitler's propaganda. The devices are still widely used in contemporary commercial and political appeals. As we attend to these devices and others that follow later in this chapter, we should try to expand our sense of the word to include as propaganda appeals toward ends that may be socially desirable as well as socially harmful: propaganda, or public persuasion using the devices of propaganda, may as easily appeal to us to stop smoking, drive on the highway at no more than 55 mph, or help the handicapped, as it does to buy a certain product, vote for a certain politician, or "buy" a particular political or social idea. Naming something "propaganda" does not relieve us of the responsibility to question and evaluate evidence, arguments, and conclusions and decide if something is good or bad, harmful or useful. The study of propaganda must ultimately depend on questions of value: To a Russian revolutionary, using slogans and symbols to appeal to the grievances of the poor, the uneducated, and the disenfranchised is certainly not seen as evil; nor is the use of the same means—symbols and slogans—for the same purpose—appealing to grievances—avoided in U.S. political campaigns. What we are looking for in studying these devices is whether they are being used responsibly or are being used to lie or mislead or urge us to act against our best interests.

*Name Calling* Also called using "snarl words," this device is the equivalent of the illogical *ad hominem* attack whereby the writer attempts to discredit the opposition by using "bad names" to appeal to hatred, fear, mistrust, or other negative emotions. Obvious examples like "fascist pig" are probably not very persuasive. Much more successful are words like "communist," which to many people simultaneously means both "member of a Marxist-Leninist party" and "enemy." Subtler still is the attempt to *give* a bad name to a group where none may have existed before: A chemical company might try to discredit "environmentalists" who oppose dumping of toxic wastes into streams by associating their cause with attacks on the U.S. economy. Former Vice-President Spiro Agnew elevated name calling into a highly popular art form. Here is an excerpt from a speech he delivered in 1970:

> As for these deserters, malcontents, radicals, incendiaries, the civil and uncivil disobedients among our young, SDS, PLP, Weatherman I and Weatherman II, the revolutionary action movement, Yippies, Hippies, Yahoos, Black Panthers, Lions and Tigers alike—I would swap the whole damn zoo for a single platoon of the kind of young American I saw in Vietnam.

*Glittering Generality* Also called using "purr words," this device is the opposite of name calling. Now the writer uses "good names" or "virtue words" to describe his side. He appeals to positive emotions like love, generosity, altruism by associating his cause with truth, justice, and the American way. Note the glittering generalities in the conclusion to John F. Kennedy's inaugural address, delivered January 20, 1960:

> And so, my fellow Americans: ask not what your country can do for you—ask what you can do for your country.
> My fellow citizens of the world: ask not what America will do for you, but what together we can do for the freedom of man.
> Finally, whether you are citizens of America or citizens of the world, ask of us here the same high standards of strength and sacrifice which we ask of you. With a good conscience our only sure reward, with history the final judge of our deeds, let us go forth to lead the land we love, asking His blessing and His help, but knowing that here on earth God's work must truly be our own.

*The Transfer* This device is the use of powerful, expressive symbols to associate a cause, idea, or product with something that is generally admired, valued, or respected. The name "Uncle Sam" is given to a laxative cereal; the silhouette of Abraham Lincoln is used as the trademark of the Lincoln National Life Insurance Company; a maker of processed foods uses the slogan "What a diamond ring does for your finger, Stouffer's side dishes do for dinner . . . the great mealtime accessories."

*The Testimonial* This device is equivalent to the illogical appeal to authority where a person's reputation or fame is used instead of evidence to support an idea, product, or candidate: A comedian or singer endorses a presidential candidate; a bald actor recommends a brand of razor blades; the daughter of former President Gerald Ford stands beside an automobile with the Capitol building in the background (a transfer device) beneath the caption "Take it from a Ford, drive Subaru."

*Plain Folks* This is a device to associate the writer and his (or her) program or product with the intended audience by appearing to be just like them. This device leads politicians to swallow ethnic food they cannot stomach, corporations to plead that they are just ordinary put-upon taxpayers like the rest of us, and a vitamin company to advertise in a health food magazine saying, "We can make better vitamins as a family-owned company than we could as part of a conglomerate. That's why we haven't sold out."

*Card Stacking* Often the most difficult device to detect, card stacking involves suppressing evidence against the propagandist's side or distorting or oversimplifying facts. Unless we are familiar with the subject, we almost always have to rely on others who are more knowledgeable coming to our rescue with the truth. Mobil Oil, for example, produced an ad that tried to prove how difficult it was to find new oil (and why, therefore, it needed higher profits) by citing as statistical evidence that only 1.7 percent of its wells ever struck oil. A Mobil critic later pointed out that the figure was only true for "new-field wildcat-discovery wells, a tiny category; of *all* wells, about sixty percent hit oil."

A variation on card stacking is the "straw man" device where the propagandist sets up as a target an especially weak and false version of his opponent, whom he then easily tears to pieces. For example, the Can Manufacturers Institute, in an extensive ad opposing beverage container legislation, asked this question: "Surely mandatory deposit laws would reduce the price of beverages to consumers?" The easily demonstrated "no" answer is set up by the use of "surely" and by the suggestion that such laws are designed to reduce costs (which they are not) instead of to reduce litter. It costs more money to take responsibility for beverage containers where they are sold or recycled instead of tossing them to the roadside or in the trash where a different cost is extracted for picking them up or disposing of them in landfills or incinerators.

*The Bandwagon* This device is the "follow the crowd," "everybody's doing it" appeal to popularity. Since everybody else is doing it or buying it or believing it, you should, too, the propagandist urges. The bandwagon is often used in conjunction with the glittering generality and the transfer to create the effect of a Fourth of July parade: "Come on, America. Baseball,

hot dogs, apple pie, and Chevrolet!" Those who refuse to jump on the bandwagon risk being branded by name calling as "reactionary" or "radical,"
"fascist" or "communist," or just "out of it."

## Reading Selections

The two political speeches that follow are "stock speeches" from early in the
1980 presidential election campaign. The texts were compiled by *The New York Times*
from actual speeches and intend to represent the central message of the candidates.

### THE BASIC SPEECH: RONALD REAGAN

When the New Deal was riding high, with a program of social experiments,
Mr. Democrat himself, Al Smith, went on nationwide radio to tell his fellow
Americans he could no longer follow the leadership of the party he had
served 20 years. He said he was taking a walk, and he asked the Democrats
to look at the record.

It is time now for all of us to look at the record—the record of Democratic
leadership.

Despite the protests about all the problems he inherited, Jimmy Carter
came into office with the economy expanding, with inflation reduced to less
than 5 percent, and with the dollar a relatively stable measure of value. In
36 months he has tripled the rate of inflation; the prime interest rate has
risen to the highest level since the Civil War; the price of gold has risen
from $125 an ounce to more than $600 and fluctuates up there at that level,
which measures the extent to which international confidence in the dollar
has fallen. And that is the indication of the collapse of confidence of economic
policies in the Carter administration.

After last summer's Cabinet massacre, the departing Sercretary of the
Treasury confessed that the Carter Administration did not bring with it to
Washington any economic philosophy of its own. So the President and his
counselors embraced the only economic philosophy they could find at hand—
the warmed-over McGovernism of the Democratic platform of 1976.

Together Mr. Carter, his Democratic Congress and his first choice for
chairman of the Federal Reserve proceeded on the premise of parallel lanes
of national prosperity, Federal deficits and easy money. Pursuing this course
together, they made a shambles of our national economy wiping out in three
years' time tens of billions of dollars of value in our private pensions, savings,
insurance, stocks and bonds.

I suggest that when one administration can give us the highest inflation
since 1946, the highest interest rates since the Civil War, and the worst

drop in value of the dollar against gold in history, it's time that administration was turned out of office and a new administration elected to repair the damage done.

But when we consider what lies ahead in this new decade, the damage done to the national economy is insignificant alongside the damage done to our national security. In May of 1977, five months after he took the oath of office, President Carter declared at Notre Dame University, "We are now free of that inordinate fear of Communism which once led us to embrace any dictator who shared that fear." We are now free, he said, of that inordinate fear of Communism which led to moral poverty in Vietnam.

Now, it's true Vietnam was not a war fought according to MacArthur's dictum, "there is no substitute for victory." It may also be true that Vietnam was the wrong war, in the wrong place, at the wrong time. But 50,000 Americans died in Southeast Asia. They were not engaged in some racist enterprise, as candidate Carter charged in 1976.

And when 50,000 Americans make the ultimate sacrifice to defend the people of a small, defenseless country in Southeast Asia from Communist tyranny, that, my friends, is a collective act of moral courage, not an example of moral poverty.

Our current Commander in Chief owes an apology to almost three million Americans who served in Southeast Asia and to the memory of 50,000 who never came home. Isn't it time we recognized the veterans of that war were men who fought as bravely and as effectively as any American fighting men have ever fought in any war? And isn't it time we told them that never again will we allow the immorality of asking young men to fight and die in a war our Government was afraid to let them win?

Since Mr. Carter dismissed his fear of Communism as inordinate, he has set about systematically to diminish and dismantle what one of his predecessors called the great arsenal of democracy:

- He junked the B-1 bomber program, which was to be the mainstay of the Strategic Air Command from now well into the next century. In doing so, he left the air deterrent of the U.S. resting on a few hundred B-52's representing the 80's with the technology of the 40's— many of them older in years than the pilots ordered to fly them.
- Bowing to Kremlin propaganda, Mr. Carter killed the neutron warhead, a credible NATO deterrent to the Soviet tank arms now massed at the eastern end of the historic invasion corridors of Western Europe.
- To show good faith at the SALT negotiating table, the President delayed or postponed the cruise missile program, the MX and the Trident submarine.
- And after all these unilateral concessions, Mr. Warnke brought home

from Europe the SALT II treaty. The Senate has so far refused to ratify, as well it should refuse.

Mr. Carter described the agreement as fair, as just, and for the security interests of the U.S. But is it fair that subsonic American bombers 25 years old are counted as strategic weapons, while supersonic Soviet bombers coming off the assembly line, one every 10 days, are not? Is it fair that severe restrictions are placed upon the range, number and deployment of our small subsonic cruise missiles, while no limits are set upon the multiple-warhead medium-range rockets the Russians are targeting at Western Europe at the rate of one a week?

How should the Americans respond to such an agreement? The President said we must ratify the SALT II treaty because no one will like us if we don't. He said we should give away the Panama Canal because no one would like us if we didn't. It is time to tell the President: We don't care if they like us or not. We intend to be respected throughout the world.

We want arms limitation. We want arms control. But the United States should never place a seal of approval on an unfair, unequal, dangerous document which legitimizes American strategic inferiority to a hostile, imperial power whose ambitions extend to the ends of the earth.

Now, you may be wondering why I bring this up. With the invasion of Afghanistan, the President says he has learned the Soviets cannot be trusted. So he's asked the Senate to hold up ratification of SALT II. But he made sure the Senate and the Soviets understood that he didn't say "no"—he said "maybe." He just doesn't want it ratified now—later on will do, when he has regained his trust in the men in the Kremlin.

For 10 years, the West has searched for détente with the Soviet Union, no one more avidly than Mr. Carter. As a consequence of this 10 years of détente with us, the Soviet Union is now fueled by Western capital, run by American computers, fed by American grain.

Where is the Soviet reciprocity? Where is the Soviet restraint promised in the code of détente of 1972? Is it visible in the Russian military buildup in North Korea? Or on the occupied islands north of Japan? Did we see it in Hanoi's annexation of Indochina? In Soviet complicity in the starvation of the people of Cambodia? The Soviet provision of poison gas used against the hill tribesmen of Laos?

Is Russian restraint evident in their military intervention with Cuban proxies in wars in Angola and Ethiopia? Is it visible in their imperial invasion of the then independent, neutral nation of Afghanistan, where they executed their own puppet president and his entire family, including even the murder of his 3-year-old daughter?

Consider the case of Cuba. When he took office, Mr. Carter extended the hand of friendship to Havana as he did to Hanoi. He had an ideological ally in Senator Kennedy, who has said, "The United States should respect the experiment that has taken place in Cuba and normalize relations with it." Will the Senator explain why free men should respect an experiment that required the elimination of human rights and political freedom?

Why should we respect an experiment of an American-hating dictator who betrayed the Cuban people and converted that country into a penal colony for the Soviet Union?

And how has Fidel Castro reciprocated the friendship offered by President Carter? Since 1976, Russian pilots have begun flying air cover over the island, Soviet submarines have been sent to Castro's navy. Nuclear-capable fighter bombers have appeared at Cuban air bases, and a Soviet combat force is discovered holding military maneuvers there. Apparently, to Mr. Carter, this was the last straw. The status quo—that's Latin for "the mess we're in"—he said was unacceptable, a few weeks later, it seems, was acceptable.

It is precisely because of this foreign policy bordering on appeasement that a student mob can hold hostage, with impunity, diplomats and marines in the American embassy in Iran.

And when viewing the Soviet empire established in Eastern Europe in the first years of the cold war, again Senator Kennedy and Mr. Carter appeared ideological and political twins. In 1976 Senator Kennedy wrote, "With exception of East Germany, Russia has no more satellites." Arriving in Warsaw in 1977, President Carter got off the plane to announce to a startled satrap who rules that country on behalf of the Soviet Union, "Our concept of human rights is preserved in Poland."

What concept of human rights can that be? Would he like to explain that to millions of Polish Americans who know better, or Czechoslovak Americans, Lithuanians, Latvians, Estonians, and Hungarian Americans who know the lands of their fathers are slave states of the Russian Gulag? But as Abraham Lincoln once said, "They only have the right to criticize who have the heart to help."

It is time for the Republican Party to come to the rescue of this country. When Woodrow Wilson delivered his inaugural address, he made a comment that applies to both the great political parties. "The success of a party means little," he said, "except when a nation is using the party for large and definite purpose."

The American people are prepared for large and definite purpose. It is many-faceted:

- It is to restore in its rightful place this society of high principle, of equality for all and special privilege for none. You do not alter the evil character of racial quotas simply by changing the color of the beneficiary.

- It is to care, shelter, and protect the least protected among us and that includes especially the unborn.
- It is to conserve the environment with which we are blessed without shackling the free enterprise system that has made a poor backward agricultural country the greatest nation on earth.
- It is to set aside forever the discredited dogma from the 1930's that an endless string of Federal deficits is the path to national prosperity.
- It is to relieve the small businessman of the burdens of excessive regulation and to energize the economy by lifting the burden of taxation from the backs of the working and middle class.
- It is to look for a solution to the energy crisis, to the genius of industry, the imagination of management, the energy of labor—not to some sprawling Cabinet office in Washington which never should have been created in the first place.
- It is to guarantee each and every American his or her constitutional and civil rights, but never to let them forget that as citizens they have responsibilities and duties as well.
- It is, lastly, to begin the moral and military rearmament of the United States for the difficult, dangerous decade ahead, and to tune out those cynics, pacifists, and appeasers who tell us the Army and Navy of this country are nothing but the extensions of some malevolent military-industrial complex.

We reject that label—that lie—against millions of American men and women who are serving in the armed forces of the United States. There is only one military-industrial complex whose operations should concern us and it is not located in Arlington, Virginia, but in Moscow in the Soviet Union.

One parting note. For years now we have witnessed the agony of refugees from Asia, starving Cambodian men, women and children, fleeing Vietnamese, struggling ashore on Malaysia from some leaky boat after a horrid passage across the South China Sea. Some of these boats make it; many do not. But all of these boats, as has been written, carry on them the same inscription: "This is what happens to friends of the United States."

If there is one message that needs to be sent to all the nations of the world by the next President, it is this: "There will be no more Taiwans and no more Vietnams, regardless of the price or the promise, be it the oil of Arabia or an Ambassador sitting in Beijing, there will be no more abandonment of friends by the United States of America." I want very much to send that message.

From *The New York Times*, February 29, 1980, p. B4.

## THE BASIC SPEECH: JOHN B. ANDERSON

We are confronted today with a vile and ruthless enemy: an enemy that threatens the vital interests of the United States, Western Europe and Japan. The enemy is well-entrenched, its forces deployed for a long battle of attrition against the major industrialized nations of the Western world.

Against this enemy, we have marshaled an army of rhetoric, a batallion of contingency plans, and a policy of containment and appeasement.

The enemy, of course, is our excessive dependence on foreign oil. The battle against this enemy has now persisted for a decade, and we are losing. Our casualties—measured not in the loss of human lives, but in the loss of purchasing powers and jobs—have been high.

The conflict has been costly, and its costs are continuing to rise. In 1970, we paid less than $3 billion for imported oil. In 1975, we paid $27 billion. This year, the price of imported oil will rise to $90 billion, and billions more will be spent in the defense of our oil lifelines and the development of synthetic and alternative fuels.

Despite this decade-long record of struggle, many Americans today still fail to recognize the enemy, because the enemy does not dress in combat fatigues, because its strength is not measured in firepower, and because its numbers are not denominated in terms of airplanes, tanks and missiles.

The enemy, however, is no less real just because its salvos come in the form of economic and political extortion, rather than bullets. And, the threat to our vital interests is no less imminent because the problem happens to be here at home.

Since the Soviet invasion of Afghanistan, the attention of the American public has been focused on the possible threat of further Soviet action against either Iran or Pakistan.

We ignore the Soviet threat at our peril, but we must not allow our concern over the situation in Afghanistan to obscure the equally important lesson of Iran. Just 18 months ago, Iran was America's trusted ally; it produced 5 million barrels of oil per day for export to the Western world; and it was relied upon to keep the Strait of Hormuz open to international commerce. Today, Iran is no longer America's trusted friend; it exports less than 2 million barrels of oil per day, and it now poses a new and dangerous threat to the stability of the region.

The political instability that has crippled Iran could also spread to the other oil-producing nations in the Persian Gulf, including Saudi Arabia. The Saudi oilfields are operated by foreign workers, including a large population of Shiite Moslems with close ties to Iran. In the aftermath of the recent radical Moslem attack at Mecca, trouble broke out in the Saudi oilfields, and 20,000 troops were dispatched to quell the disturbances. Similar troubles in the future could shut down the Saudi oil production of 9.5 million barrels per day for an indefinite period.

Thus, the threat to the security of our oil supplies stems from internal political strife in the Persian Gulf, as it does from external threat.

Whether, however, our access to Persian Gulf oil is threatened by internal or external factors, prudence requires that we take dramatic steps aimed at reducing our dependence on it.

It is important for all Americans to recognize that conflict in the Persian Gulf—regardless of its outcome—would mean an indefinite cutoff of up to 17 million barrels of oil per day to the Western powers. A shortfall of that magnitude would require nearly a 50 percent reduction in the amount of oil consumed by Western Europe, Japan, and the United States.

Now, just as before the enunciation of the so-called Carter Doctrine, the Persian Gulf is a vital interest of the Western powers.

But now, just as before the Carter Doctrine, we do not have the ability to keep oil flowing from the Persian Gulf in the event of large-scale hostilities.

So dependent are we upon the oil resources of the Persian Gulf, that any prolonged cutoff of oil supplies from that region would jeopardize our ability to defend it from internal or external threats.

Given that degree of vulnerability, it seems more than passing strange that those who would arm to the teeth in the defense of the Persian Gulf are not prepared to call for any sacrifice here at home to reduce our military and economic vulnerability in that region.

Those who define our national security in terms of guns alone commit a fatal error that invites—rather than deters—foreign aggression.

I, for one, believe in a strong national defense; but national defense, like charity, begins here at home. If we are serious about defending our national interest, we can best demonstrate that to the rest of the world by strict new conservation measures, rather than registering young men and women for the draft.

Stringent new conservation measures, however, are not required for reasons of national security alone. There exists, in fact, an equally compelling reason: our economic welfare.

In 1798, when the French Foreign Minister, Talleyrand, demanded a $2 million bribe from an American diplomatic delegation before he would consent to discuss the French seizure of American vessels on the open seas, the cry went forth, "Millions for defense, but not one cent for tribute."

Today, however, as our annual oil import bill reaches nearly $90 billion, we quietly and submissively offer up billions in tribute to the extortionist demands of the OPEC oil ministers.

The tyranny of the spot market has ended. The "leapfrogging" of OPEC price hikes have brought OPEC contract oil prices to spot market levels.

Recently, two major American suppliers—Nigeria and Algeria—announced a $4 price hike to $34.21 a barrel. Saudi Arabia, the so-called moderate of OPEC pricing, announced earlier a new fee of $26 a barrel, up 44 percent over several months and 116 percent above the price of last 1978.

And still the demand of the oil producers continue to escalate. The Saudi oil minister, Ahmed Yamani, has warned the United States that unless advanced technology transfers were forthcoming, and unless the Saudis could find inflation-proof investments for their oil earnings, they would curtail their oil production to 8.5 million barrels a day.

We are in danger of being numbed by the rapidity of the oil price shocks. Two years ago, a price hike of $2–$3 a barrel would have been the subject of front-page news; today such a price hike barely warrants mention in the financial pages. We behave like shell-shocked victims of economic warfare; we have lost our economic orientation.

The oil increases that have occurred in the past few months will add 2–3 percentage points to the Consumer Price Index, worsen the length and severity of the recession, and contribute to a further weakening of the dollar.

It is critically important that we express the cost of imported oil in terms that the average American can understand. Imagine if you will the entire population of Maine, Vermont, New Hampshire, Rhode Island, and Massachusetts working year around just to pay the nation's annual oil import bill, and you can begin to appreciate its magnitude.

It is also important to recognize the threat that OPEC poses to the stability of the international monetary system. Last year, OPEC revenues reached $186 billion, and OPEC nations had a resulting balance of payments surplus of $50 billion. This year, with the price of oil averaging $30 a barrel, OPEC revenues will rise to nearly $300 billion, and OPEC nations will have a balance of payments surplus of $90 billion.

Rimmer de Vries, the senior vice president of the Morgan Guaranty Trust Company and an internationally respected expert on monetary affairs, said in a recent Paris speech that private banks do not have the ability to recycle so vast and unprecedented a sum to the oil importing nations. De Vries warned that the huge buildup of surplus funds in the OPEC coffers threatens to create havoc in foreign exchange markets and precipitate a world monetary crisis.

The oil-consuming nations of the world are walking an energy tightrope, and, for the moment, without a safety net. Our strategic petroleum reserves are nearly empty, we have only enough for a few days. For areas like New England, we do not have even adequate plans for the construction of strategic petroleum reserves.

Despite the threat that our oil dependence poses to our economy and national security, we have yet to take the type of conservation measures that are required.

The House and Senate conferees have gutted the conservation tax incentives in the windfall profits bill in favor of generalized tax cuts.

Last summer, I recommended a tax of 50 cents a gallon on gasoline to be coupled with offsetting payroll tax reductions for working men and women, and Social Security benefit hikes for the retired and disabled. Dr. Lawrence Klein of Wharton Econometrics, one of the leading econometric forecasting firms in the country, has testified before the House Budget Committee on behalf of a tax of 50 cents a gallon on gasoline to be coupled with payroll tax reductions and a relaxation in interest rates.

Dr. Klein testified that such a package would curb inflation, reduce energy consumption by as much as 1.2 million barrels per day, strengthen the dollar, moderate the recession and enhance the recovery.

Similar policy steps have been advocated by such noted economic authorities as Nobel laureate Kenneth Arrow; Dr. Hendrik Houthakker of Harvard; Dr. McCracken at the University of Michigan; and Michael Evans of Evans Economics in Washington.

Such energy experts as Daniel Yergin and Robert Stobaugh at Harvard, Robert Pindyck at M.I.T., Robert Williams at Princeton, and Charles Ebbinger at Georgetown, have all expressed strong endorsement of a higher gasoline tax.

All have recognized that a gasoline tax would be a pre-emptive strike against OPEC pricing policies. A gas tax would help to reduce our economic and military vulnerability in the Persian Gulf by reducing our imports by as much as 700,000 barrels a day in the first year alone. The revenues from a gas tax could help to reduce regressive and inflationary payroll taxes. A gas tax could help spur the development of mass transit in urban areas and bus- and van-pool services in rural areas like New Hampshire. A gas tax, combined with offsetting tax cuts, could help to boost the dollar overseas and at home.

And yet, despite these obvious advantages, discussion of a gasoline tax remains a political taboo amongst my Republican and Democratic challengers.

Instead of trading upon glib promises of more energy production to come, we should level with the American people. In the decade ahead, there will be a world shortage of liquid fuels. Americans will have to share in that shortage. Our domestic oil production is declining. It is expected that domestic oil production will fall from 10 million barrels a day to 8 million barrels a day by the end of the decade—with or without a windfall profits tax. Our natural gas production, which peaked in 1972, is also declining with or without the deregulation of natural gas prices. Despite all the public hoopla over synthetic fuels, even its ardent proponents do not expect more than 2 million barrels a day by 1990—not even enough to offset our declining oil production.

There are, of course, alternatives to oil and natural gas. For the decade ahead, however, our best bet is conservation through more fuel-efficient cars, homes and factories. Conservation in its truest sense does not even have to mean sacrifice; it can actually save us money. Moreover, conservation can make an important contribution to our national security and reduce the chances of precipitous military involvement in the Persian Gulf.

The only question is whether we have the moral and political courage to act in the defense of our vital interests.

It is all too obvious that such courage is sadly lacking in the political leadership of this nation. Rather than confronting the issue of our energy dependence, Congressional and Presidential candidates alike prefer to traffic in the politics of vain hopes. The politicians that promise to produce our way out of the energy crisis in a few years are the same politicians that promise tax cuts *and* a balanced budget. Rather than mirroring the hopes and aspirations of the American people, it is time to reflect things as they are.

I, for one, will not perpetrate so cruel a hoax as to promise a budget that cannot be delivered, or an energy policy that cannot be fulfilled. The greatest danger that we face today is not the Soviet Union; it is our unwillingness to make the sacrifices that are necessary for the defense of our vital interests.

From *The New York Times,* March 4, 1980, p. B8.

### Questions

*Content/Meaning*

1. Is there a central theme, point, or focus to each speech?
2. What major points does each candidate make? What evidence supports these points?
3. What current problems does each candidate identify? Are solutions proposed? Do you think the solutions will work, or will they cause other problems?
4. Does either candidate define "national security," either directly or by implication? If both do, are the definitions the same? How would you define "national security"?
5. Can you find examples of all seven propaganda devices in the two speeches? Which of the two, in your estimation, relies more strongly on the use of these devices?

*Style*

1. How does each candidate establish his voice? How would you characterize that voice?
2. How would you characterize the intended audience for each of these speeches?
3. What elements of persuasion (logos, ethos, pathos) does each employ? Can you specify the paragraphs and explain the appeals?
4. Which speech in your opinion is more persuasive? Why?

## Reading Selection

The two advertisements on page 323 appeared on facing pages in a Sunday newspaper magazine section and are addressed to different audiences. As you read, consider especially what different approaches are used to appeal to the two audiences.

### Questions

*Content/Meaning*

1. What is the major persuasive point of each ad? Do both ads make the same or similar points?
2. Is the distinction between "nonsmokers" and "anti-smokers" a valid one, or is it a distinction without a difference? Is it persuasive? Does your personal experience confirm or deny the distinction?
3. What does the word "paranoid" mean? Is it used correctly in the ad addressed to smokers?

*Style*

1. These two ads are addressed to different audiences, smokers and non-smokers. Are there differences in the voices of the two ads? Are different appeals made to the two audiences? If there are differences, specify them.
2. What expository and argumentative devices are used in these ads?
3. Are there any logical fallacies or propaganda devices to notice here?
4. How do the drawings contribute to the point of the ads?
5. Are you persuaded to do or believe or buy anything as a result of reading these ads?

# A word to smokers
### (about nonsmokers and anti-smokers)

In the expressive jargon of jazz, a lot of folks are "into" segregation these days—for smokers.

If you've ridden any planes lately, you've found yourself banished to the back of them, last to be served, last to leave.

Here on the ground, there's a sudden sprouting of "No Smoking" signs. And if, by mistake, you happen to light up in the wrong place, you get a sharp reminder, annoyed frown or cold shoulder.

When that happens, it's easy to get the feeling you're being picked on, and made to feel like a social outcast.

But there's another side to this.

In Seattle some time ago, two restaurants tried segregation—an area for nonsmokers.

After a month, one had served 9,389 meals in the smoking side, and only 21 in the nonsmoker side. In the other, of 17,421 customers, only 23 asked to be segregated from the smokers.

The point is that most nonsmokers think smokers are O.K. and they like to be around us—when the choice is left up to them.

So take heart.

That doesn't mean that the tiny minority of *anti*-smokers are going to go away. They won't. Some of them have very sensible reasons for objecting. Smoke bothers them. And a discourteous smoker bothers them as much as he bothers us smokers. And then there are people, perfectly rational about everything else, who turn kind of paranoid when a smoker approaches.

We don't know what to do about these anti-smokers any more than you do—except to treat them all with the courtesy and kindness we deserve from them.

It works with our friends, the nonsmokers; it may also work with the anti-smokers.

**THE TOBACCO INSTITUTE**
1776 K St. N.W. Washington, D.C. 20006
Freedom of choice
is the best choice.

Warning: The Surgeon General Has Determined That Cigarette Smoking Is Dangerous to Your Health.

# A word to nonsmokers
### (about smokers)

A great jazz musician once said of his art, "If you don't understand it, I can't explain it."

That's the way it is with smoking.

If you've never smoked, it just *looks* puzzling—the whole ritual of lighting, puffing. What's the point?

There's really no way to explain it.

We've all heard from the people who think the 60 million American smokers ought to be, like you, nonsmokers. But even those people know there's *something* going on that smokers like.

Maybe that's the key to the whole tobacco thing from the beginning. It's a small ritual that welcomes strangers, provides companionship in solitude, fills "empty" time, marks the significance of certain occasions and expresses personal style.

For *some* people. And by personal choice, not for you. That's the way it ought to be. Whether your preference is carrot juice or bottled water, beach buggies or foreign cars, tobacco smoking or chewing gum or none of the above. Personal style.

What we're saying is that, like jazz or chamber music,

some people like it and some don't. And most of you nonsmokers understand that. It would be a dull world if everybody liked the same things.

The trouble is that some people (*anti*-smokers, as distinguished from *nonsmokers*) don't like those who march to the sound of the different drummer, and want to harass smokers and, if possible, to separate them from your company in just about everything.

And the further trouble is that even the tolerant *non*-smokers, and that's most of you, are honestly annoyed by the occasional sniff of tobacco smoke that's a little too pervasive. It annoys us smokers equally.

But it would be a shame if we allowed a tiny handful of intolerant anti-smokers, and a small group of discourteous smokers, to break up the enjoyable harmony we find in each other's personal style.

Maybe if we ignore them both, they'll go away and leave the rest of us to go on playing together.

**THE TOBACCO INSTITUTE**
1776 K St. N.W. Washington, D.C. 20006
Freedom of choice
is the best choice.

Warning: The Surgeon General Has Determined That Cigarette Smoking Is Dangerous to Your Health.

## Reading Selections

What follows is an exchange between proponents and opponents of commercial nuclear power plants.

# ⊚bservations

**Make-believe monsters.** Radioactive cattle...stillbirths... miscarriages... These and more supposed calamities were reported or predicted in the press after the accident at Three Mile Island. Well, it's been two years since TMI. Since then, state and federal experts have found that **none of these nuclear nightmares has come true.** Even honey gathered near TMI—and bees are supersensitive to contamina-tion—showed **no trace of radioactivity in the months after the accident.** So if you've been stung by the anti-nuke horror stories, now's the time to say: *"Buzz off!"*

**Witches' brew.** There's a problem all right, but it's psychological, not nuclear. That's the opinion of psychiatrist Robert L. DuPont, who nails *"nuclear phobia"* as the main culprit. According to Dr. DuPont, hysteria was spread by reporters looking for the worst *"what-if"* cases because *"fear is an upper...fear is news."* And Dr. Arthur M. Bueche, last year's winner of the American Institute of Chemists' gold medal award, sees a parallel between today's nuclear phobia and the *"17th century fear of witches."*

**Bedrock of fact.** The real news? Radiation from a nuclear power plant may be less than that in the ground you walk on, or the building you work in—especially if the bedrock or walls happen to be granite, which is often rich in radioactive uranium and thorium. This was graphically demonstrated when atom scientist Alvin Weinberg showed up with a Geiger counter to testify in the granite-sheathed Dirksen Senate Office Building. When Senate Energy Subcommittee Chairman John Glenn heard the reading, he exclaimed: *"We're getting more right here than they got downwind from Three Mile Island!"* And the presidential commission on TMI found the actual average exposure any person would get during a lifetime spent within 50 miles of the accident was the same as a Denver resident gets every week from natural background radiation.

**Click with Congress.** Unfortunately, vocal opponents, lawsuits, and government red tape can stretch to 14 years the time it takes to plan and build a nuclear plant. Now that the nuclear industry and government have spent millions of dollars on new and better safety measures, shouldn't Congress speed up procedures? For if nuclear power blossoms, America will grow—with more energy security—and less dependence on foreign oil. So if you stand with the majority of Americans who do favor continued nuclear construction (and polls say most of you do), make your voice heard. Then something will really click with Congress.

---

**It's a fact:** Using all the nuclear power plants now being built or planned could triple America's energy output from the atom by 1990, to the equivalent of $50 billion worth of oil a year at current world prices.

---

Observations, Box A, Mobil Oil Corporation, 150 East 42 Street, New York, N.Y. 10017 © 1981 Mobil Corporation

# Which Side Do You Believe?

There are two sides to the issue of nuclear power. Both sides feel strongly that their position is correct—which makes it difficult for Americans to form a responsible position on whether our country needs this source of energy.

Americans are bombarded with conflicting views and statements from numerous self-proclaimed energy experts. Some have even said that nuclear power—which currently provides 12% of the nation's electricity—should be halted altogether.

But consider the *sources* of the loudest anti-nuclear noise. Among those leading the attack on nuclear power are a host of actors and actresses, rock stars, aspiring politicians and others who think America has grown enough.

## The Issue Isn't Just Nuclear

Nuclear power is not the only thing they oppose. These are often the same people who have been against development of geothermal energy in California . . . stopped new hydro-electric plants in Maine and Tennessee . . . blocked a new oil refinery for southern California . . . opposed new pipelines to deliver natural gas to the East . . . fought the building of more coal-fired plants. And they're the same people opposed to President Carter's plan for developing a synthetic fuels program. One wonders what they are *for*, and how they propose meeting America's energy needs?

For many of these people, stopping nuclear power is but one part of a political objective to slow growth across the board in America. This no-growth philosophy of the anti-nuclear leadership was clearly expressed by Amory Lovins, one of the world's leading nuclear critics, when he admitted, "If nuclear power were clean, safe, economic . . . and socially benign per se, it would still be unattractive *because of the political implications . . .*"

## Support For Nuclear Widespread

On the other hand, consider the many organizations that have *endorsed* nuclear power for America's future. They include: the AFL-CIO . . . the NAACP . . . the National Governor's Conference . . . Consumer Alert . . . and many more. These groups recognize that America's need for electric power is growing at a rate of 4% each year.

Consider also that the health and safety record of nuclear power has been endorsed by a vast majority of the *scientific* community—including such organizations as the National Academy of Sciences, the World Health Organization, the American Medical Association, and the Health Physics Society.

We're not saying that nuclear power is risk free. The truth is that risks are involved in *all* energy technologies. However, the overwhelming scientific evidence is clear: nuclear power is at least as clean and safe as any other means available to generate electricity—more so than most.

Where will Americans get the electricity that is needed if not, in part, from nuclear power? That's the real question in the nuclear debate. It's the one for which the anti-nuclear leaders have no answer.

## Nuclear Power. Because America Needs Energy.

America's Electric Energy Companies, Department E, Post Office Box 420, Pelham Manor, New York 10803

*Nucleus,* a publication of the Union of Concerned Scientists, in which the article that follows appeared, describes itself as a "nonprofit organization of scientists, engineers, and other professionals concerned about the impact of advanced technology on society." UCS has conducted independent technical work on a range of issues including nuclear reactor safety, radioactive waste disposal, energy policy alternatives, nuclear arms limitation, liquefied natural gas transport and storage, and air and water pollution. Vince Taylor is an economist with the UCS.

## THE NUCLEAR FAITHFUL: TIME TO FACE REALITY

### *Vince Taylor*

The necessity of nuclear power is an article of faith for many. Like all true believers, the nuclear believers have been doing their best to convert everyone else to their belief; thus we are constantly exposed to ads and editorials predicting dire consequences if lagging nuclear construction programs are not accelerated. This message has been repeated so often with so much conviction that even those who fear the dangers of nuclear power may be beginning to wonder whether a nuclear future is not the best of a bad lot of choices. The cries for more nuclear power, however, appear to reflect not the energy needs of the country but the psychological needs of the criers.

The once-upon-a-time promise of nuclear power as a source of cheap energy is no longer believable, a victim of the expensive realities of attempting to make a difficult, inherently dangerous technology simultaneously safe and reliable. While this promise was evaporating, however, the energy crisis was exploding, providing the nuclear believers with a new rationale: whether expensive or not, nuclear power could now be seen as *necessary* to escape the acknowledged dangers of oil dependence.

Since Three Mile Island, TV ads sponsored by the major nuclear manufacturers and electric utilities have proclaimed that nuclear power is "needed to get that foreign oil monkey off our back"; an extended ad campaign on energy policy by the Mobil Corporation has played the theme that "power derived from the atom is essential to solving the energy problem"; and in a recent editorial, the *Wall Street Journal* cited lagging nuclear construction programs as an example of the country's lack of determination to solve the energy crisis. Clearly, the world seen by these believers in nuclear necessity is one where electric utilities consume a major proportion of all oil, have no choices except to continue to use oil or to build nuclear plants, and risk creating electrical blackouts every time they delay or cancel a nuclear plant. Consider, however, the following:

- Nuclear power is a practical source only of energy for generating electricity; thus it can reduce oil consumption only to the extent that it substitutes for oil that would otherwise be used for electrical generation or prevents electrical shortages that would discourage the substitution of electricity for oil.
- Electric utilities used less than 7 percent of all oil consumed in the United States in 1980; thus, if nuclear power were the only potential substitute for utility oil, it could displace, at most, 7 percent of U.S. oil needs.
- Between 1978 and 1980, nuclear-electric generation fell by 8 percent, while utility use of oil simultaneously declined by one-third.
- Only nuclear plants being added in areas where oil is a major utility fuel have the potential to reduce utility consumption of oil, and only 13,000 of the approximately 50,000 megawatts of nuclear capacity currently scheduled for completion by 1985 are in such oil-using areas. They would provide electrical generation equivalent to about 300,000 barrels of oil per day. This amount of oil equals 1.8 percent of 1980 U.S. consumption and 5 percent of imports. Perhaps more meaningful, it equals only one-half of the reduction in oil use achieved by utilities between 1978 and 1980, while nuclear generation was declining.
- Since 1973, electricity use has been growing at less than one-half of prior rates, and in spite of slowing their construction programs, utilities in most regions have accumulated substantial surpluses of generating capacity. For the United States as a whole, capacity exceeds maximum demand (on the hottest summer day) by 35 percent, whereas a 15 to 20 percent margin is considered adequate to assure reliable supply. Given the slowdown in electrical growth, present surpluses are unlikely to disappear much before 1985 even if cancellations and deferrals of nuclear plants continue at recent high rates—rates which reflect utility efforts to adjust to the slowdown.

Thus, in reality, utilities consume only a minor fraction of oil, are rapidly reducing even this small fraction without any help from nuclear power, and are suffering from a surfeit rather than a shortage of generating capacity. Little wonder that the nuclear believers are aggressively attempting to deny this reality.

The most important aspect of reality that the nuclear faithful refuse to acknowledge is the existence of coal as an alternative to nuclear power. Coal is by far the single largest utility fuel. Almost five times as much electricity is generated by coal as by either oil or nuclear power; thus relatively small percentage changes in coal generation can offset large percentage changes in these other sources. For example, only a 15 percent increase in coal-fired generation was required to offset the 1978–80 declines in both oil generation (33 percent) and nuclear generation (8 percent). (The total 1978 to 1980 increase in coal-fired generation, part of which went to meet growth in electrical demand, was 20 percent.)

As the experience of the last few years shows, utilities will substitute coal for oil if, for whatever reason, nuclear power is not a viable alternative. The reason is obvious: even though most oil is consumed in areas where coal is relatively expensive, the price of oil has risen to the point where it costs two to three times as much as coal per unit of electricity generated, and the savings from switching from oil to coal are large: over $100 million per year per 1000 megawatts of capacity. Utilities are moving vigorously to achieve these savings. Long-distance transmission of coal power, so-called "coal-by-wire," has become relatively cheap, and transmission lines between coal-using areas with excess capacity and oil-consuming regions are being used to their limit. Utilities are considering plans to expand transmission lines to permit still greater importation of coal (and hydro power) into oil-using regions, and expedited implementation of these plans should be expected. Many existing plants will be converted from oil to coal, and efforts will be made to accelerate completion of coal (and, it needs to be noted, nuclear) plants under construction in oil-using areas.

A continuation of recent trends, which show no sign of abating, will bring utility consumption of oil below 5 percent of total national consumption by 1982 and to 2 or 3 percent of the total by the end of the decade. Even if nuclear construction programs were to be further delayed or halted altogether, it would cause only a temporary delay in the ongoing transition of electric utilities away from oil. With or without expansion of nuclear power, consumption of oil by utilities is one part of the oil problem for which a solution seems guaranteed.

Although most of the spectres raised by the nuclear believers are without foundation, there is one contention that deserves serious consideration: the threat of greatly increased air pollution if coal is required to shoulder the entire burden of replacing utility use of oil (and eventually gas) and meeting anticipated growth in electrical demand. Coal-fired generating plants are major sources of pollution, producing half of all man-made emissions of sulfur oxides (suspected to be the primary cause of acid rain) and one-third of all smoke ("particulates"). The prospect of a large increase in this pollution burden is not a pleasant one.

If the Reagan Administration, in its drive against "unnecessary" regulation and its concern over oil dependence, moves to relax pollution standards for plants that convert from oil to coal—a move that has been endorsed and encouraged by affected utilities and coal interests—there would be a significant deterioration in air quality in some parts of the country. What needs to be recognized, though, is that *no increase in pollution need occur, even if all existing nuclear, oil, and gas generating plants were to be replaced eventually by coal*—implying a 72 percent increase in coal-fired generation. This is because the large pollution burden from coal plants is an artifact of past policies, which paid little attention to air quality. Most existing plants are many times dirtier than need be. Pollution could be reduced markedly by installing modern pollution control equipment: if all oil, gas, and nuclear plants were replaced by coal and if at the same time all coal plants were required to meet the 1979 pollution standards for new plants set by the Environmental Protection Agency, total utility emissions of oxides would decline to about one-half of current levels and emissions of smoke to one-tenth.

No matter how great the effort made on nuclear safety there can be no certainty that it will suffice to prevent a nuclear catastrophe; by contrast, the technology is in hand to reduce pollution from coal while simultaneously expanding its use. The risk with coal is not technological but political and within the power of an informed public to obviate.

From *Nucleus* Vol. 3, No. 2,
Spring-Summer, 1981, pp. 2–3.

What follows is a talk given at a rally in California against the Diablo Canyon nuclear power plants. Gofman is an M.D., a Ph.D. in nuclear chemistry, and a professor emeritus of medical physics, University of California at Berkeley. He worked on the Manhattan Project that produced the world's first atomic bombs and served as associate director of the Lawrence Livermore (radiation) Laboratory. He now chairs the Committee for Nuclear Responsibility, which printed this speech.

## RADIATION ETHICS: SOME ISSUES

### *John W. Gofman*

There's time to give you only a very, very short course in the effects of radiation on living cells, which of course are the functional unit in all our body organs.

The concept of so-called "low-dose" radiation is a planned deception, because there is *no* evidence that there exists a dose low enough to be harmless, low enough *not* to increase the risk of cancer and leukemia, low enough *not* to cause genetic and chromosome injury. When a single high-speed bullet of beta or alpha particulate radiation rips through cells in your body, it delivers enough energy to break between 250,000 and 2,500,000 chemical bonds in the supremely crucial molecules which are in the heart or nucleus of the cells. To expect adequate repair of the damage caused by a plutonium-emitted alpha particle, for instance, would be like expecting to fix a delicate Swiss watch with glue after you have sawed it in half.

Ionizing radiation can and does break off whole pieces of the chromosomes in your cells, which means that thousands of genes can be lost all at once. With enough radiation, the damage is so great that the cell simply dies. This is precisely why radiation is used to treat cancer—to *kill* cells. But any lesser dose, down to the very lowest possible dose, allows the cell to live, but unfortunately, the machinery of some cells is so screwed up that they embark on the path to cancer, or leukemia, or become a desperately injured sperm or ovum. More radiation means more cells genetically injured or on the path to cancer. Less radiation means fewer cells on those paths. But NO dose is so low as to avoid smashing the molecules of living cells.

Now let us examine the ethics of permitting any additional radiation to reach the cells of humans.

### Justified by Highway Fatalities

*Question #1:* How shall we expose the grotesque ethics of the nuclear promoters who try to *justify* the inevitable deaths from nuclear power production by comparing those deaths with an allegedly larger number of automobile fatalities. Even the National Academy of Sciences now admits nuclear power will kill thousands.

How is the argument of the promoters better than that of a murderer who argues that the *one murder* he committed was just a small matter compared with the 50,000 deaths on the American highways each year?

Moreover, the nuclear mafia is trying to compare a largely *voluntary* risk, like driving, with an *imposed* risk like nuclear power, to which many of us have not consented and to which future generations have *certainly* not consented at all.

Can the nuclear mafia justify deaths from nuclear power by pointing to deaths from fossil fuels? Do you approve of ethics which say that murder by stabbing can be justified if it replaces murder by cyanide?

Apparently, pro-nuclear ethics are low enough to argue that TWO WRONGS MAKE A RIGHT! Nuclear power promoters are polluting the *ethics* of our species as well as the planet itself!

*Never Fear: We Shall Accomplish the Impossible*

*Question #2:* We know that the nuclear radioactive garbage byproducts must be contained, through all of a very complex series of steps, at least 99.99 percent perfectly if we are to avert a cancer epidemic. How shall we cope with the ethics of scientists and engineers who blandly assert they will accomplish the impossible? These scientists are going to repeal Murphy's Law which has plagued the nuclear industry repeatedly—that law stating that "Anything that *can* go wrong *will* go wrong."

*Don't Build It Near Me*

*Question #3:* How shall we deal with the ethics of people who still tell pollsters that they approve of more nuclear power, but who also add, *overwhelmingly,* "But don't build it anywhere near me."

How is that different from their saying, "Yes, I'm willing to *kill* some other people, if that is what it takes for me to get my electric power?"

Such people would probably have second thoughts if we *help* them comprehend the moral depravity of the "build it somewhere *else*" position. BUILD IT NOWHERE is the only answer.

*A Local Matter; None of Your Business*

*Question #4:* Suppose the people at *greatest* risk from the Diablo Canyon plants—the people who live *near* it—support its opening? Do those who do not live right nearby have a right to come here and obstruct the opening?

If the harm could be locally confined, the issue is clearly for the local people to decide. But the issue here is two giant *nukes.* All Americans have the right and the *obligation* to be here and to stop these plants, because it is impossible for a nuke to be a local, one-generation problem. An accident here could kill people a hundred and more miles downwind. And even if Diablo Canyon were *never* to have a serious accident, there would be people killed who are living far away. The killing by the Diablo nukes *starts* with the mining of its fuel, which process releases radioactive radon gas which is going to kill people everywhere around the globe, and to do so over many thousands of years. That is just *one* example of why *every* nuclear plant is *everyone's* business. The people of one locality, even if they *want* a nuke for a neighbor, have no right to inflict random murder on people who live far away and certainly no right to inflict it on the future generations who have no voice, and no choice. After all, "Do unto others . . ."

*Nuclear Workers Polluting the Gene Pool of Humanity*

*Question #5:* Is it ethical for nuclear workers to pollute the genes of the human race? I am using loaded "Nazi-type" terms on purpose, to raise a difficult moral question. Even if all the byproduct radioactivity from nuclear power could somehow be kept away from the public, nuclear power would *still* create a very serious injury to public health.

The reason is simple. The nuclear industry is already irradiating the sex cells—in the gonads—of the nuclear workers. And the number of people irradiated this way will *not* be small if we tolerate nuclear power, because the industry needs lots of bodies to sop up radiation in dangerous cleanup jobs. Already "temporary" workers, even utility truck drivers, college students, and unemployed workers, are brought in to perform the especially "hot" repair jobs in radioactive areas of the nuclear plants. These men get three-month doses in three hours.

Many of these workers are going to have children, and thanks to the extra radiation, some of their children are going to have defective genes. And these defective genes will be passed into the whole population when these children have children of their own. Among the *major* miseries to which genetic defects contribute are heart disease and diabetes.

Yes, nuclear workers have the right to choose an occupation with a very high risk of cancer for themselves, if they wish to do so. But, do they have a right to pollute the genetic heritage of the population at large? Right now, I am sure that most nuclear workers understand *neither* their own cancer risk *nor* the risk they are inflicting on others. Almost without exception, they are carefully deceived by their employers.

*Deception as the USE of People*

*Question #6:* The nuclear mafia has been *deceiving* both the public and the workers about low-dose radiation, about reactor safety, and about the phony "need" for nukes. But what is so wrong about deception? There's no law against telling lies!

I think deception is really another manifestation of the slave-owner mentality, the mentality which regards other people as *objects* to be used and manipulated for one's own goals. Trickery is the prime substitute for the outright use of force to use people.

This slave-holder mentality is so widely taken for granted that if people can *not* be used as someone's objects, their very survival is in question. The Boat People from Indochina are of no immediate use to anyone. Thus they are threatened with being shot on sight, and some are being pushed to their deaths at sea. Murdered. Finally, this week, additional steps have been announced to help a *fraction* of these desperate refugees, but even *now,* the so-called civilized world is not ready to rescue them all. As I grow nauseated by the Western World's indifference to the Boat People's *survival,* I realize that it is perfectly consistent with our civilization's contempt for the inalienable right to life even of its *own* citizens. That contempt is manifest daily in the imposition of nuclear power, the spraying of dangerous herbicides, the legalized dumping of chemical poisons, and in many other ways.

Perhaps it is part of human nature for people to regard other people as objects to be used, manipulated, deceived, and even killed when convenient. We certainly see this use of people at all levels. For instance, at the small-fry level, we learn of salespeople who ruthlessly earn commissions for themselves by tricking senior citizens into buying useless medical insurance policies.

It seems to me that virtually all human problems—from nuclear power to killing of the Boat People—start with the tendency of humans to treat people as objects to be used. But even *if* this tendency is part of human nature (and some would vigorously disagree), we can deal with it in three ways:

1. By eliminating big concentrations of power, like big governments and monopolistic companies, because they *magnify* the ruthlessness of specific individuals.
2. By cultivating social *contempt* instead of social respect for people who wield power over other people, and by spotting power-lusters early and by *preventing* them from getting into positions of power.
3. By appealing to people's better nature—that part of most people which makes them feel *terrible* if they accidentally kill or even injure someone else.

I am confident that there are many, many decent people who presently hold an *indecent* position on nuclear power, and that is because nuclear power promoters have carefully obscured radiation *ethics.* That is why I appreciate *your* efforts to clarify radiation ethics, and why I'll continue my own efforts as stubbornly as I can. NO NUKES!

> From a speech delivered at San Luis
> Obispo, California, June 30, 1979.

### Questions

*Content/Meaning*

1. What are Mobil's and the electric energy companies' arguments in favor of nuclear power? How do they characterize their opposition?

2. What are Taylor and Gofman's arguments? How do they characterize their opposition?
3. Which arguments do you consider fair and valid? Which are logically flawed or propagandistic?
4. Does either side effectively counter the arguments of the other side?
5. Does either side persuade you? Which arguments are the most telling?
6. What further information would you like to have before you made up your mind? What facts are in conflict in these selections? Can you decide from these selections how to resolve the conflicts?

*Style*
1. Can you characterize the voice of each selection? What details of language establish each voice?
2. Who are the audiences addressed by each selection? Are they addressed to those who agree with them, to those who disagree, to those who are neutral, or to a general audience? How well do the voices of each match their audiences?
3. What kinds of appeals (logos, ethos, pathos) are used in each selection? Which do you find most persuasive?
4. The two pronuclear ads were sponsored by large and powerful industries and printed in mass-circulation outlets, *Time* and Sunday newspaper supplements. By contrast, the two antinuclear statements were published by nonprofit organizations in limited-circulation newsletters. Does this contrast influence your evaluation of these selections? Which selections hold more persuasive source appeal (ethos)?

## Exercises and Assignments

1. Write the copy (the verbal text) for a frankly propagandistic ad in behalf of some cause or issue you feel is socially beneficial. Assume that you are attempting to appeal to as many people as possible and so want to offend the fewest possible, either by outright attack or by insulting their intelligence. Use whatever appeals and devices you think will be effective without violating your personal ethics.

2. Write a thoroughly convincing statement about some idea or issue in which you believe. Attempt to be persuasive; use some mixture of logos, ethos, and pathos, but avoid any underhanded or misleading appeals. You may choose to address an audience favorable to your views, unfavorable to them, or to a general audience made up mostly of the uncommitted.

3. Collect examples of strongly partisan statements about some contro-versial issue and analyze the persuasive appeals, the evidence, and the reason-ing supporting the opposed positions. Research any open questions and come to some conclusion about which side is in the right or why it is impossible to decide which side is right from available information. You may use the nuclear power statements for this assignment.

# 21    COMMERCIAL PERSUASION

**W**e turn in this chapter to study advertising messages, the most pervasive form of persuasion in our society. Estimates of how many commercial messages we see in a day begin at five hundred; this would include, besides conventional print ads and broadcast commercials, our casual exposure to insignias and trademarks, billboards, the "car cards" on buses and trains, and the packaging in supermarkets and stores. But before we discuss product advertising, let us consider advertising that promotes ideas.

## IDEA ADVERTISING

Idea, or advocacy, advertising is a relatively new phenomenon in American society. It is a means by which corporations or trade groups for major industries sell not products but ideas they deem beneficial to their interests. Sometimes these ads sell the particular company or industry; they are image advertising, attempting to cast the advertiser in a good light. Other ads express a manufacturer's concern over the consequences of the use of its product. Still others are explicit pleas in behalf of corporate interests: the need for higher profits, less government regulation, or a specific piece of legislation. These ads are generally placed in magazines and newspapers read by highly paid and highly educated segments of the population: *The New Yorker, Scientific American,* the *Columbia Journalism Review,* or *The New York Times.* The ads are a form of propaganda for ideas whose social benefit is often the subject of intense debate.

## IDEOLOGICAL DOUBLESPEAK

Many people have noted that contemporary propaganda is often more subtle and sophisticated than the kind studied during the 1930s. The French thinker Jacques Ellul, for example, draws a distinction between the older, overt agitation propaganda that attempted to move people from resentment to rebellion and the newer, covert integration propaganda that attempts to make people conform to dominant attitudes and ideas. Whereas agitation propaganda was especially effective with the uneducated, integration propaganda, Ellul argues, requires both education and mass media. Whereas the old propaganda tended to use lying and deception, the new kind uses facts and information. What the educated get in modern society, Ellul says, is incoherent information, facts outside their context, wrapped up in appeals to the collective life or the mythic beliefs of the society. Such a collective belief system is one of the things meant by ideology. "Ideological doublespeak" is one term for this new propaganda.

# Reading Selection

The term "ideological doublespeak" was coined by the National Council of Teachers of English (NCTE)'s Committee on Public Doublespeak. *Doublespeak* is a portmanteau word made up of "double talk" and "newspeak," the official language of the fictional society of George Orwell's *1984*. The following is a guide to ideological doublespeak in idea advertising.

## HOW TO LOOK FOR IDEOLOGY AND DOUBLESPEAK IN ADS

### *Richard Ohmann*

**Questions to Ask**

1. Who is the advertiser?
2. What is the explicit purpose of the ad?
3. Does the advertiser have any purpose other than the explicit one?
4. What kind of person or company does the advertiser claim to represent?
5. What audience does the advertiser assume?
6. To what qualities of that audience does the advertiser appeal?
7. What self-interests does the advertiser assume the audience to have? To *think* it has?
8. How does the advertiser relate the product, company, industry, or ideas to the audience's self-interest?

9. What common interests does the advertiser claim or imply between the company or person and the audience?

10. Are there possible *conflicts* of interest between advertisers and audience?

11. Does the ad refer, directly or obliquely, to such conflicts?

12. Does the advertiser call any widely accepted values or beliefs into play in pointing to the audience's and the company or person's common interest?

13. What words does the advertiser use for such values and beliefs? How abstract are these words? How easy are they to tie down to concrete situations and events?

14. What language does the advertiser use to suggest harmony between the company or person and the audience? Is it warranted?

## Thirteen Items of Ideological Stock in Trade

Here's a highly selective list of ideological themes to look for in what American industry says:

1. Anything wrong in our society is a problem, amenable to a solution in the interest of all.

2. Corollary: all conflicts of interest are only apparent.

3. We'll all be best off if business manages the development of resources in the future.

4. It can do this only if (*a*) profits are high, and (*b*) there is a minimum of government interference.

5. Solutions to problems are generally technical; we need new technology, but not any change in the system.

6. Hence, what the experts decide is best for all. The people are often deficient in understanding.

7. On the other hand, neither business nor technocrats have much power: in the present system, *the people* are the ones who decide.

8. They decide best through individual purchases in a free market; voting is secondary, other kinds of politics a potential threat to free choice.

9. The United States can solve its problems apart from those of the rest of the world, and do so without creating problems elsewhere.

10. Freedom is good for both individuals and corporations, and pretty much the same thing for both.

11. Growth and productivity are good for all.

12. Our needs—for pleasure, love, approval, security, etc.—can best be met by consuming products.

13. Consumption should generally be done by units no larger than the nuclear family. And the nuclear family is the social ideal.

(Remember: Taken as ideas, these are of varying merit. They can be openly debated. Certainly they are not in themselves doublespeak. What earns them their places on this list is their very wide acceptance, coupled with their loose formulation: they can easily be appropriated for almost any purpose, including honest and dishonest ones. It is their abuse we should attend to.)

**Short Guide to Ideological Doublespeak**

Look for doublespeak in these areas of semantics and rhetoric:

1. *What you mean "we," paleface?* The homogenizing "we," and "us," and "our." Particularly, watch for shifts in the reference of "we," and for instances where "we" purports to refer to everyone in the society, but where what is said is in fact only true of some. (Recall the Lone Ranger's saying "There are Indians closing in from all sides, Tonto; we're in trouble." Tonto: "What you mean 'we,' paleface?")

2. *"America."* And "the people," "our society," etc. When you read "America needs . . ." stop and ask if all Americans need it, or only some, or some more than others. The use of "America" is often coercive, not referential.

3. *Abstraction away from people.* When someone proposes to fight "poverty," does that mean getting more money to poor people, and perhaps less to the wealthy? If not, what? Again, can we be for "ecology" without being against those who upset the ecological balance?

4. *Liberty. Or, the sheep and the wolf.* Both are for liberty, but one's liberty is the other's death. Watch for plus-words like "liberty," used as if they had the same meaning for all. In many situations they conceal conflict of interest.

5. *It's a problem.* An American habit of mind conceives any difficulty, crisis, disaster, social conflict—ANYthing BAD—as a problem. This move always implies that we're in it together, faced with the same problem, and all with the same interest in a solution. Remember that your solution *may* be my problem, or that your problem may even be *me*. Be watchful, especially, for distinterested formulation of "problems" by those who have helped create them, and whose livelihoods are at stake. Another thing: labeling something a problem obviously implies that there *is* a solution—but in some situations there may be no approved solution, or even no solution at all.

6. *The technological fix.* Fusion will solve our problem, or a new emission control device, or a new ingredient, or a new kind of glass, or just "research." The technological fix is usually aimed at symptoms, not causes. Now some-

times technical solutions are what we (all of us) need. But often they're *more* needed by those who supply the technology. And very often the techno-logical fix is offered as remedy for social or political problems. When some technological term is the subject of an active verb, try to put people back in the picture: Technology does nothing by itself. *Who* will set the machine going? With what interest?

7. *Experts know best.* A corollary of the above, this idea always merits some skepticism. But it leads to doublespeak especially when the ideologue says (*a*) the people must decide, (*b*) the people don't/can't understand what the experts understand, (*c*) let the experts decide.

8. *Hard facts or iron laws.* "The hard fact is that America progresses only if business prospers." Query: What makes a fact hard? Query: What issues are excluded from debate by this hard fact? Well, the equation of progress with economic growth, for one. And the question of alternatives to free enterprise for another. The hard fact move leads to doublespeak when it treats a present social arrangement as iron law, and so rules out choices that might not be good for the advertiser. Watch for law-like statements in present tense (like the invented one above), which foreclose discussion of the system itself, and its assumptions. And watch for coercive uses of words and phrases like "necessary," "only possible," "required," "essential to eco-nomic health," and "inevitable unless."

9. *There's nobody here but us chickens.* Watch for formulations like "the people will decide," or "we will all be ruled by free choices in a free market." They imply that no one has more power than anyone else in deter-mining the future—or even that big corporations have *less* power than ordi-nary people. Check these formulas against the facts of how decisions will be made on a particular issue. And remember to ask who paid for the ad, and whether ordinary people have any matching power.

10. *What can one man do?* To stop pollution, buy brand X gasoline. To handle the trash menace, dispose of your bottle properly. To deal with the energy shortage, turn your lights off when not using them. Some of this may be good advice (but not *all* of it), but none of the individual actions proposed will make a dent in the "problem." Watch for ads that urge indepen-dent acts of consumers, and stay silent about broader "solutions," like new laws, regulations of industry, etc.

11. *Corporations equal people.* A blend of 9 and 10. "We're all in this together—*you* conserve heat in your house, and *we'll* build more nuclear plants." Beware of hearty invitations to collaborate in making America better; ask whether the proposed "partnership" is one of equals, or one of chickens and foxes.

12. *Blurred ownership.* "The people's coal." "Your power company." "America's resources." "Our industrial system." And so on. Ask who, in

cold financial and legal fact, owns the thing in question, who has power to determine its future, and why the possessive noun or pronoun is so generalized.

From Richard Ohmann, "Doublespeak and Ideology in Ads," in *Teaching About Doublespeak*, ed. Daniel Dieterich (Urbana, Ill.: NCTE, 1976), pp. 44–47.

# Reading Selections

Having read the guidelines to "doublespeak," see how well you can apply them to the Monsanto and Mobil ads that follow.

## Questions

*Content/Meaning*
1. What is the main point of the Monsanto ad on page 344? What
2. What devices of exposition and argument are used here?
3. Can you express the argument here as a syllogism? Is the conclusion both valid and true?
4. What devices of exposition and argument are used here? Do you detect any logical fallacies, propaganda devices, or "doublespeak"?

*Style*
1. Who is the audience addressed by this ad? How does the ad appeal to this audience?
2. How does the picture contribute to the ad?

## THE COST OF CLEAN AIR

### *Mobil*

When a doctor gives you a prescription, you seldom ask how much the medicine will cost. But if the doctor also recommends a visit to a chic health spa, perhaps a long cruise in the Caribbean or a trip around the world, you probably start thinking hard about the bill—and whether it's worth the price. This kind of economic question, unfortunately, is one that the Clean Air Act fails to deal with when it specifies what emission controls are necessary.

The Environmental Protection Agency, by law, now establishes air quality standards with little regard to cost. Not surprisingly, the cost has turned out sky-high. By the government's own estimates, environmental controls required by the Clean Air Act from 1970 to 1987 will cost over $400 billion at current prices. Yet serious questions can be raised as to whether the nation would be getting its money's worth.

# Mother Nature is lucky her products don't need labels.

All foods, even natural ones, are made up of chemicals. But natural foods don't have to list their ingredients. So it's often assumed they're chemical-free. In fact, the ordinary orange is a miniature chemical factory. And the good old potato contains arsenic among its more than 150 ingredients.

This doesn't mean natural foods are dangerous. If they were, they wouldn't be on the market. The same is true of man-made foods.

All man-made foods are tested for safety. And they often provide more nutrition, at a lower cost, than natural foods. They even use many of the same chemical ingredients.

So you see, there really isn't much difference between foods made by Mother Nature and those made by man. What's artificial is the line drawn between them.

© Monsanto Company 1980

For a free booklet explaining the risks and benefits of chemicals, mail to:
Monsanto, 800 Lindbergh Blvd., St. Louis, Mo. 63166. Dept. A3NA

Name _____

Address _____

City & state _____Zip _____

# Monsanto

Without chemicals,
life itself would be impossible.

Simple cost analysis shows that America could buy an equally effective air quality package far more cheaply. In some cases we're paying through the nose just for fancy wrapping. And sometimes we don't even know how much we're paying.

Current regulations, for example, require new coal-fired electric generators to remove 70 to 90 percent of the *potential* sulfur oxide emissions in any coal they use—regardless of how "clean" the coal already is. Thus, utilities using low-sulfur coal must install multimillion-dollar scrubbers just like power stations burning high-sulfur coal. The result: heavy expenditures to clean up emissions from coal that isn't that "dirty" to begin with.

Moreover, the law comes down heavily on new plants, which bear most of the burden of achieving air quality goals. It would make better economic sense to encourage power companies to spend their environmental dollars where they do the most good—whether on new plants or existing ones in the same region. A Business Roundtable study estimates that utilities could reduce their sulfur abatement costs by nearly 50 percent within the next decade—*without any loss in air quality*—if the clean air rules were more flexible.

While greater flexibility in implementing the Clean Air Act definitely could save the country money, the more fundamental question is whether all the emission control requirements are worth the price America is being charged. Some of the more recent air quality standards seem to be classic examples of the law of diminishing returns. Regulations in the 1970 Act, for example, required utilities to remove more than 98 percent of the particulate matter emitted by coal-fired burners. According to estimates by National Economic Research Associates, a private consulting firm, 1977 Clean Air amendments mandating an additional one percent increase in the removal of particulates increased the cost by nearly 25 percent.

Up until now, the law hasn't required EPA to ask dollars-and-cents questions when determining national air quality standards. We think the American people should at least know what they're being charged—*before* standards are set. Such a revision would make good sense. Society—like individuals—does not have unlimited wealth, and it must allocate its recources wisely. Given the enormous incremental costs of such higher standards, America might be better off directing its resources into other areas. A frontal attack on cancer or heart disease, say, could affect many more people than the small groups singled out for "fail-safe" protection by many of our national air quality standards. Such policy questions, and alternate values, must be weighed in any discussion of the Clean Air Act.

We all want, and insist upon, clean air standards that protect human health. But can we really *afford* standards that jeopardize economic growth and energy development without a corresponding health benefit? Congress must steer a course that balances environmental needs with other national objectives—at a cost America can afford. The Clean Air Act needs fine tuning. Let's hope Congress does its job wisely. It's time to make the Clean Air Act work for America.

From *The New York Times,* August 13, 1981, p. A23.

### Questions

*Content/Meaning*
1. What is the central point of the Mobil ad? How is it supported?
2. Does the ad employ any logical fallacies, propaganda devices, or "doublespeak?"

*Style*
1. Can you characterize the voice in the ad? To whom is the ad addressed?
2. How does the voice appeal to its audience? How are logos, ethos, and pathos used?

## Reading Selection

The ad on page 347 appeared as you see it in *The New York Times* for October 20, 1975.

### Questions

*Content/Meaning/Style*
1. To whom is the ad addressed? What is it selling?
2. Who is the speaker of this ad? How thoroughly can you describe her? What are her values? Are any contradictory?
3. How does the speaker of this ad appeal to the audience? Are the appeals persuasive?
4. What is the ad's message? What does the ad want you to think or do? Who would benefit from this message?

## Assignment

In 500 to 1000 words analyze one industry ad defending its product, or one idea ad, considering its persuasive value and checking closely for examples of propaganda, "doublespeak," and logical fallacies. Demonstrate

I was asleep for 29 years.

Are you sure you're awake while you're reading this?

Maybe you're in the kind of trance I used to be in: get up, go to work, come home. Get up, go to work, come home. You know what I'm talking about:

The 20th Century trance.

If I wanted to do something new and different, I'd think: tomorrow.

Get involved in the community ecology meetings: tomorrow. Go shopping for a portable color TV: tomorrow. Make reservations for a week in the sun: tomorrow.

I used to spend my life going through the motions today, and putting things off until: tomorrow.

Nothing happens in your life unless you make it happen. I started thinking that way once I stepped back and looked at my life.

Self-knowledge is powerful stuff. It can make you throw away a lot of things in your life, and flip the switch to go after the new things you really want.

I have my new color TV now. In fact, a whole living room full of new furniture. I've been away twice this year, not counting long weekends. And not only am I going to community meetings, I'm organizing them.

I woke up to the fact that you have to live your life today, even though you're always planning for tomorrow.

In fact, I feel secure about the future.

But today is where I live.

## I live my dreams today, not tomorrow.

the truth and validity of the arguments or demonstrate that the arguments are flawed, misleading, or untrustworthy. State first exactly what ideas or attitudes the ad is selling. You will find Ohmann's guides (p. 339–343) valuable in analyzing your ad.

You may use one of the ads included in this chapter or find an ad of your own. If the latter, submit a copy of the ad with your paper.

## THE LANGUAGE OF ADVERTISING

Advertising has been called the modern substitute for argument. As a substitute, advertising defies simple logic and ordinary understanding. Superlatives like "best" and "most," for example, are not really superlative in the advertising world. "Best" means "the same as all the rest" or "none better"; "better" means "best," and, legally, an advertiser who claims to be "better" than the competition has to be able to prove it. That is why so few advertisements ever actually make direct claims of superiority; they rely instead on creating the impression of superiority by verbal and visual subterfuge. "Minute Maid Orange Juice. The best there is" actually says only that Minute Maid is like all the rest. Similarly, "The most refreshing taste in any cigarette" asserts only that this cigarette tastes like a cigarette, whose "refreshment" is the body reacting to the effects of the drug nicotine. One toothpaste company asserted its equality more subtly with "Only a dentist can give him a better fluoride treatment." It does not follow from this statement that the toothpaste is the best on the market. Beware of claims that imply superiority: None may be better, but probably none is worse.

Another technique for creating the misleading illusion of superiority is the *qualified* or *ambiguous statement.* When advertisers say "helps suppress cold symptoms," they hope that a sizable portion of the audience will hear "cures colds." A more subtle example comes from a journal written by a student studying advertising:

> A few days ago I was preparing lunch for my four-year-old son and myself, under his discerning eye. As I started to open a can of tuna fish, my son grabbed my arm and said accusingly, "That's not Star Kist, Daddy. Good-tasting tuna only get to be Star Kist." I noticed right away that he had misquoted the T.V. advertisement which says, "Only good tasting tuna get to be Star Kist," and I couldn't help wondering if my son's interpretation of the line was the one the ad men hoped we would all perceive.

Casual or naive viewers much older than four have transformed an ad's literal message into its implied meaning in the same way as "Star Kist never tastes bad" was transformed into "all other tuna fish tastes bad."

Other techniques designed to mislead are the *incomplete statement:* "You can be sure if it's Westinghouse" (sure of what?); what Jeffrey Schrank has called the *"water is wet" claim:* "Rheingold—the natural beer" (as are all others); and the *pseudo-scientific* or *statistical statement:* "Ford LTD—700% quieter," which is also an incomplete statement. When the Federal Trade Commission asked the Ford Moter Company "quieter than what?" Ford replied that the inside of the LTD was 700 percent quieter than the outside.

For the most part, advertising copy for national brands depends upon non-logical claims such as "It's the real thing" or "A fresh new slice of apple pie" (for a Chevrolet automobile) both *meaningless statements.* Also popular is the *unprovable statement:* "You're gonna love our great little car" or "Lips have never looked so luscious." Yet another category is the *complimentary statement:* "You deserve a break today" and "I'm worth it." The insincerity of such appeals can be seen in a slogan such as "You've come a long way, baby" used to illustrate a series of cigarette advertisements whose background of small, antiqued photographs depict women being punished for smoking. In the foreground stands a beautiful model liberated to endanger her health without fear of humiliation. The use of the trifling "baby" betrays the ad man's true feelings; the ad perpetuates the stereotype of woman as plaything even as it ostensibly celebrates feminism.

Advertising has also been called "sponsored poetry" in tribute to its precision, conciseness, and word play; both poetry and advertising, says semanticist S. I. Hayakawa, give "imaginative, symbolic, or ideal dimension to life and all that is in it." There is no denying that advertising employs many of the devices of poetry: *rhythm and rhyme:* "I like Ike," "Blizzard Wizard," "Danskins are not just for dancing"; *alliteration:* "Peppery, pretty, pure Revlon 'pow'!" *puns and double entendre:* "I'm a thinner" (for Silva Thins cigarettes), "WomenSports has balls" (for a women's sports magazine). Occasionally advertising copy turns literary by developing a story line or by using devices like interior monologue. The following example, from an advertisement for perfume, also uses indentation and short lines to imitate the form of a poem:

> If there's anyone who
> really knows me, it's Michael.
> He says he loves the smell
> of my skin, and he likes my perfume
> because he says it brings out what
> I am to him.
> More of a woman. More honest.
> More open. Less helpless.

> I used to think being more
> of a woman
> meant acting hard to get.
>> Today I think it means not
> acting at all.

The appeals of advertisers are seldom based on reasoning and evidence; words themselves seldom occupy the greatest amount of space in most ads. Instead, colors, symbols, pictures, and images dominate and exert powerful nonrational appeals whose effects are often subliminal. That is, ads can work on us below the level of our conscious awareness.

For this reason, product advertising is especially interesting to study and analyze. Many ads function simultaneously on several levels: verbal, visual, symbolic, and subliminal. As preparation for analyzing ads, consider these guidelines and the analysis that follows them.

### Guides to Interpreting Overt Content

Look at the ad. What is the title or headline? It will provide you with your first clues to the ad's appeal. What do the words suggest? What do they claim?

Notice the background. It may be a landscape stretching to a horizon, a scene of activity, or just a single color. Whatever it is, it has been put there to raise such sensitive and abstract issues as love, pleasure, security, success, freedom, individuality, youth, and many others in order to arouse your hopes and fears.

The attempt to establish an emotional relationship with you continues and becomes more explicit in the *foreground* of the ad. The product may be shown alone, but more often an ad shows people admiring or using the product. Study those people: Who are they? What are they doing? What are their expressions? Are they married? Single? Blue collar? Professional? Happy? Sad? Young? Old? The ad invites you to identify psychologically with the people in the ads, to enter the idealized world the ad depicts, and to relate yourself to the product the way people in the ad have. Observe other *visual techniques* used in the ad. How are light and shadow, color and contrast, photography, drawing, and design used? Are any details, objects, or people exaggerated, out of proportion, or otherwise distorted? Why are such techniques used?

Finally, look again at the whole ad. How does the emotional impact of the ad relate to the product? Most advertising is an attempt to manipulate your emotions so that you will buy one product instead of another just like it, or any product whether you need it or not.

Highly paid and talented artists and researchers have put together these ads. In analyzing their appeals, you are working from the finished ads back to the original plan and intention. The success of your analysis depends on how consistent your interpretation is in each area you discuss.

### Mother's Day at Bloomingdale's

To see how these factors interact, let us look at an ad that appeared in *The New York Times Magazine* on May 2, 1976, one week before Mother's Day (see Fig. 21.3). Bloomingdale's is an exclusive New York department store known for its fashion-conscious ads and clientele.

The eye-catching appeal of the ad lies in its contrast. The can in the picture is all too familiar—an item so identified with common American life that the artist Andy Warhol in the 1960s used it as an important subject for his pop-art paintings. We recognize it instantly, but we are also stopped by its alterations and its context. "This isn't Campbell's soup," we say, "It's Soup by Bloomingdale's!?" "And what is 'Halston Peretti Bean Soup'?" We don't know. The ad has hooked us; we must find out.

We also have to find out something else. Why is this familiar item of food packaging with its opened top displayed in such an elegant setting? If we could see the ad in color, we would find the usual red and white can with its gold highlighting on a lush field of green. Above it are three manicured fingers, with nails painted a shimmering rose, holding a gold chain from which a large golden bean is suspended over the open can. The whole ad is mystifying. Who is selling what here?

If we turn to the copy, we see the heading with the Campbell's motto "mmm mmm . . . good" and below we discover that the product being sold is perfume made by Halston and that Elsa Peretti has designed the containers and the jewelry offered as a bonus for Mother's Day. Having answered our initial questions, we have still to account for all the extraordinary visual and symbolic details. Someone has gone to a great deal of expense and effort to concoct this appeal. What makes it so compelling?

"love remembered . . . mother's day at bloomingdale's." There is probably no other brand name food product more closely associated with mother, kitchen coziness, and warm nourishment than Campbell's soup. Is there a person in the country whose mother has not at one time or another served Campbell's soup? In place of the usual gold seal at the center of the soup label there appears the partial image of a wistful, dreamy-eyed, chic young woman. She is the Bloomingdale's woman, but the yellowish color of the circle suggests nostalgia, antiquing. Is this Mom in the days before she became Mom, before she was encircled by the family responsibilities that can also be represented by the soup can? Besides the picture of the female on the

*21.3*

can, and the role of Campbell's soup in the kitchen, there is also the psychological sense in which circles and cylinders can be symbolically female to suggest that the soup can is meant to stand for Mom.

We have, then, in the can both the elegant world of high fashion and the unpretentious domestic world of Mom in the kitchen. If we pursue the symbol interpretation, the ad not only says, "Bring some elegance into Mom's drab domestic life," it also suggests rebirth. On one level the Bloomingdale's can has just been opened and the Halston/Peretti bonus bean is being removed. On the symbolic level Mom is giving birth: The chain extends umbilically from the can to a bean that seems to enclose a fetuslike shadow! The rich green background reinforces this sense of birth, renewal, and springtime. Give Mother the best gift of all—you again. And give yourself the security of being put once more into her hands. The ad is rich in symbolism and in subliminal emotion both appropriate to Mother's Day.

## Exercises and Assignments

1. The claims in many ads—both commercial and ideological—can be recast in the form of a syllogism. This exercise sharpens your ability to detect arguments and demonstrates how often the arguments in advertising are unstated or stated by implication only. Consider this slogan:

Want him to be more of a man?
Try being more of a woman.
Emeraude
by Coty.

> PREMISE: *If you want him to be more of a man, you should be more of a woman.*
> PREMISE: *Using Emeraude perfume will make you more of a woman.*
> CONCLUSION: *Using Emeraude perfume will make him more of a man.*

This argument, while logical, does not address what "being more of a man" or "being more of a woman" mean, and its premises are also open to question for vagueness and ambiguity.

Often several sets of premises and conclusions are buried in a single brief appeal:

I think a woman can be both strong and sexy. And, I like my hair to be strong and sexy, too. That's why I use Wella Kolestral, the deep conditioner preferred by so many professional hair stylists. . . .
   Try Wella Kolestral. And let your hair reflect the strong, sexy woman in you.

> PREMISE: *Strong and sexy women have strong and sexy hair.*
> PREMISE: *Wella Kolestral makes hair strong and sexy.*
> CONCLUSION: *Wella Kolestral will make you a strong and sexy woman.*

PREMISE: *You want to use on your hair what professional hair stylists use.*

PREMISE: *Professional hair stylists use Wella Kolestral.*

CONCLUSION: *You want to use Wella Kolestral.*

Anything wrong with these premises or conclusions?

Bring to class several examples of advertising copy whose claims can be restated in syllogism form. Construct the syllogism and analyze the premises and the reasoning.

2. Identify the major selling strategy (the theme) in the following ads (pp. 355–360) and comment on how the words, pictures and symbols all contribute to that strategy. Are there subliminal messages?

3. In 500 to 1000 words analyze one product ad from a newspaper or magazine. Choose an ad of your own or pick one from the examples on pp. 355–360. Your analysis should include:

a. A *description* of the ad, its verbal and visual content.

b. The *aim* of the ad. To whom is the ad addressed? How does it make its appeal?

c. An evaluation of the ad's appeal. What is its effect? Include a copy of the ad with your analysis, where possible, and specify the source (magazine or newspaper and the date).

# SEVEN LUXURY FEATURES THOUGHTFULLY LEFT OFF THE VOLVO 164.

You can't create a luxury car by tacking on "luxury features." One of the things that makes the Volvo 164 truly elegant is a total absence of tackiness.

**1 NO OPERA WINDOWS** Tiny side windows are all the rage. But to Volvo, they're outrageous. The 164 has big windows that let you see out instead of little ones that keep outsiders from seeing in.

**2 NO FANCY INTERIOR DECOR GROUP** Volvo's bucket seats were designed by an orthopedic specialist, not an interior decorator. They adjust to your every inclination, even "soft" or "firm." The driver's seat is heated. And there's leather everywhere you sit.

**3 NO 400 CUBIC INCH V-8** Volvo's 3-litre six has enough "go" for any well-balanced person. And enough economy—22 mpg on the highway.* Volvo's computerized fuel injection has electronic sensors that monitor speed, altitude and temperature to determine proper fuel mixture.

*U.S. Gov't. EPA figures, 9/74

**4 NO FAKE WOOD VENEER** Volvo covers its dashboard with instrumentation. A tachometer, trip mileage indicator and electric clock are standard. There's even a light that warns if an important light goes out.

**5 NO STATUS HOOD ORNAMENT** The Volvo driver doesn't require constant reassurance. Nor does he need to be reminded what car he's driving. Unlike other cars today, the 164 isn't a copy of anything.

**6 NO DECALED-ON PIN STRIPING** Volvo concentrates on what's under the paint. 8,000 spot welds fight rattles. The metal is magnetically charged to soak up rustproofing. There are two separate coats of undercoating.

**7 NO LONG OPTIONS LIST** Instead, the 164 provides a long standards list. Air conditioning, automatic transmission, power-assisted steering, power front windows, 4-wheel power disc brakes and steel belted radial whitewalls.

## VOLVO
The luxury car for people who think.

© 1975 Volvo of America Corporation.

# Is Tsingtao winning the cold war?

Recently (as those who've been watching television, reading newspapers and listening to radio are aware) China's greatest vodka, *Tsingtao*, has become embroiled with the Russian vodkas in a war for supremacy.

*Tsingtao* (pronounced "ching dow") has taken the offensive and invaded Russian vodka strongholds previously regarded as secure.

But unlike wars fought on rough terrain, this war is being fought in the posh surroundings of some of the most elegant "to be seen in" restaurants in New York.

There, where one can find what little *Tsingtao*

vodka is available in the United States, vodka purists are subjecting *Tsingtao* to every imaginable test of the palate. And from recent reports, *Tsingtao* is winning more than its share of the battles.

At a famous uptown watering hole (need we mention its name) a political journalist quipped: "*Tsingtao alone was reason enough to grant China favored-nation trading status.*"

And at an up-and-coming SoHo bar, a Russian-vodka diehard, having just finished extolling the virtues of Russian vodka, tried his first *Tsingtao* and announced:

"*I needed two good reasons to stop drinking Russian vodka. Russia gave me one, and China just gave me the other.*"

When China first allowed *Tsingtao* to be exported to the United States, they hardly expected it to become the toast of the town. (At $10 a bottle, they were convinced only the wealthy would be able to afford it.) Besides, who even knew that China was already distilling spirits 1000 years before Russia ever existed?

But China has been known for keeping things secret.

And *Tsingtao*, much to the Russian's regret, seems to have been China's best-kept secret.

Imported from the People's Republic of China exclusively by Monarch Import Co., N.Y., N.Y. 11232. Tsingtao Vodka, 80 Proof. Distilled from grain.

## Is Tsingtao winning the cold war?

Recently (as those who've been watching television, reading newspapers and listening to radio are aware) China's greatest vodka, *Tsingtao,* has become embroiled with the Russian vodkas in a war for supremacy.

*Tsingtao* (pronounced "ching dow") has taken the offensive and invaded Russian vodka strongholds previously regarded as secure.

But unlike wars fought on rough terrain, this war is being fought in the posh surroundings of some of the most elegant "to be seen in" restaurants in New York.

There, where one can find what little *Tsingtao* vodka is available in the United States, vodka purists are subjecting *Tsingtao* to every imaginable test of the palate. And from recent reports, *Tsingtao* is winning more than its share of the battles.

At a famous uptown watering hole (need we mention its name) a political journalist quipped: *"Tsingtao alone was reason enough to grant China favored-nation trading status."*

And at an up-and-coming SoHo bar, a Russian-vodka diehard, having just finished extolling the virtues of Russian vodka, tried his first *Tsingtao* and announced: *"I needed two good reasons to stop drinking Russian vodka. Russia gave me one, and China just gave me the other."*

When China first allowed *Tsingtao* to be exported to the United States, they hardly expected it to become the toast of the town. (At $10 a bottle, they were convinced only the wealthy would be able to afford it.) Besides, who even knew that China was already distilling spirits 1000 years before Russia ever existed?

But China has been known for keeping things secret.

And *Tsingtao,* much to the Russian's regret, seems to have been China's best-kept secret.

Imported from the People's Republic of China exclusively by Monarch Import Co., N.Y., N.Y. 11232. Tsingtao Vodka, 80 Proof. Distilled from grain.

# CRITICISM

The word "criticism" has at least two general meanings, one negative and the other neutral. In its negative sense, it means "the passing of unfavorable judgment" or "finding fault," an extension of the adjective "critical," as in the phrase "to be critical of someone or something." Our use of the term here is not in the negative but in the neutral sense. "Criticism" thus refers simply to "the act of making judgments"—any judgments, whether positive or negative, personal or impersonal, well documented or impressionistic.

Criticism in the neutral sense of the term is an essential part of our lives. It is practiced everywhere. We find it, for example, in college classrooms, and we certainly find it in the mass media. In our educational progress we move ideally from gathering and assimilating information to forming opinions about it. Specialists in any field must also be critics; they must know which sources they can trust and which they must reject, which ideas are morally acceptable and which are not. Scientists, for example, often have to question the products of their research ("Is splitting the atom good when it can lead to the development of the atomic bomb?"). In the broadest terms, the educated person must learn to challenge ideas in all realms all the time. We must be impatient with the commonplace, with ideas and slogans that impress us only because we have heard them so often, such as "crime doesn't pay," "marriage is a fifty-fifty proposition," "progress is our most important product," "childhood is a blissful state." The educated reader and writer learns to discriminate and to look beneath the surface for meaning. Criticism has to do with this way of looking at the world.

# 22

# THE SHORT SUMMARY AND CAPSULE REVIEW

**T**he task of writing a review requires careful attention to the substance and meaning of the work to be evaluated. A useful preliminary step for reviewing is, therefore, the writing of a summary account of the work under consideration. That account may be descriptive, expository, narrative, or a combination of these modes depending on the nature of the work being reviewed.

The short narrative summary is usually called a *synopsis,* which in strictest terms is simply a plot summary. Synopses can thus be written for short stories, novels, plays, films, TV serials, and any other narrative forms. The short expository or descriptive summary is usually called an *abstract. Expository abstracts* typically summarize arguments as presented in essays, articles, or books; *descriptive abstracts* concentrate on such subjects as paintings, sculptures, works of architecture, musical performances, items of fashion, restaurants, and foods or wines. Some subjects are mixed in form, such as opera or ballet, and may be rendered in a combination of synopsis and abstract. Summaries can also be called by other names, for example *precis* or *digest.* Generally, a precis is an expository abstract or synopsis presented essentially in the order of the original work; a digest implies a longer summary than either an abstract or a synopsis.

A good illustration of the term digest is its use in the title of *The Reader's Digest,* a magazine that reproduces works in a cut-down version but in their original language. In this chapter we give no further attention to the digest.

## ABSTRACTS AND SYNOPSES

Both the abstract and the synopsis depend on our ability to reproduce essential ideas and facts in precise and carefully chosen detail. They demand close attention in listening to, viewing, or reading the original work. Such attention is naturally desirable and useful for the complex job of writing a critical review, for we must know our subject intimately before we can offer a responsible opinion about it. When we compose expository abstracts or synopses of written works, we must perform the difficult but important task of *paraphrasing*, which in the abstract or synopsis is a form of shorthand translation of an author's wording into our own. Successful paraphrase depends on close reading; it establishes the need for the act of reading as a preliminary step to the act of writing. While most abstracts and synopses are, in fact, succinct paraphrases of the works summarized, one may on occasion extract a direct quotation from the original. Such quotations must never distort the context of the original, and they should be used with discretion, usually to preserve a memorable phrase.

# Reading Selection

As an illustration of how to write a summary, in this case an expository abstract, we have chosen a selection on *People* magazine by Nora Ephron from her book *Scribble, Scribble*. As you read the essay, underline what you consider to be essential ideas, facts, or both, and make marginal notations about content that you would consider for inclusion in an abstract. Also try to formulate what you consider to be the central point.

### *PEOPLE* MAGAZINE

#### *Nora Ephron*

The people over at *People* get all riled up if anyone suggests that *People* is a direct descendant of anything at all. You do not even have to suggest that it is; the first words anyone over there says, *insists*, really, is that *People* is *not* a spin-off of the *Time* "People" section (which they are right about), and that it is *not* a reincarnation of *Life* (which they are, at least in part, wrong about). *People*, they tell you, is an original thing. Distinctive. Different. Unto itself. They make it sound a lot like a cigarette.

*People* was introduced by Time Inc. a year ago, and at last reports it was selling 1,250,000 copies a week, all of them on newsstands. It is the first national weekly that has been launched since *Sports Illustrated* in 1954, and it will probably lose some three million dollars in its first year, a sum that fazes no one at Time Inc., since it is right on target. *Sports Illustrated* lost twenty-six million in the ten years before it turned the corner, and *People* is expected to lose considerably less and turn the corner considerably quicker. There is probably something to be said for all this—something about how healthy it is for the magazine business that a thing like this is happening, a new magazine with good prospects and no nudity that interests over a million readers a week—but I'm not sure that I am the person who is going to say it. *People* makes me grouchy, and I have been trying for months to figure out why. I do read it. I read it in the exact way its editors intend me to—straight through without stopping. I buy it in airline terminals, and I find that if I start reading it at the moment I am seated on the Eastern shuttle, it lasts until shortly before takeoff. This means that its time span is approximately five minutes longer than the *New York Post* on a day with a good Rose Franzblau column, and five minutes less than *Rona Barrett's Gossip*, which in any case is not available at the Eastern shuttle terminal in La Guardia Airport.

My problem with the magazine is not that I think it is harmful or dangerous or anything of the sort. It's almost not worth getting upset about. It's a potato chip. A snack. Empty calories. Which would be fine, really— I like potato chips. But they make you feel lousy afterward too.

*People* is a product of something called the Magazine Development Group at Time Inc., which has been laboring for several years to come up with new magazines and has brought forth *Money* and two rejected dummy magazines, one on photography, the other on show business. The approach this group takes is a unique one in today's magazine business: Most magazines tend to be about a sensibility rather than a subject, and tend to be dominated not by a group but by one editor and his or her concept of what that sensibility is. In any event, the idea for *People*—which was a simple, five-word idea: let's-call-a-magazine-*People*—started kicking around the halls of Time Inc. a couple of years ago. Some people, mainly Clare Boothe Luce, think it originated with Clare Boothe Luce; others seem to lean toward a great-idea-whose-time-has-come theory, not unlike the Big Bang, and they say that if anyone thought of it at all (which they are not sure of), it was Andrew Heiskell, Time Inc.'s chairman of the board. But the credit probably belongs, in some transcendental way, to Kierkegaard, who in 1846 said that in time, all anyone would be interested in was gossip.

From the beginning, *People* was conceived as an inexpensive magazine— cheap to produce and cheap to buy. There would be a small staff. Low overhead. Stringers. No color photographs except for the cover. It was intended to be sold only on newsstands—thus eliminating the escalating cost of mailing the magazine to subscribers and mailing the subscribers reminders to renew their subscriptions. It was clear that the magazine would have to have a very strong appeal for women; an increasing proportion of newsstands in this country are in supermarkets. Its direct competitor for rack space at the check-out counter was the *National Enquirer.* A pilot issue of the magazine, with Richard Burton and Elizabeth Taylor on the cover, was produced in August, 1973, and test-marketed in seven cities, and it is the pride of the Time Inc. marketing department that this was done in the exact way Procter & Gamble introduces a new toilet paper. When Malcolm B. Ochs, marketing director of the Magazine Development Group at Time Inc., speaks about *People,* he talks about selling "packaged goods" and "one million units a week" and "perishable products." This sort of talk is not really surprising—I have spent enough time around magazine salesmen to know they would all be more comfortable selling tomatoes—but it is nonetheless a depressing development.

The second major decision that was arrived at early on was to keep the stories short. "We always want to leave people wishing for more," says Richard B. Stolley, *People's* managing editor. This is a perfectly valid editorial slogan, but what Stolley does not seem willing to admit is the reason for it, which is that *People* is essentially a magazine for people who don't want to read. The people at *People* seem to believe that people who read *People* have the shortest attention spans in the world. *Time* and *Life* started out this way too, but both of them managed to rise above their original intentions.

The incarnation of *Life* that *People* most resembles is not the early era, where photographs dominated, nor even the middle-to-late period, when the photography and journalism struck a nice balance, but the last desperate days, when Ralph Graves was trying to save the magazine from what turned out to be its inevitable death. This is not the time to go into Graves's most serious and abhorrent editorial decision, which was to eliminate the *Life* Great Dinners series; what I want to talk about instead is his decision to shorten the articles. There are people over at the Time-Life Building, defenders of Graves, who insist he did this for reasons of economy—there was no room for long pieces in a magazine that was losing advertising and therefore editorial pages—but Graves himself refuses to be so defended. He claims he shortened the articles because he believes in short articles. And the result, in the case of *Life,* was a magazine that did nothing terribly well.

*People* has this exact quality—and I'm not exactly sure why. I have nothing against short articles, and no desire to read more than 1500 words or so on most of the personalities *People* profiles. In fact, in the case of a number of those personalities—and here the name of Telly Savalas springs instantly to mind—a caption would suffice. I have no quarrel with the writing in the magazine, which is slick and perfectly competent. I wouldn't mind if *People* were just a picture magazine, if I could at least see the pictures; there is an indefinable something in its art direction that makes the magazine look remarkably like the centerfold of the *Daily News*. And I wouldn't even mind if it were a fan magazine for grownups—if it delivered the goods. But the real problem is that when I finish reading *People*, I always feel that I have just spent four days in Los Angeles. *Women's Wear Daily* at least makes me feel dirty; *People* makes me feel that I haven't read or learned or seen anything at all. I don't think this is what Richard Stolley means when he says he wants to leave his readers wanting more: I tend to be left feeling that I haven't gotten anything in the first place. And even this feeling is hard to pinpoint; I am looking at a recent issue of *People*, with Hugh Hefner on the cover, and I can't really say I didn't learn anything in it: On page 6 it says that Hefner told his unauthorized biographer that he once had a homosexual experience. I didn't actually know that before reading *People*, but somehow it doesn't surprise me.k0

Worst of all—yes, there is a worst of all—I end up feeling glutted with celebrity. I stopped reading movie magazines in the beauty parlor a couple of years ago because I could not accommodate any more information about something called the Lennon Sisters. I had got to the point where I thought I knew what celebrity was—celebrity was anyone I would stand up in a restaurant and stare at. I had whittled the list down to Marlon Brando, Mary Tyler Moore and Angelo "Gyp" DeCarlo, and I was fairly happy. Now I am confronted with *People*, and the plain fact is that a celebrity is anyone *People* writes about; I know the magazine is filling some nameless, bottomless pit of need for gossip and names, but I haven't got room in my life for so many lights.

*People's* only serious financial difficulty at this point is in attracting advertisers, and one of the reasons the people at *People* think they are having trouble doing so is that their advertisers don't know who the *People* reader is. Time Inc. has issued a demographic survey which shows that *People's* readers are upscale, whatever that means, and that 48 percent of them have been to college. I never believe these surveys—*Playboy* and *Penthouse* have them, and theirs show that their readers are mainly interested in the fine fiction; in any case, I suspect that *People's* real problem with advertisers is not that they don't know who's reading the magazine, but that they know exactly who's reading it. In one recent issue there are three liquor ads—for Seagram's Seven Crown, Jim Beam and a bottled cocktail called the Brass Monkey, all of them brands bought predominantly by the blue-collar middle class. It's logical that these brands would buy space in *People*—liquor companies can't advertise on television. But any product that could would probably do better to reach nonreaders through the mass-market women's magazines, which at least sit around all month, or on television itself.

"The human element really is being neglected in national reporting," says Richard Stolley. "The better newspapers and magazines deal more and more with events and issues and debates. The human beings caught up in them simply get squelched. If we can bring a human being out of a massive event, then we've done what I want to do." I don't really object to this philosophy—I'm not sure that I agree with it, but I don't object to it. But it seems a shame that so much of the reporting of the so-called human element in *People* is aimed at the lowest common denominator of the also-so-called human element, that all this coverage of humanity has to be at the expense of the issues and events and ideas involved. It seems even sadder that there seems to be no stopping it. *People* is the future, and it works, and that makes me grouchiest of all.

From Nora Ephron, *Scribble, Scribble*
(New York: Knopf, 1978), pp. 13–18.

As we reexamine this essay, let us, first, decide what we consider to be its central point. Which of the following statements, in your estimation, summarizes that central point most accurately?

1. Nora Ephron thinks that *People* magazine is a cheap spinoff of the *Time* "People" sections.
2. Nora Ephron considers *People* a badly written, cheap version of *Life* magazine, directed essentially to blue-collar middle-class readers.
3. Nora Ephron objects to *People* because it is produced and marketed as a slick, empty gossip magazine.
4. Nora Ephron objects to the compromise made by the publisher of letting neither pictures nor stories dominate its articles.

If you marked statement 3 as the most accurate paraphrase of the article's central point, you would have agreed with our reading of the essay. Statement 1 is a point specifically denied in the first paragraph. Statement 2 includes some acknowledged facts—*People* resembles the late, poor format of *Life* and is addressed to blue-collar tastes—but these facts are at least partially distorted, and they do not restate Ephron's central point. Moreover, statement 2 contradicts one point actually made: Ephron says that she has "no quarrel with the writing of the magazine." Statement 4 is an accurate restatement of an implication in the article (see paragraph 7), but it is certainly not the central point.

The central point, then, can be paraphrased as follows: "Nora Ephron objects to *People* because it is produced and marketed as a slick, empty gossip magazine." Such a summary statement is a necessary starting point for the writing of an abstract. As a supplementary matter of interest, we could establish further what Ephron's purpose was in writing the piece. She tells us that directly (paragrah 2): She wanted to figure out why she reads the magazine. Her conclusion is, by implication, that she reads it because, like the million and a quarter other readers who buy it on the newsstands, she has been unconsciously influenced by its marketing strategy. Once recognizing this fact, she concludes that *People* is like other "junk" products, for instance, potato chips, which give you calories without taste and make you "feel lousy." To paraphrase this interesting analogy one has to find the right descriptive adjective. We have chosen to use the words "slick" and "empty" because they properly transfer the "potato chip" quality to the magazine as a consumable product.

Once the central point and the purpose have been established, the abstractor must engage in yet another critical act to produce an abstracted paraphrase. Which facts are essential for inclusion in the abstract and which unessential? For instance, is it important to mention that *People* lost approximately $3 million in its first year of publication, that either Clare Boothe Luce or Andrew Heiskell was the inspirational force of the magainze, that Richard Burton and Elizabeth Taylor were on the cover of the pilot issue, or that Ralph Graves instituted the policy of shortening articles to save *Life* magazine? These seem to us unessential facts for inclusion in the abstract. On the other hand, we think that two facts are extremely important, and obviously should be included in our abstract: (1) that the magazine was designed to be inexpensive, and (2) that its stories were to be kept short. Why do we think these facts are essential? Because, for one thing, the writer tells us so. Note the beginning sentence of paragraph 6; "The second major decision that was arrived at early on was to keep the stories short." Words like *major, significant, important, crucial,* and others registering the writer's sense of priority must be carefully noted in the writing of abstracts. Incidentally, we are never told explicitly in this essay what the first major decision was. To discover that we must infer—but in this instance the inference is obvious. Since the "second major decision" starts a paragraph and forms part of the topic sentence, the first ought to be the topic sentence of the preceding paragraph, as indeed it is. The art of writing abstracts depends vitally on the interpretation of such signals.

What follows is our attempt to write a one-hundred-word abstract of the Ephron essay. Read it critically, and try to decide whether you would have made the same decisions concerning what to include and exclude from your paraphrase.

In characterizing *People* magazine Nora Ephron states that the publisher considers it an original magazine, not a spinoff from *Life* or *Time,* and that it sells 1,250,000 copies a week, a figure showing that it is a success among weeklies that avoid nudity. *People,* according to Ephron, was marketed much like a new perishable product. Its essential unifying feature is gossip. The two basic ideas in its creation were to keep it inexpensive and its articles short. Ephron argues that the marketing decisions have created slick and empty articles, as well as a glut of celebrities, and consequently an appeal "aimed at the lowest common denominator."

Before we leave the Ephron piece, we should note one more feature of the abstract. The preceding summary is essentially objective in its *paraphrase*. Its wording is meant to be neutral. We know from it that Nora Ephron dislikes *People* magazine, but we cannot gather from it how strongly and personally she dislikes it. The personal intensity of her dislike is finally a matter of tone and style. Since the nature of our feelings is often as important as the content of the message we have written, an abstract might attempt to mirror the tone of the original. It is one thing to say *People* magazine is "slick and empty"; it is another to call it a potato chip. In an effort to convey a sense of Ephron's tone, we have written a second abstract. Read it and decide how successfully and by what means this abstract mirrors the tone of the original. Also, decide under what circumstances the second option of abstracting is preferable to the first.

Nora Ephron thinks that *People* magazine is about as nourishing as a potato chip and as culturally exciting as spending four days in Los Angeles. Its editorial policy was set by a corporate body known as the Magazine Development Group, an organizational offshoot of Time Inc. Its interest was to package an inexpensive product, like a tomato, and to appeal to the tastes of the blue-collar public. The magazine, as its name tells us, is simply about "people," with no editorial rationale, lots of pictures and short, gossipy articles. It's a junk product that markets unnoteworthy "celebrities."

## Exercises and Assignments

1. Abstracts occur frequently both in the media and in less widely circulating publications. Find at least three examples of abstracts and record their sources. Bring your list to class. Your instructor may wish to have the class assemble a list so that the widespread uses and kinds of abstracts become evident.

2. From your list of three abstracts, choose one expository abstract and xerox it. Then read and xerox the original. Write a short paper analyzing the success of the paraphrase, both in terms of its inclusiveness and its tone.

3. Choose a selection that you have previously read in this book, and

write two abstracts of it: one neutral in phrasing, the other registering the tone of the original.

4. Choose a chapter from a textbook you are reading for another class. Write a 100-word abstract of it.

### Writing the Synopsis

The principles that apply to writing a successful abstract also apply to writing synopses. In this form, as in the abstract, one must strive to write a succinct paraphrase of key details. The difference is that the synopsis is a plot review, and as such it must follow the narrative sequence of the original. Synopses are generally ordered chronologically, but since they should reflect the order of the narrative as told or performed in the original, the time order can be scrambled: They can begin in the middle or at the end, and they can include flashbacks.

Synopses must focus on the important characters, events, and settings in a story. One way of preparing a complete synopsis is to use the reporting formula of the "5 W's" (i.e., to ask Who? Where? When? What? and Why?). Bearing in mind the narrative sequence of the story, we can ask these questions concentrating on central details and the synopsis will virtually write itself. A good illustration is the following straightforward synopsis of Alfred Hitchcock's classic film *Psycho.* Using the question, we would sort out the following details:

|  |  |
|---|---|
| *Who?* | Marion Crane, the heroine and victim |
| | Norman Bates, the strange young man and murderer |
| | Sam Loomis, the hero |
| | Lila Crane, the victim's sister |
| | Milton Arbogast, the detective and second victim |
| | The Psychiatrist |
| | (Note that we haven't bothered with such minor characters as the Policeman, the Millionaire, the Car Salesman, Marion's Boss, and her co-worker.) |
| *Where?* | From Phoenix to a remote, deserted motel that is adjacent to an old gothic house. Three specific settings of importance are the shower in Marion's motel room, a nearby swamp, and the basement of the old house. |
| *When?* | The action begins on an afternoon when Marion leaves work. It shifts to the same night in the motel. The rest of the action takes place some days later. |
| *What* (How)? | Marion is stabbed to death by what appears to be an eerie-looking old woman. The detective is stabbed by the same |

person. Lila finds the body of the old woman in a basement rocker only to be confronted by Norman dressed just like the old woman and wielding a butcher's knife. Sam captures and disarms him.

*Why?*     Norman has a split personality, resulting from the murder of his mother. He has turned his ire against women and has now totally assumed the persona of his mother.


# Reading Selections

With these basic facts in mind, we could easily have written the following synopsis, which was published in the journal *Filmfacts*.

## SYNOPSIS OF *PSYCHO*

In Phoenix, Arizona, a young woman named Marion Crane steals $40,000 from her employer's real estate firm and then leaves town, planning to join her lover in another city. She stops for the night at a remote, deserted motel operated by one Norman Bates, a strange young man interested in taxidermy and dominated by a possessive, crippled mother who lives with him in an adjoining Victorian house. Late that night, as Marion showers, she is suddenly attacked and stabbed to death by the shadowy figure of a woman. A short time later Norman appears, dumps her body and belongings—including the $40,000—into the trunk of her car and then sinks it in a nearby swamp. When Marion's disappearance becomes known, her lover Sam Loomis, her sister Lila, and a private detective named Milton Arbogast begin an investigation. The latter traces Marion to the motel but before he can make a positive discovery he too is stabbed to death by the female assailant. When he fails to return, Sam and Lila register at the motel and begin snooping. While Sam detains Norman, Lila investigates the old house, hoping to find Mrs. Bates. What she does find is the old woman's cadaver, partially preserved through Norman's knowledge of taxidermy. Suddenly Lila is confronted by Norman—wearing a wig and his mother's clothing—wielding a murderous butcher's knife. But before he can claim another victim, Sam appears and apprehends him. Later, a psychiatrist explains that Norman has a split personality, a mental aberration stemming from the day he murdered his mother upon finding her in bed with a lover. For years he has lived a double life—his own and his mother's—but now, as a result of the shocking turn of events, the dominant personality has emerged and Norman has, in effect, completely assumed his mother's personality.

From *Filmfacts*, July 29, 1960, p. 153.

In the synopsis of *Psycho,* we have a straightforward chronological plot. Note how flashbacks are recorded in the following synopsis of Arthur Miller's *Death of a Salesman,* taken from *The Reader's Encyclopedia of World Drama,* which is a good source for synopses of plays. Reference books like *The Reader's Encyclopedia* are useful for those who wish to recall plots they have forgotten or for potential reader/spectators of a play. Synopses by their nature are never a satisfactory substitute for the original work.

### SYNOPSIS OF *DEATH OF A SALESMAN*

**Death of a Salesman** (1949). A play by Arthur Miller. The scene is Brooklyn. Willy Loman, a salesman of sixty, is undergoing a nervous breakdown. He can no longer go out on the road to make sales, and he is upset by the presence of his older son, Biff, who scorns his father's dream of achieving success by being well liked and prefers to be a cowboy out west. On the same day, Willy tries to get a transfer to his firm's home office, while Biff looks for a job. Both fail, and Willy is fired. Biff and his brother, Happy, meeting their father for dinner at a restaurant that night, pick up two girls and desert Willy. The next day, Biff argues that their failure in business has proved Willy's conception of success to be false. Willy kills himself in an automobile accident, having announced that he will do it in order to leave the insurance money that will give Biff a start in business. At his funeral, Biff asserts that Willy's best self was reflected in his work with his hands, Happy praises his father's philosophy of success, and their mother, Linda, expresses her bewilderment. The present action of the play is accompanied by Willy's recollection of the hopeful past, when Biff was growing up. He recalls also his brother Ben, who preaches aggressiveness as the means to success, and his neighbor Charley, whose son Bernard became a real success, as a lawyer, without subscribing to any myth. Willy's reminiscences culminate in the incident that, years before, ruined his close relationship with Biff: Biff found him in a hotel room in Boston with a woman.

From The Reader's Encyclopedia of World<br>Drama (New York: Thomas Y. Crowell,<br>1969) p. 17.

# Exercise

Choose a film, short story, play, or book that you know well in which the story is not told in straight beginning-to-end, chronological order. Note how details from the past are worked into the plot. Good illustrations of plots with considerable dependence on "flashbacks" are Sophocles' *Oedipus Rex,* Shakespeare's *The Tempest,* and contemporary works of fiction like William Faulkner's short story "A Rose for Emily" or the movie *Godfather*

*II.* Choose one such work and write a synopsis giving special attention to integrating the flashback details—either at the end or in proper chronological sequence.

### The Uses of Abstracts and Synopses

Without doubt, both abstracts and synopses are used widely in virtually every sort of writing. Often their purpose is simply to inform a body of readers about the central content of important articles, books, films, dramas, or musical works. In this capacity they are aids to the serious reader or researcher who may wish or need to know just what has been written on a given subject. At other times, the synopsis (or abstract) may help prepare the reader or viewer to understand more fully a work he or she is about to experience. A synopsis of the opera *Aida,* especially if the opera is sung in the original Italian, will aid the uninitiated spectator to understand the action on stage.

Another use of the abstract or synopsis is to persuade the reader (or more generally, consumer) to buy a copy or replica of the work being summarized. Blurbs for books often work that way. Here is an illustration from the back-cover description of a paperback edition of the Pulitzer-prize-winning novel *A Confederacy of Dunces* by John Kennedy Toole.

> Ignatius J. Reilly is a thirty-year-old self-proclaimed genius out to reform the entire twentieth century, which doesn't leave him much time for an ordinary nine to five job! Then one day, Mrs. Reilly pushes her reluctant son out of the nest and into the working world—a decision with unforseeably hilarious results. The born-to-clash Ignatius takes on a colorful cast of characters as he roams through the city of New Orleans, leaving chaos in his wake. (Quoted from back cover of Grove Press edition, copyright 1980.)

Notice that this synopsis differs in approach and content considerably from those of *Psycho* and *Death of a Salesman.* Try to determine just how and why this synopsis is different from the others.

## Exercise

Find two or three synopses or abstracts used either as part of advertisements or in other forms of communication in order to sell a product. What methods do these abstractors or writers of synopses use to stimulate their readers' interests? Make a close analysis of their techniques in writing the abstract or synopsis.

Finally, abstracts and synopses are of essential use to reviewers and critics. The chapters that follow show us how the paraphrase, as practiced in the abstract or synopsis, becomes an important part of a work of criticism. We hasten to add, however, that abstracts and synopses are not in themselves substitutes for criticism. They are often embedded in one form or another within a review. And perhaps most important, they can serve in the writer's mind as a summary and an orientation from which the review can be launched.

## THE CAPSULE REVIEW

Most Americans got their reviews in the form of capsule summaries and evaluations. Examples of such reviews abound; they appear as features in most newspapers and general circulation magazines and also as part of daily news programs on radio and television. Some periodicals, like *New York Magazine* in its "Cue" entertainment guide, include an entire section of short notices, many of which present capsule evaluations. Others, like the *Library Journal,* consist in large part of capsule reviews. The general public and, in some instances, the specialist have come to rely on such quick reviews as a way of keeping up with notable events and publications. Capsule reviews cover a wide assortment of topics, from movies, theater, books, art exhibits, radio, television, concerts, recitals, recordings, restaurants, and nightclubs to any number of noteworthy happenings, products, or establishments.

Because capsule reviewing is so varied, we here look at only two of the more popular examples of the type: short reviews of books and films. For books, the capsule review is virtually mandatory if only to single out from a large list of daily publications those that are most prominent and of greatest interest to particular readerships. Over 36,000 books are published annually in the United States. This means that nearly 100 new titles flow from our presses *every day.* Of some 20,000 new publications each year that come to the attention of major book review organs, like the *Los Angeles Times,* perhaps a mere 450 to 500 get full-length daily or Sunday reviews. Obviously, then, the capsule review has an important place in keeping the reading public informed about new titles that did not attract enough attention to gain full-scale reviews in daily newspapers and general circulation magazines.

The *Library Journal* provides us with some excellent illustrations of capsule book reviews. The purpose of this journal is to provide information and feature articles that are of professional interest to librarians; it also includes in each issue a "Book Review" section that consists entirely of capsule reviews of newly published books in major fields of knowledge and in such

general categories as "The Contemporary Scene," "Reference," "Fiction,"
and "Sports and Recreation." Reviews in this part of the journal usually
consist of approximately 100 words; they are written by specialists from all
over the country (who are reimbursed for their reviews simply by retaining
their review copies). Frequently they try to project as much of the flavor
of the book as they can, and sometimes they concentrate on special points
of interest: the circumstances under which the work was composed, facts
about the author, comparison or contrast with other books in the same field
or on the same subject, matters of format (e.g., the use of illustrations or
photos), special biases of the author, a notable failing or achievement, a
recommendation for particular readers.

## Reading Selections

The following abstracts were published in the *Library Journal.* Read them and
study carefully their methods of presentation.

Calder, Nigel. **The Comet Is Coming! the feverish legacy of Mr. Halley.**

Viking Apr. 1981, 160p. illus., some color, bibliog. index. $12.95.
                                                SOC SCI/ASTRONOMY

Folk tales say it carried off Mark Twain and signalled the Norman invasion
of 1066. It is coming back in 1985. What is it? Halley's Comet, of course.
Calder's book is the first account written to meet the interest that is likely
to arise as 1985 approaches. The author originally wrote the text as a BBC
television script, and its jaunty tone should appeal to all star buffs of high
school age or older. In Calder's view, all comets are pesky celestial snowballs
that have been blamed for toppling dynasties, ending the age of dinosaurs,
and generally plaguing life on earth. He debunks the mythology of comets
while he highlights the human side of scientific discovery. The text is accurate,
but rather brief. For example, Charles Messier, an 18th-century discoverer
of comets whose work is still important to sky-watchers, is barely mentioned.
The book's layout is attractive and the illustrations are appropriate. Recommended for most libraries.—*William W. Elison, Univ. of Montana Lib., Missoula*

From *Library Journal,* March 1, 1981, p.
567.

Gregory, Neal & Janice Gregory. **When Elvis Died.**

Communications Pr. 1980. 292p. photogs. bibliog. index. LC 80-19862.
ISBN 0-89461-032-5. $13.95.                     MUSIC/MEDIA

More than a study of Elvis Presley and his music, this is an examination of the phenomenal reaction to the death of an idol. Using numerous personal interviews and a vast array of primary sources, the Gregorys focus on the response of the media to the event. When Elvis died, most major networks made the death their lead story on the evening news: President Carter issued a formal statement to the press; newspapers in some areas sold five times as many copies as they had after JFK's assassination; and media representatives from all over the world rushed to Memphis, where the atmosphere was like that "among journalists at a space shot." The authors' treatment is more reportorial than analytical, and their writing style is sometimes choppy, but the book is filled with fascinating information and the extensive research is impressive. Recommended for social science, music, and media collections.—*Judith Sutton, "Library Journal"*

From *Library Journal,* February 15, 1981, p. 448.

### Questions

*Content/Meaning*

1. To what extent are the two selections straightforward abstracts? To what extent are they reviews? Does the reviewer support his or her opinion?
2. Does the reviewer demonstrate competence in the subject treated by the author?

*Style*

1. Is the reviewer's language geared to the general reader? Do you find the vocabulary general or specialized, simple or complex?
2. Would you call the review relatively objective?
3. How does the reviewer build interest in the book being reviewed? How much do you learn of the content of the book? Is the review itself interesting? Why or why not?

## Exercises and Assignments

1. Write a 100-word capsule review of a book you have recently read. (You may, if you wish, choose a textbook, including this one.) Be sure to include an informative abstract or synopsis (whichever applies). Use the general format of the capsule reviews in the *Library Journal.*

2. Be prepared to explain what strategies you intended to use in the abstract. In other words, be able to justify the choice of your style, the method of incorporating your opinion into the review, and any extraneous

facts that you bring to the review (e.g., comparison with other books, background of the author).

The capsule film review tends to be less informative, less directly concerned with synopsis, and more intent upon rendering a snap judgment than the capsule book review of the sort we have been examining. The reasons for this difference are essentially two: First, far fewer new films than new books are marketed each year, and in consequence, each film released is almost certain to receive some attention in regular newspaper and magazine review columns. Hence the capsule review tends to serve more nearly as an attention-getter than as a means of imparting information. Second, the capsule film review is almost invariably directed to a mass audience, which tends to be much less demanding than the readers of such magazines as the *Library Journal* or even of book sections in Sunday newspapers. The typical capsule film review thus demands slightly different skills of its writer. It tends to emphasize judgment, often done in wordplay, more than plot review and analysis. And because of the difference of the medium, a capsule film review also requires attention to the performances of actors, the use of cameras, and the skills of the director.

## Reading Selection

The following capsule review by Rex Reed appeared in *Vogue* magazine. Read it critically and note what sort of details it includes. After you have read it, decide how informative it is and whether you consider its style effective.

### HESTER STREET

#### *Rex Reed*

A first feature film by Joan Micklin Silver about simple, coarse-as-muslin Russian immigrants adjusting to a changing life-style in the ghettos of New York in 1896, this warm little surprise filters through the big, bloated, dull, noisy flotsam that now passes itself off as entertainment like morning sun.

Filmed in thirty-four days for only $400,000, a mere fraction of the budget of most of the awful movies that are churning out of Hollywood, *Hester Street* has more humor, charm, and decency than I thought possible in an age of cinematic chaos. And it is amazing to see how Mrs. Silver turned tree-lined Morton Street in Greenwich Village into a completely authentic period setting. She has a keen eye for detail and a deft way with actors; the burnished rub of almost grainy black-and-white gives the look and feel of faded attic-trunk family memoirs, circa *A Tree Grows in Brooklyn.*

A fine film with a heart from an important new feminist director on the rise and moving, hearty performances by Carol Kane and Doris Roberts go with it.

From *Vogue,* November 1975, p. 66.

Obviously, the Reed review forgoes synopsis almost entirely. We know something about the setting of the film but almost nothing of its plot. The emphasis is clearly on evaluation. In Reed's view, *Hester Street* is an unpretentious, well-directed, decent, charming, and humorous little film, which he recommends for its authentic period setting. About all that we know of its plot is that it deals with immigrant life in New York at the turn of the century. We realize that Reed admires the film because it comes as a refreshing surprise at a time when big, lavish, and usually dull films receive all the critical attention. In terms of content, then, this capsule review is quite successful: it characterizes the film and recommends it for certain specific qualities. That, typically, is what one should expect to find in the capsule review directed to a mass readership.

The style of Reed's review, on the other hand, is not nearly as successful. What is wrong mainly is that Reed wastes words. Amplification through metaphor is a form of writing that capsule reviewers ought to avoid, for the purpose of the short review is to say as much as possible in the fewest words. When we are told that "this little surprise filters through the big, bloated, dull, noisy flotsam that now passes itself off as entertainment like morning sun," we are overwhelmed with useless and confusing imagery. "Flotsam" refers to wreckage floating on the sea. It is difficult to conceive of flotsam as "noisy" and even more difficult to give shape to the "little surprise" that is said to "filter" through this flotsam "like morning sun." Are we underwater? Why "filter"? These ill-chosen metaphors are wasteful and confusing. Reed, himself, seems to recognize this flaw, for the next sentence tells us explicitly what the superfluous metaphor had jumbled up. A careful editing would probably have removed the "flotsam" metaphor and perhaps also the word "feminist," which seems to be simply a synonym for "woman," and the word "circa," which means "approximately" and not "like."

## Reading Selections

The film synopses that follow appeared in a variety of sources. The first review was originally published in the monthly "Spotlights" section of the *Saturday Review,* a quality mass-circulation magazine for readers with serious interests in the arts. The very selection of the film, one by Federico Fellini, gives some indication of the readership of "Spotlights." The second comes from the "Movie Classics" section of *Esquire.* The review clearly addresses itself to a more general public, but it also limits itself to classics and thus speaks to readers who may or may not be familiar with the film under consideration. The third review comes from Gene Shalit's column, which appeared in the *Ladies Home Journal.* Shalit is one of America's best-known capsule reviewers, an art he developed for ninety-second spots on television. As resident critic of the *Today* show, he reaches an audience in the millions.

## SPOTLIGHTS: FILM

Federico Fellini's sexual phantasmagoria **City of Women** will burst upon American screens this month. Marcello Mastroianni plays Snaporaz, a battle-scarred soldier in the war of the sexes who, in pursuit of an elusive beauty, stumbles upon a convention of angry feminists. There, some practice karate, while one sixtyish woman with seven husbands expounds upon the joys of polygamy. Spotted lurking in the corner, Snaporaz is set upon. He escapes only to have his life imperiled by a carload of teenaged punk rockers; and is eventually rescued by the aging, rifle-toting Dr. Zaübercock (Ettore Manni), who announces a party that night to celebrate his 10,000th romantic conquest.

*City of Women* is sure to enrage feminists. But as always Fellini is, without apologies, Fellini. "Going to the cinema," he says, "is like returning to the womb." Of women he declares, "They represent myth, mystery, diversity, fascination, the thirst for knowledge and the search for one's own identity. Women are everything."

From *Saturday Review,* April 1981, p. 8.

## MOVIE CLASSICS: The Bride of Frankenstein
*In which the monster's love is unrequited*

### Edward Sorel

Mary Shelley's novel has been recycled over and over on film (beginning with a 1910 one-reeler by Thomas Edison Studios), but the best of the bloody lot remains James Whale's 1935 *The Bride of Frankenstein.* This sequel to Whale's 1931 *Frankenstein* boasts two mad scientists: Henry Frankenstein (Colin Clive) and Dr. Praetorius (Ernest Thesiger). It is Praetorius who promises to create the rampaging monster (Boris Karloff) a nice lady monster if he'll just calm down and stop killing people. The hideous creature, desperately unhappy because of his poor self-image, cottons to the idea and follows Praetorius to Henry's laboratory. There, with the aid of giant kites to attract electricity (and with Franz Waxman's spooky music), the mummified bride (Elsa Lanchester) comes to life. One look at her scarred groom and she recoils in horror. The monster, hopes dashed, goes berserk, tears apart the laboratory, and pulls the switch that blows the entire castle tower to smithereens.

In real life the monster's demise was much worse. Universal used him in six more features, putting him to rest only after he had suffered the indignity of appearing in *Abbott and Costello Meet Frankenstein* (1948).

From *Esquire,* May, 1981, p. 112.

## REVIEW OF THREE FILMS

### *Gene Shalit*

The Journal cheers *The Orient Express,* one of the year's most elegantly entertaining movies. The cast reads like a Hollywood directory: Lauren Bacall, Ingrid Bergman, Michael York, Sean Connery, Richard Widmark, Anthony Perkins, Vanessa Redgrave, John Gielgud, Rachel Roberts and Albert Finney. Finney is fine as Hercule Poirot, Agatha Christie's fastidious detective, and the film is indeed based on one of Miss Christie's most famous stories. A marvelous movie—mysterious and chic—proving how good movies can be when they get back on the track. *The Orient Express* is another victory for trains over airplanes, especially planes caught in dopey disasters as they are in *Airport 1975.* This picture may set a trend: it may start buses and trains showing movies. You can bet *this* one will never be shown on a plane. *Airport 1975* is about a jumbo jet that is smacked in the fog by Dana Andrews' private plane, ripping it open and turning the jumbo cockpit into a convertible. The crew is wiped out, which leaves it up to Karen Black, a stewardess, to pilot the plane to safety. Charlton Heston helps by leaping into the jet in mid-air from a helicopter. Meanwhile the passengers are in various stages of panic. All except Jerry Stiller, the only person in the movie who is funny on purpose. He is also the smartest, because he sleeps through the whole movie. Maybe he thought he was supposed to be playing a member of the audience.

As soon as Charlton Heston rescues Miss Black (well, of course you *knew* he would), he sets out to save half of the population of Los Angeles in *Earthquake.* The city has been invaded by special effects men who destroy buildings, burst dams, and hurl various locals to their demises. When the earthquake strikes, the audience is enveloped in the noisiest movie on record (or maybe it's on tape). This will make a lot of money, but it's not a good movie, because *Earthquake* has too many faults.

From *Ladies Home Journal* 92 (February 1972): 6.

### Questions

*Content and Style*

1. What does the tone of the review tell us about the Fellini film *City of Women?* Does the capsule reviewer make a comment about the film by the selection of details that he chooses to put into the synopsis? Do we learn anything about the characterization of Snaporaz (Marcello Mastroianni)? What do words like "stumbles" or "spotted lurking in the corner" contribute to our picture of him? Does the reviewer

seem to support the contention he anticipates that the film will "enrage feminists?" How does this capsule review compare with the one by Rex Reed of *Hester Street?*

2. There is a suggestion in the capsule review of *The Bride of Franken-stein* that the movie has to be viewed, for full enjoyment, as camp or as a spoof of the genre of horror movies. In what way does the synopsis, which at first glance might seem to be a fairly objective plot description, help in the creation of this tone? To what extent is the capsule review "critical" (in the neutral sense of the term)? What effort does the reviewer make to provide a "historical context" for *The Bride of Frankenstein?* Does the subtitle help prepare us for the tone of the review?

3. To what extent does the Gene Shalit column depend on synopsis? How does this review differ, in content and tone, from the other capsule reviews you read in this chapter?

## Exercises and Assignments

1. Choose a classic movie, preferably one you have seen often, and write a capsule review on the model of the review of *The Bride of Frankenstein.*

2. Watch a movie on television or a movie currently playing in a movie theater on campus or in the neighborhood. Immediately after seeing the movie, write a synopsis, giving emphasis to the plot line, the names of principal characters and the names of the actors who play these roles. Then proceed to write a straightforward capsule review directed to the general reader, one who might read the daily newspaper of your hometown or a general circulation magazine like *Esquire* or *Vogue.*

3. Using the same synopsis you devised in exercise 2, write a capsule review of the movie for a reader of *Saturday Review.*

4. Using the same synopsis once more, try to write either a humorous review of the movie or a highly charged one. You might concentrate your efforts especially on changing the language of the synopsis to accommodate this purpose.

5. Make a point of watching five or more films on television during the coming week or two, then pretend that you are doing a preview column for your college newspaper in which you prepare your readers for the week's bill of fare. Organize your capsule review into a coherent article, focusing either on your recommendations or similarity of films reviewed in topic or approach. Concentrate on providing interesting transitions between the various capsule reviews. You might, in the course of your composite review, try your hand at making a Shalit-type quip.

# 23

# THE POPULAR REVIEW

**N**ow that we have examined the art of summarizing and capsule reviewing, we are ready to explore the standard newspaper or magazine review. For lack of a better term, we have chosen the name "popular review" to describe the typical appraisal of books, films, television programs, musical performances, theatrical productions, exhibits, buildings, recordings, restaurants, wines—in short, all activities and products that receive critical coverage in the realm of what most newspapers and magazines call "Arts and Leisure."

The popular review is distinguished from other kinds of review in part by size and in part by timing: It usually ranges from 500 to 2,000 words (typically 800 words), and it is published as soon as possible after the item being reviewed has been made available to the public. On occasion the popular review is a revisitation by the newspaper of, say, a theatrical performance when the major roles have been assumed by new actors or when a restaurant, previously noticed, has come under new management. The important fact, however, about the popular review is that invariably it is addressed to a general audience to provide it with a critical estimate, either by a staff reviewer or a free-lancer, of something new and noteworthy in the world of arts and leisure.

It is worth repeating at this point that a review is not simply an abstract or a summary. In fact, it must not be. Simply to offer a plot synopsis for a new movie or book is to violate the mandate of the reviewer, which is not only to acquaint the readership with the subject of the review but also to provide relevant and important background information—that is, to put it in its context—to discuss its significance, and to appraise its qualities. What, then, of the abstract or synopsis? Despite the fact that it will, most likely, not be incorporated per se in the popular review, it nevertheless can play a very important role in the preparation for writing such a review. Moreover, parts of it will no doubt find a place in the finished draft. Therefore, as a first step in writing the popular review, you should write an abstract or a synopsis of your subject.

We have said that usually the popular review is aimed at a general readership in order to respond to something new and noteworthy. This readership is implicitly defined by the nature of the publication. Small-city newspapers cannot afford to hire specialist reviewers, and because the arts have a limited exposure in such a setting, reviewing tends to receive minimal emphasis. National newspapers, like *The New York Times* and the *Washington Post,* employ specialists as staff reviewers and devote regular columns, even sections, to book, film, theater, music, and other kinds of reviews. The readership of such newspapers tends to be relatively sophisticated. Hence, less time will be devoted to basic facts (the assumption will be made, for example, that the reader knows who Federico Fellini is) and plot reviewing. National and metropolitan newspapers geared to a generally educated readership make every effort to avoid the practice of "puffing." This practice is to "sell" what is being reviewed, and sometimes it simply repeats what a publisher or movie studio has released as a kind of "prepackaged" critique and sent to the newspaper for the general information of the reviewer (no doubt with the hope that he or she will be influenced by it).

As we have tried to make clear, effective reviews do much more than simply approve or disapprove of their subjects. The statement "I liked it" or "I hated it" may in some subtler form find its place in the review, but it never suffices. Responsible reviewing means, first, that the reader must be informed. Reviewers are in some respects teachers and "tastemakers." They are obliged, if they practice their profession with integrity, to point out mistakes and illuminate weaknesses in argument, structure, style, and execution. They also serve to raise the level of appreciation, taste, and understanding of their readers. Further, they assume the role of consumer guides: They inform their readers where best to spend their "arts and leisure" dollars. A critic who finds that, for example, a film is totally unworthy of the public's attention renders a consumer service by warning the reader to stay away from it. Effective reviewers, moreover, are stylists. They must draw and hold the attention of the general reader. Often their more spectacular phrases are removed from the context and put into advertisements.

The following paragraph describes what a good popular review is and underlines what we have said. Since this paragraph was written by a journalist, it gives you an idea of what practitioners—in this case book reviewers of the Sunday "Book Review" section of the *Los Angeles Times*—accept as their obligation toward their readers. The paragraph establishes that good reviews must both summarize and evaluate the book under consideration.

> "We are almost at peace in the balance of powers between summary and analysis. A responsible reviewer cannot simply deliver a synopsis of where the author went, from chapter one to conclusion. A respectable critic cannot turn in a mere argument on where the author went wrong along the way. A book section owes its audience more than clues to content and attacks on assumption. Every author deserves the benefit of intent as well as doubt. A proper book review makes room for intention, substance, interpretation and evaluation. (Art Seidenbaum, "Endpapers," *Los Angeles Times,* May 24, 1981, p. 12.)

Note especially the prescription for a "proper book review"—a prescription that will apply equally well to other kinds of reviews. It must deal with: intention, substance, interpretation, and evaluation. These categories, though they need not and, indeed, should not be discussed invariably in that order or even as separate entities, should nevertheless guide you in the writing of your own reviews.

## DEVELOPING THE REVIEW

In preparing to write a review, you must know your subject. The preparatory steps in writing an abstract or synopsis and formulating a central idea are of primary importance in getting the first draft under way. To develop your review, you might well ask some or all of the following questions. You will recognize that they recapitulate the four categories stressed in Seidenbaum's requirements for "proper" reviewing:

1. *What did the writer, director, artist, musician, architect intend? Did he carry out his intention?*

To find the "intention" of the work, you obviously have to get inside of it. If you are reviewing a local event or product, you may discover the intent by interviewing someone connected with it. Mike Hale, the reviewer of a Stanford University theater production of Shakespeare's *Twelfth Night* probably spoke with the director or some of the actors before writing his column for the *Stanford Daily*. He explains that "the emphasis . . . here is almost entirely on the plot, that is, on the most immediately accessible elements of the play" (Mike Hale, *"Twelfth Night* is Successful," *The Stanford Daily,* May 21, 1981, p. 8), and he goes on to show how the intent of this production is much more to give a theatrical than a philosophical interpretation of the play. Sometimes, the intent is so clearly built into the event being reviewed that it becomes the central point of the review. When the New York City Opera gave a gala performance with hundreds of famous guest artists as a farewell to Beverly Sills, its most famous singer, the reviewer in *The New Yorker* used the occasion to survey Miss Sills's remarkable career. The intent, in this instance, was to pay respect to Miss Sills and to honor her. The reviewer matched the intent of the gala with a backward glance at her career. To find the intent of the work under consideration, reviewers may rely on their own insights or seek outside authorities either through interviews or background reading.

2. *What is the substance of the work under review? What is its genre and context?*

The first of these questions is easily answered by the prepared abstract or synopsis. The context and genre are also easily discoverable. In the case of a performance, the context is, of course, the event itself: the season's first theatrical production, the first time Elizabeth Taylor appeared on Broadway, or the visit of the Cleveland Symphony to Russia. The context of a new novel may be its subject: the civil war in Ireland, the assassination of John F. Kennedy, the publication of a new edition of *Webster's International Dictionary.* The genre, in turn, is the kind of item being reviewed. The work should be placed in its class: The film is a typical (or atypical) Western, another spoof on fraternity life, a spy thriller with a twist; the painting is abstract-expressionist or cubist or pop art; the restaurant is typically (or atypically) Chinese Kosher; the novel is another of the sort of sweeping historical chronologies that James A. Michener writes.

3. *What exactly is the meaning of the work? How does it contribute to our understanding or appreciation of its subject?*

These questions move us away from paraphrase, factual summary, or the reporting of relevant information, and toward analysis. Some years ago, a film called "The Watermelon Man" presented what seemed to be just another amusing contemporary account of black-white relations in suburbia.

The plot focused on a bigoted white commuter who suddenly, unaccountably, turned into a black man. We see him, thereafter, at first seeking every chemical means in his local pharmacy to regain his white appearance; later, after all sorts of misadventures, he becomes a black revolutionary. The emphasis of the film throughout is on innocent comedy. But *underneath,* the film made a serious statement: In the person of its main character, it traced the history of black consciousness in America. The recognition of this submerged and implicit statement is vitally a part of the interpretative act. The reviewer owes the public an interpretation of the work under review. When the work reviewed is a performance, the reviewer has a choice of interpreting the "text" itself (e.g., the play, ballet, concerto), this particular rendition of the text, or both. In reviewing a concerto, let's say Bartok's Concerto Number 2 for Violin and Orchestra, the reviewer knows that Bartok, in this concerto as in numerous other works, was intent on merging Hungarian folk idioms with the art music of contemporary Europe—of letting the gypsy violin resonate the people's music of his native Hungary at a time, in 1937, when Hitler's fanaticism did not respect any folk tradition except his Aryan myth. A performance that fails to make prominent the Hungarian rhythms in the great solos of the Concerto thus would destroy an important effect that the musically aware audience would have expected. An informed reviewer would no doubt call attention to such a breach in interpretation between performance and text.

4. *How do reviewers assess the works under consideration? Do they recommend them to their readers? Do they express reservations?*

Too often, criticism is thought of simply as a statement of approval or disapproval. The responsible critic is, of course, obliged to render an opinion. But the critic need not make a direct or even an overall evaluative comment. To point out that a performance fails to fulfill the artist's intent or perverts that intent in some significant way is in itself a statement of evaluation. Sometimes, of course, a work is so vapid and inconsequential that the reviewer chooses through clever and humorous language to devastate it. The emphasis in such a situation is almost entirely on evaluation.

## WRITING THE LEAD PARAGRAPH

There is no formula for beginning a review. Yet, with the essential preparation out of the way—that is, a well-written abstract or synopsis, a statement of the central idea, concept, or interpretation, and critical notes—the most difficult step in writing a review is, without question, the problem of getting started. There are about as many ways of beginning a review, that is, of writing the lead, as there are different subjects, styles, and individual critical voices. Hence, rather than set down artificial rules, we prefer to look at some actual examples of opening paragraphs from a variety of reviews.

Here is the introduction to a review of the Franklin D. Roosevelt Post Office in New York City. The reviewer, John Russell, who regularly writes a column for *The New York Times* entitled "Design Notebook," had recently revisited this post office.

> "A Garden is a lovesome thing," the poet said. He was entitled to his opinion, no doubt, but I prefer a post office any day. A Post Office, to be precise, with a big P and a big O. (*The New York Times,* Aug. 3, 1978, p. C10.)

The emphasis in the overall review that follows this introduction is not on the particular post office revisited by the reviewer but on the history of post offices as structures and of their functions. As the lead paragraph makes clear, Mr. Russell likes spacious and lofty post office buildings, man-made structures that, unlike gardens, have much to say about the busy commercial world they serve. He spends a great deal of time on the grand European post office of the nineteenth century, which came close to resembling a Gothic cathedral and to being the communication center of the city. Now that the post office no longer serves such a vital function, it too often is architecturally boring and physically uncomfortable. The Franklin D. Roosevelt branch of New York City is fortunately not like that. The article goes on to describe what makes this post office a successful building in the eyes of the reviewer. You may have noted that the opening paragraph was designed to prepare the reader for the progression of the critical argument.

Vincent Canby begins the following film review outrightly with a judgment:

> "Nothing Personal," which opens today at the Cinerama 2 and other theatres, is a skimpy, poorly paced feebly populist comedy about a college professor, played by Donald Sutherland, who fights Big Business to save an endangered species of Alaskan seal. Suzanne Somers of television's "Three's Company" plays the Washington lawyer who helps the professor. (*The New York Times,* April 18, 1980, p. C6.)

In the remainder of the short review he concentrates on performances. He singles out Miss Somers as a mechanical actress who in plain words is "terrible" and compares her to "one of those rubber dolls you order through the mail and inflate with a tire pump." Clearly, here the reviewer found no worthwhile qualities in the movie and deliberately set out to warn his public that the movie fails not merely because it is a cliché but because it lacks credible actors. The emphasis is on bad taste.

A "Winetalk" column in the *Times-Picayune* of New Orleans began as follows:

> From lakeside during the night came a persistent clanking, almost like the dull ringing of a ship's bell, and now it was morning and time to investigate. It was a quiet lake in the Adirondack mountains of northern New York, a remote place where the stillness normally is broken only by the cry of a loon or the splash of a rising fish. A few yards from the dock I saw a partly submerged bottle bobbing against a mossy rock. (Terry Robards, *The Times-Picayune/The States-Item,* Nov. 6, 1980, Section 8, p. 9.)

This is a playful, teasing introduction based on what we presume was Mr. Robards' actual experience. How, we ask, does such a lead coherently develop into a critical review of a particular wine? Well, it turns out that the floating, bobbing bottle contained a Soave wine (apparently having floated away from its owner, who intended to chill it in the lake). Robards uses this lead to say that Soaves these days can be found anywhere, they are so popular. He then reviews the wine for its taste, the comparative qualities of different vineyards, and its origins.

A review by John Leonard of James A. Michener's *The Covenant* begins as follows:

> What must be said for James A. Michener is that he wears you down. He numbs you into acquiescence. Page after page of pedestrian prose marches, like a defeated army, across the optic tract. It is a Great Trek from platitude to piety. The mind, between the ears, might as well be the south African veld after one of the devastations of Mzilikazi or the "scorched earth" policy of the British during the Boer War. No bird sings and the antelope dies of thirst. (*The New York Times,* November 14, 1980, p. C28.)

Leonard here promises to show the truth of a generally perceived opinion that bad books make a good review. Certainly he has fun with Michener from the outset. He addresses a reader who knows Michener's penchant for writing extremely long, tediously plotted novels, like *Hawaii* and *Chesapeake.* By cleverly drawing on specific incidents from the book (Mzilikazi), he connects the assault of the African land by various forces with Michener's assault on the reader's mind. If the book finally wears you down, as Leonard thinks it does, we can expect the review to be thoroughly unflattering about the plot but grudgingly admiring of the historical coverage (which, after all, will bring it on the same best-seller shelf as its predecessors). The lead captures not only the tone and content of the review but also skillfully prepares us for the overall evaluation.

We have seen from the foregoing illustrations that while all sorts of options are open to the reviewer, an effective lead paragraph almost always contains two basic ingredients. First, it arrests the readers attention. Second, it forecasts, either implicitly or explicitly, the central critical point of the review.

## Reading Selection

The following review is about a production of Macbeth performed at the Lincoln Center in New York. Frank Rich, the reviewer, is the regular daily drama critic of *The New York Times,* an assignment that has unrivaled power in the world of theater criticism. In the tradition of his noted predecessors, Brooks Atkinson and Clive Barnes, Rich can close a show with a bad review. In contrast, his raves are often partially quoted in newspaper ads and usually add significantly to the financial success of a play. In this instance Rich takes serious issue with a production of *Macbeth.*

### *MACBETH* RETURNS

#### *Frank Rich*

To put it simply, there can be no "Macbeth" without Macbeth.

Such is the sad case with the Lincoln Center Theater Company's production of the play, which opened Thursday night. The evening is by no means without its incidental merits. Sarah Caldwell, the director, has conceived a commanding physical production that at times solves the problems of the Vivian Beaumont's vast stage. Her supporting cast is often outstanding, and Shakespeare's text rings through the huge auditorium with nary a word lost. But without a Macbeth, the audience might just as well go home. Miss Caldwell has erected a gargantuan theatrical contraption only to leave out the motor that would make it fly.

The nominal Macbeth of the evening is Philip Anglim, the young actor who triumphed as the physically deformed "Elephant Man." Here he tries to play one of the most demanding mental cripples in theatrical literature and sinks without a trace. The problem is not his youth: there have been other young Macbeths. Nor is it his voice: declaiming diligently from his diaphragm, Mr. Anglim is capable of sounding the bass notes that are essential to the character. What's missing from this performance are merely the bread-and-butter qualities of good acting: feeling, stage presence, physical, vocal and facial expressiveness.

I don't know what this actor is up to in "Macbeth," and I doubt that he does, either. In the early scenes, he is so shifty-eyed and bonkers that one expects him to be arrested for suspicion of murder before he actually commits one. He shows us none of Macbeth's equivocation or false faces until the Banquo's ghost scene, at which point his sudden, quirky smiles earn unwanted laughs. As he charges into his doom, his performance changes not a whit: there is no discernible difference between his flat, pop-eyed reading of the dagger speech and his final droning of the "Tomorrow, and tomorrow, and tomorrow" monologue.

It's not that Mr. Anglim is misinterpreting the hero; there is no interpretation here at all. This is a Macbeth bereft of emotions—unless utter, dead coldness counts as such. The star's eyes neither make contact with those of his fellow actors nor look inward. His face is fixed in a blank, unchanging pose of mild nervousness, as if he feared he might be late for a train. His voice rarely varies in tone, and his body, which was so expressive as John Merrick, clumps about woodenly. His one, tardy attempt to summon up passion is the beginning of a sob on the line with which he greets news of his wife's death ("She should have died hereafter"). It's debatable whether the then-dazed Macbeth would start to cry at that point; in any case, Mr. Anglim turns his back on the audience rather than letting us see even the most tentative stirring of his heart.

There are lots of ways to play this tragically ambitious Scotsman—sympathetically, neurotically, wittily or even (in desperation) as a one-note blackguard. It says a lot about Mr. Anglim's Macbeth that he not only fails to inspire pity but that he also fails to arouse even the easy response of pure hatred. He is instead a strolling vacuum that swallows up the rest of the production. Though Miss Caldwell must bear partial responsibility for her star's performance, she deserves better.

Miss Caldwell does, however, inflict some wounds of her own on this "Macbeth." In her debut as a theater director, she at times betrays her roots as an iconoclastic opera impresario. Much of the staging is too stately, and there are sequences that sacrifice the text for pointless visual conceits. The banquet table in the ghost scene is set perpendicular to the audience, thereby making it impossible for us to see the reactions of the guests to Macbeth's "strange infirmity." The goings-on surrounding Duncan's murder unfold on a high, "Sweeney Todd"-style bridge that puts the actors out of visual reach and also causes them to do a lot of breathless running up and down stairs.

Indeed, most of the Beaumont's Act I (three acts of Shakespeare) can be written off. Mr. Anglim is on stage much of the time, and his performance constricts the range of Maureen Anderman's well-considered Lady Macbeth. Duncan (Neal Vipond) and the drunken porter (Roy K. Stevens) are both inadequate, and surprisingly enough, Miss Caldwell does nothing of interest with the witches. These weird sisters include a man, whatever that means, and they sing some of their verses to "Exorcist" music that merely blurs the words.

But, in Act II, Duncan and the Porter are gone, and so, for much of the time, are Macbeth and the witches. As a result, Miss Caldwell's "Macbeth" starts to get going. Kaiulani Lee proves to be an extraordinary Lady Macduff: in her single scene, her voice careers from anger to grief to horror, and her murder provides the evening's only gooseflesh. J. Kenneth Campbell's fierce (if overslouchy) Macduff, James Hurdle's coolly cynical Rosse and, especially, John Vickery's magnetic, quixotic Malcolm transform their difficult reunion scene in England into a compelling battle of complex sensibilities. Freed of Mr. Anglim, Miss Anderman's Lady Macbeth becomes a somewhat harrowing sleepwalker—a pale, frazzled Edvard Munch figure imprisoned in nihilistic pain.

With the considerable aid of the handsome black-and-steel void of a set by Herbert Senn and Helen Pond, Miss Caldwell also creates some rending images. Miss Anderman ascends to her bedroom on a labyrinthine, winding staircase that mirrors the turmoil of her soul. The attacking army, camouflaged by Birnam Wood, comes to Dunsinane from the smoky rear of the stage like a haunted, advancing forest. The subsequent battle scenes cascade forward in mad bursts of violence that are faithful to the jagged rhythms of Shakespeare's shortest, most abruptly composed tragedy.

But by then the impassive Mr. Anglim has reappeared to die, like a crumpled toy soldier, in the distracting midst of Miss Caldwell's sound and fury. One would like to say that nothing became this "Macbeth" like the protagonist's leaving it—but in this doomed production, I'm afraid, Macbeth never even arrived.

From *The New York Times,* January 24, 1981, p. 15.

### Questions

*Content/Meaning*

1. Which aspect of the review—intention, substance, interpretation, or evaluation—does Rich stress?
2. Which receives the least attention? Why?
3. What, in your view, is the central point of Rich's review?
4. *Time* magazine reviewed the play at about the same time. After drawing a good deal of attention to the theater and the series in which this production appeared—the lately reopened Vivian Beaumont The-

atre at Manhattan's Lincoln Center—it made the following statements. How many of these contradict Rich's point of view? Is there evidence here that the reviewing of plays is at best a subjective endeavor?

a. "Caldwell stresses the lust for power and the power of lust."

b. "Rarely have two actors so young and so full of animal magnetism played the two key roles."

c. "Philip Anglim . . . brings to his Macbeth the boundless energy of a fledgling Henry V."

d. "The guests at the feast where Banquo's ghost appears are seated on one side of a long refectory table resembling the one in Da Vinci's *The Last Supper,* thus carrying resonances of sacrilege." (*Time,* Feb. 2, 1981, p. 80.)

*Style*

1. There is evidence in the Rich review that he not only knows the play well but also is writing it for readers who are familiar with it. Can you discover two or three illustrations from the review that project this familiarity? If so, what stylistic choices did Rich make to speak intimately with a reader who knows the play? In what ways would the review have to differ if it were addressed to a reader who had never read or seen the play?

2. Do you find Rich's lead paragraph effective? Does it relate well to the central point of the review?

3. Rich gives us a very specific description of Philip Anglim's portrayal of Macbeth. Focusing on that description, how would you comment on the reviewer's effectiveness of word choice and figures of speech? Can you discover two or three examples of each that, in your mind, summarize the performance as perceived by Rich?

# Reading Selection

The review you are about to read was written by John Leonard in the early 1970s under the pseudonym "Cyclops," a *Life* magazine TV review column. In reading the review, note especially John Leonard's distinctive style. What aspects of it do you find especially noteworthy? Also notice the organization of the review and try to outline the progression of main points.

## BIGOTRY AS A DIRTY JOKE

### John Leonard

*All in the Family* is a wretched program. Why review a wretched program? Well, why fix the septic tank or scrub the sink with a magic scouring pad?

Every once in a while a reviewer must assume the role of a Roto-Rooter, stick himself down the clogged drain of the culture he happens to live in, and try to clean away the obstruction.

Carroll O'Connor plays the part of your friendly neighborhood bigot, the American workingman as Norman Lear and CBS conceive of him, William Bendix with a bad mouth, going on for half an hour every Tuesday night about the spooks and spics and wops and fags. He mugs a lot. Jean Stapleton plays his wife, slightly out of sync, one of those women—like Ruby Keeler—who never seems to belong in the situation in which they find themselves but who tries hard, thereby earning from the audience an admiration heavily laced with contempt. Sally Struthers plays their daughter; she's married to Rob Reiner (Carl Reiner's son), who plays a slightly long-haired Polack college pinko. Sally and Rob live with Carroll and Jean. They are always having Sunday dinner, the occasion for Mr. O'Connor to spit out his snappy one-liners on the inferiority of alien races, colors and creeds.

Just as most TV commercials are not really insulting to women (they are insulting to *people*), *All in the Family* is not merely insulting to minorities; it is insulting to Mr. O'Connor, Miss Stapleton, Miss Struthers, Mr. Reiner, the American workingman, CBS and everybody who watches the program. Bigotry becomes a form of dirty joke. We are invited to snigger. Invited, hell—we are *instructed* to snigger, like morons in a nursery school, before each episode. And we are piously assured that laughter cures, cauterizes, exorcises, even when it's canned. Fearless programming! About as fearless as the underground press's decision to use men's-room graffiti as a model for newspaper illustration, which in turn is about as fearless as pinching your little sister.

Take a recent, typical example. Mr. Reiner brings home a long-haired friend whom Mr. O'Connor suspects of being a homosexual. Mr. O'Connor complains about it at his local beer parlor. Mr. O'Connor is made to intuit that one of his drinking buddies, a heavily muscled ex-college football star, just may be, well, *that* way too. Mr. O'Connor refuses to believe it. End of program, after much mincing around. Mr. O'Connor always winds up refusing to believe; how else could the sit-com drag its asininity on to next week?

And what are *we* supposed to believe? That limp-wristed longhairs may look like homosexuals but aren't necessarily so disposed, while the short-haired athlete on the next stool lapping up draught beer and bellowing at the TV set is suspect? Don't say nasty things about homosexuals, your best friend may be one? Very funny. Cauterizing. Implicit in the sit-com is stasis; it's a condition, not a movement toward or away from revelation, and therefore it's naturally immune to theories of drama, abstractions about catharsis. OK.

But what *is* the condition of *All in the Family?* Why is what Archie Bunker says considered to be laughable?

I don't object to this vulgarity because of my ideological delinquencies, my toilet training, my SAT scores, my Higher Seriousness or my chromosomatic complexion. I object because the program is a double-edged lie. Cutting one way, the lie tells us that workingmen are mindless buffoons; their opinions, unlike ours, are unrelated to social, psychological or political conditions; their knee-jerk responses to stimuli are so farcical as to be amusing. (See Studs Terkel on "The Great American Dream Machine" for evidence overwhelmingly to the contrary.) Cutting the other way, the lie tells us that Mr. O'Connor's Archie is, anyway, charming. Forgivable. Purely a premise, a *given*, in no way dangerous, certainly incapable of roughing up antiwar demonstrators. A bad mouth, maybe; a sloppy mind, yes; but somewhere anterior to this style of speaking and thinking is an essential decency, or harmlessness, that makes him a figure of fun. Bigotry out loud, like scatology out loud, robs the words of their subterranean power to shock or destroy— or so we are told. (Meet George Wallace; he's a *fun* person.)

But the words to begin with were only approximations of feelings which are in no way defused or defanged by making a sly joke out of them. Even as the complexities of individuals are reduced to a cartoon, so the cartoon is legitimized. A double-edged lie and a two-way pandering (we—CBS and the audience—are better than he is; he is ridiculous; but then, people actually say these things) . . . just who is the joke on?

From Life, March 19, 1971; reprinted in<br>John Leonard, This Pen for Hire (New<br>York: Doubleday, 1973), pp. 237–39.

### Questions

*Content/Meaning*

1. How is the review organized? Do you detect an ordered plan by which it is developed?
2. Who are William Bendix, Studs Terkel, and George Wallace? (If you don't know, look up the names in an appropriate biographical dictionary.)

*Style*

1. We asked you to examine closely Leonard's style as a reviewer. What special characteristics in word choice would you single out? What personality does Leonard project? Do you find him caustic, arrogant, chummy, candid, outspoken? Does he speak down to his reader?
2. What do you make of Leonard's use of the analogy of fixing a septic

tank in paragraph 1? Or his intention of calling the program a "double-edged lie"? How, for example, might the latter phrase be applied to the example involving the alleged homosexuals?

3. Does Leonard resort to synopsis in the review? If so, where and how? Is the column necessarily addressed to the *Life* reader who is familiar with the program?

## Reading Selection

The following review was written by one of America's outstanding film critics, Pauline Kael, who regularly appears in the pages of *The New Yorker*. Read the review closely, noting especially Ms. Kael's central point and the subtopics she covers in her review. A commentary of the Kael review immediately follows it. In effect, this commentary is a critical review in itself—one might call it "a review of a review." Such criticism is often written in college classrooms, and it can serve as an example for a similar exercise that your instructor may ask you to undertake of another film review.

### FATHERS AND SONS

#### *Pauline Kael*

At the close of *The Godfather*, Michael Corleone has consolidated his power by a series of murders and has earned the crown his dead father, Don Vito, handed him. In the last shot, Michael—his eyes clouded—assures his wife, Kay, that he is not responsible for the murder of his sister's husband. The door closes Kay out while he receives the homage of subordinates, and if she doesn't know that he lied, it can only be because she doesn't want to. *The Godfather, Part II* begins where the first film ended: before the titles there is a view behind that door. The new king stands in the dark, his face lusterless and dispassionate as his hand is being kissed. The familiar *Godfather* waltz theme is heard in an ambiguous, melancholy tone. Is it our imagination, or is Michael's face starting to rot? The dramatic charge of that moment is Shakespearean. The waltz is faintly, chillingly ominous.

By a single image, Francis Ford Coppola has plunged us back into the sensuality and terror of the first film. And, with the relentlessness of a master, he goes farther and farther. The daring of Part II is that it enlarges the scope and deepens the meaning of the first film; *The Godfather* was the greatest gangster picture ever made, and had metaphorical overtones that took it far beyond the gangster genre. In Part II, the wider themes are no longer merely implied. The second film shows the consequences of the actions in the first; it's all one movie, in two great big pieces, and it comes together in your head while you watch. Coppola might almost have a pact with the audience; we're already so engrossed in the Corleones that now he can go on to give us a more interior view of the characters at the same time that he shows their spreading social influence. The completed work is an epic about the seeds of destruction that the immigrants brought to the new land, with Sicilians, Wasps, and Jews separate socially but joined together in crime and political bribery. This is a bicentennial picture that doesn't insult the intelligence. It's an epic vision of the corruption of America.

After the titles, the action begins in Sicily in 1901, with the funeral procession of Michael's murdered grandfather, and we realize that the plaintive tone that was so unsettling in the opening music is linked to funeral drums and to a line of mourning women. The rot in Michael's face starts here, in his legacy from his father. The silent nine-year-old boy walking behind the coffin with his strong, grief-hardened mother is Vito, who will become the Don, the Godfather (the role played in the first film by Marlon Brando). Shots are heard, the procession breaks up—Vito's older brother has just been killed. And in a few minutes Vito, his mother dead, too, is running for his life. The waltz is heard again, still poignant but with a note of exaltation, as a ship with the wide-eyed child among the hordes in steerage passes the Statue of Liberty. The sallow, skinny boy has an almost frightening look of guarded intelligence; not understanding a word of English, he makes no sound until he's all alone, quarantined with smallpox on Ellis Island. Then, in his hospital cell, he looks out the barred window and, in a thin, childish soprano, sings a Sicilian song. As he sings, we see the superimposed face of another dark-eyed little boy, a shining princeling in white with a pretty flower-face—Michael's son, the little boy who had been playing in the garden with the old Don Vito when he died. It is the rich princeling's First Communion, and there is a lavish celebration at the Corleone estate on the shore of Lake Tahoe. The year is 1958, and the surviving members of the Corleone family, whose base of operations is now in Nevada, are gathered for the occasion.

The first film covered the period from 1945 to the mid-fifties. Part II, contrasting the early manhood of Vito (played by Robert De Niro) with the life of Michael, his inheritor (Al Pacino), spans almost seventy years. We saw only the middle of the story in the first film; now we have the beginning and the end. Structurally, the completed work is nothing less than the rise and decay of an American dynasty of unofficial rulers. Vito rises and becomes a respected man while his son Michael, the young king, rots before our eyes, and there is something about actually seeing the generations of a family in counterpoint that is emotionally overpowering. It's as if the movie satisfied an impossible yet basic human desire to see what our parents were like before we were born and to see what they did that affected what we became—not to hear about it, or to read about it, as we can in novels, but actually to see it. It really is like the past recaptured. We see the characters at different points in their lives, with every scene sharpening our perception of them; at one moment Michael embraces his young son, at another Vito cradles young Michael in his arms. The whole picture is informed with such a complex sense of the intermingling of good and evil—and of the inability to foresee the effects of our love upon our children—that it may be the most passionately felt epic ever made in this country.

Throughout the three hours and twenty minutes of Part II, there are so many moments of epiphany—mysterious, reverberant images, such as the small Vito singing in his cell—that one scarcely has the emotional resources to deal with the experience of this film. Twice, I almost cried out at acts of violence that De Niro's Vito committed. I didn't look away from the images, as I sometimes do at routine action pictures. I wanted to see the worst; there is a powerful need to see it. You need these moments as you need the terrible climaxes in a Tolstoy novel. A great novelist does not spare our feelings (as the historical romancer does); he intensifies them, and so does Coppola. On the screen, the speed of the climaxes and their vividness make them almost unbearably wounding.

Much of the material about Don Vito's early life which appears in Part II was in the Mario Puzo book and was left out of the first movie, but the real fecundity of Puzo's mind shows in the way this new film can take his characters further along and can expand (and, in a few cases, alter) the implications of the book. Puzo didn't write the novel he probably could have written, but there was a Promethean spark in his trash, and Coppola has written the novel it might have been. However, this second film (the script is again by Coppola and Puzo) doesn't appear to derive from the book as much as from what Coppola learned while he was making the first. In Part II, he has had the opportunity to do what he was prevented from doing before, and he's been able to develop what he didn't know about his characters and themes until after he'd made the first picture. He has also been able to balance the material. Many people who saw *The Godfather* developed a romantic identification with the Corleones; they longed for the feeling of protection that Don Vito conferred on his loving family. Now that the full story has been told, you'd have to have an insensitivity bordering on moral idiocy to think that the Corleones live a wonderful life, which you'd like to be part of.

The violence in this film never doesn't bother us—it's never just a kick. For a movie director, Coppola has an unusual interest in ideas and in the texture of feeling and thought. This wasn't always apparent in the first film, because the melodramatic suspense was so strong that one's motor responses demanded the resolution of tension (as in the restaurant scene, when one's heart almost stopped in the few seconds before Michael pulled out the gun and fired). But this time Coppola controls our emotional responses so that the horror seeps through everything and no action provides a melodramatic release. Within a scene Coppola is controlled and unhurried, yet he has a gift for igniting narrative, and the exploding effects keep accumulating. About midway, I began to feel that the film was expanding in my head like a soft bullet.

The casting is so close to flawless that we can feel the family connections, and there are times when one could swear that Michael's brother Fredo (John Cazale), as he ages, is beginning to look like a weak version of his father, because we see Marlon Brando in the wide forehead and receding hair. Brando is not on the screen this time, but he persists in his sons, Fredo and Michael, and Brando's character is extended by our seeing how it was formed. As Vito, Robert De Niro amply convinces one that he has it in him to become the old man that Brando was. It's not that he looks exactly like Brando but that he has Brando's wary soul, and so we can easily imagine the body changing with the years. It is much like seeing a photograph of one's own dead father when he was a strapping young man; the burning spirit we see in his face spooks us, because of our knowledge of what he was at the end. In De Niro's case, the young man's face is fired by a secret pride. His gesture as he refuses the gift of a box of groceries is beautifully expressive and has the added wonder of suggesting Brando, and not from the outside but from the inside. Even the soft, cracked Brando-like voice seems to come from the inside. When De Niro closes his eyes to blot out something insupportable, the reflex is like a presentiment of the old man's reflexes. There is such a continuity of soul between the child on the ship, De Niro's slight, ironic smile as a cowardly landlord tries to appease him, and Brando, the old man who died happy in the sun, that although Vito is a subsidiary character in terms of actual time on the screen, this second film, like the first, is imbued with his presence.

De Niro is right to be playing the young Brando because he has the physical audacity, the grace, and the instinct to become a great actor—perhaps as great as Brando. In *Mean Streets,* he was a wild, reckless kid who flaunted his being out of control; here he's a man who holds himself in—and he's just as transfixing. Vito came to America to survive. He brought nothing with him but a background of violence, and when he believes the only choice is between knuckling under to the gangsters who terrorize the poor in Little Italy—just as gangsters terrorized his family in Sicily—and using a gun, he chooses the gun. In his terms, it's a simple matter of self-preservation, and he achieves his manhood when he becomes a killer. Vito has a feudal code of honor. To the Italians who treated him with respect he's a folk hero—a Robin Hood you can come to in times of trouble. No matter what he does, he believes he's a man of principle, and he's wrapped in dignity.

The child's silence is carried forward in the adult. De Niro's performance is so subtle that when he speaks in the Sicilian dialect he learned for the role he speaks easily, but he is cautious in English and speaks very clearly and precisely. For a man of Vito's character who doesn't know the language well, precision is important—sloppy talk would be unthinkable. Like Brando's Vito, De Niro's has a reserve that can never be breached. Vito is so secure in the knowledge of how dangerous he is that his courtliness is no more or less than noblesse oblige.

The physical contrasts between De Niro's characterization and Pacino's give an almost tactile dimension to the theme. Driving through the streets of Batista's Havana, which he's buying into—buying a piece of the government—Michael sees the children begging, and he knows what he is: he's a predator on human weakness. And that's exactly what he looks like. He wears silvery-gray nubby-silk suits over a soft, amorphous body; he's hidden under the price tag. The burden of power sits on him like a sickness; his expression is sullen and withdrawn. He didn't have to be what he is: he knew there were other possibilities, and he chose to become a killer out of family loyalty. Here in Part II he is a disconsolate man, whose only attachment is to his children; he can never go back to the time before that moment in the restaurant when he shot his father's enemies. In the first film, we saw Don Vito weep when he learned that it was Michael who had done the killing; Michael's act, which preserved the family's power, destroyed his own life. Don Vito had recoiled from the sordid drug traffic, but since crime is the most competitive business of all (the quality of what you're peddling not being a conspicuous factor), Michael, the modernist, recoils from nothing; the empire that he runs from Nevada has few links with his young father's Robin Hood days. It's only inside himself that Michael recoils. His tense, flaccid face hovers over the movie; he's the man in power, trying to control the lives around him and feeling empty and betrayed. He's like a depressed Brando.

There are times when Pacino's moodiness isn't particularly eloquent, and when Michael asks his mother (Morgana King) how his father felt deep down in his heart the question doesn't have enough urgency. However, Pacino does something very difficult: he gives an almost immobile performance. Michael's attempt to be the man his father was has aged him, and he can't conceal the ugliness of the calculations that his father's ceremonial manner masked. His father had a domestic life that was a sanctuary, but Michael has no sanctuary. He cannot maintain the traditional division of home and business, and so the light and dark contrasts are not as sharp as in the first picture. His wife knows he lied to her, just as he lies to a Senate investigating committee, and the darkness of his business dealings has invaded his home. Part II has the same mythic and operatic visual scheme as the first;

once again the cinematographer is Gordon Willis. Visually the film is, however, far more complexly beautiful than the first, just as it's thematically richer, more shadowed, more full. Willis's workmanship has developed, like Coppola's; even the sequences in the sunlight have deep tones—elegiac yet lyrical, as in *The Conformist,* and always serves the narrative, as the Nino Rota score also does.

Talia Shire had a very sure touch in her wedding scenes in the first film; her Connie was like a Pier Angeli with a less fragile, bolder nature—a spoiled princess. Now, tight with anger, dependent on her brother Michael, who killed her husband, Connie behaves self-destructively. She once had a dream wedding; now she hooks up with gigolo playboys. (Troy Donahue is her newest husband.) Talia Shire has such beauty and strength that she commands attention. It's possible that she didn't impose herself more strongly in the first film because Coppola, through a kind of reverse nepotism (Miss Shire is his sister), deemphasized her role and didn't give her many closeups, but this time—pinched, strident, whory—she comes through as a stunningly controlled actress. Kay (Diane Keaton), Michael's New England-born wife, balks at becoming the acquiescent woman he requires, so he shows her what his protection means. It's dependent on absolute fealty. Any challenge or betrayal and you're dead—for men, that is. Women are so subservient they're not considered dangerous enough to kill—that's about the extent of Mafioso chivalry. The male-female relationships are worked out with a Jacobean splendor that goes far beyond one's expectations.

There must be more brilliant strokes of casting here (including the use of a batch of Hollywood notables—Phil Feldman, Roger Corman, and William Bowers—as United States senators), and more first-rate acting in small parts, than in any other American movie. An important new character, Hyman Roth, a Meyer Lansky-like businessman-gangster, as full of cant and fake wisdom as a fund-raising rabbi, is played with smooth conviction by the near-legendary Lee Strasberg. Even his breath control is impeccable: when Roth talks too much and gets more excited than he should, his talk ends with a sound of exertion from his chest. As another new major character, Frankie Pentangeli, an old-timer in the rackets who wants things to be as they were when Don Vito was in his heyday, Michael V. Gazzo (the playwright-actor) gives an intensely likable performance that adds flavor to the picture. His Pentangeli has the capacity for enjoying life, unlike Michael and the anonymous-looking high-echelon hoods who surround him. As the bland, despicably loyal Tom Hagen, more square-faced and sturdy now, Robert Duvall, a powerful recessive actor, is practically a genius at keeping himself in the background; and Richard Bright as Al Neri, one of Michael's henchmen, runs him a close second.

Coppola's approach is openhanded: he doesn't force the situations. He puts the material up there, and we read the screen for ourselves. But in a few places, such as in the double-crossing maneuvers of Michael Corleone and Hyman Roth, his partner in the Cuban venture, it hasn't been made readable enough. There's a slight confusion for the audience in the sequences dealing with Roth's bogus attempt on the life of Pentangeli, and the staging is a little flatfooted in the scenes in which the Corleone assassin first eliminates Roth's bodyguard and then goes to kill Roth. Also, it's a disadvantage that the frame-up of Senator Geary (which is very poorly staged, with more gory views of a murdered girl than are necessary) comes so long after the provocation for it. Everywhere else, the contrapuntal cutting is beautifully right, but the pieces of the Senator Geary story seem too slackly spaced apart. (The casting of G. D. Spradlin in the role is a juicy bit of satire; he looks and acts like a synthesis of several of our worst senators.) These small flaws are not failures of intelligence; they're faults in the storytelling, and there are a few abrupt transitions, indicating unplanned last-minute cuts. There may be too many scenes of plotting heads, and at times one wishes the sequences to be more fully developed. One never wants less of the characters; one always wants more—particularly of Vito in the 1917 period, which is recreated in a way that makes movies once again seem a miraculous medium.

This film wouldn't have been made if the first hadn't been a hit—and the first was made because the Paramount executives expected it to be an ordinary gangster shoot-'em-up. When you see this new picture, you wonder how Coppola won the fights. Maybe the answer is that they knew they couldn't make it without him. After you see it, you feel they can't make *any* picture without him. He directs with supreme confidence. Coppola is the inheritor of the traditions of the novel, the theater, and—especially—opera and movies. The sensibility at work in this film is that of a major artist. We're not used to it: how many screen artists get the chance to work in the epic form, and who has been able to seize the power to compose a modern American epic? And who else, when he got the chance and the power, would have proceeded with the absolute conviction that he'd make the film the way it should be made? In movies, that's the inner voice of the authentic hero.

From *The New Yorker,* December 23, 1974, pp. 63–66.

Miss Kael's review of *The Godfather, Part II* is in many respects typical of her art as a film critic. She never overwhelms her reader with technical observations or with weighty erudition. Her method is to look closely at the film, to discover its essential structure, and to talk about its larger significance (when it has one). She is usually a demanding reviewer, and it is not often that she can give a nearly unqualified endorsement as she does here. Above all, Miss Kael is an elegant writer whose style is marked by an interesting mixture of straightforward sentence style and a ranging vocabulary, which can move in one sweep from academic language to colloquialisms. She is widely known as the finest stylist among the major critics now writing film reviews.

The review of *Godfather II* was originally written for *The New Yorker* and later reprinted unchanged in Miss Kael's collection of reviews entitled *Reeling*. In both the magazine and the book, she clearly addresses her remarks to the educated reader. *The New Yorker* caters generally to sophisticated townspeople (one of its regular features is called "The Talk of the Town"); its advertisements feature expensive merchandise; its emphasis is on the cultural scene; its style is marked by urbanity and wit. The book *Reeling*, of course, would have selected its own audience—Kael buffs and readers with a serious interest in film would likely be its most frequent buyers and readers. One test of the audience for whom a piece is written is a sampling of the vocabulary. Here are some words taken from Miss Kael's review: epiphany, fecundity, Promethean spark, presentiment, transfixing, noblesse oblige, tactile, predator, amorphous, sordid, conspicuous, contrapuntal. While it is highly unlikely that even typical *New Yorker* readers can define all these words, they probably have seen them before. Clearly when Miss Kael warms up to her subject, as she seems to in paragraph 10, her vocabulary can become quite academic and her style dense. To appreciate her reviews the reader must be alert and attentive.

While it is not always easy to find a single sentence that will sum up the thesis of a piece of critical writing, in this particular review there does seem to be such a sentence. At the end of the second paragraph, Miss Kael calls the film "an epic vision of the corruption of America"—a sentence that summarizes the central idea of the review, one that she restates and returns to repeatedly. She had told us shortly before that the completed work (meaning Parts I and II) "is an epic about the seeds of destruction that the immigrants brought to the new land, with Sicilians, Wasps, and Jews separate socially but joined together in crime and political bribery." Later, she returns to this idea, slightly restated: "the completed work is nothing less than the rise and decay of an American dynasty." After various references in various forms to the empire of the Corleones and the rot which eats away at it, she returns at the end of the review to a direct statement once more about "the epic form" of the film. An epic has been defined as a "series of adventures which form an organic whole through their relation to a central figure of heroic proportions and through their development of episodes important to the [growth] of a nation or race." [W. F. Thrall and A. Hibbard, *A Handbook of Literature* (New York: The Odyssey Press, 1936), p. 155]. Miss Kael suggests precisely such an organic structure in the two *Godfather* films, with young and old Vito Corleone as the heroic patriarch who seems to decay before our eyes in his son Michael's face. The whole of this progress is an episodic narration of an immigrant family gone wrong—one that can stand as a symbol for many others and a signpost of a larger deterioration that is eating away at the America left by immigrant adventurers. The review notes especially and repeatedly the "rot" in the face of Michael, the character played by Pacino, who, at Kael's best, is described as wearing "silvery-gray nubby-silk suits over a soft, amorphous body; he's hidden under the price tag." Has the essence of a character ever been re-created more tellingly? While "rot" is the dominant metaphor for Miss Kael, the epic view she takes allows her to bind up the three parts (*Godfather I,* Vito in *Godfather II,* and Michael in *Godfather II*) into one coherent whole—one dramatic structure that in the final analysis gives us a single epic.

In terms of the general conventions of the film review, one finds some more prominently than others in Miss Kael's work. She is not much obsessed by technique. While she speaks knowledgeably about certain camera angles (e.g., her reference to "contrapuntal cutting") and about musical references ("the Nino Rota score"), she does not give us a technical reading of the film. She is, however, persistently concerned with the viewer's response to the film as a visual work. We are told to "read the screen" to see pictures before our eyes, to perceive an "operatic visual scheme." Her emphasis is constantly on *seeing, perception, images, vision, eyes.* While technical achievements claim relatively less of her attention, acting is tremendously important to her. Her paragraphs comparing and contrasting the performances in the two films of Brando, DeNiro, and Pacino together with the roles that they play are packed with close observations of acting styles and the achievement of effects that lend additional unity to the film.

Only once does Miss Kael step out from behind her cloak of authorial anonymity. This is when she tells us how she personally responded to the violence of the film—about her "powerful need to see" that violence. But less directly, her images reveal a good deal about the force of her imagination as when she tells us that about midway, she "began to feel that the film was expanding in [her] head like a soft bullet." There is in this voice of the reviewer a dramatic revulsion against violence but also a recognition of its hypnotic and necessary presence in the film.

Miss Kael is not in any systematic sense in *auteurist* critic, that is, a critic who judges the director to be the author and hence the central intelligence of the film. Yet she does see a film functionally as the work of its director. In her eyes, *Godfather II* is the product of Francis Ford Coppola's artistry. She has said that bad books make good films, a point that she subscribes to here, at least indirectly, in paragraph 6. But despite these essentially antiliterary views toward film there can be little doubt about the literary sensibility that guides Miss Kael's critical energy in this review (as in most of her others). She does here what has made her an important commentator: She not only reviews a film but renders a comprehensive critical statement.

### Questions

*Content/Meaning*
1. Only once in the review does Kael give her reader a straightforward synopsis. Can you find the passage and comment on its scope and purpose in the review?
2. The central idea of Kael's criticism is that *Godfather II,* together with its predecessor, forms an "American epic." How, specifically, does she support this idea? In what sense does *Godfather II* elevate the meaning of *The Godfather?*

*Style*
1. There are two excellent descriptions of performances in Kael's review—of Robert deNiro's young Vito Corleone (paragraphs 8 and 9) and Al Pacino's Michael Corleone (paragraphs 10 and 11). Can you summarize Kael's descriptions? What stylistic devices does she use to give them life and authenticity?
2. Collect a sampling of Kael's figures of speech. What would you say about their variety and effectiveness?
3. How does the lead paragraph prepare the reader in tone, content, and style for the review that follows?

## Exercises

1. Using the *Reader's Guide* or the *Card Catalogue* in your library, read some additional reviews of Pauline Kael. You might select reviews of films you have seen and know well. Then write a commentary of one of her reviews.

2. Compare Kael's form and manner of film reviewing with the regular film reviews of your daily newspaper. What essential differences do you find? What assumptions do each of the reviewers make about their readers?

## Reading Selections

The following two reviews of John Kenneth Galbraith's memoirs, *A Life in Our Times,* appeared in the Sunday book review sections of two important metropolitan newspapers. Sunday book reviews, often written by free-lancers, tend to be longer and more detailed than daily reviews. Because they are published as part of a full newspaper section devoted to books, they also tend to speak to a more selective audience—one that normally buys and reads books. Both newspapers obviously considered the Galbraith book important; both reviews appeared on the front page. Note that *The New York Times* review appeared three weeks earlier than the review in the *Los Angeles Times*. This may be the result simply of the relative promptness of reviewers in delivering their manuscripts, but it may also reflect the eagerness of *The New York Times* to bring the review of an important book to its readers as soon as possible.

As you read the reviews, note that they differ considerably not only in their evaluation but also in their coverage and attitudes. Make careful marginal notes as you read and then turn to the questions that follow.

## A LIFE IN OUR TIMES

### Memoirs by John Kenneth Galbraith

#### *James Fallows*

His fellow economists have traditionally condescended to John Kenneth Galbraith, appearing to believe that anyone whose views could be expressed so clearly could not be considered first-rate. Forces on the political right, taking his ideas more seriously, have seen in Mr. Galbraith the source of much error in the modern world. Such arguments aside, this long memoir, Mr. Galbraith's 22d book, re-establishes the fact that as a raconteur and a literary stylist, he stands with the best. At age 72, he has produced one of his most enjoyable books.

Even before this volume of memoirs was published, Mr. Galbraith's life story was hardly a mystery. This book is laced with cross-references to tales he has told in his other works, especially "Ambassador's Journal," which was an account of his service in India. It is a measure of the diversity of his experience that there is still so much new to go around.

Mr. Galbraith was reared as a farmer, in southern Ontario, in a family that had left Scotland years before: "Our forebears were expelled from the Highlands between 1780 and 1830 when their lairds discovered that sheep were both more profitable and, as they moved over the hillside, more rewarding to the eye." His later identities have included the following: Student of animal husbandry at Ontario Agricultural College; aspiring economist at Berkeley, Princeton, Cambridge (in the age of Keynes's sainthood) and Harvard; Government bureaucrat during World War II and eventually, as he describes it, the man who more or less singlehanded controlled prices in the wartime economy; member of the Strategic Bombing Survey; staff writer for Fortune; speechwriter for Adlai Stevenson; co-founder of Americans for Democratic Action; the rich and famous author of "The Affluent Society" and "The New Industrial State"; friend and servant of the Kennedys, and tour guide for Jackie Kennedy when she traveled to India; figure of controversy for his political views; television performer (through his BBC series "The Age of Uncertainty"); and last the veteran who watches bemused from the stands.

As entertainment, the book is a total success. Its charm comes from the combination of Mr. Galbraith's smooth comic timing and his not-always-charitable wit. He makes a familiar point about television news in an unfamiliar way: "On the morning following the 1978 Congressional elections, I was asked in urgent tones by an NBC commentator who I thought would win a yet unresolved electoral contest in Ohio. I said that it was a silly question; he had only to wait for a few hours and he would know for sure. The great man trembled with indignation." He mentions that Richard Nixon, who like Mr. Galbraith served during the war in the Office of Price Administration, later grew apprehensive about being identified with this classically New Deal organization. Instead, "he said he had worked for the Office of Emergency Management. The latter was the administrative shell for all the war agencies. It was much as though a marine had said that he worked in the public sector."

As a work of economics, the book alludes to rather than attempts to re-prove Mr. Galbraith's well-known views about the structure of modern economic society and the contending powers of corporations and state. (An example of the allusions: "The city of Berkeley, in the days before Messrs. Jarvis and Gann and Professor Milton Friedman made the spending of money on urban sanitation an infringement of personal liberty, was sparkling clean and covered with geraniums.")

Such argumentative and instructional passion as the book contains is usually attached not to economic questions but rather to the nature of bureaucracy and organizational life. On these matters Mr. Galbraith has demonstrated his sophistication before. (His novel "The Triumph" can be read as a parable of the way that the mechanics of daily life in the Government can lead the nation to misadventure overseas.) Here he dispenses rules-of-survival lessons on practically every page. Of the struggle over the Muscle Shoals T.V.A. project in 1940, for example, he says: "One should remember that most Washington battles are won not out of one's own strength but from loss of confidence in others and the resulting rush to cover. One should never threaten to resign; that only tells one's allies that one might abandon the field. One should never, never accept as final the word of an expert. He can be wrong, careless, or politically motivated. Finally one should, if possible, have the President on one's side." Or, "After death and dismemberment, idleness was the nightmare of World War II and much the greater threat in Washington. . . . Nothing in wartime Washington was so feared by so many as having space in an office, a shared secretary, and no function at all. The most ruthless and most frequent of jurisdictional battles in those years were waged not by people who wanted power but by people who wanted something to do."

As history, the book is a modest addition to the public record, primarily through its portraiture. For instance, Mr. Galbraith depicts Bernard Baruch in his heyday as a relentless publicity agent for himself, who visited the White House "on all possible occasions, partly to advise the President of the United States, partly to show the rest of the government (and the country) that he was the kind of man who visited the President. . . . Baruch's comments to the press on emerging from the Oval Office—his use of the Presidency for echo and amplification—was the highest development of a notable art." He says that in 1961 he arranged for Baruch to call on President Kennedy. "I also suggested to Kennedy that he would be enchanted by a level of vanity for which not even his service in the Senate would fully have prepared him." There is also a passage explicitly billed as new historical information, concerning the inner wranglings between the United States and India, to which Mr. Galbraith as Ambassador was privy, during the border war between India and China in 1962.

The one startling revelation in the book is Mr. Galbraith's contention that it was he who persuaded Lyndon Johnson to woo Arthur Goldberg off the Supreme Court so that Mr. Goldberg could take Adlai Stevenson's place as Ambassador to the United Nations: "It was a poisonous thing I did. Goldberg's resignation cost the Court a good and liberal jurist. . . . I did little for liberalism that morning."

This particular story also illustrates what is most wrong with the book, which is that Mr. Galbraith's estimation of his own importance has exceeded all reasonable bounds. Mr. Galbraith is contrite for what he did to Mr. Goldberg; but is not the real point of his anecdote that it was within Mr. Galbraith's capacity to work such mighty deeds? Yet it is possible to imagine that the same incident looked somewhat different when seen through Lyndon Johnson's eyes. Johnson was desperate to find a place for his friend Abe Fortas on the Court; he knew that there were few better ways to flatter a man than to let him think that he'd changed your mind. Why not string the professor along?

Perhaps Mr. Galbraith's version of this episode is historically impeccable. Still, similar moments occur with such frequency that Mr. Galbraith has either confirmed the worst fears of those who think a cabal of pointy-headed Eastern liberals has been running the country or he has lost his sense of proportion. The face Mr. Galbraith chooses to wear in this, as in his previous works, is that of the wry, detached observer, who can be depended upon to come up with a precise, deflating one-liner that will combine wit with seriousness—and who knows just how apt his comments are. "Truth is not

always coordinate with modesty," he jokes at one point. Neither party would
be pleased by the comparison, but such jokes, in sufficient quantity, sound
not unlike Henry Kissinger's ceaseless wisecracks about his own omniscience.
After the 30th or 40th repetition, you realize that their purpose is not self-
depreciation but the reverse.

Mr. Galbraith's sardonic tone also means that this book, which tells
so much about the author's activities, is curiously unrevealing about his inner
life. The life he describes, while on the whole hugely enviable, seems not
to have been unrelievedly pleasant. In 1943, for example, he was a 35-year-
old former professor whose contract had run out at Harvard, who had been
driven from the O.P.A. because he had become too controversial, who briefly
held a make-work job at the State Department and who finally decided to
jump into journalism at Fortune magazine. Entire novels have been based
on far slighter disruptions in the human condition; Mr. Galbraith passes
such moments by with a joke or with the stoic remark that "on the next
few months I do not find it altogether pleasant to dwell."

If the reader is looking for a soul in torment, he won't find it here. If
he is looking for laughter, style, sophistication, plus a dose of self-aggrandize-
ment, he won't easily do better than this.

"An Economist with Style," The New York<br>
Times Book Review, May 3, 1981, pp. 1 ff.

## MEMOIRS OF AN UNRECONCILED LIBERAL THINKER

### *A Life In Our Times* by John Kenneth Galbraith

### *Lowell Ponte*

From 1941 until 1943, John Kenneth Galbraith was economic dictator of
the United States.

This, at any rate, is how his merchant critics described the Canadian-
born economist picked by President Franklin D. Roosevelt to devise and
command price controls and, briefly, the rationing of goods in the United
States.

Midway through World War II, Galbraith was ousted from this post
during the political infighting that had turned wartime Washington, D.C.,
into a battlefield for the ambitious. He never regained great power or position,
but Galbraith retained influence among the powerful, particularly with the
Kennedy family. And as a best-selling author and crusader, he has continued
to be one of the most articulate and faithful spokesmen for New Deal liberal
economics and values.

In these memoirs, Galbraith sketches the path his life has taken and
the leaders, great and small, he has known. That path passed through the

University of California at Berkeley, where in 1931 he came to study and teach agricultural economics at age 23.

Then as later, Berkeley was a hotbed of new ideas. There Galbraith caught a lifelong enthusiasm for John Maynard Keynes, the British economist who held that government intervention in the marketplace could eliminate the roller-coaster ups and downs of the business cycle, the ride from boom to bust that seemed the bane of capitalism. With the world in economic depression, Keynes' prescription to remedy such ills was eagerly embraced by many young economists. For Ken Galbraith, prescription became missionary passion.

The New Deal made Keynesianism the official economic faith, and a growing government bureaucracy swelled with its true believers. Galbraith was called to Washington in 1934 to help entrench the new dispensation of the New Deal.

No theoretical economist, he was (and remains) determined to put the faith into practice, converting the nation by word and, where knees were slow to bend to government dictum, by punishment. Keynesianism was for him not merely an idea but rather an ideology to be made triumphant through unquestioning loyalty to F.D.R. and the New Deal. His mission was "evangelism."

"After a lifetime in public office, self-censorship becomes not only automatic but a part of one's personality," writes Galbraith. "Only in the most infrequent cases can there be escape for autobiography or memoir. And what there passes for candor is only a minor loosening of the chains; it cannot be more, for the individual is rarely aware of his manacles."

True enough, and this helps explain why these memoirs are generally unsatisfying. Galbraith exposes here too little of himself, revealing the wheels and cogs he has known but concealing the pivots around which his mind and heart turned.

But to his credit, Galbraith has striven for candor and insight, and in so doing he offers the reader glimpses into the dark side of his life. He is cavalier about telling untruths to a congressional committee, about using coercion to silence critics, about his own deceit and abuse of power in government office. But he does explain, here, his willingness to do such things to advance his cause.

He writes approvingly of a liberal Princeton department chairman who "had never allowed the promotion to tenure of any economist in his department who testified on behalf of a corporation in an antitrust case, for such behavior meant the man's views could be had for money. He was, I think, right." For Galbraith the liberal, academic freedom apparently means the freedom to hold views in accord with his own. Heaven help the career of any young economist at Harvard, where Galbraith long has taught, who takes the side of any company against government regulators.

Galbraith has long been called "arrogant," even by close friends. Throughout these memoirs he preaches, and apparently believes, that no person of good will could hold views opposed to his own. "When an economist argues for lower taxes on the affluent," Galbraith assumes that "he has been bought." All who advocate free enterprise he depicts as knaves, fools, pawns, prostitutes or scoundrels.

What is it we smell burning in Galbraith's hot invective, in his propagandistic pronouncements branding liberals as angels and conservatives as devils? Could it be smoldering resentment? He never has been named a Nobel laureate, as have his chief free-market economist rivals Friedrich A. Hayek and Milton Friedman. He attacks both of them.

As a thinker, Galbraith has made major contributions to the economic arguments of our time. As a writer who learned economy of prose and a brilliant wry style at the elbow of Henry Luce when Galbraith was an editor at Fortune magazine, he has transformed "the dismal science" of economics into the vibrant stuff of best sellers in books such as "The Affluent Society" and "The New Industrial State." In such volumes, he has advanced the idea that free enterprise has given way to governmentlike bureaucratic corporations, and that capitalist and communist systems are becoming more alike, converging. His original insights into modern economies do merit Nobel consideration.

As he was for Roosevelt, Kennedy and Eugene McCarthy, Galbraith was a speech writer for Democratic presidential nominee Adlai Stevenson during the 1950s. Liberals may be startled here to read that Galbraith thought Stevenson "a committed elitist. He ran for President not to rescue the downtrodden but to assume the responsibilities properly belonging to the privileged."

However pragmatic Galbraith has been, he has consistently pursued liberal ideals. In 1968, he joined a principled McCarthy effort to unseat Lyndon Johnson over the issue of Vietnam, even though this helped put Richard Nixon in the White House. And now that the liberalism he championed is generally regarded as a failed and flaccid dream, Galbraith with vigor and dedication is working to control nuclear weapons. "Economics is not durable truth," he writes here. "It requries continuous revision and accommodation. Nearly all its error is from those who cannot change."

From the *Los Angeles Times Book Review*,
May 24, 1981, pp. 1 f.

## Questions

*Content/Meaning*
1. On which major points do the two reviews agree and disagree? Do they agree less often than they disagree?

2. Do you notice a political or social bias in one or both reviewers? Does this bias seem to influence the opinions they express about the man or the book? What do you know about the two reviewers? Which is more likely to have a bias about a liberal economist?

3. Since Galbraith's book is an autobiography, the reviewer may at times have difficulty separating the man from the book in his evaluation. At one point, Fallows in *The New York Times* review writes that "what is most wrong with the book" is that "Mr. Galbraith's estimation of his own importance has exceeded all reasonable bounds." Considering Fallows' development of this point, do you think that he is here primarily reviewing "the man or the book"? Does Ponte express a similar criticism? If so, which of the two does he emphasize?

*Style*

1. A synopsis for an autobiography is essentially a sketch of the writer's life. Do you find such a sketch in either review? If so, what does it add to the quality of the review and our understanding of the book?

2. What are the relative merits of the two leads? Does each prepare you for the substance, style, and tone of the reviews they introduce?

3. Study the use of direct quotations in the two reviews. How does each reviewer use them? Also examine the kinds of quotations included in the two reviews. Which reviewer, in your mind, makes the more effective and responsible use of quotation?

# Exercise

Choose a recently published book and read any two reviews, preferably in comparable publications (like *Time* and *Newsweek* or the Sunday book sections of two major metropolitan newspapers). Compare and contrast the reviews by focusing on the overall critical judgment, background information, factual support, and the reviewers' styles, including complexity of vocabulary, strategies of organization, and revelation of their personalities.

# Reading Selection

The following review focuses on an architectural design exhibit entitled "Place, Product, Packaging: A Look at Four Popular American Building Types" at the Cooper-Hewitt Museum in New York. As you will see, it takes the reviewer some time before she even mentions this exhibit. One may rightly surmise that she is less interested in reviewing the show than in discussing critically the idea that it fosters or promotes. In this quality of moving outward to contemplate a subject rather than strictly "reviewing" a show, event, or artifact, Ada Louise Huxtable's piece is properly a critical essay rather than a review per se. Much popular criticism, especially in highbrow journals like the *New York Review of Books* or the *Boston Review,* takes this broader option—enlarging upon themes and ideas prompted by the subject being reviewed. An essay, in its most general sense, is a "trial" or "attempt," often quite personal, of interpreting or analyzing a given subject. In the essay that follows, Ms. Huxtable, a noted critic of architecture, examines the publications of modern design in architecture to promote the sale of products. She asks whether such design can truly be considered as esthetically pleasing. The article appeared originally in *The New York Times Magazine,* a Sunday supplement addressed to educated readers that features a good many critical essays.

## ARCHITECTURE FOR A FAST-FOOD CULTURE

### *Ada Louise Huxtable*

Tired of the New Nostalgia? Had it with the 30's, 40's and 50's? Been through camp, kitsch and all the stylish ghosts of the recent past? Too bad, because we're in for more of the Brave Old World. The fascination is still with the artifacts of near-history. Those who set the esthetic and intellectual fashions— and this is not to denigrate the seriousness of the intent or the result—are still engaged in an orgy of rediscovery of the familiar. The vernacular environment, the transient buildings of the highway, the Pop visions of the Strip, the signs and symbols of suburbia, Main Street then and now, the commercial world of fast food and service and the esthetics of expediency are being spotlighted with increasing seriousness.

This new architectural vision can be looked on as the revelation of great truths or a cultural disaster, but it should come as no surprise. It is closely related to the ascendancy of Pop Art and the development of those ironic sensibilities that have changed the way we look at the everyday world.

With the antihero now in fashion, could the antimonument be far behind? The current philosophies of populism and pluralism have found easy echoes in the multiple movements of the architectural world. This is a world that exerts a peculiar fascination, with its visual one-liners and genuine insights into sociocultural history. And the understanding of this world is reinforced by the 1960's' discovery of the environment, a real place that includes un-planned chaos and "antiarchitecture," in addition to more conscious efforts at art and order. That this architectural underworld with its esthetic and intellectual perversities has become the focus of the taste makers who ignored or reviled it for so long is a significant cultural irony of our time.

There is one important change, however, in the present excursions into the Pop environment and the recent past: They are no longer just a sentimental journey, a fashionable trip, or a skimming of surface sensations. We are treating the Pop scene now as serious art and history. A few pioneers have always seen it that way, but there is a growing movement to try to sort things out, to decide what is art, and what is history in the world we have built in the last half century. There is increasing scholarly analysis, an attempt to establish perspective, to evaluate intent and result, and to apply standards of judgment. Some thoughtful critics say Pop architecture is neither all art nor all junk, and others believe that its degree of qualitative success can be determined rationally within a given pragmatic and esthetic framework.

The process began a dozen years ago with Robert Venturi's seminal book "Complexity and Contradiction in Architecture," published by the Museum of Modern Art, which made an erudite plea for an "inclusionist" rather than an "exclusionist" view of architectural styles and asked for the recognition of the diverse components of the real environment. More of Venturi's proselytizing appeared in "Learning from Las Vegas," done with Denise Scott Brown and Stephen Izenour, and also in "Learning from Levittown." If you could not learn to love these Pop phenomena—and, by extension, the Strip, Miami and the clichés of suburbia and the shopping center—you could at least learn to see them as a valid cultural manifestation.

Today there is an established body of documentation in the field: John Margolies has become the apostle of the gas station with his articles and lectures on "Pump and Circumstance"; Jeffrey Limerick may be the leading historian of resort architecture, from spas to motels; John Baeder has made a perceptive career of photographing and painting diners; Françoise Bollack and Tom Killian have amassed an epic collection of photographs of "everyday masterpieces" on the streets of New York.

There have been fine collections of the commonplace for some time, from Berenice Abbott's superb photographs of New York in the 1930's to today's photo-realism. But most of the earlier essays on the ordinary were filtered through refining sensibilities to be seen as high art. Today the banal is supposedly presented on its own terms. Actually, it is being transformed into a sophisticated set of cultural and esthetic symbols.

Architecture exhibitions have been bringing this subject and this point of view to public attention for the past decade. The Architectural League of New York outraged its members in the 1960's with a deadpan show of Morris Lapidus's Miami hotels, and, at about the same time, the Whitney Museum made a brief excursion into the vernacular world of Venturi and Rauch. Pop architecture finally made it into an official Washington showcase, the Smithsonian's Renwick Gallery, in 1976, with Venturi and Rauch's "Signs of Life: Symbols in the American City." Meanwhile, the Museum of Modern Art has served up Shinjuku, the multi-level underground rail and subway concourse in Tokyo, complete with plastic samples from its fast-food restaurants. Shinjuku features four huge department stores, thousands of shops and restaurants, and diversions ranging from movies to "love" hotels. Ad-

mired as an "ad hoc" environment, it covers the whole range of newly discovered "Process" architecture and design.

Right now, the chief outpost of this burgeoning architectural concern is the Cooper-Hewitt Museum in New York, which reopened in 1976 in the renovated Carnegie Mansion at Fifth Avenue and 91st Street as the Smithsonian Institution's official Museum of Design. Lisa Taylor, director of the museum, and Richard Oliver, curator of architecture and design, have sponsored a series of small, lively exhibitions in the contemporary-design gallery housed in the basement. The themes and insights are far bigger than the shows that contain them.

The latest exhibition, which will be on view through March 19, is called "Place, Product, Packaging." It is subtitled "A look at four popular American building types: fast-food restaurants, diners, gasoline stations and museum villages."

That's right—museum villages. Something else has been added to the Pop environment. Mr. Oliver—with his assistant, Nancy Ferguson, who has worked with him on the show and catalog—puts Colonial Williamsburg in Virginia (not to mention such historical complexes as Sturbridge Village in Massachusetts) in the same frame as McDonald's and Texaco. The point being made is that all of these architectural examples, from the restored village to franchised fast food, are essays in style; each is a highly successful exercise in packaging and selling a specific product and place.

Every one of these building types, whether it be a historic house-museum or a diner, presents a characteristic image through design. The product being packaged and sold may be commercial, cultural or educational. The line can be crossed easily from Williamsburg, with its real ties to history, to Disneyland, which makes up history out of whole cloth, at slightly less than life size. But salesmanship through design works equally well in the identifica-

tion of the product, be it packaged history or packaged food. All are supreme examples of the American design and merchandising talent, and ultimately, of a unique architectural phenomenon.

The individual design is presented as a calculated totality through skillfully related architecture, artifacts, graphics and costumes. The ladies in mob caps and sprigged muslin at Williamsburg have their counterparts in McDonald blazers and Mobil jumpsuits. (The theme of vernacular types and traditions in American architecture is being explored in a series of lectures related to the show at Cooper-Hewitt, through March 29.)

This thesis, of course, has shock value; to compare a gas station and a diner with Williamsburg is a kind of heresy, even though all three may exhibit "colonial" forms. The museum village is a sacrosanct and authoritative culture icon. But influences have ricocheted from the museum village reconstruction—Williamsburg was a powerful design force in this country from the 1920's on—to the highway and the shopping center. The ultimate Williamsburg statement may be the colonial A&P.

What is becoming increasingly clear as time passes, however, is that the museum village is a creation, a rebuilding to a pattern, with immense attention to "re-created" history and something called, with sublime scholarly ambiguity, "authentic reproduction." This ranges from measured copies to educated guesswork and wishful thinking. But the result is essentially a stage set, an evocation of the past as we wish to see that past today, for our present tastes and needs. It is all seductively unreal. The very title "Colonial Williamsburg" immediately sets an artificial image and an arbitrary cutoff date. The museum village is a most artfully packaged place, a product that satisfies our craving for high-class cultural and educational entertainment and instant roots. After 50 years of evolution and success, it is beginning to be recognized as legitimate 20th-century architectural history.

The style and packaging of most vernacular architectural forms have been profoundly affected by changing tastes in every decade. Only the museum village established a rigidly controlled character and stayed with it for obvious reasons, the idea and style fixed in false time, the game marvelously well played.

Commercial buildings, however, all show significant stylistic changes from the 1920's on. They modify both their look and their presentation techniques with perfect pitch for changing taste and fashion. In gas stations, designers of the eclectic 20's and 30's dealt equally facilely with American Colonial and Spanish Colonial types, often applied to the same basic building form. There were also Moorish, Elizabethan and classical models for the stations, just as there were for domestic architecture of the time.

The 30's also brought st[r]eamlining and visions of the future from the Chicago and New York World's Fairs. The "modernistic" gas station sported "fast" curves, sleek baked enamel, and chrome trim. It was the High Period of the streamlined Art Deco diner. Building was at a standstill during World War II but the 50's saw an explosion of free-wheeling eclecticism in suburbia, as well as the conversion in official circles to the moral and esthetic imperatives of modern architecture. At that time, the oil companies got architectural religion and began to invest in "good design," with emphasis on modular prototypes that could be used across the country. The much-publicized efforts of industrial designers Norman Bel Geddes and Walter Dorwin Teague were probably the first examples, but other architects of stature were called on for prestige purposes, from Frederick G. Frost, who designed the International Style Mobil station of the 1940's to Eliot Noyes who produced a national model for Mobil in the 1960's.

But as these buildings moved from the highway to the suburbs and the city, and as environmental awareness became a popular movement in the 60's, protest mounted against their aggressive or disruptive presence. Gas stations conceived as independent stylish objects were a problem in older residential neighborhoods. The 1970's model is therefore "environmental." It stresses "suitability" over style. When possible, it resembles a ranch house, or at least suggests a rustic romanticism; it wins prizes for landscaping.

The fast-food restaurant has gone through a similar metamorphosis. Designed in the 1950's to catch the motorist's eye at a minimum speed of 50 miles an hour, it stressed the most raucous visual images it could devise. Boldness and garishness were the design criteria. McDonald's and Jack in the Box unfurled their neon and Day-Glo banners and architectural containers against the endless sky.

These, too, have been toned down with the changing taste of the 60's and 70's. Increasingly domesticated, they now feature an overlay of a shingled mansard roof, or at least the vestigial, clip-on mansard trim that is today's

universal vernacular motif. Jack in the Box, for example, has "Mark II" and "Mark III" models with progressively subdued signs and shapes and growing mansards.

Scholarly exercises in the iconography of these building types is based on the techniques of conventional art history. It is not unrelated to the study of the stylistic development and facade changes of cinquecento churches. Such objectivity inevitably leads to the conclusion that it is possible and proper to judge vernacular and Pop architecture as "good" or "bad" examples of the type—a competent Williamsburg theme, for example, versus an inept one, instead of a scathing dismissal of both.

In the Cooper-Hewitt presentation, Mr. Oliver cultivates a cool and quietly delighted aloofness; he prefers not to puff this kind of architecture as "art," although it is currently popular to do so. But though he does not treat it as high art, he takes it very seriously as a legitimate vernacular expression, while carefully avoiding either an elitist or a populist stance. He acknowledged that there are esthetic standards involved, however, saying that the Cooper-Hewitt show uses examples that "seem well designed," and that act "as mirrors of our culture." That happens to be a pretty good definition of art.

Among the more striking examples of "good" design are some of the "theme" interiors of McDonald's in California or Texas. Outstanding are a biplane motif with cockpit booths in Garden Grove, Calif., designed by Al Gordon; anthropomorphic trees and mushroom seats in an outdoor eating area in Chula Vista, Calif., by Setmakers, Inc., and a revolving, giant, plastic, see-through hamburger in a setting of disco glitter and mirrors in Los Angeles, by Sharon Landa Associates. Theme architecture is clearly the new eclecticism

of the 70's. Significantly, while themes change, the standardized, formula food is unvaryingly the same.

Theme architecture is in fact the universal vernacular today, from instant American "English pubs" and stagily ethnic or overdesigned restaurants (where the food rarely matches the stylistic aspirations) to "old" fishing villages newly built for tourism on the Sardinian coast. Inevitably, these styles are a trickle-down from some form of high art, as they always have been. But they are unique in that everything from hard-sell, high-style and stage-set romanticism to genteel historicism is used in the service of predominantly American marketing skills.

The results are no longer being viewed as universal travesties; they are considered to be an art phenomenon that is the result of legitimate cultural and esthetic interaction. Today we are revising, and rewriting, contemporary art history, and in particular the history of the uses of art and taste. It is a little like a trick with mirrors, because we are also making history in the process. What has evolved in this country in particular is a contemporary consumer esthetic in which art is co-opted for a marketable product, and its packaging and merchandising are done with consummate expertise.

Is today's "environmental" theme just another style or is it the final triumph of this ingenious exploitation of the creative act? Stay tuned for the next American decade, and see.

From *The New York Times Magazine,*
February 12, 1978, p. 23 ff.

### Questions

*Content/Meaning*

1. The Cooper-Hewitt show reviewed in this article focused on four kinds of buildings: fast-food restaurants, diners, gas stations, and museum villages. In what way does the last kind relate to the preceding three? Does Huxtable agree with this grouping? What point, in essence, does she make about museum villages in relation to the other architectural designs? Would she group Williamsburg and Disneyland as museum villages? Can you think of examples that you could add to the category?

2. In paragraphs 17 through 19, Huxtable traces the evolution of gas-station design. Can you summarize her discussion? In what manner would she compare or contrast the development of the fast-food restaurant?

3. At one point, specifically in paragraph 22, Huxtable observes that the study of the styles of modern commercial buildings like gas stations is not unlike the study of fifteenth-century Italian ("cinquecento")

churches. What major point is she making with this observation? How does this point relate to her main argument?

4. In paragraph 24, Huxtable mentions "theme architecture." What does she mean by this turn? Can you find some illustrations for it from your own observation and experience?

*Style*

1. The fact that Ms. Huxtable is writing for a relatively educated reader is evident throughout the article. Taking a close look at paragraph 15, can you demonstrate in what particular features she is speaking to a literate reader? (You might, for example, ask yourself what she means by the metaphor "stage set" and how she integrates that metaphor with her major point. You might also take a close look at the vocabulary and the sentence structure of the paragraph.)

2. What words used in the essay are not in your vocabulary? What phrases or sentences did you have difficulty understanding (possibly, "With the antihero now in fashion, could the antimonument be far behind?" or "What has evolved in this country in particular is a contemporary consumer esthetic in which art is co-opted for a marketable product . . .")? Using your desk dictionary, can you figure out the meanings of these words and phrases? Which words and phrases do you still not fully understand?

## Exercises and Assignments

1. Plan to see a play, film, musical performance, or TV program, or to read a book, in order to review it. Follow the steps we have outlined on the preparation for popular reviewing and then write an 800-word review aimed at the typical readership of your local newspaper. As a postscript, write a brief paragraph describing the kind of audience to which your local newspaper is addressed. Include the name of the paper, its circulation figures, and the means by which you have inferred the nature of its readership.

2. You have read a sample television review in this chapter focusing on a form of entertainment that is peculiar to television (though it used to be broadcast over radio as well). Television reviewers have to be extremely versatile and knowledgeable because their area of expertise is much more a medium than it is a particular form of art or leisure, as is usually true of other reviewers in the mass media. Television reviews can easily range over such diverse subjects as opera, art history, interviewing, sportcasting, educational TV, documentaries and news, comedy, advertising—literally anything that might be televised at any time. To experience something of the challenge that faces the television reviewer, choose a program or series that is peculiar to television—the "Today" show, a crime show, a minidrama series, a presi-

dential press conference—and write an 800-word review of it. Where possible, emphasize the media aspects of the program (i.e., the use of cameras, the special visual effects, the use of conventional formats and set designs).

3. Your instructor might ask the class to form into various groups according to interests and then send the groups out as reviewers to a well-defined community near the campus to compile collectively a review of the arts and leisure available in the immediate university environment. Teams of from two to five could focus on such topics as restaurants (possibly divided into subcategories like ethnic, fast-food, gourmet), museums and art exhibits, musical concerts, dramatic performances (including ballets and modern dance), libraries and book stores, films, buildings of special interest, campus fashions, churches as architecture, local entertainment, local television offerings, or local disc jockeys. You might even add some offbeat assignments such as evaluating prominent graffiti and other forms of "street art," or campus and off-campus food vendors, or the hot food and beverages dispensed by vending machines, or the best disco dancers (a la *Saturday Night Fever*) in the area. Whatever you do, place the emphasis on questions of taste. Groups should parcel out assignments to be written up in no more than 500 words. One member should serve as editor and put the whole project together into a coherent paper.

4. If it is too difficult to undertake the assignments in exercise 3 as a group, choose one of them to do on your own. Preferably, choose an offbeat topic where you must rely strongly on your own investigative efforts and evaluative responses. Write a two- or three-page review.

5. The following is a definition of *kitsch,* a word used by Huxtable: "Art, writing, etc., of a pretentious, but shallow kind, calculated to have popular appeal" (*Webster's New World Dictionary*). Usually, kitsch is a tasteless attempt to imitate or mimic high art. It is typically pretentious, stereotyped, sentimental, and simplistic both in style and content. Kitsch appears in many forms: sentimental greeting cards, porcelain figurines, paintings of electric-blue cityscapes or ships, fake period furniture, suburban shopping-center architecture, funeral parlor decorations, etc. Choose one or more objects of kitsch and write a 500-word review geared for a popular audience. Explain what makes the object kitsch.

6. For lack of space, we have been unable to include popular reviews of restaurants, fashions, foods, wines, dance, works of art or exhibits, opera, photography, and design. Choose one of these areas (or another we may have missed) and read four or five popular reviews in newspapers and magazines that concentrate on one of these specialties. Be prepared to discuss what special demand these categories make of the reviewer. (For example, a restaurant review ideally should include an evaluation of the physical environment, or "ambiance," the quality of the food, emphasizing specialties of

the house, and the service.) Then write a short review of a subject in a category of your own choosing.

7. In the selections in this chapter, you have seen that reviewers are not required to agree with one another's judgments. Select one of these reviews and if you are familiar with the subject, write a review representing an opposing point of view. If you find nothing to disagree with in the foregoing reviews, find a popular review with which you take issue in a newspaper or magazine and write a review with an opposing point of view. Limit your review to 800 words. If you choose a review from a newspaper or magazine, include a xerox of it when you turn in your paper.

8. In a book entitled *How to See* (New York: Little Brown, 1978), we are told by the author, George Nelson, that the average adult in the United States is afflicted with "visual illiteracy," that we fail not only to understand but to appreciate the design of some of the more common objects we look at daily, from a building to a piece of furniture, even to an entire city. Choose some item, large or small, important or trivial, and carefully study its design. If you wish, read some books or articles on principles of design before making your final choice. It will be best, of course, to choose an item that is generally familiar to you. (For instance, if you like to play a guitar, you may want to evaluate the design of a particular guitar. Or you may wish to choose an automobile, a van, a record jacket, a pair of shoes, a belt buckle, a particular type of suburban house, a boat, a piece of jewelry—any item that interests you.) Remember, you are to write about its visual appeal, its design, *not its function*. Address your review to a readership of "visual illiterates." The purpose of your essay is both to inform and evaluate.

9. Choose one reviewer in areas other than films or books who contributes a regular review column to a newspaper or magazine. Read at least five of his or her columns and then write an analysis of the reviewer's style, apparent biases, and knowledge of the subject. End your analysis by evaluating the reviewer's critical judgment. If you wish, and are able to do so, compare him or her with other reviewers.

10. Write an evaluation of arts and leisure reviewing in a newspaper or magazine of your choice. What areas are well represented? Which are neglected? Are the review columns written by experts? How much local coverage is there in contrast to national and international? To what kind of audience are the review articles addressed? Are some geared to a more knowledgeable readership than others? Would you recommend this newspaper to a fellow student as one to read daily for its critical coverage of the arts and leisure?

11. In place of a newspaper, choose a television station or your local campus newspaper and make an analysis similar to the one outlined in exercise 10.

# 24

# THE CRITICAL RECEPTION STUDY AS TERM PAPER

**A** useful way of getting to know the world of reviewing is to choose a famous book, film, drama, television program, opera, ballet performance, symphony, painting, exhibition, or building and research its reception by the critics. The emphasis can be on immediate or later reception, on popular or scholarly criticism. In the case of a film like *Psycho* or a philosophical novel like Herman Melville's *Moby Dick,* the immediate critical response would hardly have led one to believe that each would eventually become a classic in its field. To compare and contrast the immediate and long-range impact of a work of art can make an interesting and useful research project.

In this chapter, because we are limited in space, we concentrate on the critical reception of books. We chose this concentration because a guide to book reviewing should be of use to you in a general way throughout your college career. We further concentrate in our guide to book reviews on bibliographic aids and journals aimed for a contemporary mass readership. Thus, for example, we do not provide you with a guide to researching the critical reception of *Moby Dick* or *Das Kapital* in their own time. For such information you have to consult specialized, scholarly bibliographies about which your reference librarian can inform you. If you are engaged in a project of this nature, especially if it is done in conjunction with other classes you are taking, you might also consult your instructor and, of course, the card catalogue for specialized books on the work and the author.

What follows, then, is a listing and description of bibliographic guides and journals that will be of use to you in a critical reception study. While it is clearly impossible to list and describe all such sources here, we can attempt a selective classification and look at some examples.

## BOOK REVIEW JOURNALS

In this category we have placed those journals that deal exclusively with books and book news. The journals differ in sponsorship and quality, but all make an attempt to bring the more notable new books to the attention of the public. Here is our list with comments:

*Publishers Weekly:* A journal reflecting in essence the interests of the book publishing trade, it contains a whole section of capsule summaries and reviews describing the plot or content of newly published books. Most bookstores and many book reviewing departments in the mass media subscribe to *Publishers Weekly* if only to find out what the industry itself is highlighting. *Publishers Weekly* also gives business information about new books—concerning the dollar value of contracts, paperback affiliations, film rights, etc.

*Library Journal:* Apart from specialized articles of interest to librarians, this journal prints capsule reviews, usually written by experts, indicating the nature and quality of newly published books with an eye toward giving librarians information on the basis of which they can place their orders.

*Bookviews:* This is a commercial publication directed to the book trade in an attractive format. A recent Christmas issue, for example, featured a special section on "The Year's Best Gift Books," a timely commercial feature. The same issue also contained more than 200 short reviews in 23 categories, including both fiction and nonfiction. Capsule reviews are aimed at the general reader and are almost always favorable. (They resemble the kind of information we are likely to find on book jackets.)

*New York Times Book Review:* Published as part of the huge Sunday *Times,* the "Book Review" has no vested interests and therefore presents an assortment of independent-minded, authoritative reviews in each weekly issue of the latest important books of general interest to the public. Reviews are done by experts, who usually are free-lancers and often academics. Each issue gives reviews of 20 to 25 books. It also includes short listings of crime books, nonfiction in brief, and paperbacks "new and noteworthy." Most metropolitan Sunday newspapers, like the

*Los Angeles Times* (see pp. 409–411), have Sunday book review sections. The *New York Times Book Review* is simply the best known and the most widely read among newspaper book sections.

*New York Review of Books:* This magazine, which ironically appears in the shape of a tabloid, is the most "high-brow" of the specialized book review publications mentioned so far. It may well be the most "high-brow" general periodical in America. Its reviews appear essentially as critical essays, written by professional critics, many of whom have become regular reviewers for the *New York Review*. Articles often make original contributions to the topic of the book being reviewed. Opinion about the nature of the *New York Review* is strongly divided, even among specialized readers. Some think it is a pretentious and narrow-minded organ for New York liberals. Others regard it as the only truly intelligent cultural voice in American mass media criticism. Its articles are almost always provocative—whether in the good or bad sense of that term.

*Times Literary Supplement:* The *Times* in this case is not the one from New York but from London. The *TLS* (as it is known in the trade) is read widely on both sides of the Atlantic. In format it is a mix between the *New York Times Book Review* and the *New York Review of Books*. It covers significant publications—hence mostly books published by university presses—and concentrates on books published and distributed in England. Most discriminating readers consider it an important source of literary opinion.

There are undoubtedly many other review journals, but this list contains some of the more important of the species. Readers seeking serious and well-formed opinions of books should consult especially the last three on the list.

## SPECIALIZED JOURNALS WITH BOOK REVIEWS

Virtually every field of study has its specialized review journals, many of which put primary emphasis on reviewing recently published books. These journals differ from the general ones mainly in their level of specialization. Their reviews are written by specialists for specialists, and their subject matter is the product of still other specialists. Here is a typical instance: A book by Robert M. Jordan entitled *Chaucer and the Shape of Creation: The Aesthetic Possibilities of Inorganic Structure* published by Harvard University Press in 1967 was reviewed in *Modern Language Quarterly* (itself a scholarly publication of the University of Washington) by the late Francis Lee Utley, a specialist in early English literature who at the time taught at the Ohio State University. The review was probably read by some 200 to 300 readers, mostly students of Chaucer. It is unlikely that Jordan's book would have been reviewed in any of the general periodicals we been talking about. Most scholarly books are not. Moreover, the Utley review appeared two years after the publication of Jordan's book. In scholarly reviewing, time is not of the essence. While the general reader is not likely to be interested in or to profit from such specialized reviewing, students in particular fields of study should increasingly become aware of its existence.

Certainly college seniors should on occasion consult journals in the field of their major, and graduate students must. It would be impossible to present even a representative list of specialized journals here. We therefore confine ourselves to mentioning a few titles:

*American Economic Review*
*American Journal of Public Health and the Nation's Health*
*American Journal of Sociology*
*American Political Science Review*
*Architectural Forum*
*Bulletin of the Atomic Scientists*
*Chronicle of Higher Education*
*Classical World*
*Columbia Review of Journalism*
*English Historical Review*
*Harvard Educational Review*
*Journal of Anthropological Research*
*Journal of Home Economics*
*Journal of Popular Culture*
*Journal of the Warburg and Courtauld Institutes*
*Journal of Philosophy*
*Modern Philology*
*Musical Quarterly*
*Poetry*
*Scientific American*
*World Politics*

Obviously some of these titles are more specialized than others, but all address readers with some knowledge and interest in the field of specialty. If you have never looked at this kind of journal, it might be useful for you to examine an issue in a field that holds special interest for you, perhaps your major. You will find that while some of the articles and reviews may at this point be beyond your understanding, others will be easily comprehensible. Cultivating such sources of information will serve to enrich your knowledge and give you a greater range of source material to use as background for your own writing.

## GENERAL PERIODICALS WITH BOOK REVIEWS

In addition to newspapers, most general magazines contain reviews. Some, in fact, began exclusively as book review journals. *Saturday Review* is one such journal; it used to be known as the *Saturday Review of Literature,* and its main substance was the reviewing of books. Today, *Saturday Review* still concentrates on reviews, and you will find that at least a few major books are reviewed in each issue. Reviews in general journals vary in size and quality. Class magazines are certainly on a par with *The New York Times Book Review,* the major difference being that they review fewer books per issue and therefore are more selective. Some of these magazines, however, do greater in-depth book reviews than the Sunday *Times.* Among the magazines that you should get to know as sources for book reviews, we would include the following:

> *American Scholar*
> *Antioch Review*
> *Atlantic*
> *Commentary*
> *Commonweal*
> *Encounter*
> *Harper's*
> *Nation*
> *National Review*
> *New Republic*
> *New Yorker*
> *Saturday Review*
> *Yale Review*

Many of these journals use free-lance book reviewers—experts drawn from varying fields—though a few have their own reviewers. The newsweeklies might be added to this list, specifically *Time* and *Newsweek,* although in general their interests turn more toward the mass market. Nevertheless, their arts and book reviewers can be excellent, and these magazines should certainly not be neglected in a search for responsible opinion about recently published books.

## BOOK REVIEW DIGEST

We have saved for separate coverage a special bibliographic aid in the area of book reviewing, the *Book Review Digest*, which is published annually by the H. W. Wilson Company. It is actually much more a bibliographic index, along the lines of *The New York Times Index*, than it is a digest. Most college and university libraries subscribe to it and keep copies, year by year, in the Reference or General Periodical Room. As a guide to recent reviews of selected books, it is an indispensible source.

The *Book Review Digest* is an index to book reviews published in some seventy-five journals, mostly drawn from the lists of the three categories we have just discussed. For a book to be included as an entry in the *Digest* it must have received two or more reviews in the source journals if it is nonfiction and four or more if it is fiction.

In some ways, the exclusion of popular books from the *Digest* is a preliminary comment on their quality; they lacked stature or sufficient general interest to receive reviews in the more prestigious review journals. To qualify for inclusion in the *Book Review Digest*, a book must either have been published or distributed in the United States. Inclusion guarantees that the book will have been reviewed within eighteen months of its publication.

Generally speaking, an entry in the *Book Review Digest* will list all necessary bibliographical information of source journals that have reviewed the book. The information is given in the same form and style as that of *The Reader's Guide*. The following is an illustration of a strictly bibliographical entry:

Nat R 26:489 Ap. 26 '74 850w

This entry means that a review appeared in the *National Review*, one of the source journals listed at the front of the book, in volume 26, on page 489, in the issue of April 26, 1974. The review of the book in question was 850 words long.

Most important, the *Digest* lives up to its name not only in listing bibliographical information but also in citing short excerpts from selected reviews to give the reader an indication of the book's character and critical reception. The rule is that it will cite three such passages for a work of fiction and four for nonfiction, except when the book has received an unusual amount of critical attention. Formerly, the *Book Review Digest* printed a plus or minus next to its entry to indicate whether the reception was basically favorable or unfavorable. This practice has been discontinued, probably because the decision was too difficult to make.

To cite one illustration, we have chosen the entry in the 1974 volume on Aleksandr I. Solzhenitsyn's *The Gulag Archipelago, 1918–1956,* as translated into English by Thomas P. Whitney. Study the entry to get an idea of the usefulness of the *Book Review Digest.* You will notice that after citing the publishing information about the book being reviewed, there follows either a synopsis or an abstract, which can be drawn from any of a number of sources—a review, a blurb, a description from a publisher's list, the foreword to the book, and so on. Note that in the case of *The Gulag Archipelago,* 16 of the source journals published reviews, ranging in size from 170 words (in *Choice*) to 4,350 words (in the *New York Review of Books*). Of these, 5 reviews were excerpted, an indication of how important the book was judged by the editors of the *Book Review Digest.*

**SOLZHENITSYN, ALEKSANDR I.** The Gulag archipelago, 1918–1956; an experiment in literary investigation; tr. from the Russian by Thomas P. Whitney. pt 1, 2 660p il $12.50; pa $1.95 '74 Harper.

365 Political prisoners. Russia–Politics and government–1917
ISBN 0–06–013914–5;  0–06–080332–0 (pa)
LC 73–22756

The 'Archipelago' of the title refers to the Soviet "system of forced labor camps run and augmented by the secret police and its institutions. . . . ['Gulag'] is the acronym of the central office that administered the penal camps. . . . [This volume], containing only two of seven projected parts, is structured loosely as a journey to the 'thousands of islands of the spellbound Archipelago.' The reader follows scores of victims . . . from arrest to first cell and 'interrogation,' then onward through transit prisons, across the vast country . . . to the ports and ships of the Archipelago. . . . The journey and book end upon arrival at the forced camps." (N Y Times Bk R) Glossary, Index.

Reviewed by Catharine Hughes
    **America** 131:89 S 7 '74 1300w
Reviewed by W. J. Parente
    **Best Sell** 34:174 Jl 1 '74 1200w
    **Choice** 11:1201 O '74 170w
"What distinguishes this account is its particular quality of moral outrage. Precisely because of his moral vision [Solzhenitsyn] has been able to probe the underbelly of totalitarian society and he has limned it perfectly. . . .

But 'Gulag Archipelago' is not a literary masterpiece. Solzhenitsyn's moralism, his strong sense of 'ought' gets in his way as an imaginative artist. . . . He is pre-occupied in this book with non-resistance. . . . Solzhenitsyn condemns [the conduct of the prisoners of Lenin and Stalin] . . . and his own—so sternly that he seems not to grasp what it is that makes some men capable of resistance while others are not. . . . Nor is the book an historical masterpiece—as some critics claim. Solzhenitsyn is only diminished as an historian when he suggests, for example, that the Soviet penal system sprang more or less entirely from the head of Lenin, with flourishes added on by Stalin." Priscilla Macmillan
    **Christian Science Monitor** pll Jl 24 '74 950w
    **Economist** 251:127 Je 29 '74 650w
    **Encounter** 43:39 O '74 2100w
Reviewed by George Charney
    **Library J** 99:1948 Ag '74 200w
Reviewed by Francis Russell
    **Nat R** 26:877 Ag 2 '74 1550w
Reviewed by Joshua Rubenstein
    **New Repub** 170:21 Je 22'74 2350w
Reviewed by V. S. Pritchett
    **New Statesman** 87:924 Je 28 '74 1100w
"The book has its faults. . . . The historical parts are heavy. That some inaccuracies should occur, and some statements be open to challenge, was inevitable in a work of this size and nature. . . . Here, as in the First Circle, [BRD 1969] Solzhenitsyn, incomparable in his treatment of the ordinary victims of the

system, shows himself curiously helpless when it comes to picturing the senior figures of the regime: they emerge as caricatures, not as real human beings. . . . [But this work] achieves, in its massiveness, its fierce frankness, and its compelling detail, an authority no amount of counterpropaganda will ever be able to shake. . . . [It emerges] as the greatest and most powerful single indictment of a political regime ever to be leveled in modern times. . . . It is impossible to believe that this book can have anything less than a major effect on the Soviet regime. This would be true even if no more of the total work were to appear than the two parts to which this review [based on the original Russian text] is addressed." G. F. Kennan

N Y Rev of Books 12:3 Mar 21 '74 4350w

"As a chronicle of . . . holocaust [this book] is an extraordinary achievement. As historical explanation, it is less successful. . . . Solzhenitsyn's reconstruction of this secret 'country' within the country is itself a heroic accomplishment under Soviet conditions. The main sources are his own prison experiences from 1945 to 1953 and those related to him by 227 other survivors. Their testimonies are supplemented by information from official, *samizdat*, and even several Western publications. They are assembled in a powerful narrative which combines the prose styles of epic novelist, partisan historian and outraged moralist, interspersed with Russian proverbs, black humor, prison camp language and parodies of Soviet bureaucratese. The sardonically polemical tone throughout the book suits Solzhenitsyn's subject and anger." S. F. Cohen

N Y Times Bk R pl Je 16 '74 1250w
Reviewed by George Steiner

New Yorker 50:78 Ag 5 '74 3300w

"Understatement is no part of Solzhenitsyn's repertory: he writes instead breathless, exclamatory sentences ('Piles of victims! Hills of victims!'); his tone is sarcastic, indignant, and his prose . . . seems here to be hurried. He reaches for abstractions and generaliza-

tions; he seems to accept without question whatever he is told; indeed, his manner might provoke skepticism had not the principal lines of his story been sketched before by such disparate historians as Robert Conquest, Adam Ulam and Roy Medvedev. . . . More important than the recitation of atrocities is the author's carefully buttressed argument that . . . indiscriminate political persecution resulting in show trials and wholesale extermination of regional groups, was not a pathological Stalinist deviation, but a result of Lenin's belief in the necessity of terror, a program that began in 1918 and continues even now. More evidence, presumably, will be forthcoming in the succeeding volumes, but the prima facie case made by Solzhenitsyn in these pages is nothing short of staggering." P. S. Prescott

Newsweek 84:65 Jl 1 '74 1000w

"[This book] is written by a man whose courage, whose integrity, and whose experience will give it overwhelming authority throughout the world. It is a truly exceptional work: For in it literature transcends history, without distorting it. . . . What is there about Gulag Archipelago that made it a kind of last straw and that drove the politburo to its reckless and arbitrary arrest and expulsion of the author? First of all, Solzhenitsyn does not put the blame solely on Stalin and the 'personality cult.' He traces the long evolution of terror . . . back to early Soviet times. . . . [He] breaks totally with the myth . . . of a constructive and humane Lenin. Solzhenitsyn compounds this 'blasphemy' by a comparison between Soviet standards of terror and those of czardom. . . . Solzhenitsyn, it is true, denounces the terror with passion; but even more intolerable from the point of view of the *apparat* is the stinging contempt that he expresses for all concerned." Robert Conquest

Sat R/World 1:22 Ap 20 '74 2250w (Review of Russian text)
Reviewed by Timothy Foote

Time 104:90 Jl 15 '74 650w

From *Book Review Digest*, ed. Josephine Samudio, New York, The H. W. Wilson Co., Vol. 70 (Mar. 74 to Feb. 75 incl.), p. 1145.

## Assignments

1. In groups of five to seven members from your class, visit the library reference room and draw up a list of journals in which specialized reviews might be found on the following topics. Each person should be responsible for a short description of the general contents and typical coverage of several journals.

Art
Drama
Architecture
Film
Musical Performances
Radio and Television

Include in your coverage both general periodicals (among which you will find many of the ones we listed as also carrying book reviews) and specialized scholarly journals. Make a master list to be xeroxed for each member of the class, and in a group discussion, discuss your findings.

2. Do a content review of one of the book review journals. Cover all relevant points by trying to answer the following questions (and any others that may occur to you): How many books are reviewed? Does the journal specialize? How many major fields of interest do the books it reviewed cover? Who are the reviewers? Are they regulars or free-lancers? How would you describe the style of the journal? For what kind of readership is the journal aimed? What is the typical length and format of the reviews? What departments besides book reviews does the journal cover? Does it have ads? If so, to whom do they appeal? Who are the major advertisers? After answering these questions, write an analysis of the journal for the purpose of informing potential readers of its coverage and quality. Choose any journal you wish, as long as its major subject is book reviewing.

## Term Paper Project

Using the *Book Review Digest* as a starter and any other specialized bibliographies you may know of or learn about from your instructor or librarian, choose a book with an established reputation that was published in the past and do a study solely based on its immediate critical reception (i.e., newspaper and journal reviews upon publication or its overall reception.) You should obviously read the book yourself so that you can understand the specific comments made about it. Be sure to take careful notes and to attribute in proper footnote form all language and opinions that are not your own. Your paper should be 1,500 words long (approximately 7 typewritten pages), and it should include a bibliography. Here are some posssible subjects:

Norman Mailer, *The Naked and the Dead*
James Joyce, *The Portrait of the Artist as a Young Man*
Malcolm X, *The Autobiography*
William Shirer, *The Rise and Fall of the Third Reich*
Ernest Hemingway, *Across the River and Into the Trees*
Roger Angell, *Five Seasons*
Susan Brownmiller, *Against Our Will: Men, Women and Rape*
J. D. Salinger, *The Catcher in the Rye*
Samuel Schoenbaum, *Shakespeare's Lives*
Irving Howe, *The World of Our Fathers*
Truman Capote, *In Cold Blood*
Thomas Mann, *Death in Venice*
David Riesman et al., *The Lonely Crowd*
Gabriel Garcia Marquez, *One Hundred Years of Solitude*
F. Scott Fitzgerald, *The Beautiful and the Damned*
Erich Segal, *Love Story*
John Gardner, *The Life and Times of Chaucer*
John F. Kennedy, *Profiles in Courage*
E. L. Doctorow, *Ragtime*
Mark Lane, *Rush to Judgment*
William Faulkner, *Light in August*
John Hersey, *Hiroshima*
Adolf Hitler, *Mein Kampf*
W. D. Cash, *The Mind of the South*
James Baldwin, *The Fire Next Time*
Carl Sagan, *Cosmos*
Arthur Schlesinger, Jr., *Robert Kennedy and His Times*
Alex Haley, *Roots*

# AUTHOR/TITLE INDEX

# SUBJECT INDEX